All Poets Welcome

D1571029

The publisher gratefully acknowledges the generous contribution to this book provided by the General Endowment Fund of the University of California Press Associates.

The
Lower
East Side
Poetry
Scene

All Poets Welcome

in the

1960s

Daniel Kane

UNIVERSITY OF CALIFORNIA PRESS BERKELEY LOS ANGELES LONDON

University of California Press
Berkeley and Los Angeles, California

University of California Press, Ltd.
London, England

For acknowledgments of permissions, see page 289.

Library of Congress Cataloging-in-Publication Data

Kane, Daniel, 1968–
    All poets welcome : the Lower East Side poetry
 scene in the 1960s / Daniel Kane.
        p.   cm.
    Includes bibliographical references and index.
    ISBN 0–520–23384–0 (acid-free paper).–
    ISBN 0–520–23385–9 (pbk. : acid-free paper)
    1. American poetry–New York (State)–New
 York–History and criticism.   2. American poetry–
 20th century–History and criticism.   3. Lower East
 Side (New York, N.Y.)–Intellectual life.   4. Lower
 East Side (New York, N.Y.)–In literature.   I. Title.

PS255.N5 K36   2003
811'.540997471–dc21   2002012704

Manufactured in the United States of America
12   11   10   09   08   07   06   05   04   03
10   9   8   7   6   5   4   3   2   1

The paper used in this publication is both acid-free
and totally chlorine-free (TCF). It meets the minimum
requirements of ANSI/NISO Z39.48–1992 (R 1997)
(Permanence of Paper).

For Rachel Turner and for my parents

Contents

Plates follow page 172

Acknowledgments ix

Introduction xiii

1   Community through Poetry 1

2   Oral Poetics on the Lower East Side 27

3   The Aesthetics of the Little 57

4   The Poetry Project at St. Mark's Church 123

5   Anne Waldman, *The World,* and the Early Years at the Poetry Project 153

6   Bernadette Mayer and "Language" in the Poetry Project 187

Epilogue: Bob Holman, the Poetry Project, and the Nuyorican Poets Café 203

Notes 209

Bibliography 273

Sources and Permissions 289

Index 295

Playlist for compact disc follows page 308

Acknowledgments

I GRATEFULLY ACKNOWLEDGE ALL THE POETS, WRITERS, SCHOLARS, AND READING series organizers who took the time to share their stories and ideas with me through interviews, phone calls, and e-mails: Bruce Andrews, John Ashbery, Carol Bergé, Bill Berkson, Charles Bernstein, Sara Blackburn, Jerry Bloedow, Peter Cenedella, Paul Chevigny, Tom Clark, Steven Clay, Andrei Codrescu, Clark Coolidge, Kirby Congdon, Stephen Cope, Michael Davidson, Allen DeLoach, Rachel Blau DuPlessis, Marcella Durand, George Economou, Andrew Epstein, Clayton Eshleman, Steve Facey, Larry Fagin, Ed Foster, Kathleen Fraser, Ed Friedman, Lyman Gilmore, John Giorno, Peter Gizzi, Alan Golding, George Greene, David Henderson, Bob Holman, Lisa Jarnot, Hettie Jones, Pierre Joris, Robert Kelly, Kenneth Koch, David Lehman, Michael Magee, Jackson Mac Low, Theresa Maier, Gerard Malanga, Jack Marshall, Bernadette Mayer, Taylor Mead, Alice Notley, Rochelle Owens, Ron Padgett, Rodney Phillips, Ishmael Reed, Libby Rifkin, Jerome Rothenberg, Mark Salerno, Ed Sanders, Susan Sherman, Ron Silliman, Joel Sloman, Michael Stephens, Lorenzo Thomas, Diane Wakoski, Anne Waldman, Lewis Warsh, Eliot Weinberger, and John Wieners. Extra thanks go to those of you who gave me permission to quote from our correspondence and other archived materials. My apologies as well to anyone whose name I may have inadvertently omitted.

I am especially grateful to Carol Bergé, who was adamant in her insistence that I research and learn about the Les Deux Mégots and Le Metro reading series as precursors to the Poetry Project, and to Bob Holman, who produced an oral history of the Poetry Project and who generously let me cite his unpublished manuscript. Bob wanted me to ensure that everyone knew that the Comprehensive Employment and Training Act (CETA)—a federally funded reeducation program for the unemployed, which resulted in the largest federally funded arts project since the WPA—enabled Holman to write his piece on the Poetry Project. To all those poets who met with me two, three, or more times: for your enthusiasm and generosity in our many interviews, on top of all those phone calls and e-mails, I thank you again. Without your input, this project would have lacked the kind of human vitality I was hoping to include. To the faculty at Kingsborough Community College and the staff at Teachers and Writers Collaborative: your intellectual, social, and technical support will always be deeply appreciated.

The assistance and support of Richard Sieburth was invaluable in guiding the theoretical impulses behind this study and its overall framework. I thank Richard for reading through the various drafts and for providing excellent suggestions for revision. I am indebted to Reva Wolf, whose study on Andy Warhol's relationship to the poetic community in the 1960s was extremely influential in my own work, and who generously took time out of her busy schedule to read through an unwieldy initial draft. To friends and colleagues Libbie Rifkin, Peter Gizzi, Rachel Turner, Lisa Jarnot, Stephen Cope, and Alice Robinson: thank you for pointing me in the right directions and for suggesting ways to revise the text. Of course, thank you to my colleagues at the University of East Anglia in Norwich, England, for their support of my research.

This work would not have been possible without the generous and enthusiastic help of the staff in the following libraries: Bradley D. Westbrook and Lynda Classen at the Mandeville Special Collections Library at the University of California, San Diego (which provided me with two research grants that helped me explore their incredible archive of new poetry); Rutherford Witthus at The Thomas J. Dodd Research Center of the University of Connecticut Libraries; Jean Ashton at the Rare Book and Manuscript Library at Columbia University; Rodney Phillips at the Henry W. and Albert A. Berg Collection of English and American Literature at the New York Public Library; Marvin Taylor at the Elmer Holmes Bobst Library, Fales Library at New York University; and Tara Wenger at the Harry Ransom Center at the University of Texas, Austin. Additionally, the City University of New York generously provided me with a PSC-CUNY faculty research award that allowed me to sit for weeks in the Mandeville Special Collections Library in San Diego, where I had the honor and pleasure of listening to tapes of poetry readings on the Lower East Side originally recorded by Paul Blackburn. From that collection, I culled most of the material presented on the compact disc that is included in this book. Many thanks to my old friend Joe Lizzi for producing the compact disc; such a favor will never be asked of you again. Finally, thanks to the English Department at New York University, which started the ball rolling by backing me both financially and intellectually when I began this project as a Ph.D. thesis and to Linda Norton, Kristen Cashman, Rachel Berchten, and Randy Heyman at the University of California Press for their dedication to this project.

Introduction

IN THE EARLY TO MID-1960S, A GROWING POETRY-READING SCENE WAS DEVELOP-
ing in dozens of cafés and lofts around Manhattan, particularly in the neigh-
borhood known as the Lower East Side. Especially significant reading series
in this area were centered, chronologically, at Mickey Ruskin and Ed Kaplan's
Tenth Street Coffeehouse, at Ruskin and Bill Mackey's Les Deux Mégots coffee-
house on East Seventh Street, at Maurice Margules's Le Metro coffeehouse
on Second Avenue, and finally, at the Poetry Project at St. Mark's Church. The
readings served as self-consciously inscribed meeting grounds, think tanks,
and community spaces for poets working outside the mainstream of contem-
porary American poetry. The poetics and politics associated with the loosely
defined New York School, Beat, San Francisco Renaissance, and Black Moun-
tain schools were adopted, argued over, and developed by poets who ultimately
founded the Poetry Project, which Allen Ginsberg described as an "immedi-
ate neighborhood community and family" that "served and still serves to for-
mulate local public opinion."[1]

Recovering, in the pages of this book, the Lower East Side poetic com-
munity—a community that despite its significant influence on American
poetry since the 1960s has not been the subject of a book-length exegesis—
will, I hope, serve several valuable functions. Placing the Lower East Side scene
in historical context adds to our overall understanding of 1960s Lower East
Side as a radical center and of the role the twentieth-century avant-garde
played in developing a politics of joy and resistance. As we will also see, the
Lower East Side poetic community was a fascinating microcosm of a coun-
terculture that helped define the 1960s as a time when experiments in com-

munity building were crucial to forming an alternative and at times dissident sensibility.

Framing poetry as a communal effort parallels community-building work typical of the 1960s and changes established notions of what constitutes authorship and literary production. Most obvious, Ginsberg's naming of poets as "community and family" underscores the tacit acceptance of poetry as a group phenomenon and threatens the prevailing romanticized conception of the author as a solitary inspired figure. In chapter 1, I suggest that what defined the group dynamic of the Lower East Side poets was their sense of engagement in an "alternative" literary and social project in opposition to an official conservative verse culture (Charles Bernstein's term). In an effort to define what poets actually meant when they used words like *academic* and *alternative,* I have traced the manifestation of these terms not in relation to questions specific to familiar binaries including "formalism" vs. "avant-garde" but within the context of literary and political history and reception as they played themselves out within circumscribed poetic communities.

Relying on an array of previously unpublished material including letters, recordings of readings, and personal interviews, I describe how poets on the Lower East Side favored a *kind* of literary heritage (including the work of Stein, Whitman, and Pound; European dada and surrealism; and poetry produced by ancient oral traditions) that defined them against the critical mainstream at that time. Inspired by Pierre Bourdieu's belief that "[q]uestions of the meaning and value of the work of art, like the question of the specificity of aesthetic judgment, can only find solutions in a social history of the field,"[2] I continue by pointing to the social and literary connections among the Lower East Side poetic community, the earlier San Francisco Renaissance phenomenon, and Grove Press, which was notorious during this period for publishing material that was often deemed "obscene" by courts across the country. Associations with Grove Press and a "dangerous" literary milieu inadvertently assisted poets on the Lower East Side in further defining their poetry as an alternative to formalist writing and, by extension, to conservative or complacent political ideologies.

Beyond discussing the kinds of writing the Lower East Side poetic community claimed as an inheritance, I show that poets associated with this scene employed extraliterary practices to emphasize their dissent from the mainstream. Local fashions, including the "cowboy" aesthetic that some writers inherited both from popular culture and from the poet Charles Olson, music-listening habits, and connections to other social scenes are all analyzed in light of their potential impact on reader reception to indicate what Bourdieu has referred to as the "socially constituted categories of perception and appreciation."[3] It is my belief that the personal behavior and social formations exhibited at poetry readings, cafes, and bars played a role in determining future reception of a given text, as did the more conventional distribution of published material designed for solitary reading.

The second chapter serves a historical function; as far as I know, no extended analysis and description of the reading series taking place at Les Deux Mégots and Le Metro has been published. While occasional articles and a small amount of published personal reminiscences refer to these series, Le Metro and Les Deux Mégots have not received due recognition as the meeting grounds for poets to develop and present their craft or as predecessors of the Poetry Project at St. Mark's Church. Poets associated with these two coffeehouses were central in setting up the initial conditions for the poetry reading as a staging ground for an alternative community. Associated poems, mimeograph magazines, and the readings themselves circulated within a social system that determined a poet's place in and knowledge of the Lower East Side scene. For example, an issue of the mimeograph magazine series *Poets at Les Deux Mégots* included a text by Ed Sanders, owner of the Lower East Side bookstore the Peace Eye and eventual lead singer in the rock band the Fugs. Sanders's text here is not really a "poem" in a conventional sense; instead, it is a collection of Greek mythological icons, a spurting penis, the word ZAP! written to the left of an illustration of a genital crab, and phrases including "HOMAGE TO RA / in the sun-disc / HAIL RA / ON THE PEAKS OF THE EAST" scattered on the page. However, this piece of writing was not an unwitting example of semantic chaos. With its Egyptian hieroglyphics and references and its explicit sexual content, the text would have immediately cued its in-the-know readers to associate it with Sanders as publisher of the popular *Fuck You / a magazine of the arts* as well as with Sanders's bookstore the Peace Eye, a radical gathering place whose storefront was covered in graffiti, including Egyptian hieroglyphics.

Poets at Les Deux Mégots and Le Metro received pleasure from recognizing one another's cues published in the mimeograph series. These cues were often so hermetic that they excluded anyone not personally familiar with the poets or the underground literary gathering places of the Lower East Side alluded to by Sanders. The inclusive impulses characteristic of Lower East Side writers were balanced by strategies of exclusion central to the identity of any community and helped establish the predominantly libertarian and/or politically leftist tenor of the participants in the scene.

Events related to Les Deux Mégots and Le Metro also situated poets within an overall history of artistic resistance characteristic of twentieth-century downtown Manhattan bohemia. As the second chapter shows, readings at Le Metro were targeted by city authorities and shut down on the pretext of vaguely worded code violations under the so-called coffeehouse license law.

Poets often interpreted these attacks as initiated by the authorities' fear of the renegade texts and political beliefs promoted within coffeehouses. The behavior of city authorities reminded poets of earlier police misconduct associated with the infamous "cabaret laws." Used widely beginning in 1926, the cabaret laws often served to prohibit performances in mostly black-owned jazz clubs.[4] Indeed, the coffeehouse license law was developed after West Village coffeehouses featuring poetry readings, prior to 1961, were issued summonses under the cabaret law. The strictures of the cabaret law were found not to apply to coffeehouses, so city authorities cleverly developed the coffeehouse license law essentially as an extension of the cabaret law. Thus, poets on the Lower East Side were aligned with a black underclass by virtue of being subjected to the same kinds of attacks used against small clubs and African American musicians, including Billie Holiday and Charlie Parker.[5]

Such phenomena continued to position the Lower East Side poetic community as an alternative to the more conservative and aesthetically formalist verse culture dominant in the universities and lecture halls at the time. The city-sanctioned crackdowns also solidified the poets' sense of themselves as a renegade group bound by an ethos of political resistance and artistic innovation. What is particularly striking about the nature of the crackdowns is their similarity not only to earlier enforcement of cabaret laws but also to recent enforcement by former New York City Mayor Rudolph Giuliani's administration. During Giuliani's terms in the late 1990s through 2002, obscure statutes similar to the earlier cabaret laws were invoked primarily against the Lower East Side's smaller nightclubs and bars in order to prohibit unauthorized dancing. The neighborhood as a whole has historically served as a site for competing interpretations regarding the limits of acceptable speech and conduct, and thus one can see how place itself helped determine a subversive identity for poets reading at Les Deux Mégots and Le Metro.

In chapter 2 I also suggest that public readings in New York during the early 1960s were crucial in terms of determining future reception of individual poets. John Ashbery has expressed a rather mixed appreciation for the role of public readings. Nevertheless, his comments below indicate how the developing oral tradition initiated in part by Beat poets and the Lower East Side coffeehouse scene established the poetry reading—and by extension his and his compeers work—as a necessary locus for the dissemination and reception of poetry:

I enjoy promoting my poetry up to a certain point, which is reading it, but not dramatically with masks or festoons or anything. I want people to be aware of my writing and read it and hopefully like it. On the other hand it's embarrassing and uncomfortable to be the focus of attention and perhaps disfavor as well as applause. But it's all part of the great plan, I suppose. In 1963, when I returned from Paris where I had been living for five years, I wasn't aware that anyone was reading my poetry. When I left, poetry readings were solemn and official events given by elder statespersons of poetry, like Auden or Eliot and Marianne Moore. Then the "Beat revolution" happened to take place while I was away, and when I got back—although I wasn't aware of it—everyone was giving poetry readings everywhere. I was astonished at being asked to give one, until I realized I was one of about a hundred poets one could have heard that night in New York.[6]

Beyond the Lower East Side poetic community's resuscitation of the community-based oral reading, of which Ashbery rather quizzically found himself a part, the community was also responsible for reinvigorating and reimagining publishing practices by producing more than fifty magazines, many of which were mimeographed. Unlike their academic counterparts, these magazines were determinedly gossipy, often sloppy, and inclusive of ephemera superficially unrelated to poetry. One could turn to these magazines and learn of readings, job openings for secretarial work for Allen Ginsberg, who was sleeping with whom (or who wanted to sleep with whom), directions on growing marijuana, and more.

In many ways, these magazines are the most lasting records of this poetic community and its place within the counterculture, which is why chapter 3 focuses entirely on a representative sampling. Ed Sanders's mimeo *Fuck You / a magazine of the arts* is read as indicative of the socially libertarian strain on the Lower East Side; Lorenzo Thomas, Tom Dent, and David Henderson's *Umbra* is read as representative of the role a distinctly African American poetics (both informed by and informing a developing postmodernity) played within the community; Jerome Rothenberg's *Poems from the Floating World* and George Economou and Robert Kelly's *Trobar* are examined for their function in developing the "deep image" poetic quasi-philosophy, reinvigorating the troubadour aesthetic, reaching out to the international poetic community, and articulating links between the contemporary avant-garde and ancient oral traditions; Ted Berrigan's *C: A Journal of Poetry* is analyzed in terms of its role in developing the so-called Second-Generation New York School, whose "members" were to have a huge influence on the development of St. Mark's Poetry Project and on the promotion of aesthetic values associated with First-Generation New York School poets Kenneth Koch, John Ashbery, Frank O'Hara, and James Schuyler. Ultimately, these small-press and mimeographed magazines, along with even more ephemeral documents, including letters and flyers, played a major role in institutionalizing the Poetry Project—and the Lower East Side of Manhattan—as a forum for avant-garde poetics and the resulting politics associated with the poetic community.

In many ways, these chapters serve as a narrative of emergence for the Poetry Project at St. Mark's Church, which is discussed at length in the fourth and fifth chapters. There are good reasons to focus extensively on the import of the Poetry Project to contemporary American poetry. Since the fall of 1966, St. Mark's has had about three poetry readings a week, along with related poetry workshops and special events, making it a place that, on average, has perhaps held more readings than any other reading series in the twentieth century. Currently, a vital group of younger poets continues to read, socialize, and attend events at the Project regularly, and all publish in related if geographically dispersed small magazines. Poets of all ages and from all over the avant-garde spectrum really want to read at St. Mark's. Relatively established writers (after learning of my involvement in writing this book) have actually called me to help "get them a reading" at the Project, despite the fact that I have no influence at the Poetry Project and that in 2001 no poet was paid more than $150 per reading—including Ashbery, Creeley, Ferlinghetti, and so on. The Poetry Project serves as a nerve center, social meeting ground, and barometer of the contemporary American alternative poetry scene, and one looks to it to see in part what has happened and what will happen.

It is important to ground the Poetry Project in the overall poetic community of the Lower East Side. Without the earlier reading series and magazines, it is unlikely that the Poetry Project (now in its third decade) would have had the community support it needed to organize and run its programs, and it might not have so easily inherited the kinds of politically radical ideals typical of the period. Chapters 4 and 5 discuss the increasingly politicized nature of the Poetry Project. Ironically, this politicization, which coincided with growing national dissent in response to the Vietnam War and to the civil rights, drug legalization, and sexual liberation movements, existed in tandem with initial federal government funding of the reading series. The fascinating story of the grant that funded the Poetry Project is rife with literary politics and repercussions that leaked into the poetry readings themselves. Drug-bust release funds, the surprise arrival of theatrical dada assassins in the middle of a poetry reading, the results of and reactions to a days-long LSD bacchanalia were all on one level or another related and responding to the inevitable institutionalization accompanying a government-funded program.

Chapter 5 also studies texts found in early issues of the Poetry Project's "official" publication *The World* and points to the poems as indicative of the overall ascendance and evolutionary styles of the New York School during the early years of the Poetry Project. Finally, it marks the first shift in poetics and social life at St. Mark's by discussing and analyzing the significance of mainstream publishing successes and the migration of key figures, including Ted Berrigan, to other urban and rural areas including Chicago and Bolinas, California. I argue that this shift allowed for the Poetry Project to maintain a certain level of dynamism it may have otherwise lacked had it relegated itself to publishing and promoting its founding figures.

The last chapter suggests that Lower East Side–related literary events, including Bernadette Mayer and Vito Acconci's mimeographed magazine *o to 9* and Mayer's own workshops held at the church, played at least a partial role in shaping literary values associated with those poets participating in the production of *L = A = N = G = U = A = G = E* magazine and associated groupings. Finally, the epilogue draws on Bob Holman's work at the Poetry Project during the early 1970s to suggest that the Poetry Project also influenced and encouraged the development of "slam" or "spoken-word" poetry, perhaps the most popular—and populist—poetry movement of the late twentieth century.

There are other reading series, poetic communities in and outside New York, and individual poets, books, and magazines that, had they been included, would have enhanced this project. It was not my aim, however, to write a conclusive survey of the poetry scene on the Lower East Side during the 1960s. Rather, I petition my readers to see the chapters of this book as various views of the Lower East Side poetic community, while acknowledging that the full picture can never be wholly seen from such a distance.

Community through Poetry

An "Alternative" Poetic Community on the Lower East Side

During the early to mid-1960s, before the founding of the Poetry Project at St. Mark's Church in 1966, a series of poetry readings based in various coffee-houses on the Lower East Side of Manhattan began to receive growing attention from the local press and the wider literary community. These readings, the most important of which began at Les Deux Mégots (on East Seventh Street) and then at Le Metro (on Second Avenue between Ninth and Tenth Streets), were not funded by any government, foundation, or corporate grants, as most long-term reading series are today. They did not charge much, if any, admission, and they were characterized by a boisterous and literary audience. Poets attending the coffee shop readings represented an increasingly established number of often ill-defined and porous poetic "schools." In the highly social environments of Les Deux Mégots and Le Metro, many writers could be found reading, discussing their work, and collaborating, among them, Beat poets Allen Ginsberg and Peter Orlovsky; Black Mountain poets Paul Blackburn and Joel Oppenheimer; New York School poets Ron Padgett and Ted Berrigan; "Deep Image" poets Jerome Rothenberg, Robert Kelly, and George Economou; Umbra poets David Henderson and Lorenzo Thomas; as well as Kathleen Fraser, Jackson Mac Low, Diane Wakoski, and Carol Bergé.

The actual literary production of many of the poets involved in forming this complicated and at times contentious poetic community on the Lower East Side was contained initially within a self-enclosed world of readings, small-press publications, and related social gatherings. Major commercial publishers, university presses, and the like were simply not interested in incorporating the developing literary scene into their own distribution apparatus. This lack of mainstream interest was primarily due to the experimental nature of much of the Lower East Side poets' work. However, this marginalization was also linked extensively to the very place in which poets on the Lower East Side were situated. Since the turn of the twentieth century downtown Manhattan as a whole has served as an environment where artists have developed politically and artistically radical communities. Steven Watson's description of the art and life of the early-twentieth-century avant-garde of New York illustrates the possibility for geographical place to be incorporated into an overall avant-garde signifying system, one in which radical critiques of prevailing morality and politics emanate from a specific urban space:

> The alienation of this avant-garde from bourgeois taste and morality demanded an alternative society. New York's Greenwich Village became its center. . . . *Both a geographical entity and a state of mind,* the Village was where individuals could go to reinvent themselves through psychoanalysis, feminism, fashion, revolutionary politics, and unorthodox sexual relationships. . . . It was commonly remarked that "all revolution is synonymous," and Margaret Anderson went so far as to declare "Revolution *is* Art."[1]

While the West Village would generally remain a center for the avant-garde throughout the first half of the twentieth century, the postwar era saw a gradual shift of the downtown artistic community toward the Lower East Side, particularly the section north of Houston Street and below Fourteenth Street, bounded by Fourth Avenue on the west and the East River on the east. This shift was precipitated primarily by economics (high rents) but also had roots in artists' resistance to being co-opted by the kinds of mainstream activity commodifying the late 1950s West Village arts scene. This commodification took forms as various as increased police harassment of drug users, organized tours bringing suburban residents wanting to experience bohemia into the West Village for a day, sugar-coated media representations of bohemian theater and poetry, and deflationary or dismissive attitudes toward the often-revolutionary beliefs underpinning the avant-garde.[2]

As a result of the changing environment in Greenwich Village, by the late 1950s artists of all kinds had redirected and revitalized the downtown arts scene by establishing themselves as a presence in the tenements and neighboring bars, coffee shops, and restaurants of the Lower East Side. There artists temporarily avoided larger media scrutiny by keeping their "scene" politically insular and socially marginal through their absence in community, academic, artistic, and literary establishment circles.[3] Avant-garde artists beginning to break from the earlier dominant (and established) abstract expressionist movement; poets associated with the Beat, Black Mountain, and New York Schools; and musicians developing the new languages of free jazz began congregating in bars, including the Five Spot on Cooper Square. The block of Tenth Street near Fourth Avenue became a center for innovative art as artists such as Willem de Kooning and Franz Kline showed their work in the street's numerous galleries.[4]

Beyond the aesthetic changes taking place in the new literary, artistic, and musical movements, the neighborhood itself maintained representations of alterity. The Lower East Side was well-known for its history of Latino, Ukranian, Jewish, and other minority poor-to-working-class long-term residents, generations of whom had spent the better part of the century establishing a community in the face of repeated attempts by the real estate industry to transform the Lower East Side into a middle-class professional haven.[5] Thus, the newly arriving artists on the Lower East Side were defined both by their rejection of the West Village as overpriced, bourgeois, and co-opted and by the Lower East Side's tradition of working-class radicalism and resistance. This condition gave substance to the scene's reputation as an alternative to middle-class cultural consumption and expression.[6] Particularly in terms of the growing poetry scene, the Lower East Side *as a neighborhood* proved helpful in lending "alternative" status to artistic production.

An Alternative Poetics

In poetry, the word *alternative* suggests a binary system. To be "alternative" means to reject, dissent from, or mock a conventional or "academic" aesthetic—that is, a formalist aesthetic employing regular meters and purportedly transparent paraphrasable narratives or messages—in favor of writing that is indebted to innovative laws of prosody; that uses unusual typography; that beatifies scandalous or licentious behavior; that threatens generic distinctions between prose, poetry, performance, and visual art; and so on. Poets on the Lower East Side used their position in a marginal neighborhood to sustain their developing poetics, a poetics in which the word *academic* was transformed into a pejorative term. Poet Amiri Baraka (formerly LeRoi Jones) recalls in his autobiography: "The various 'schools' of poetry we related to were themselves all linked together by the ingenuous. They were a point of departure from the academic, from the Eliotic model of rhetoric, formalism, and dull iambics. Bullshit school poetry. All these I responded to and saw as part of a whole anti-academic voice."[7]

In hindsight, one could argue that alternative poets' hostility toward the academic was somewhat ironic. Many poets associated with the Lower East Side scene ended up in tenure-track jobs in the academy, including Baraka. Indeed, by the late 1960s and early 1970s alternative poets were being welcomed, if cautiously at first, into college and university faculties throughout the United States.[8] Nevertheless, writers associated with the Lower East Side scene maintained and championed an alternative status that included both a familiar bohemianism (with its associations of lighthearted criminality, liberated sexual relations, and social threat contained within a specific urban space) as well as a more complicated and often truly marginalized literary genealogy. To achieve this sleight of hand, poets who worked in some capacity in academia positioned themselves as infiltrators as opposed to traitors and used material directly related to the Lower East Side poetic community to assist them in this task.

Poet Kirby Congdon illustrated this phenomenon in a letter to Ed Sanders (poet, editor, and lead singer of countercultural rock band the Fugs) requesting copies of Sanders's Lower East Side–based magazine *Fuck You / a magazine of the arts.* Congdon, an active participant in the Lower East Side reading series, informed Sanders that he was "trying to collect a reference library of all non-academic poets and poetry," not for his personal use but for Brown University: "I have been getting hold of little known things for them that reflect the real activity that is going on outside the walls of schools and commercial publishing houses."[9] The fact that the "real activity" was being gathered by Congdon for use *inside* the trim walls of Brown University points to the way poetry was being positioned by Congdon as infiltrating and enlightening the stodgy universities.

One should consider this letter in light of how the poetry reading was eventually used by student activists in the latter part of the 1960s. To name just two of hundreds of examples, Allen Ginsberg was invited by students at University of California, Berkeley, to read during campus unrest associated with the Free Speech movement, and Joel Sloman (the first assistant director of the Poetry Project at St. Mark's Church) distributed his poem "Strike" throughout Harvard University's campus during student demonstrations in 1969.[10] Using readings and texts as tactical if benevolent weapons, designed in part to challenge the assumed conservatism of the academy, assisted poets in their complicated relationships with academic institutions. As Congdon's letter indicates, alternative poets could be responsible for setting up the conditions for alternative poetry's combined threat to and absorption into the university.[11]

Poets associated with Les Deux Mégots and Le Metro often looked to and discussed earlier alternative literary movements that promoted oral presentation and typographical innovation, thus situating themselves within a literary genealogy. Influenced by their reading and recuperation of earlier avant-garde experimental work, including Italian and Russian futurism, dada, and the texts of radical modernist figures, many writers at the coffee shops highlighted the poem as a spoken phenomenon and typed or "scored" their writing to emphasize its place on both page and stage.[12] For example, poet Jackson Mac Low, a consistent presence on the Lower East Side, has written many works that use unusual typography to encourage audience participation. We can look to a Mac Low text in which the page is filled entirely with words drawn from the letters in the name of his friend Peter Innisfree Moore—words like *smite, opinion, fen, minister,* and *smote* circle around one another in various hand-drawn shapes and sizes. Of this piece, Richard Kostelanetz writes, "This visual-verbal text can then become a score for a live performance in which any number of readers are encouraged to read aloud whichever words they wish, at whatever tempo they wish, for indefinite durations; and Mac Low's instructions for this particular piece suggest that the individual letters can be translated into certain musical notes (and, thus, that the same text can be interpreted as a musical score)."[13] Mac Low conceived of typographical innovation as structurally useful in terms of encouraging collaborative and exciting performance. Poet John Giorno also encouraged spectacle and collaboration during his performances, employing technological as opposed to typographical means to project his poetry into a live environment. His work during the latter part of the 1960s often featured a series of blueslike repetitive lines containing slight variations that tended to push the narrative forward. An early instance of this is found in his poem "I'm Tired of Being Scared":

An unemployed
machinist
An unemployed machinist
who travelled
here
who travelled here
from Georgia
From Georgia 10 days ago
10 days ago
and could not find
a job
and could not find a job
walked

into a police station
walked into a police station
yesterday and said
yesterday
and said:

"I'm tired
of being scared
I'm tired of being scared."[14]

Like the Italian futurists before him, Giorno often embraced technology as an aid in his presentation of such a text.[15] In performance, Giorno would heighten the effects of the repetitions in a poem like "I'm Tired of Being Scared" by playing them on various tape machines, filling the reading area with reverberating sound through speakers installed throughout. At times, Giorno used fog machines that belched out smoke as he distributed drugs, including marijuana and LSD, to audience members to elicit particularly animated participation in the performance. Additionally, Giorno's friendship with Bob Moog, inventor of the Moog analog synthesizer, led him to combine the vocal reading of poetry with the new sounds available through the synthesizer.[16] As Giorno recalls, he used the Moog to produce some rather unusual effects:

> I'd do a poem, using multilevels, oscillations, all kinds of things like that. At the same time, it was the beginning of radical politics. We learned that the U.S. Army was experimenting with a certain kind of synthesized oscillation that loosened your sphincter muscle. We tried endlessly to figure out what that oscillation could be, and incorporate it into the performance of a poem. You know— read the poem, include that oscillation, so that everybody's asshole would loosen as we read![17]

As Giorno's anecdote illustrates, poetry on the Lower East Side could be interpreted as depending partly on the physical presence of a gathered audience— that is, if one were to receive that poem in a variety of manifestations that stretched beyond print into what sound poet and artist Dick Higgins called "intermedia."[18] Like experimental poets in the early part of the twentieth century, Giorno, Mac Low, and others treated the page not so much as a site of preservation as a score ready to be performed.[19]

Looking Up to "Grampaw"

Alternative poets on the Lower East Side also strengthened their sense of identity by acknowledging and publicizing their debt to predecessor modernist poets, especially Ezra Pound and William Carlos Williams.[20] Evidence for Lower East Side poets' recognition of the debts they owed Williams and Pound is clear not just from the championing of Pound's and Williams's poetics as seen in various publications related to the scene but also from the slightest of social rhetorical gestures found throughout the documents specific to the neighborhood.[21] As early as 1950, Paul Blackburn (one of the most active organizers of reading series in New York) was hatching plans for a chain magazine destined to end up in the hands of Pound and Williams:

Dear Olson:
There's a scheme afoot we would like you to come in on. A circular packet
of mss. oddments by young writers, experiments which editors might dodge,
poems with tough technical problems etc. Anything with new ideas or
methods which might not otherwise have circulation, will have circulation,
readers, critics. . . . Pound and Williams in for the deal and will get the
stuff last.[22]

That the magazine would end with Pound and Williams points to the practice that many of the poets associated with the Lower East Side used in live poetry readings: treating pagination as a metaphor for a poet's status in the community. Just as the more famous poet often read last at a double-bill poetry reading, so Pound and Williams were given the chance to have the final, definitive say.

Ezra Pound took on a patriarchal and advisory role in the poetic community of New York, as he did with poets all over the world, going so far as to refer to himself as Paul Blackburn's "grampaw."[23] Pound encouraged the formation of new friendships and helped build a fertile collaborative environment. In a letter to Blackburn and poet Harold Dicker, Pound writes in a characteristically eccentric curmudgeon's drawl:

O.Kay

Blacker an Dickburn , contact mr DUDEK (Louis)

500@. 122 St. N.Y. 27

also Jxn MacLow , 152 Ave. C. N.Y. 9
civ/n not a one man job/
note also Clara de Chambrun's "Shadows Lengthen" as means of
damagin yr/ (presumabl?) iggurunce.[24]

Pound's sentence "civ/n not a one man job" has particular resonance if one considers that Blackburn would spend the following two decades ensuring that the poetry scene in New York was a collaborative enterprise by consistently running open readings, introducing poets to one another, and generally promoting the value of oral poetry readings. Additionally, Pound's reach extended into the lives of those poets who did not have the benefit of actual correspondence with "grampaw." As one sees when looking at letters and mimeos of this era, multitudes of Poundian contractions dot the mimeographed magazines of the Lower East Side. Words like *would* and *should* are transformed into *wd* and *shd*, a practice that is a typical Poundian conceit and is found throughout the poetry of Charles Olson, Robert Creeley, Joel Oppenheimer, Carol Bergé, and others. In fact, *The Letters of Ezra Pound* was originally published in 1950 and was very likely read by many of the poets associated with the Allen anthology and the subsequent reading scenes in the Lower East Side.[25]

These Poundian contractions were not just a passing whimsy on the part of the Lower East Side poets, but a very real, conscious, and easily recognizable link to an alternative tradition. Ishmael Reed (a regular presence during the Le Metro scene and the first years of the Poetry Project), while poking fun at his earlier writing practices, nevertheless reminds one about the significance of *wd*:

> I was living in New York when my early poems were written, and the thing then was to be experimental. We thought that using slashes and "wd" instead of "would" was experimental writing. I finally asked Joel Oppenheimer, who was well known for this, why he used slashes instead of apostrophes and he told me that it was because he was a typesetter and the typesetting machine had no apostrophes. So I guess it wasn't all that avant garde after all.[26]

Additionally, incorporating the American vernacular and a precise use and description of everyday objects—stereotypical if imprecisely defined components in William Carlos Williams's poetics—were effected by many of the poets reading at Les Deux Mégots and Le Metro. Ted Berrigan made this connection literal in his "Sonnet LVIII" (first published in his magazine, *C*) when he recycled William Carlos Williams's dictum "no ideas but in things":

> A glass of chocolate milk, head of lettuce, dark-
> ness of clouds at one o'clock   No truth except
> in things![27]

Of course, allegiances were not limited to the twentieth century. Ron Padgett defines an alternative tradition by going chronologically through "O'Hara, Koch, Ashbery, Schuyler, Elmslie, Ginsberg, Cesaire, to Kenneth Patchen, Hart Crane, Williams, Pound, Stevens, to early Eliot, Lorca, Mayakovsky, Neruda, the surrealists, the dadaists, Hopkins, Apollinaire, Jacob, Reverdy, Cendrars, Larbaud, St-Pol-Roux, Mallarmé, Lautréamont, Rimbaud, Baudelaire, Whitman, Dickinson, Hölderlin, Blake, Ariosto . . . let's go back to Aristophanes!"[28] Additionally, George Economou states, "For Paul Blackburn and Robert Kelly and me especially we also placed a high value on medieval poets. Not just Chaucer and Dante but also the troubadours."[29] Almost all the figures mentioned in these lists shared a commitment to formal innovation, as well as a tendency to include provocative content (like scatological humor or homosexual themes). Most important—for a community in which live readings were an essential part of poetic transmission and reception—many of the figures on these lists had articulated and championed a conception of the poem both as text and performance. The Lower East Side scene's dependence on live readings as a primary staging ground for distribution was related to a lineage, as opposed to being treated as a purely contemporary phenomenon or fad.

Grove Press, San Francisco, and the Alternative Outlaw Tradition

Poets on the Lower East Side were strongly allied with Grove Press, particularly since Grove edited the *Evergreen Review* (which published poets living on the Lower East Side including Allen Ginsberg, Amiri Baraka, and Frank O'Hara) and especially because Grove published Donald Allen's groundbreaking anthology, *The New American Poetry*.[30] Along with alternative representations afforded to poets through associations with the Lower East Side itself as a radical space, the affiliation with Grove Press was to prove crucial in Lower East Side poets' development of a general aura of political dissent and avant-gardism. When the Allen anthology was attacked by mainstream critics, many Lower East Side poets defended it in print through the mimeos that were coming out of various basements, apartments, and storefronts.[31] Writer Cecil Helmley's early attack on the Allen anthology (found in the relatively conservative and expensive *Hudson Review*) was quickly rebutted by Baraka in his and Diane di Prima's free mimeographed magazine *The Floating Bear.* Helmley savaged most of the writers included in the book, ending his review by insisting, "Since the editor has made such vast claims for what he is offering, there is an inclination not only to withdraw but to laugh."[32] In his response, Baraka argued against Helmley as he defined a new, insurrectionary poetics:

> Recently someone handed me some pages which had been taken from the latest *Hudson Review,* which contained a review of Donald Allen's anthology *The New American Poetry: 1945–1960,* written by Cecil Helmley. . . .
>
> Helmley says first "Anyone who has had a serious interest in American Poetry from 1945 to 1960 must see that this is a very eccentric version of what has been going on. It represents Mr. Allen's private view, and that is all and it

shows what happens when a narrow, dictatorial taste attempts to assert itself as authoritative."

Liberals are disparaged by anyone attempting to demonstrate Taste or Feeling (sensibility) as separate from Situation. Nothing shd present itself *outside* of certain recognized conditions. The Negroes in the south cannot utilize violence to achieve their ends (whatever? schools, homes, jobs? Why bother? But if you don't want another man to *handle your life* . . . you might, just might, mind you, have to kill him) because they admit (officially) that there is some common utopia each of them wants/ collectively. If this is true, they are stuck, perhaps, for another hundred years. But the minute some intrepid soul prints up, say, a manifesto, detailing exactly what, just he, himself, alone, uncontrolled by the NAACP or KKK or Fischer Baking Co, wants . . . (t)hen perhaps these "wants" will not be so *common:* and then perhaps, someone's list might definitely have to do with homicide.

The Liberal, also, cannot help but be academic . . . And it, the review, certainly is within that same "walking grove (of trees)". Peripatetic academicism, is certainly another name for, like, American Liberalism.[33]

In Baraka's response to the Helmley piece, we find a distinction being made between a "liberal" naively inclusive poetics and a poetic revolutionary activity. The Allen anthology is reframed as manifesto, and as such it is incompatible with liberal notions of consensus. Baraka makes a metaphor out of Helmley's reaction. Here Helmley is a "liberal" who, while feeling some sympathy for alternative/black poets, nevertheless prefers to see them absorbed into the dominant culture. Baraka suggests that acts of resistance (be they alternative anthologies or effective political manifestoes) are rooted in the conditions or the situation of the oppressed, and that taste and feeling as defined by liberals are always seen as existing outside such situations. Therefore, the Allen anthology is read by Baraka as a violation of the social code that critics like Helmley need to maintain for their own professional safety. Since Allen undertook the anthology in an attempt to change the situation of marginalized poets, Helmley needed to dismiss such a revolutionary attempt as offensive to appropriate aesthetics. Baraka roots the anthology in social relations, politics, and conditions—that is, in the dissident community rather than in the abstract academic realm of taste and feeling.

The New American Poetry (its front jacket bearing the imprint *Evergreen Original*) would inevitably generate criminal or "outlaw" significations simply by virtue of being published by Grove Press. Grove was notorious for a series of obscenity trials throughout its early history. Perhaps most famously, Ginsberg's *Howl* was the target of obscenity proceedings. The trial ended on October 3, 1957, with Judge Clayton W. Horn of the San Francisco Municipal Court handing down the decision that *Howl* did have "some redeeming importance" and was not obscene.[34] An issue of the *Evergreen Review* (published by Grove and edited by Donald Allen and Barney Rosset) included an account of the *Howl* trial written by Lawrence Ferlinghetti:

> Fahrenheit 451, the temperature at which books burn, has finally been determined not to be the prevailing temperature in San Francisco, though the police still would be all too happy to make it hot for you. . . . When William Carlos Williams, in his Introduction to HOWL, said that Ginsberg had come up with "an arresting poem," he hardly knew what he was saying . . .
>
> On May 29 1957 Customs released the books it had been holding, since the United States Attorney at San Francisco refused to institute condemnation proceedings against HOWL. Then the police took over and arrested us, Captain William Hanrahan of the juvenile department (well named, in this case) reporting that the books were not fit for children to read . . . As one paper reported, "The Cops Don't Allow No Renaissance Here."[35]

The "one paper" that Ferlinghetti speaks of probably used the phrase "the cops don't allow no renaissance here" in reference to a famous earlier issue of the *Evergreen Review*. Entitled "The San Francisco Renaissance," this issue featured work by Robert Duncan, Jack Spicer, Gary Snyder, Philip Whalen, Jack Kerouac, Allen Ginsberg, and others.[36] This particular issue, by its very title and its organization of names as representative of a specific geographic milieu, raised the possibility for an organized, nameable urban microcommunity centered on the production of poetry and the defense of its various members (in this case Ginsberg).[37] The very fact that the word *renaissance* was used in reference to a group of San Francisco–based experimental writers was certainly as much a tongue-in-cheek acknowledgment of the literary milieu in which these writers found themselves as it was a political challenge to the literary establishment at that time. After all, the dominant New Critics in the United States during this period were, through the "conservative" influence of T. S. Eliot, responsible for pointing to writers like John Donne and Andrew Marvell—poets of the British Renaissance—as the ideal models for a closed, formal poetics. By referring to themselves as "renaissance," the San Francisco poets resolutely connected themselves to an alternative notion of renaissance and coterie, one that depended far more on immanence and social engagement than it did on the New Critical values of impersonality, irony, and "distantiation."[38]

The critique of the New Critics helped define the San Francisco scene as a nameable cultural community complete with aesthetic and political rules, leaders, and acolytes. Kenneth Rexroth, in the introduction to the *Evergreen* "San Francisco Renaissance" issue, rejected those academic poets whose aesthetics fell on the side of the New Critical divide. Instead, he favored the New American poetry of which Ginsberg had become a kind of standard-bearer: "Ginsberg is almost alone in his generation in his ability to make powerful poetry of the inherent rhythms of our speech, to push forward the conquests of a few of the earliest poems of Sandburg and of William Carlos Williams. This is more skillful verse than all the cornbelt Donnes laid end to end."[39] The phrase "cornbelt Donnes" would likely have been interpreted by knowledgeable readers as referring to those "academic" poets and teachers in universities and colleges, including Kenyon College in Ohio. Kenyon College was a particular stronghold of the New Criticism—it was home to John Crowe Ransom, who in essays collected in his book *The New Criticism* argued that the poem has a "paraphrasable core" and "a context of lively local details."[40] The New Critical approach positioned the poem as an object to be identified and studied in order to determine a conclusive meaning for the static text. On the other end of the spectrum was the orally based San Francisco scene, where poets including future Lower East Side reading series regulars Taylor Mead, John Wieners, and Allen Ginsberg situated their poetry as inherently public and affective documents by reading consistently in the art galleries and coffee shops of North Beach.[41] This communal approach to the distribution and reception of poetry was clearly in conflict with the New Critical approach, which Christopher Beach has defined as "ostensibly dissociated from the social context of either poet or reader: the particularity of the poetic audience was seen as irrelevant to any 'correct' reading of the poem."[42]

Along with emphasizing San Francisco poets' dissident aesthetics, editors, publishers, and the popular press interpreted many of the "nonacademic" poets associated with the *Evergreen Review* as political agitators. They had help, since many of the poets published in Grove Press and *Evergreen* defined their writing as part of an overall subversive social and political life. An excerpt from Kenneth Rexroth's introduction to the *Evergreen Review* "San Francisco Renaissance" issue quite literally defines the work of the modern writer as a revolutionary project:

> No literature of the past two hundred years is of the slightest importance unless it is "disaffiliated." Only our modern industrial and commercial civilization has produced an elite which has consistently rejected all the reigning values of the society . . . The special ideology of the only artists and writers since the French Revolution who deserve to be taken seriously is a destructive, revolutionary force. They would blow up "their" ship of state—destroy it utterly.[43]

Here literary production in the San Francisco Renaissance is synonymous with political insurgency, and thus the poetic community, through rhetoric like Rexroth's, continued to attack the assumptions behind New Critical ahistoricity. The conscious conflation of experimental aesthetics with leftist politics was continued on the Lower East Side. Writers including Lorenzo Thomas insisted that "the avant-garde is less about change in the arts than it is about genuine experimentation in social relations."[44] Amiri Baraka connected aesthetics with the contemporary political condition of the mid-1960s: "I was always interested in Surrealism and Expressionism, and I think the reason was to really try to get below the surface of things. . . . The Civil Rights Movement, it's the same thing essentially, trying to get below the surface of things, trying to get below the norm, the everyday, the status quo, which was finally unacceptable, just unacceptable."[45] Such dissident stances held by poets on the Lower East Side stemmed in part from San Francisco poets' earlier connection of avant-garde poetry and progressive politics in opposition to New Critical hegemony.

Part of blowing up the ship of the literary and political status quo meant associating poet and publisher as a subversive group that stood in overt opposition to the "southern agrarian" conservatism felt to be at the core of much New Critical writing.[46] Mainstream publishing institutions including Meridian Books, which published the successful academic anthology *New Poets of England and America* edited by Donald Hall, Robert Pack, and Louis Simpson, in no way suggested venality, danger, and corruption in the popular imagination.[47] On the other hand, Grove Press and its associated magazine the *Evergreen Review* unavoidably represented a dangerous collection of writers and writing designed to signify a threat. This was further evidenced by Grove's practice of associating their stable of poets to predecessor "outlaw" writers. The *Evergreen Review,* for example, published politically radical writers including Artaud, Jean Genet, and earlier French surrealists, alongside Lower East Side figures including Ginsberg, Baraka, and O'Hara. Perhaps Grove Press's greatest alignment with a historical lineage of literary criminality came with the publication of the unexpurgated version of D. H. Lawrence's *Lady Chatterley's Lover,* released one year before the publication of *The New American Poetry.*

Grove Press's Tactics in Creating a Profitable Naughty Reputation

The Comstock Act of 1873 had made it a crime to employ the mails to distribute obscenity. Citing this law, Washington police charged that the Grove Press unexpurgated edition of D. H. Lawrence's *Lady Chatterley's Lover* was obscene. "A deputy chief in charge of the Washington vice squad had heard the book was on sale. He telephoned Brentano's [book store], and asked whether it was true. The clerk said it was. The deputy chief told him to get a copy, turn to a particular page and read the page aloud over the phone. . . .

The press reported that the deputy chief was considering seizure of the book and criminal prosecution."[48] Charles Rembar, the attorney for Grove Press, sued the Washington police in an attempt to get the book cleared. On April 30, 1959, two days after the Washington suit was filed, Robert K. Christenberry, former chairman of the Boxing Commission and candidate for mayor working as postmaster of the City of New York, "ordered the interception of twenty-four cartons of the book that Grove had mailed . . . a few days after the seizure Grove heard about it informally, and a few days after that got an official notice. The notice set a trial for May 14."[49]

Saul Mindel, counsel to the postmaster, actually used the precedent case of James Joyce's *Ulysses* (a book that was cleared of all obscenity charges) against Grove, arguing that *Ulysses* contained more literary merit than obscene sex, whereas *Lady Chatterley's Lover* contained more obscene sex than literary merit: "[I]t is our position that whatever literary merit may be found in the unexpurgated edition, it is outweighed by the obscenity; that the dominant effect of the book, taken as a whole, is one which appeals to prurient interests."[50]

The trial took place within the post office department and was covered fairly extensively by the media. Grove Press called in Alfred Kazin and Malcolm Cowley to testify, and Jacques Barzun, dean of faculties at Columbia University, sent a letter in support of Grove.[51] Malcolm Cowley testified that Lawrence "thought he could accomplish (the removal of sentimentality re: the sex act) by using what seemed to him the absolutely hard, definite Anglo-Saxon words for physical function."[52] However, despite all the major literary figures present at the Grove Press trial, Summerfield, the postmaster general, concluded, "The contemporary community standards are not such that this book should be allowed to be transmitted in the mails . . . any literary merit the book may have is far outweighed by the pornographic and smutty passages and words, so that the book, taken as a whole, is an obscene and filthy work."[53] Lawyers for Grove Press then filed suit in the federal district court in New York. While the court of appeals ultimately judged in favor of Grove, Grove's problems with censorship continued throughout the late 1950s and early 1960s as Donald Allen's *The New American Poetry* went through its various reprints.[54] As a result of this publicity, *any* book featuring the Grove imprint during the 1960s essentially guaranteed a reader response characterized in part by expectations of aesthetic daring, shocking content, unique or "avant-garde" textual practices, or at the very least titillating good times.[55] Grove's editorial practices also helped to ensure that poets on the Lower East Side, as they continued to be published in the *Evergreen Review* and associated with *The New American Poetry,* would also generate significations of aesthetic and social boldness by virtue of association.

As earlier San Francisco–based writers suffered legal assaults for their "obscene" literature, alternative poets in the early to mid-1960s found New York a somewhat dangerous place for the avant-garde. Prosecutors in Manhattan could look back on the trials City Lights and Grove Press faced for ideas on how to prosecute their own local poets and estimate the extent to which a given text or image could be deemed obscene. In a rather unfriendly assessment of Grove Press's legal troubles during the 1960s, Richard H. Kuh—the prosecutor responsible for initiating legal proceedings against comedian Lenny Bruce in New York City—provided a compendium of "criminal" literature that the company was responsible for disseminating:

In the spring of 1964 Grove Press's avant-garde monthly, *Evergreen Review,* featured a photographic portfolio of mixed nudes, processed as if taken under water or through a bubbly haze. The pictures showed bodies so juxtaposed that sexual contact of various sorts were not improbable, but the distortion left wholly to the imagination precisely who was doing what (if anything), how, and to whom. (Criminal litigation charging that issue of Evergreen Review with obscenity was disposed of on procedural grounds). Grove's presses had accelerated. Its imprimatur was to be seen on such widely distributed "pornographic classics" as Frank Harris's *My Life and Loves,* the collected writings of the Marquis de Sade (an anthology of luridly depicted group sex of every imaginable variation, only pallidly intimated by the word "sadism"), more of Henry Miller's work, and the Victorian era's contribution to pornographic literature, the anonymously authored *My Secret Life.* It also published an assortment of that rancid contemporary writing that seems indigenous to the years of Western culture: writing that ranged from the savage, eloquent *Our Lady of the Flowers* of Jean Genet, through Selby's *Last Exit to Brooklyn* and Burroughs's *Naked Lunch.*[56]

These suggestions of dissolution and criminality were very useful in setting up some of the writers of the Lower East Side poetic community with alternative credentials, since they provided morally minded prosecutors with enough evidence to make arrests. Writers in the Lower East Side poetic community would face legal trouble throughout the late 1950s and 1960s. Amiri Baraka and Diane di Prima were charged with distributing obscenity by sending copies of *The Floating Bear* through the mails, Ed Sanders was brought up on obscenity charges, Ron Padgett's editorial choices were censored by the Columbia University administration, and reading series themselves were under constant threat of being shut down by law-enforcement officials.[57] As late as 1967, editors from *The East Village Other* became sufficiently alarmed by legal proceedings being initiated against poets that articles including the following (headlined "Legalize Poetry") were written with increasing frequency:

Big Brother has been watching the poets, and with prurient interest yet. Numerous recent arrests and indictments for obscenity brought against poets here and abroad indicate that the methods of the public defenders are often repulsive, offensive to decency, and ill-omened—the precise definition, in fact, given in Webster's for "obscene."[58]

The Poetry Project extended this tradition of associating downtown New York–based avant-garde art with politically and socially unconventional performance. On the most basic social level, the Poetry Project administration was generally permissive regarding the kinds of behavior that could go on in its parish hall. In an interview with Lisa Jarnot, poet Bernadette Mayer recalled, "People used to make love in the church belfry and on the pews. You know, it was a lot of fun."[59] This kind of behavior would in no way have been tolerated in more established reading series such as the one taking place concurrently at the 92nd Street Y. The "Y" series, featuring mostly established and relatively formal poets who read from a raised stage to an audience seated in rows, was not amenable to such activity.

However, rebellious behavior attendant to poetry went beyond the kinds of sexually libertine behavior to which Mayer refers. On a more complicated and politically engaged level, the Poetry Project prominently featured poets included in Grove Press–related publications reading at fund-raisers for other poets and political activists who were in jail for reasons as varied as political dissidence and drug charges. For example, on October 10, 1968, poets anthologized in *The New American Poetry,* including Paul Blackburn, Kenneth Koch, Ron Loewisohn, and Joel Oppenheimer, along with their younger peers Ron Padgett and Michael Palmer, read at a benefit for the Catonsville 9. The Catonsville 9 were brought to trial for burning draft cards, which they had appropriated from Draft Board 33 in Catonsville, Maryland. The activists doused the cards with homemade napalm, set them afire, and waited for the police. The 1968 Catonsville event marked a new phase in the growing antiwar movement, in which resistance moved "from mere demonstrations to burning draft cards, inciting civil disobedience, and using the courtroom as a platform. Their leader was Phil Berrigan, a strapping Josephite priest who'd been an army officer in World War II but was determined to stop the slaughter in Vietnam. His brother Dan, a Jesuit priest-poet, was also involved; after Catonsville, Dan went underground, evading J. Edgar Hoover's minions for months."[60]

By supporting such political fugitives, poets reading regularly at the Poetry Project continued a kind of alternative tradition through their organized readings. This tradition both complemented and was sustained by the history of the Lower East Side as a site of resistance, since it linked up to clearly defined literary predecessors in earlier avant-garde groupings and national avant-garde publications, including Grove Press's *Evergreen Review.* Acts of revolutionary (if mostly pacifist) activity on the part of political insurgents like the Berrigan brothers certainly inspired the performance of art and the progressive establishment of a poetic community. While the content of many of the poems read at the events described above may not have been overtly political, nevertheless the social environment in which such work was projected helped position it as an alternative to the dominant discourse manifested in the literary and political establishment.

Charles Olson and the "Cowboys" of the Lower East Side

Donald Allen's choice to begin *The New American Poetry* with poems by Charles Olson was a prescient and politically useful decision made by an editor eager to absorb a disparate group of poets into an oppositional, avant-garde sign. Olson wrote the immensely influential essay "Projective Verse" (included in the back of Allen's anthology under the "Statements on Poetics" section). Much has been written about this essay already, but more should be said about how the tone and attitude of the essay was received, interpreted, and applied specifically by poets on the Lower East Side.

Olson's essay suggested what Anne Waldman, poet and former director of the Poetry Project, has called an "outrider" poetry aesthetic. Literally, an outrider is a cowboy who serves as an advance scout; the iconography of the cowboy and his place on the frontier would play a real part in the discursive environment of Lower East Side poets. This sense of going beyond the frontier is meant both in terms of the experimental nature of much of the Lower East Side poets' work and in their role as bohemian "colonizers" of the Lower East Side. The Lower East Side was seen in the early 1960s as a kind of no-man's-land ready to be conquered, especially by those mostly young artists attracted by cheap rents and the historically progressive reputation of the neighborhood. In an interview with Lisa Jarnot, poet David Henderson, an editor of the predominantly African American Lower East Side–based magazine *Umbra,* drew a connection between being an outsider and place, race, and poetics. "*Umbra* workshops were amazing because, it wasn't about 'is this a good poem?' or 'does it have iambic pentameter' or 'the rhyme scheme is great.' They were all poems really about . . . not all of them were about social things, but a lot of them were about being black, *or being an outsider,* which is exactly what we were. We were on the lower east side, and over on Avenue C and 2nd Street."[61] Hettie Jones, Baraka's wife during the early 1960s, wrote of the Lower East Side, "The real estate broker D. D. Stein offered his twenty-five-dollar bathtub-in-kitchen apartments on Avenue B with the slogan 'Join the Smart Trend,' and the café Les Deux Mégots on Seventh Street advertised 'Come East Young Man.'"[62]

Note the inverted Western slogans—"Come East Young Man" replaces the iconic "Go west young man," and D. D. Stein's offer hearkens back to pioneer-era posters promising riches to those willing to take a risk by making the move out west. Those poets who didn't move to the Lower East Side could be perceived as akin to nineteenth-century city dwellers in the urban east who remained in relative safety as their more adventurous or desperate peers moved west. For example, the poet James Schuyler saw the Lower East Side as a kind of wild country by which he was certainly impressed. However, as one sees in this excerpt of a letter from Schuyler to Gerard Malanga, Schuyler wasn't quite ready to put on his boots and hop on a horse to make his way "out there" to the Lower East Side: "It's a remarkably dreary day out here and I think I'll soon be staying more at my New York pad, on East 35th—a nice blah sort of neighborhood, unostentatious middle class, my dish exactly. I admire my friends who [have] the courage to live on the lower East side; I certainly haven't."[63]

Slogans like "Come east young man" casually if unselfconsciously echoed colonialist rhetoric used by predecessor settlers of the American Wild West in that they suggested an uninhabited space ripe with low-cost artistic lebensraum. Of course, as the "frontier" American landscape was populated in the eighteenth and nineteenth century by Native Americans, the Lower East Side was settled, before the bohemian influx, by Latino, African American, Jewish, white-ethnic poor, and working-class people. Nevertheless, the presence of this population did not dissuade artists looking to carve out a new community, but instead added to the overall anti-middle-class cachet crucial to forming an alternative sensibility. "The representation of the Lower East Side as marginal, exotic, and different suited the image and the identity of romantic artists as 'frontier scouts' of culture, moving ahead of their contemporaries into uncharted territories where they would undergo privation and sacrifices." On the one hand, the aura of the frontier—abetted by the presence of a long-term ethnic residential majority—proved irresistible to artists looking for cheap rents and a sense of artistic community. On the other, the incursion of artists into the Lower East Side began to attract real estate developers excited by the possibilities for eventual gentrification.[64]

This problematic adoption of a frontier mentality as it related to developing alternative formations was extended throughout the bohemian population of the neighborhood. The emerging fashions visibly projected and codified a "look" for the Lower East Side scene that depended on signs related to traditional American values of self-sufficiency, bravery, and the ability to make order out of "uncharted" territory. In John Gruen's *The New Bohemia: The*

Combine Generation, one finds that the "New Bohemia" of the Lower East Side took its cues from frontier myth:

> Out of the American tradition of the barn dance, has come a kind of salvation. This ironic tie to the past has its parallel in the sense of frontiersmanship that seems to be an integral part of this New Bohemia. Take its mode of dress: strictly boots and saddles. New Bohemia likes leather jackets, Levis, western boots, work shirts, long hair, beards, moustaches . . . The whole thing is like a romantic revival of the wild, wild, West. From the single vigilante to the hell-bent posse, they ride in search of something that used to be known as "justice" and "vengeance," but which seems now to be a confrontation with LIFE, which is "out there."[65]

The typically American cowboy look, visible as one of the fashions displayed throughout the Lower East Side, extended into the poetry and writing coming out of and favored by the Lower East Side scene. In Berrigan's *The Sonnets,* one found lines including "my dream a drink with Ira Hayes we discuss the code of the west," "As I am a cowboy and you imaginary / Ripeness," and the aggressive if ironically posturing line found throughout *The Sonnets,* "I like to beat people up."[66] Even a poet like George Economou, who wrote modern-day versions of Virgilian georgics and held a Ph.D. in medievalism and comparative literature, wrote cowboy poems. The poem "Crazy-Eyed Cowboys" reconciled Economou's interests in courtly literature with Lower East Side cowboy "talk": "Those crazy-eyed cowboys / Lady, who romp you fantastically / have sharp little knee caps / beneath their horse sweat stinky."[67] These are just two examples out of many texts and fashions associated with the Lower East Side poetic community that recycled and adapted cowboy language complementary to the rhetoric found in Olson's "Projective Verse."[68]

Olson's *Projective Verse* anticipated the adoption of this cowboy aesthetic among the group of younger poets living full- or part-time on the Lower East Side. Olson used a wholly fraternal "yee haw" language in his essay, such as "go by it, boys, rather than by, the metronome," "there it is, brothers, sitting there, for USE," "get on with it, keep moving, keep in speed . . . keep it moving as fast as you can, citizen," "(f)rom the moment he ventures into FIELD COMPOSITION—puts himself into the open."[69] This sense of fraternity manifested itself in both productive and unfortunate ways within the Lower East Side poetry community before the founding of the Poetry Project. Olson's sociability, support, and patrimonial influence extended to predominantly male writers—Fielding Dawson, Amiri Baraka, Joel Oppenheimer, and Paul Blackburn, to name just a few who were active in the Lower East Side—and many of these writers went on record referring to Olson as a father figure.[70] It is possible that Olson's extensive influence on Lower East Side poets—both through his actual friendships and the resulting dissemination of tough-guy if erudite rhetoric—was partly responsible for creating an initial male-centered environment within the poetic community. Aldon Nielsen has pointed out, "The coteries of avant-garde poetry in America were largely operated as male enclaves, even when, as in the case of *Yugen,* one of the coeditors was a woman."[71] While Nielsen adds, "Clearly the male avant-garde poets did encourage and assist some women poets (indeed, each 'school' seems to have had its requisite token woman)," during the early 1960s women poets, while active live performers, were generally denied the establishment status afforded by book publication.

Women poets on the Lower East Side certainly existed before the advent of the Poetry Project and were active participants in the reading series at Les Deux Mégots and Le Metro. Poets including Diane Wakoski, Kathleen Fraser, Carol Bergé, Barbara Moraff, and Leonore Kandell were published in mimeograph magazines and occasionally in books throughout the early to mid-1960s. However, male editors who published them often sexualized their presence, even as their presence on the stages of the poetic community was equal to that of the men with whom they shared the spotlight. A particularly egregious example of this can be found in the magazine *Femora,* which on the surface appeared somewhat progressive. Edited by George Montgomery, *Femora* featured only women poets. An introduction to *Femora* 2 written by Albert Ellis (who signed his article "Albert Ellis, Ph.D." in an effort, one supposes, to lend academic credence to his comments) indicates the attitude these "enlightened" male literati held toward their female counterparts:

> George Montgomery has made several significant contributions to the field of modern poetry during the last few years, both as a poet and a publisher. One of his most remarkable ideas is the publication, FEMORA. I suppose that there have been other magazines which exclusively featured female poets; if so, I can't recall any; and I shudder to think of what their overfeminized (not to mention, over-lesbianized) contents might have been. Not so, with FEMORA. This is hardly a journal replete with the chrysanthemum and rosebud type of stuff for which many of our popular lady poets are justly infamous. Nor does its cup runneth over with masculine protest, penis envy, and other shades of even-though-I'm-a-woman-I-can-be-as-big-a-shit-shit-as-you-are. Maybe I'm over-optimistically nutty, but I seem to find in FEMORA an unusually heavy and heady potion of honest, gutsy female heterosexuality. These poetesses like to be females; but they also like to have, both figuratively and literally, a good fucking time with males; and they do. Long may they continue to femorate and fuck.[72]

One should keep in mind that Ellis was speaking as a *progressive* in his depiction of women poets, since *Femora* published sexually explicit and "obscene" language in an environment that had previously resisted new realist writing by women. In a radio interview with David Ossman, Olson protégé Paul Blackburn went so far as to suggest that women should naturally avoid using "common" speech in their poetry. "If we start from the point of view that common speech is a very fair and valid medium for poetry, you're going to find some people whose common speech is commoner than most. I think that would include especially a lot of the male members—the ladies usually watch their language very carefully. That's only right, too."[73] In light of such attitudes about the proper speech for ladies, perhaps *Femora was* a step up for female poets in the early 1960s.

Olson's "Projective Verse" indirectly perpetuated this male-centered literary environment. As a social document within the Lower East Side community, "Projective Verse" circulated and was eventually canonized as a primary manifesto in the alternative scene, and it helped to sustain an environment where poetry was gendered male. As DuPlessis writes in her discussion of "Projective Verse":

> The Olson manifesto . . . rings with its own homosocial enthusiasms. "There it is, brothers, sitting there, for USE." Here too, poetry and poetics are gendered male. As a condition of the employment called poetry, pretenders to poetry who are inadequate are, to say it short, not-men . . . Although made as dissent, and effective as a terrific blast against academic poetries of the "New Critical" period . . . Olson's is not a poetics that undermines the poetic compact of male mastery. Those apparent males positioned as "not-men" are dismissed, and the speaking female is missing."[74]

Beyond seeing how Olson's language (as DuPlessis recognizes) gendered his poetics, one can argue that the adamantly macho and exhortative tone in "Projective Verse" also helped generate social response among Olson's acolytes that was, in hindsight, heterosexist.[75] The essay's language, as received on the Lower East Side, may have helped sustain the "poet as cowboy" motif that was taking hold in the neighborhood. Olson protégé Paul Blackburn walked around the Lower East Side in a trademark black cowboy hat. This hat was so familiar to fellow poets that "for awhile, Oppenheimer affected a white cowboy hat, a self-mocking response to Paul's familiar black hat. The smile widens. In 1961, 'The Great American Desert' opened at Judson Church, with Paul Blackburn playing Doc Holliday, who 'is dressed in black.' Joel wrote the play."[76] The visual spectacle of the frontier-poet in his cowboy hat, aided or at the very least complemented in part by Olson's rhetoric including, "Go by it, boys" and "get on with it, keep moving," coincided with the continuing popularization of the Western movie genre. As Blackburn and others walked around the streets in cowboy hats and boots, actors including John Wayne and James Stewart appeared throughout the late 1950s and early '60s in director John Ford's or Anthony Mann's wildly popular Western movies. The motif of the hard-*acting,* hard-drinking cowboy resonated in the literary scene of the Lower East Side and affected the way in which women's writing was received. Sara Blackburn, Paul Blackburn's wife at the time, insists:

> This was very much a boy's community. It was the style. There was a great deal of drinking, and male camaraderie, and there was an enormous amount of "fucking around." It was almost a parody of machismo for these guys. I didn't think it was funny. Nobody ever knew where to put me—I wasn't a poet, though I was reputed to be an editor. I was known mostly as "wife of Paul." People like Carol Bergé and Diane Wakoski, who were enormously articulate and extraordinary people, were taken seriously by a few people, but for the most part I think these men were scared of women. They didn't know what to do with them except have sex. And women poets in that scene didn't have the aching, longing, necessity to screw everybody in sight that these virile male poets had (and I exclude poets like George Economou, Armand Schwerner, and Jerry Rothenberg from this characterization—I don't want to tar everyone with this old brush).[77]

Nevertheless, one should be cautious not to focus too obsessively on the historically typical heterosexism implicit in Olson's language. Women poets during the 1960s took what they needed from Olson, and as a whole Olson continues to influence innovative women's writing. While poet Susan Howe has written, "Had [Olson] been my teacher in real life, I know he would have stopped my voice," she nevertheless insists, "Charles Olson's writing encouraged me to be a radical poet. When I was writing my first poems I recall he showed me what to do." Howe continues to temper Olson's negative influence by solidifying his poetic achievement. "But where would American poetry be now without 'The Kingfishers,' 'The Death of Europe,' 'At Yorktown,' 'As the Dead Prey Upon Us,' parts of *Maximus,* some of the essays, letters, and speeches? They are a necessary concentration of energy."[78]

While essentialist in its gender-based assumptions, Olson's oeuvre or "concentration of energy" was useful as a source for a radical impulse in contemporary American writing. As Edward Foster points out, Olson himself was, in the 1940s, politically active both in the Roosevelt administration and in the Common Council for American Unity, "a New York-based organization that fought the kind of ethnic and racial prejudice [Olson] had known in New England." Foster argues that "Olson's opposition to New England white Anglo-Saxon Protestant culture ran very deep." Foster also suggests that Olson was at least friendly to the concept of the gay liberation struggle, and refers to Olson's poem "Diaries of Death," in which Olson writes of his homosexual former teacher F. O. Matthiesen's suicide: "go free / from places where the strictures are too much, too much / for you and me to bear!"[79] Olson's resistance politics leaked into his poetry and proved crucial in assisting poets to link an antiauthoritarian ethos to their writing projects. Many of the poets of the Lower East Side made an overt connection between Charles Olson's writing and its relationship to what was seen as a flabby, corrupt American society, as this excerpt from Amiri Baraka's autobiography makes clear:

> What fascinated me about Olson was his sense of having dropped out of the U.S., the "pejoracracy." He said in his poems we should "Go Against" it. That we should oppose "those who would advertise you out." It was a similar spirit that informed the most meaningful of the Beats, and Olson was a heavy scholar. His "Projective Verse" had been a bible for me because it seemed to give voice to feelings I had about poetry and about society.[80]

In the context of Baraka's statement, one sees that Olson's rhetoric helped avant-garde poets to situate themselves as living on the margins of their society. Lower East Side poets used Olson's ideas, their own developing poetics, and the alternative representations generated by the neighborhood they populated to "Go Against" it.

The New York School as Corrective to Machismo

At the memorial service for Charles Olson held at the Poetry Project, Ted Berrigan discussed Olson as a great reconciler of previously competing "schools":

> It's nice to be here with everybody, even on such a sad occasion. I thought not to read since I thought that the reading would be restricted to Vincent [Ferrini] and John [Wieners] and Ed [Sanders] and the kind of the first circle of Charles's friends and fellow poets, but Anne [Waldman] pointed out quite properly that Charles is more than just that. He was the father of us all. He was one of my legendary heroes. My wife and I were going to hitchhike to Maine, we were going to have an adventure. We were invited by John [Wieners] and Dana to come and visit them in Gloucester. [By the time we got to Wieners' house], Charles came for dinner, and stayed all night. At 10 in the morning, Charles was still talking. At one point I was getting very excited about the way he was talking and I started interrupting and saying things. He kind of smiled and put his hand on my shoulder and said "Let the old man talk, son, your time will come."

Later on in his talk, Berrigan explained,

> Frank O'Hara met Charles when Frank went to Buffalo to give a reading. I guess everybody always thinks that there are big feuds in the poetry world and

that the Black Mountain Poets don't like the New York School and vice-versa. Well, it's all true, but it's true in a special way. Frank went to read—Frank the epitome of the New York School. Frank told me that Charles came up to him after the reading. Frank had a very cocky way of reading, especially when he didn't know the audience. It wasn't personally cocky, it's that the poems were cocky, they were good and he knew it, even if he was in maybe the enemy camp. He said that Charles came up after the reading and put his arm around him and said "Good for you, you gave them just what they didn't want to hear."

The tension that Berrigan describes—that Olson and O'Hara are in "enemy camps"—is certainly true in terms of the poetic histories involved. The fey and at times campy language and antics associated with the New York School—many of whose members, especially in the so-called First Generation, were homosexual—were correctives to the machismo so often associated with poets like Joel Oppenheimer and Paul Blackburn of the Black Mountain milieu.[81] New York School poets had poked fun at and deflated machismo in 1957, for example, when artists Larry Rivers and Fairfield Porter created, respectively, a portrait and sketches of Frank O'Hara. Rivers's portrait, entitled *O'Hara Nude with Boots* featured a large image of O'Hara standing, nude except for a pair of army boots. The portrait shows O'Hara with his arms curled effeminately above him, his hands interlocking at the top of his head. Porter's sketches, *Untitled Male Nude (in Boots)* features similar, smaller-scale images of O'Hara. By undermining machismo with representations of male nudity that were feminized with a "faggy" gesture, Rivers's and Porter's images tended to disable the macho associations an urban dweller might hope to contain as a result of wearing army boots.

Resistance to machismo, as exhibited by the paintings described above, became a kind of legacy the New York School passed on to younger poets. As the poetic community of the Lower East Side progressed throughout the 1960s, New York School poets—especially Ashbery, Koch, O'Hara, and Schuyler—became a kind of alternative influential patrimony for a growing group of writers in distinction to the Olson-centered crowd. John Shoptaw has written how "Ashbery thinks of the New York School of the 1950s as establishing 'a geographical reality and an intellectual opposition with the Black Mountain poets, implanted in North Carolina.'" Later, Shoptaw notes that "Schuyler, who was editing the premier issue of *Locus Solus,* wrote to Ashbery that 'part of its unstated objective is a riposte at THE NEW AMERICAN POETRY, which has so thoroughly misrepresented so many of us—not completely, but the implications of context [with Olson opening the anthology] are rather overwhelming.'" After quoting Schuyler's letter, Shoptaw rightly distinguishes between the two schools: "Unlike the Black Mountain school, the New York

School had no campus or lessons or poetics, other than the absence of a poetics, the very rules by which group discipline might be maintained. None of these founding members wrote anything like the manifestoes coming from Black Mountain."[82]

Perhaps one of the reasons that O'Hara and other poets associated with the New York School held Olson and company in suspicion was Olson's attachment to mythic and powerful icons. There's Olson's towering "Maximus" figure, as well as lines found throughout the shorter poems that rely on mythic substance to lend gravitas to the texts, including the following from Olson's "La Préface": "Open, the figure stands at the door, horror his / and gone, possessed, o new Osiris, Odysseus ship."[83] New York School poets and their "descendants" (including Ron Padgett, Ted Berrigan, and Joe Brainard) resisted incorporating familiar figures of the Western literary tradition into their poetry; the use of mythic, Homeric allusions was too reminiscent of "academic" poetry.[84] Kenneth Koch has referred to his poetic project as working against poetry "about the myth, the missus and the midterms."[85] Koch and O'Hara especially saw humor, lightheartedness, and feyness as a way of interrogating or destabilizing the sense of import attached to myth and, by extension, poetry too reliant on the authority of canonical Western texts. A typical example of this can be found in "Fresh Air," the second poem of Koch's included in *The New American Poetry.*

"Fresh Air" is divided into five sections and set initially at a meeting of an academic poetry establishment known as the "Poem Society." Koch describes these academic poets as "assembled mediocrities." Several poets attending the meeting stage a kind of avant-garde rebellion, and, by the end of the meeting, the once-powerful "mediocrities" and "professors" have either "left the room to go back to their duty" or "wilted away like a cigarette paper on which the bumblebees have urinated." The remaining victorious avant-garde poets sing "a new poem of the twentieth century" which, "though influenced by Mallarmé, Shelley, Byron, and Whitman, / Plus a million other poets, is still entirely original."[86] As if in response to the success of Eliot's *Waste Land,* with its now legendary footnotes and references to texts in the Western epic tradition, "Fresh Air" goes on in its third section to feature a "Strangler" whose job it is to "annihilate the students of myth!" and whose ear is "alert for the names of Orpheus, Cuchulain, Gawain, and Odysseus."[87] Berrigan's description of O'Hara's reading style as "cocky" applies just as well to Koch's poem, in that the rebellious avant-garde poet is literally cocky in the face of an unappreciative audience as he embodies a kind of gay (cock-y?) lighthearted wit typical of O'Hara and Koch and generally atypical of a poet like Olson, who tended to position himself in public as an impassioned, possessed, and wholly male figure.

Nevertheless, Berrigan insists that the feuding that existed between these schools was "special." Perhaps this was so because Olson in many ways was responsible for propagating the poem as a spoken and even *social* event. Michael Davidson points out: "Olson and other poets of his generation hoped to defeat Cartesianism by restoring the physiology of the poet's breath, musculature, movement—in the composition process."[88] The poem as speech act was a concept that was actively extended into the multischool reading series at Les Deux Mégots, Le Metro, and the Poetry Project at St. Mark's Church. It is important to pay special attention to Davidson's phrase "other poets." As the next chapter will show, many of Olson's students and admirers—and even those poets who were at odds with Olson aesthetically, socially, and politically—were to make good on lines from Olson's "Projective Verse," including "the line comes (I swear it) from the breath, from the breathing of the man who writes"[89] by developing a vibrant community centered on the presentation of poets reading their poems in the coffee shops on the Lower East Side.

Oral Poetics on the Lower East Side

Different Collective Ends

Poets of the Lower East Side directed attention to the function of art in society by reinvigorating the tradition of the poetry reading. Readings were not just public presentations of texts, but events that defined a contemporary avant-garde as they redefined the way poetry was used in contemporary American culture. Amiri Baraka's description of his writing practice helps us see how a conception of the poem as speech act determined writing: "I don't mean that I write poems completely the way I'm talking now, although I'm certain that a great deal of my natural rhythm dominates the line, where I break the line of the poem, for instance where I'm breathing, and I have to stop the line to inhale or exhale. I have to break the line there. I'm trying to get closer to the way I sound."[1] Baraka was essentially manifesting Olson's theorized poetics, in which line breaks are determined by the "natural" rhythms of the individual human body and breath as opposed to a preordained formal template. As long as the reader was part of an interpretive community aware of the significance of breath as it related to composition, the reading of the poem necessarily served to direct part of the reader's attention to the poet's situated body. Reading a line with the understanding that the author treated it as a unit equal to his or her particular breath tended to emphasize authorial presence. Reading a poem in this fashion therefore engaged the senses in a variety of ways. While the poem was still a text on a page, the ideal reader accepted a tacit invitation to conceive of the poet's body articulating the lines. Silent reading became an event, a poetry reading taking place in the imagination.[2]

The new focus on the role of breath in determining phrasing, line length, and line placement was tied to the historical conditions of the postwar American avant-garde poetry scene.[3] Robert Duncan recalled that, circa 1950, poets in San Francisco "really preached the doctrine of reading a poem aloud. We weren't even interested in publishing, and we had already by 1950 an audience going."[4] The San Francisco reading scene welcomed peripatetic poets including Allen Ginsberg and John Wieners into its fold. The public reading tradition was thus extended as these poets traveled to other locations and encouraged or participated in the formation and promotion of café and bar readings, most notably the reading series taking place on the Lower East Side at Les Deux Mégots and Le Metro. The San Francisco jazz-poetry tradition even influenced New York School poet Kenneth Koch, who did not read very often in public until the founding of the Poetry Project. Koch remembers that his friend Larry Rivers organized jazz-poetry readings at the Five Spot Café near Cooper Square: "Rivers knew a lot of jazz musicians. The Beat poets, and Rexroth out on the West Coast, were reading poetry to jazz. I thought this absurd. The beat of music is so much stronger than that of poetry that you could read the telephone book to music and it would sound good. I did that once. The other thing I thought was 'I want to do that too!'"[5]

The debt that poetry coming out of the Lower East Side owed to jazz is clear from recordings of the readings themselves. Poets at Les Deux Mégots (and at later reading series) consistently used the word *set* to describe their readings, as in "I'll read two sets" or "For my next set, I'll read two long poems." Linking poetry to jazz both emphasized performativity—the poets performing their work or "set" in front of an audience—and reminded listeners that writing was a peculiarly collaborative endeavor. After all, a set in jazz refers to a *group* playing together, not to an individual soloing on his or her instrument. Referring to a poetry reading as a set ushered in representations of a group project into Les Deux Mégots and related spaces. Calling a poetry reading a set was also irreverent. A poetry that was tied to jazz and its attendant associations of active, collaborative crowd response (that is, cheering, clapping, booing, yelling epithets and praise) strengthened the Lower East Side scene's alternative status. As Michael Magee has pointed out, jazz sets were social models for poets:

> Monk and Coltrane were among a handful of musician-composers regularly playing at The Five Spot in the late 1950's. . . . That music, as Nathaniel Mackey

has argued, "proposed a model social order, an ideal, even utopic balance between personal impulse and group demands." Monk's influence on the young jazz avant-garde which congregated at the Five Spot . . . was profound. . . . Moreover, Monk's influence extended beyond young jazz musicians to include young poets such as Baraka, Spellman and Creeley.[6]

Additionally, in terms of racial politics, it is important to note that jazz language was used by poets to underscore the overall aesthetic of the Lower East Side poetry reading, particularly since jazz was mostly associated with African American performers. Like the so-called Beat poets before them, Lower East Side poets adopted jazz language to ally themselves with artists (such as Thelonious Monk, Charlie Parker, and Dizzy Gillespie), who, being black in pre–civil rights America, were unavoidably outsiders in a white hegemonic culture. It helped that figures like Charlie Parker were outsiders in terms of race and of their ostensibly dissident social behavior. "Charlie Parker represented the ultimate in hipster mystique: frantic genius, coupled with romanticized overindulgence."[7] Such racialized representations of excessive and illicit behavior attached themselves by association to the word *set,* and thus poetry readings, partly transformed through language into jam sessions, gained a valuable dissident allure.[8]

Performativity in jazz as it found a parallel in the poetic community was augmented by an increasing emphasis on the human voice as shaper of poetic form. As readings became increasingly popular on both coasts, the ideas in "Projective Verse" served as a kind of theoretical foundation for the readings. Poets linked conceptions of voice as delineated by Olson to jazz performance and theory. "Recognizing the possible connections between Olson's theory of projective verse ('projectile, percussive, prospective') and Parker's jazz, Creeley kept urging the older poet to hear the 'New Sounds' of music."[9] While Olson himself was never particularly interested in bebop, his ideas of phrasing found their complement in the new jazz popular among many of the New American alternative poets.

Olson's theories also corresponded to the material conditions of Lower East Side poets in the early 1960s. In his essay Olson insisted, "What we have suffered from, is manuscript, press, the removal of verse from its producer and its reproducer, the voice."[10] One can imagine that such a sentence served to romanticize and ennoble the lack of conventional publishing opportunities many of the San Francisco, Beat, and Lower East Side poets initially faced, while encouraging those same writers to consider live readings (sets) as a viable alternative to the printed page. Paul Blackburn used the cafés and bars of Greenwich Village and its eastern environs to promote live readings vigorously.[11] A reading Blackburn organized in 1960 along with his associates

George Economou, Jerome Rothenberg, and Robert Kelly at the Café Cino illustrates the pedagogical role Blackburn played in transmitting information about poetry. Alluding to the fashions of the time, the organizers linked poetry to jazz performativity by calling the reading "New Jazz for Old—*Trobar* Magazine Presents a Poetry Reading with Music: Medieval and Early Renaissance Poetry." This event featured an unidentified drummer and the poet Armand Schwerner playing clarinet as Robert Kelly read the troubadour poetry of Arnaut Daniel and Blackburn read his translations of Provençal poems by Marcabru.

This reading of troubadour poetry is of considerable interest, especially in terms of the discussion linking the jazz group to a social and theoretical model for poetic community, the poets' conception of breath as it relates to the poetic line, and the subsequent direction of the knowledgeable reader's attention to the individual writer. One could argue that the poetry reading, with its mostly unavoidable focus on the author as the center of attention, appears to serve a rather conservative function. Combine this focus with the discourse on individual breath as an essential ingredient in composition, and we seem to end up with a strengthened image of the individual writer speaking his or her Word as only he or she could speak it. However, Peter Middleton offers a way out of the individualist paradigm associated with the poetry reading: "Is [the poetry reading] a ritual to reestablish the authority of authorship in the face of its downsizing by the academic industry, or is the performance of authorship not an attempt to resist this delayering after all, but tacitly working for different collective ends?"[12]

With the phrase "different collective ends," we can return to the significance of the troubadour aesthetic in the poetic community of the Lower East Side, particularly in terms of how that aesthetic was employed by Paul Blackburn at public readings. Laura Kendrick has pointed out, "For the medieval reader, the written text of a lyric was only a *semblance* or visible sign of the oral text; in order to be understood, the images on the manuscript page needed translation into sounds."[13] The troubadour representation of the merely *written* poem as an incomplete product was a similar conception held by many of the poets of the Lower East Side. The poetry reading itself became not so much a space for the performance of an individual genius or windbag as a site for the ongoing fulfillment of a poem actualized in its aural/oral form as it was performed and received in communal territory.

The Sociability of Poetry Readings

John Glassco has complained about the "naive listener's belief that he is getting 'closer' to a poem by hearing it from the poet himself." He writes that

"not only is [the listener] listening to [the poet] more than to what he is say-
ing but, as part of a crowd, one is not so much having an aesthetic experience
as participating in a communal one."[14] However, here one can suggest that
the very distinctions Glassco makes (private reading verses public reception,
aesthetic experience verses communal experience) are hollow. Public readings
could assist the reader in his or her private readings, and vice versa. Reading
and listening, speaking and seeing, are all interrelated activities surrounding
the social experience of poetry.

Public readings on the Lower East Side, while often dramatic, tended to
focus as much on the immediate community at the readings as they did on
the poet reading. Many people in the audience at Lower East Side readings
knew one another and commented on one another's work during the read-
ings themselves. A typical example of this dynamic can be heard on a tape of
a reading given by John Wieners at Le Metro. In his weekly radio show, Paul
Blackburn emphasized the community of poets responding to one of their
own in an irreverent and funny fashion:

> This particular evening [John Wieners] arrived late with his glasses broken.
> The frame had snapped exactly in the middle over the nosepiece. Embarrass-
> ingly enough we taped it with some scotch tape, and it broke almost immedi-
> ately when he started reading. He ended up borrowing somebody else's glasses,
> Marguerite Harris's, I think. Something you may not get on the tape after it's
> edited is the audience's very sympathetic response to Wiener's presence, even
> to all the evidences of goof-city, whether that be New York or Boston where
> John comes from is up to you. In any case it was a lovely man reading beauti-
> ful poems, which you will hear.[15]

The tape of the Wieners reading indicates that Le Metro was a familiar
environment for those in attendance. Wieners interrupted himself consis-
tently. In the middle of the poem "Mole Proposes Solitude," Wieners's glasses
broke. Wieners stopped his reading and said, "I have to get some more pow-
erful glass, I'm sorry. Do you think I could try your glasses, Ted?" Near the
end of the reading (during the poem "Acts of Youth") Wieners began to ac-
company himself in a vaguely rhythmic way by what sounded like banging
on a pot. In the background, laughter and the occasional yell of encourage-
ment could be heard.[16]

The preponderance of extraliterary speech evident in the Wieners reading
and generally associated with the poetry scene had an effect on the writing
itself. Poetic language in the writing of downtown poets became increasingly
informal in tandem with the increasingly unofficial environment surround-
ing the production and reception of poetry. In a radio interview with David
Ossman, Blackburn hypothesized that the use of the vernacular in poetry had

a direct effect on the social life on the Lower East Side: "I think that's one rea-
son for instance that readings in coffee shops and bars and readings to friends
have become so much more common in the last five years than they were be-
fore. Poetry is less removed from its audience."[17] As one can see when read-
ing and listening to the essays, tapes, and correspondence of the poets in the
Lower East Side poetic community, the link between poetics and social life
is brought up repeatedly. This is interesting since it reiterates what might be
unfairly dismissed as unimportant. "All the essays on contemporary poetry
readings stress, with varying degrees of approval, that the poetry reading 'brings
together an audience which wishes to participate in consuming poetry with
others who also wish to do so, to acknowledge poetry, and to feel part of a
community,' and in doing so they are recognizing what readers have always
known. Reading aloud is a form of sociality."[18] Reading aloud on the Lower
East Side was a method for at once absorbing new aesthetic influences, mak-
ing new friends, and continuing relationships established at previous readings.
In terms of community building through the poetry reading and its effect on
poetic production and reception, a homologous relationship was established
between Le Metro as a dissident, communal space and the poetry itself. Bour-
dieu's discussion of earlier avant-garde art social scenes is certainly applicable
to this scenario, in that the *place* of Le Metro, much like the places of earlier
avant-garde "galleries, theatres, publishing houses," served to "mark the cul-
tural products that [were] associated with [it], among other reasons because
through [it] a public is designated which (on the basis of the homology be-
tween field of production and field of consumption) qualifies the product con-
sumed."[19] The specific physical space of Le Metro, consciously organized as
avant-garde, reflexively marked and certified work produced and performed
within that space with avant-garde and community status.

Of course, the reality of using readings as opportunities for "networking"
did not necessarily distinguish Lower East Side poets from their more academic
counterparts, who also used parties, readings, and other events to make the
necessary publishing connections. To maintain their irreverent culture, poets
had to reject the social conservatism they associated with the rarefied atmos-
phere of the academy and the academic reading series taking place uptown.
Some of the strategies they used included connecting their project to other
nascent artistic genres, particularly the "Happening." In an interview with
Lisa Jarnot, Ed Sanders recalls that his rock-poetry band the Fugs "came out
of those concepts of a happening. You'd go to these galleries and there'd be
people jumping up and down in barrels full of grapes and then somebody
naked covering their head with pieces of ticker tape. And you could call that
art. Easy rules—all you had to do was bring youthful genius and will."[20] Poet
Jackson Mac Low connected the spontaneity of the Happening to the activ-

ity of the poetry reading, eliciting audience participation to guarantee the communal production of a poem. At a reading at St. Mark's Poetry Project, Mac Low handed out copies of his work "The Bluebird Asymmetries" to audience members and directed them in a performance of the text. Mac Low clearly privileged oral reading, as one sees when considering his introduction to this particular event:

> The method here is to be silent during whatever white spaces there are on the page, and the length of the silence is relative to the size of the white space. You can extend the length of the silence as it seems to fit in to what's happening. Listen always to what's happening. You can extend the phonemes, such as "blue." When you have repeated letters—they're never repeated sounds, like "oo-oo-oo-oo," but continuing sounds, like "ooooooo" or "ooommmm" or "lllll," whatever is indicated. Roughly you can judge the length of it by what's printed—the words that fit in the length of the space. When you finish one of them, exchange it with somebody else as soon as they've finished. We'll do about two exchanges, so that each person will have read three.[21]

As Michael Kirby has recognized in reference to Happenings, such interactive routines had an historical precedent in Italian futurist performance. Mac Low's "Bluebird Asymmetries" shared with futurism a disavowal of realism in favor of "alogical structures" and "an interest in the physical audience-performance relationship and in a physicalization of performance."[22] Audience response to Mac Low's directions supports this historical connection. In listening to the tape, one hears what sounds like controlled feedback and guttural drones as well as facts about bluebirds being voiced in sing-song cadences reminiscent of a round. Phrases including "a beneficial bird," "bluebirds are speckled," "Fulva," "starlings in winter," and the sound "sssssss" were repeated in a variously incantatory, whimsical, and hilarious fashion. The collaborative *vocal* relationship between audience members and author was clearly crucial to the ideal manifestation of the text.

Anecdotes like the descriptions of Mac Low's and Wieners's reading—hundreds like them are available on tapes of readings recorded throughout the 1960s—demonstrate that many poetry readings on the Lower East Side were more than just opportunities to hear original authors read their original works. They were social, aesthetic, and experimental meeting grounds for a community of people whose main organizing principle was poetry. Writers in this community designed poems that were partially conditioned by an expectation that a live audience—as opposed to a solitary author—would determine *both* reception and ideal manifestation of text in a specific social space like Le Metro or St. Mark's.[23] The types of events described above simply did not occur for the most part in the lecture halls of universities. This fact was as much owing to the logistics of the raised stage, the isolated proscenium, and the fixed rows of assembly-style chairs as it was to the academic poets who read their formal verse to the quiet and respectful audience. This distinction was not universal. For example, in 1965 dozens of alternative poets organized a mass reading in London's Royal Albert Hall, where audience members danced, sang, openly consumed drugs, and so on.[24] Nevertheless, for the most part, the 1960s saw a relatively clear line being drawn between the kinds of poetry and audience behavior acceptable in the space of the café and bar and that acceptable in the space of the lecture hall, concert hall, library reading room, and museum. The readings that occurred at Les Deux Mégots and Le Metro were partly responsible for drawing this line.

"All Poets Welcome to Come and Read": The Scene at Les Deux Mégots

In June 1961, an ad in the Village Voice read, "THE WEDNESDAY POETRY READINGS at the 10th Street Coffee House have been moved to the DEUX Mégots Coffee House, 64 East 7th St, nr. 2nd Ave. All poets welcome to come and read every Wed. 8:30 P.M."[25] According to poet and reading-series organizer Howard Ant (who has since disappeared from the poetry scene), the initial group readings in the Lower East Side poetic community were planned by him and by Ree Dragonette in the early fall of 1960 at Mickey Ruskin's Tenth Street Coffeehouse, on the gallery block between Third and Fourth Avenues. In June 1961, Ruskin and his partner Bill Mackey opened Les Deux Mégots in a storefront on 64 East Seventh Street.[26] Les Deux Mégots was named after the famous Café Des Deux-Magots in Paris, which was renowned as the meeting place for writers including Verlaine, Rimbaud, and Mallarmé in the nineteenth century and Breton and Artaud in the early part of the twentieth century, as well as later writers and artists including Sartre, Simone de Beauvoir, Malcolm Cowley, and Picasso.[27]

The concept behind the reading series at Les Deux Mégots was a poetry scene based on inclusiveness or what might romantically be termed a gathering of the avant-garde tribes. The series was a conscious effort on the part of organizers including Howard Ant, Carol Bergé, and Allen Katzman to eliminate distinctions that might alienate individuals from collaborating with one another:

> "The Deux Mégots had tremendous energy," Katzman continues. "The reason it had tremendous energy, though, was there were so many different types of poetry. Deep Image, Black Mountain, Beat, 1920's—that was even interesting, it gave you such a historical perspective on the Village, East and West."
> "The funny thing is it's a family," says Bergé. "You have to get that feeling.

It's something so tribal that even now, supposing I should say that I don't like somebody's poetry, it wouldn't matter. That's family. We didn't think about who was going to make it and who wasn't. I don't think anyone did."[28]

Ultimately, the Lower East Side social phenomenon helped to erase even further the geographical distinctions Donald Allen's *The New American Poetry* anthology made between disparate groups of poets and other artists. The social environment that Allen DeLoach has termed the "East Side Scene" in his eponymous anthology helped override earlier categorizations:

> Paul Blackburn, Allen Ginsberg, Joel Oppenheimer, Peter Orlovsky, and John Wieners have been previously anthologized by Donald Allen to represent the "post–World War II generation" (or third generation) of Twentieth Century avant-garde poets; and although according to Donald Allen these poets variously represent either *Black Mountain College,* the *Beat Generation,* or an engagement with the *San Francisco Renaissance,* they maintained a principal involvement later with the East Side scene.[29]

The open readings were held every Wednesday evening. The only rule poets had to follow was to limit their "sets" to three poems and five minutes of reading time. Of the open reading, Howard Ant warned, "A poet's work may receive violent attack from the audience at its conclusion—and by reading he impliedly offers himself to such attack, or to a corresponding praise and acceptance—but no artistic criteria—or pseudo-criteria—will be applied to preclude him from reading it."[30] The Wednesday open readings were supplemented by a series of Sunday solo readings by individual poets who were almost always "name" poets—that is, poets who had published and been anthologized more frequently than the regulars at the open readings.[31]

Many poets on the Lower East Side who read during the 1960s traced the Lower East Side reading series history beginning at either the Tenth Street Coffeehouse or at Les Deux Mégots and continuing through to Le Metro and the St. Mark's Poetry Project. Jackson Mac Low writes:

> People I met at the Tenth Street Coffeehouse after that (many became close friends of mine) included, besides Carol [Bergé] and Howard [Ant], Jerome and Diane Rothenberg, Armand Schwerner, George Economou and Rochelle Owens, David and Eleanor Antin, Robert Kelly and his wife then, Joan, and Paul Blackburn . . .
>
> The coffeehouse readings moved, while I was participating in them, from the 10th Street Coffeehouse to Les Deux Mégots . . . and then after several years to a place on Second Avenue called Le Metro, and finally, about 30 years ago, to St. Marks Church, where they became the present Poetry Project.[32]

Taking Mac Low's comments into consideration, one can suggest that Les Deux Mégots was crucial in the development of St. Mark's Poetry Project. St. Mark's Church started its reading series in the spring of 1966 with the help of a group of poets, including Paul Blackburn, Jerome Rothenberg, and Carol Bergé, who originally served as members of a Reading Series Committee at St. Mark's Church just six months before the inception of the Poetry Project. Basic numbers point to the Poetry Project's debt to the preceding Lower East Side reading series. As listed in the Poetry Project's archived readings list, during the first four years of the Poetry Project, Blackburn was to read six times, Ed Sanders ten times, and Oppenheimer eight times alone, while many of the names mentioned so far read at least once during the early years and more than once after 1970.

Rexograph at Les Deux Mégots

At the Les Deux Mégots readings, poet Dan Saxon collected hand- and typewritten manuscripts from the readers and, collating these pieces, produced a rexograph magazine he circulated for free called *Poets at Les Deux Mégots*.[33] Saxon's work ensured that every reading would in turn be a publishing event. The magazine contained the poems that were read out loud at Les Deux Mégots, as opposed to poems solicited from outside the scene. By the standards of any professionally bound "glossy" magazine, this magazine looked ragged at best. Additionally, poems ranged from texts resembling Hallmark greeting card verse to carefully delineated, scored pieces by Mac Low and Blackburn. All the pages were handwritten and were blue because of the stencil, allowing for a lot of expression that would otherwise be limited if typeset. For example, a Jack Micheline poem published in *Poets at Les Deux Mégots* consisted of five words:

Happiness
Happiness
Happiness

Jelly Roll!

The look of the text on the original page, with its big blue, centered, and loopy script, lent it a charm that otherwise is lost in the cold form of the uniform typed font above. The inclusion of this kind of handwritten text in a "poetry magazine" tended to emphasize the poem as visual art; and the enthusiastic scrawl served as a kind of staging of an energetic live performance.[34] Additionally, the rexograph's capacity to contain actual handwriting also suggests concrete poetry combined with a scored musical page; one could treat the size of the letters as cues providing the reader with an idea of how loudly he or she should read the words.[35] The poems in rexograph and mimeo magazines were really enactments of oral readings, as opposed to finished presentations of "closed" poems.[36]

Micheline's poem serves as a reminder that the main reason people came to Les Deux Mégots was to hear one another read. Before the café series, the belief that listening to a poem was a significant mode of literary reception was developed through editorials, essays, footnotes, and poems in small alternative magazines from the mid- to late 1950s. For instance, after describing how *Origin* editor Cid Corman consistently published articles and poems related to orality and speech-based poetics, Alan Golding writes:

> This emphasis on the oral or performative appears in many forms throughout *Origin,* consistently enough to show it to be a consciously articulated editorial stance. It appears in details as small as the invitation to oral performance contained in Duncan's footnote to a line of his poem "Africa Revisited": on the line "bbbbbbbbbbbbbbbbbbb" Duncan comments, "this sound is a voiced labial trill held for the duration indicated in the rhythmic structure of the poem."[37]

The rexographed *Poets at Les Deux Mégots* series extended the job that *Origin* and other earlier magazines had started by emphasizing, both directly and indirectly, the poem's relation to actual speech and performance. This use of the page, which invited the reader to consider the poem in terms of utterance, reminds us that Les Deux Mégots was a space where avant-garde poetics were linked to earlier troubadour and oral traditions.[38] Laura Kendrick's writing on troubadour graphology is helpful in articulating a connection between troubadour poets and the poets of the Lower East Side, all of whom used the page far more actively than did their academic counterparts:

> A medieval scribe did not necessarily transcribe, like a modern typist, the graphic formulas from the exemplar before him . . . He heard the text he read, and he represented the sounds he heard according to the graphic formulas he habitually used for representing those sounds; thus his new text often differed from the text he was reproducing.[39]

That is, in troubadour writing and in much of the writing associated with the Lower East Side, it was important to represent the way a poem *sounded* using the text as a visual medium. Poems like Micheline's "Happiness" were in this sense enactments of orality and cues for performance.

Of course, the inclusiveness of the reading series at Les Deux Mégots often resulted in the recording of some terrible poems—the curse of any open reading. Nevertheless, some of the less-than-astonishing poems in these rexographs are interesting from an historical standpoint, in that they contain clues about the kinds of literary experiments going on in the Lower East Side poetic community. Allen Katzman's "Poem for the Poet" (excerpted below) contains the parenthetical phrase "(From the Poetry Machine)" attached to the title:

Poem for the Poet (From the Poetry Machine)

Even
As I
devour gold/proof
black coincides gull-like
and effectively reproaches.[40]

Jerry Bloedow is credited with having invented the Poetry Machine, which he described in an interview: "Around that time I invented this thing called 'the Poetry Machine.' I made about fifteen or twenty of them. It was a long strip of balsa wood, with another piece of board with dowels pasted down to make a carrier for loops of film. I wrote the words down on a piece of transparent film, and sent it in for a print. Then I cut the words up and pasted them and cut them up so that they'd form loops. It was a collaborative thing— I'd say 'Now, you and I have collaborated on a poem because you couldn't have written it without me and yet I couldn't have written it without you,' and so forth."[41] The tradition of chance or automatic procedures typical of earlier surrealist groupings and extended in the 1950s through the work of composer John Cage and choreographer Merce Cunningham (both of whom had worked and taught in collaboration with poets at Black Mountain College) was continued on the Lower East Side through new methods of arriving at chance-determined works. Writing practices associated with the Beats were also evident in Bloedow's Poetry Machine. Bloedow's use of the phrase "cut the words up" evokes earlier works of the 1950s associated with Beat predecessors William Burroughs and Brion Gysin. These writers formed texts out of randomly selected words culled from cut-up newspaper articles, advertisements, and the like.[42] Bloedow's Poetry Machine in many ways continued these experiments in sense and nonsense, which—contextualized in light of chance-determined work of the 1950s as well as dada and surrealism—provided depth, complexity, and historical resonance to the practices of the Lower East Side poetic community.

From Les Deux Mégots to Le Metro

Mickey Ruskin and Bill Mackey co-owned Les Deux Mégots, but by late 1962 Ruskin had had enough of the business. As David Henderson remembers, "Mickey Ruskin was always on record . . . he hated the place, he hated poetry, he wasn't making any money. I think he wanted to make more money. . . . Bill Mackey felt the same way. It was simply a coffeehouse . . . we used to walk in there, bring our bottles of wine, buy a cup of coffee, drink the coffee, and then pour the wine in. So we weren't even buying the coffee . . . they weren't making any money. It was a poetry hangout."[43]

At that point, the coffee shop had been robbed twice. Ruskin quit to open what would turn out to be a very successful restaurant, the Ninth Circle (located in the West Village); he would ultimately open the legendary Max's Kansas City.[44] The Deux Mégots crowd attempted to continue the readings at the coffee shop. However, according to Bergé and others, the poets "chafe[d] under the new regime."[45] The negative response to Les Deux Mégot's management after Ruskin's departure was widespread, at least according to published and epistolary reports regarding the ending of the reading series. In Ed Sanders's mimeo *Fuck You / a magazine of the arts,* Nelson Barr awarded a "Bouquet of Fuck You's" to "*Les Deux Mégots*—new management—banisher of poets—caterer to the obtuse—lapdog of the monied—patron of art (only if it sucks up gelt) / may the hip vomit thee forth from their mouth!"[46] While readings at various locations throughout the Lower East Side occurred during January and February, the poets ended up finding a much larger space for their readings, and by March 1963 Les Deux Mégots poets could claim a new home. That was Le Metro, located at 149 Second Avenue, just one block south of St. Mark's Church.

"I Remember 'Le Metro'"

In his book *I Remember,* Joe Brainard wrote, "I remember 'Le Metro.' (A coffeehouse on Second Avenue that had poetry readings.) Paul Blackburn. And Diane Di Prima sitting on top of a piano reading her poems."[47] Brainard, artist, poet, and close friend of poets Ron Padgett and Ted Berrigan, shows in this small excerpt the interplay between those writers and artists associated with the "New York School" (both first and second generation) and the larger poetry community, including "Black Mountain" (Blackburn) and "Beat" (di Prima). These various groups became increasingly interrelated socially at Le Metro, recognizing the common ground they shared in their allegiances to modernist predecessors, including Williams and Pound. Indeed, these allegiances were particularly clear in terms of the history of Le Metro. No matter what "school" the poets purportedly belonged to, their debt to the primary figures of American modernism remained strong. On March 4, 1963, William Carlos Williams died. Two days later, the first reading at Le Metro was held. In a letter to Williams's wife, Flossie, Paul Blackburn wrote, "I have a reading series at Le Metro Café on Second Ave. and the first reading happened to fall on Wednesday March 6. Joel Oppenheimer reading. After reading a rough of a poem for Bill, he read only Bill's poems, ones he loved. Gil Sorrentino did one set also of Bill's work, and Brother Antoninus one also. It was a beautiful evening."[48]

There were several differences between Les Deux Mégots and Le Metro in basic physical makeup and changes in scheduling. Open readings at Le Metro were on Mondays, and the featured readings on Wednesdays.[49] Additionally, Le Metro was a much bigger space than Les Deux Mégots and was located on a city avenue as opposed to a city street. This meant that there were more passers-by. The series at Le Metro attracted far more attention than the preceding series had. This attention was welcomed by many of the earlier reading series organizers and regular participants, and resented by others. Jerry Bloedow remembers that "there was a lot of drug dealing going on at Le Metro. I say this for the record. [William] Burroughs showed up back in town. He went off back in the corner, and people were clustered around him. All that was happening was that people were dealing drugs. And the thing is, Le Metro was probably run by the cops. It was part of the shady world of the Lower East Side."[50] In response to being asked why he had a bad reputation among many poets, Moe Margules (the owner of Le Metro) replied, "I had to kick out the guys shooting up in the bathroom. I was the bad guy."[51] Whereas Les Deux Mégots was in many ways a clubby scene, Le Metro managed to attract a far greater number of poets included in the Allen anthology, as well as a newer, slightly younger generation of writers who had little to no exposure to the reading scene at Les Deux Mégots and who were now ready to join what was certainly becoming a larger poetry community. Ron Padgett remembers what it was like walking into and out of Le Metro for a poetry reading:

> Paul Blackburn organized the readings at Le Metro and was really the stalwart there. He came with his tape recorder, and he also stood at the door of Le Metro, so you could get in to the readings fine, but to get out you had to confront Paul about making a donation. He didn't specify any amount, but he was kind of insistent you contribute "something for the poet." If it was a dime, that was fine. But he insisted that the poet get something. You had to figure out how little you dared put in, because actually we didn't have much money. At Le Metro, coffee was a quarter, which was a lot for a cup of coffee. Normally it was a dime.[52]

Ed Sanders provides a picture of what a person would see stepping inside the premises:

The group organizing the readings had élan and spirit, and more of a sense of anarchy in the Barcelonan sense, in the Spanish Civil War/Syndicalist spirit in the sense of people joining into groups but with the sense of freedom, so that was the strength of it, in that you had Marguerite Harris and Dan Saxon and George Economou and Rochelle Owens and Armand Schwerner and Paul Blackburn and Carol Bergé and Susan Sherman and myself and Allen Ginsberg and Ted Berrigan, Ron Padgett, fifty or a hundred more clutching their spring-binders from many different schools and thought patterns and different worldviews and different educations and different intelligences and focuses all in the same room appreciating the different schools of poetry being presented . . . that to me is more important than how they were run. I did not believe in factions and I printed a vast cross-section of those poets who were hanging out there. I ran the readings in the summer of 1964 at Le Metro. Huncke, Carl Solomon, those were the people I got to read.[53]

Le Metro was owned and managed by Moe and Cindy Margules as a regular coffee shop, and the proprietors saw the poetry series as a chance for guaranteed crowds and greater exposure.[54] Allen Katzman, Paul Blackburn, Carol Bergé, and Susan Sherman formed a quorum to run the open readings, and Paul Blackburn was responsible for running the solo readings on Wednesday evenings.[55] Open readings were as attractive to the name poets as the featured readings, and poets including Allen Ginsberg, Diane di Prima, Peter Orlovsky, John Wieners, and Amiri Baraka would read or listen in regularly.

The New York School and More at Le Metro

The New York School poets—Koch, Schuyler, Ashbery, Guest, and O'Hara—really weren't part of the Les Deux Mégots scene and were, in fact, considered by some to be a bit too "uptown" for the downtown crowd. The writer Jim Brodey,[56] who knew Paul Blackburn during the 1960s, said of Blackburn's attitude toward the New York School, "Paul Blackburn & I didn't get along very well. He had this side of his personality that indulged in discouraging or competitiveness at least. MOMA/Edge of the Big Money school is what Blackburn called the New York School at that time."[57] Some of the writers associated with the Lower East Side poetic community viewed the poets of the New York School as perhaps a little too urbane, witty, and chatty to be welcomed fully into the relatively macho heterosexual scene that initially dominated the Lower East Side scene.[58]

The New York School would nevertheless prove to have an enormous impact on poets reading regularly at Le Metro and particularly at St. Mark's Poetry

Project, which would in its first year alone feature a memorial reading for Frank O'Hara (June 22, 1967), a reading by John Ashbery (December 6, 1967), and various readings by poets associated with the so-called Second-Generation New York School, including Anne Waldman, Ron Padgett, Ted Berrigan, Dick Gallup, and Lewis Warsh. Ron Padgett and Ted Berrigan were especially able, metaphorically, to bring the New York School downtown, mostly by extending the aesthetics of chattiness, wit, surrealistic playfulness, and a commitment to the visual arts in their own poetry and by publishing Ashbery, Koch, O'Hara, Guest, and Schuyler in the mimeographed magazine *C.* Berrigan and Padgett, perhaps more than any of the other poets associated with the earlier Deux Mégots readings, helped convince the downtown poetic community that New York School poets were part of the alternative poetics scene. As Brainard referred to Beat and Black Mountain icons in his own charming, chatty, faux-childish, and therefore typically New York School passage from *I Remember,* Ted Berrigan (who would run the solo-reading series at Le Metro during the summer of 1965) consistently recognized and referred to group affinities between Beat and New York schools: "My own line of descent is Beatnik cum Frank O'Hara. That's the way I've always seen it: Beats, with O'Hara on the left & Creeley on the right."[59] Additionally, Padgett promoted members of the New York School as nonacademic outsiders (despite the fact that Kenneth Koch was a professor at Columbia University), as is evident in Padgett's review of a "Faculty Poetry Reading" held at Columbia University. Here Padgett begins by lightly critiquing Leonie Adams, Babette Deutsch, and Stanley Kunitz before going on to laud Koch and others:

> Kenneth Koch's poems show a constant interest in creating a brilliant, exciting surface through fresh language. What might be "beneath" the surface of his poems is for everyone to decide for himself. Critics have been obviously correct in pointing to his extremely beautiful and energetic imagination, but none seem to have noted that imagination without sensibleness produces silly results. The three poems he read, although "abstract" and of course impossible to logically paraphrase, were very sensible. While most English and American poets writing today manage to bore us by bottling up experience, commenting on it, and handing it to us in the form of a lecture, Mr. Koch attempts to incorporate—that is, give body to—as much of the excitement of being alive as he can. He is one of the three best American poets writing today, the other two being Frank O'Hara and John Ashbery.[60]

Padgett is clearly taking a potshot at academic poetry. The sentence "most English and American poets writing today manage to bore us by bottling up experience, commenting on it, and handing it to us in the form of a lecture" manages to refer slyly to the famous Hall, Pack, and Simpson academic anthologies (*New Poets of England and America*) as it ties this "boring" poetry to the academy through the use of the word *lecture*. Additionally, Padgett places Ashbery, Koch, and O'Hara on the periphery of contemporary writing—the place where all avant-garde writers by definition belong—by taking them out of the sphere of "most English and American writing." In an interview, Padgett admits that he essentially made up the line "Critics have been obviously correct in pointing to his extremely beautiful and energetic imagination": "I was creating a mythology there. Most critics were dismissing [Koch] as being frivolous."[61] Padgett understood that New York School poets—for all their apparently "uptown" accouterments like university teaching positions, Harvard educations, curatorial jobs at the Museum of Modern Art, and so on—were still nevertheless largely unrecognized, underappreciated, avant-garde writers.[62]

One of the ways that New York School influences came into Le Metro—besides the fact that Berrigan and Padgett often attended and that both O'Hara and Koch are listed as having given readings there—was through the continuation of Dan Saxon's *Poets at Les Deux Mégots* magazine series, reincarnated for the occasion as *Poets at Le Metro*. The first mimeo to come out of the developing scene was entitled *Volume III: Poets at Le Metro*. Padgett recalls how these magazines were put together:

> Dan Saxon would come in to Le Metro during the readings and hand out rexograph sheets, and we would get one stencil sheet each. Some people would take them home and type on them, but a lot of us wrote by hand on one of the old wooden tables at Le Metro. Some would spontaneously write a poem by themselves or collaborate with somebody. Or they would draw a poem picture. A few people would come in occasionally and write from memory a poem they had written recently. Then Saxon would take all these sheets home, print them up, collate them, and hand them out the following week. *Poets at Le Metro* was kind of a free-flowing record of the readings that went on there. Some of the poems were awful, but that didn't matter. It was more the sense of spontaneity that was important to me.[63]

The spontaneous, rough-edged nature of this magazine illustrates an anarchic, spirited reading environment. Lorenzo Thomas adds to Padgett's memories by emphasizing that *Poets at Le Metro* was not so much important for its literary quality as it was emblematic of a scene and community. "After the first couple of issues, all these bad poets started saying 'Hey, I'm taking the page home with me,' and they'd type their great works. Everyone else took it for what it was, which was a joke. In the Poundian tradition, you knew what you were supposed to do was improvise, or the bebop/Provençal tradition which was to improvise something extraordinarily beautiful and clever on the spot, and not take the damn thing home and type up some poems you wrote all those years ago. Something as silly as Dan Saxon's *Poets at Le Metro* certainly captured what the moment was about."[64]

The magazine grew alongside the developing scene and neighborhood. More and more poets, artists, and members of the growing hippie counterculture were taking rooms and apartments on the Lower East Side. Increasing inroads into the neighborhood were being made by predominantly white bohemians, helping to transform the area both culturally and semantically. What was once known as the Lower East Side was now being referred to—especially as the artistic community, in combination with the hippie movement, established itself as a presence in the area—as the "East Village." The years between 1964 and 1968 in particular found the area between Houston and Fourteenth Streets increasingly marked by "a cultural explosion of art, music, theater, film, writing, and, most significantly, public performance, all of which were linked to the loosely connected hippie movement . . . [for] four years [the East Village] became the key East Coast site of a countercultural spectacle that had an enduring influence on the cultural history of the United States and the struggle over neighborhood restructuring on the Lower East Side."[65] Le Metro played a role in the transformation of what had formerly been a working-class neighborhood with an artistic underground. As Le Metro—via its larger, more accessible space, its more catholic group of poets, and resulting public and media attention—promoted its poets on a far larger scale than the earlier Deux Mégots series had, so the counterculture as a whole began to make its presence felt in the Lower East Side much more overtly than it had previously.[66]

As poets, artists, and hippies rented more and more of the then-available and cheap cold-water flats, the bohemian population of the neighborhood grew exponentially. Le Metro served as a kind of community center where poets attached to this scene could trade information crucial to disseminating news about their subculture within a subculture, including where to get the latest issues of related publications. From an issue of *Poets at Le Metro,* a poem by Ed Sanders (featuring the familiar spurting penis symbol and signed "Ed Sanders, the spurting phantom") conveniently shows the functions a mimeographed magazine served in the poetic community. Sanders's poem was entitled "Poem Describing the Cover of the Next Issue of *Fuck You,* Issue 5 Volume 5." This text contained lines like "Nūt with the moon at her tit / under the lactating spurts / & the stars spraying / out of her twat / Her feet are the claws of birds / wings are her crown."[67] In this case, Sanders wrote a characteristically lively poem as an enticement to pick up the next issue of *Fuck You,* which regular attendees at Le Metro were sure to know could be found at such community sites as Ted Wilentz's Eighth Street Bookshop or Bob Wilson's Phoenix Bookshop.

Since magazines had always served as metaphors for the Lower East Side poetic community, *Poets at Le Metro* moved along with the environment it was a part of and reflected the progressive demographic changes. Volume five of *Poets at Le Metro* was the first issue indicating that the poetry scene was in some ways getting more "serious." For the first time in the history of the *Poets at Les Deux Mégots/Le Metro* series, the cover was made out of heavy stock paper, and the titles of the poems were typeset. New names to the scene included Lawrence Ferlinghetti, publisher of City Lights Books and author of *A Coney Island of the Mind.* Ferlinghetti's presence here shows that the Lower East Side poetic community was being visited by writers and artists outside the neighborhood, lending it a more cosmopolitan air than it had previously enjoyed. By late 1963 and early 1964, by-now established counterculture icons were participating in Le Metro events. "The Fugs were born there. Getting the picture? Ferlinghetti, Brion Gysin, Lou Reed, all there. Warhol. Stockhausen. Are you ready? Bob Dylan."[68]

Berrigan at Le Metro

Blackburn, Bergé, and Dan Saxon were featured in almost every issue of the *Poets at Le Metro* series, indicating their continuing centrality as organizers of the poetry community. However, volume seven of *Poets at Le Metro* featured Ted Berrigan, who would go on to be published in nearly every issue of *Poets at Le Metro* until its eventual demise. By this simple standard, Berrigan was in place to become (as Allen Ginsberg would later characterize him in a blurb on the back cover of the Penguin edition of Berrigan's *Selected Poems*) "big Father Figure Lower East Side." A diary entry dated Friday September, 13, 1963, marks the first time that Berrigan mentions Le Metro, though it is clear from the content of this note that he had read there previously: "Went yesterday to see John Wieners read at Le Metro . . . I seem to be a 'literary light' now—half the people there greeted me, John announced he was working on the preface for the Edwin Denby issue of *C,* etc."[69]

The Berrigan poems in volume seven contain a note at the bottom reading "Improvised Monday, Sept. 23rd 1963," indicating the accuracy of Padgett's depiction of the readings at Le Metro as "spontaneous." There are six poems in all, in six little boxes. The first three are numbered one to three on the left and the next three are numbered four to six on the right. These "improvisations" are particularly interesting in that Berrigan's now-characteristic method of repeating lines and phrases throughout a series of poems (most notably in his book *The Sonnets,* copyrighted in 1964) is in evidence even in a live, apparently improvised spontaneous performance:

1.

The moths are playing
misty croquet. Come home.
My beard is a broth of owls
The stars were a blunder.

2.

It had not wanted to marry
"The Owl." But in "Croquet"
He did. So instead vast brothels
Opened to his beard. He became a mist
In "Croquet," with "The Owl,"
    and was staggered.

3.

Croquet of vast
Beard staggering blunders,
Star-steaming mists
Are a brothel. Signed:
"The Owl."

4.

Vast steaming brothels
Were a blunder. My beard
Is an open mist. Out among
The stars, owls are playing croquet.

5.

Croquet of owls
Vast steaming moths
blunder into my beard.
THE BROTHEL OF MIST IS OPEN—
Stars are staggering home

6.

"Brothels are for the owls.
Croquet is what really staggers me.
Stars don't wear beards."
—He missed his home.[70]

Beyond Berrigan's characteristic use of variations and repetitions of lines, his practice of lifting lines from poems or using lines reminiscent of poems originally "belonging" to John Ashbery and other First-Generation New York School poets might very well be in evidence here. The line "THE BROTHEL OF MIST IS OPEN" could refer to John Ashbery's poem "Last Month," which contains the lines "The academy of the future is / opening its doors."[71] Berrigan would go on to use the lines "The academy of the future is / opening its doors" in his book *The Sonnets.* One can tentatively suggest that Berrigan practiced writing methods evident in *The Sonnets* by using the techniques of improvisation and appropriation employed at Le Metro.

Berrigan also used *Poets at Le Metro* to welcome certain poets entering the scene. One of Berrigan's poems found in *Poets at Le Metro* refers to another member of the Second-Generation New York School, Jim Brodey:

Homage to James Brodey

Garbo is back!
among the serious spastic poets

"Man, you gotta do something
about your handwriting. It's disgusting!"

Lorenzo Thomas, there—dead serious
        half spastic

    writes poems about Habbakuk and
    a lot of dead Roumanians

Hmmm!
    while the rest of the quarter poets
    write about fucking. They call it
    "Love" or "Philosophy"
    We call it "Hygiene."

    I like lady poets best of all.

Like Great Garbo.[72]

While it is difficult to detect precisely how this poem is a homage to Jim
Brodey, the text is noteworthy for several reasons. Besides echoing, through
content and tone, the celebrated Frank O'Hara poem "Poem (Lana Turner Has
Collapsed!)" this "homage" serves as a social document in that it records what
was probably an evening at Le Metro.[73] The lines "Man, you gotta do some-
thing / about your handwriting. It's disgusting!" were likely spoken to Berri-
gan by another attending poet commenting on Berrigan's handwriting (which
was sloppy) reproduced in Dan Saxon's *Poets at Le Metro* series. Additionally,
Berrigan uses the poem to provide the reader with a short review of Lorenzo
Thomas's performance: "Lorenzo Thomas, there—dead serious / half spastic /
writes poems about Habbakuk and / a lot of dead Roumanians." Perhaps pok-
ing fun at the poets in attendance that particular evening, Berrigan describes
"the rest" of them as "quarter poets." Since the Left Bank of Paris was com-
monly referred to as the intellectual quarter of the city, and since Le Metro
was a French name, Berrigan seems to be implying that the poets perhaps
pompously perceived themselves as Parisian-style Left Bank *artistes*.

Poets associated with the new New York School participated in ever-
increasing numbers at Le Metro. Aram Saroyan, Ted Berrigan, Ron Padgett,
and Gerard Malanga were included in *Poets at Le Metro* volume nine. These
poets would go on to be strongly associated with the St. Mark's Poetry Project;
Berrigan as the unofficial éminence grise, Saroyan as publisher of the mimeo
Lines, Padgett as regular presence and (eventually, in the 1970s) director of

the Poetry Project, and Malanga as regular presence and link to the Andy Warhol scene. Additionally, while poet and future Poetry Project director Bernadette Mayer never read at Le Metro, she remembers: "I used to go to Le Metro with Ted to eat chocolate cake."[74]

Berrigan would continue somewhat obsessively to record lists of names associated with the poetry reading scene at Le Metro. These lists clearly show the interplay between figures associated with pop art, First- and Second-Generation New York School poets, and those poets who started the regular, long-running reading series traditions beginning at Mickey Ruskin's Tenth Street Coffeehouse. Referring to a reading he gave at Le Metro on Wednesday, April 8, 1964, Berrigan listed possibly everyone who was in attendance, pointing out that he "had a good reading at the Metro last night. 55 or 60 people were there. I got about $20.00. (first money I ever made off of poetry)."[75]

In Berrigan's diaries, the lists of names continue and expand in relation to the increasing presence of Berrigan and other Second-Generation New York School poets in the Le Metro scene. One learns that Berrigan was at this point playing a part in organizing both the open readings and the solo readings. By April 1964 Berrigan had joined Diane Wakoski and Jerry Rothenberg to participate in the Metro reading series committee, and he was responsible for scheduling Dick Gallup, Kenward Elmslie, and David Henderson as featured Monday-night readers. Berrigan also ran the summer reading series in 1965, scheduling Kenward Elmslie, Dick Gallup, Ron Padgett, Ed Sanders, Lorenzo Thomas, and himself. Since Berrigan arranged some of the final readings at Le Metro before the readings moved to St Mark's and read regularly from the early years of the Poetry Project through the 1970s, it is not surprising that New York School poets and their younger Second-Generation associates would end up playing primary roles in the overall tenor and administration of the Poetry Project.[76]

Harassment of the Arts at Le Metro

Le Metro rose to prominence and appealed to figures not immediately related to the Tenth Street/Deux Mégots scene partly because the Le Metro reading series found itself entangled in a years-long city-sanctioned crackdown on "unlicensed" entertainment. Music clubs in New York had suffered for years under the notorious cabaret laws, which determined that only "'incidental musical entertainment' by up to three live musicians, provided they played only keyboards and strings" was allowable.[77] Throughout the late 1950s and early 1960s, the Department of Licenses, encouraged by the success of the cabaret laws, aggressively cited various cultural establishments in the West and East Village for breaking fire and zoning laws, even though these establishments were not "cabarets" as defined in the cabaret laws.[78] In 1959, cabaret laws were used to issue summonses against coffeehouses that held regular poetry readings. At times police actually shut down regular poetry readings throughout the West Village, including one at the Epitome on 165 Bleecker Street.[79] By 1960 police continued to "issue summonses to the coffee houses as *unlicensed cabarets*. There were a lot of them by contemporary standards; in May of 1961, the *New York Times* reported that sixty summonses were pending against coffeehouses."[80] Cafés, including the Café Wha?, the Gaslight, and the Café Bizarre had all been padlocked, cited for various infractions, and threatened with closure for minor offenses that went unnoticed elsewhere.[81]

However, "the proprietors of several establishments had protested . . . that the readings [did] not constitute entertainment within the strict meaning of the [cabaret] law." Legal proceedings initiated by the owners of the Epitome were judged in the owners' favor: "Magistrate Walter J. Bayer . . . ruled that the Epitome . . . had not violated the [cabaret] law by holding regular poets' sessions."[82] Because of the city's legal inability to shut down poetry readings by using the cabaret laws, a new statute was eventually written into the Administrative Code of the City of New York in March 1961 that redefined what a coffeehouse was.[83] Under this law—legally distinct from the almost identical regulations of the cabaret laws—the owner of a restaurant or coffee shop was required to obtain an expensive and administratively onerous license if his or her establishment wished to feature performances including "instrumental music, folk, popular or operatic singing, *poetry or other literary readings or recitals,* dramatic or musical enactments."[84] What this meant was that the owner would then have to jump through a series of complicated bureaucratic hoops to qualify for the coffeehouse license, including having the license commissioner determine that the owner was "a fit and proper person"; "that the premises to be licensed are a safe and proper place to be used as a coffee house"; that "all applicants for licenses . . . shall be fingerprinted"; and finally, that a yearly fee "for each such coffee house license shall be seventy-five dollars for each year or fraction thereof."[85] The coffeehouse license law resulted in a number of sites being ticketed for presenting illegal performances—including poetry readings.

Many members of the downtown community interpreted the coffeehouse license law as a throwback to the earlier set of racist and politically motivated cabaret law policies on the part of the New York City police force.[86] Considering that many poets on the Lower East Side incorporated "obscene" words into their writing and held relatively libertarian attitudes toward sexuality and drug use, the alarmingly vague and subjective language of the law must certainly have added to artists' paranoia: "A license may be suspended or revoked by the commissioner for any violation of law, or upon the ground that *disor-*

derly, obscene, or immoral conduct is permitted on the licensed premises, or for other good cause."[87] In reaction to the coffeehouse license law, poets and journalists in Manhattan responded with a flurry of newspaper articles, calls for demonstrations, and behind-the-scenes politicking. In her article "Fuzz's Progress," Diane di Prima outlined a general contemporary history of police repression of arts organizations and performance spaces:

> The term "harassment of the arts" is relatively new but it has already become a byword in New York and other cities of this country. Four theatres alone have been closed; writers and painters are spending more time in the courtroom than at the typewriter or easel. The current outbreak is merely an acceleration of a process which has been building for some time. One of the more publicized cases from that earlier phase was the federal government's seizure of the Living Theatre for back taxes on October 17, 1963. Contrary to popular impression, co-director Julian Beck stated he had been paying these taxes in small installments. . . . It may be useful to point out that the three main law-enforcement agencies at work are: New York City's Department of Licenses; the New York State Division of Motion Pictures (under the Board of Education) which licenses films; the New York City police and occasionally fire, building or other municipal authorities.[88]

In this article, di Prima also described how, in December 1963, the city administration "broke its 1961 agreement with the Artist-Tenants Association and began denying applications for Artist-in-Residence permits—which allow artists to live in lofts—on the basis of the new zoning laws." Additionally, one learns that on December 7, 1963, "A performance of Jack Smith's film *Flaming Creatures* was scheduled at the Tivoli Theatre. A crowd of 600–800 people was kept waiting and finally dispersed: the manager had been warned by a phone call from the Bureau of Licenses not to open that night." The Bread and Puppet Theater and Jerry Bloedow's Hardware Poets Theater (located in the Upper West Side) were threatened with closure, though Bloedow conveniently sidestepped the potential trouble by transforming his theater into a private club. Department officials also targeted Mort Lewis's theater, which was based in his own apartment and held seats for only sixteen people (all invited). Finally, on February 2, 1964, "Maurice Margules of the Metro Coffee Shop received a summons for presenting 'entertainment'—poetry readings— without a coffeehouse license."[89]

As di Prima makes clear, Le Metro was in no way alone in facing harassment by the city. While di Prima mentions mostly East Village institutions, one should remember that the West Village had faced similar trouble a number of years earlier. Clearly, harassment of the arts in the East Village was actually part of a years-long struggle between city bureaucrats on the one hand

and artists on the other in both the West and East Village. Visible targets including comedian Lenny Bruce (who was arrested in the West Village at the Café Au Go Go in April of 1964 on obscenity charges) were being threatened with the same intensity as the poetry series at Le Metro, which had its first taste of trouble on February 2, 1964, during Carol Bergé's Sunday poetry reading series.[90] On that particular Sunday, a group of poets happened to be gathered at Le Metro to participate in a collaborative performance or "simultaneity" of Jackson Mac Low's.

Mac Low remembers, "Early in 1964 (I remember this because I had just gotten a bundle of copies of the first Fluxus newspaper, *V Tre,* from George Maciunas, and had distributed copies of it to the people that showed up at the rehearsal at Carol Bergé's apartment on East 9th Street), I gathered a large group of people together for a performance at Le Metro. Each performer was at a table just as the members of the audience were. All participants performed from their seats in the audience. Nevertheless, a policeman gave the proprietor a summons for having 'entertainment' without having a cabaret license."[91] Mac Low recalls that Moe Margules, the proprietor of Le Metro, "said to the cop that it wasn't 'entertainment' at all; just customers who liked to read their poetry out loud at their tables when they were drinking their coffee or whatever. The cop didn't buy it, and gave the proprietor a summons for breaking the cabaret law."[92] Ed Sanders adds, "In those days, the buildings department was very corrupt and it was just gigantically expensive, so one couldn't afford to do all the bribing and engineering work and blueprints and specs and more bribes in order to transform something into a cabaret license. No one wanted to undergo what Billie Holiday had to go through, where you had to get a card, and the police are then in on it and make a determination where you work."[93]

The response by poets in the Lower East Side to the legal action initiated by the City was swift, Mac Low recalls:

> A number of us, including Allen Ginsberg, Allen Katzman, Ed Sanders, and, I think Carol Bergé, got up a "Committee on Poetry" to get the cabaret law changed. We somehow reached Ed Koch, the future mayor, who was then the heroic district leader who had toppled the evil former district leader Carmine De Sapio. A group of us, including the two Allens and me, and possibly Ed, visited Koch in his apartment, then on Barrow Street, near Hudson St. (I remember particularly that Koch's place was on the same floor as that of a woman with whom I had had an intermittent relationship from about 1953 to 1957). Koch—who was by then a prominent member of the City Council for the West Village—was completely charming and supportive (and showed he knew his modernist poets by heart by quoting from Eliot et al. as we talked). He had

his friend Henry Stern (for many years the head of the Parks Department) take us to visit the City Councilman and a number of relevant city commissioners for the part of the East Side in which Le Metro was located. The upshot was that the cabaret law was changed to allow poetry readings.[94]

Sanders, Mac Low, Ed Koch, and the rest of the committee participated in meetings with members of the Department of Licenses and discovered that the indictments against Le Metro and other coffeehouses were arranged simply by ordering functionaries at the Department of Licenses to read through publications including the *Village Voice* in order to find announcements of poetry readings. Mac Low, Sanders, and the others argued that such a policy was tantamount to harassment and violated their First Amendment rights. Ed Sanders stated, "Once we realized they were just scanning newspapers and sending people in, we wanted to just intercept that concept. You know, just don't pay fifteen cents to buy the *Village Voice*. It takes one J. Edgar Hoover type, one public official, one Joe McCarthy, one person upset . . . you know, there was no censorship, so some of the poetry was frankly erotic, and politically out there too. A lot of left-wing poems, about the civil rights movement, about racism, a lot of antiwar stuff."[95] In light of the free speech issues raised by the case, the New York Civil Liberties Union also came to the defense of Le Metro. The N.Y.C.L.U. submitted a court brief that stated no government agency "may regulate or license the reading of poetry by means of a prior restraint and that the imposition of criminal sanctions for the reading of poetry is violative of the federally guaranteed right of free speech."[96] The ensuing legal battles and media attention resulted in Le Metro becoming a nationally known establishment, which of course produced greater crowds and more media attention. This was not surprising; after all, the moment an artistic phenomenon—be it a painting, a photograph, a performance, or a poetry-reading series—becomes defined as illicit or dangerous, it will immediately attract a level of attention far higher than it otherwise would.[97]

The summons handed out to Margules at Le Metro was just part of what was to become a months-long offensive by the Department of Licenses to shut down a number of downtown performance spaces. As the months wore on, more and more venues were being faced with city-sanctioned harassment. The *Village Voice* reported, "The current zeal of the City's Department of Licenses for the strict enforcement of licensing regulations against small avant-garde creative ventures has so far resulted in the temporary closing of three off-Broadway theatres, the suspension of poetry readings at Le Metro, and a general malaise among culturally minded New Yorkers as to what may be afoot."[98] Responses among the artistic community in Manhattan to the above harassment included editorials in various mimeographed magazines, as well as announcements for the following demonstration:

> The Committee for Freedom
> of the Arts invites you to a
> FLASHLIGHT PARADE
> AND RALLY
> to protest
> Harassment of the Arts
> in New York City

Marchers will gather on 6th Avenue at 41st Street at 6:00 P.M. on Wednesday, April 22, 1964 and march across 42nd Street and up Broadway to Lincoln Center. Marchers are asked to carry flashlights and wear black as a token of mourning for the Death of Freedom in the city.

This particular march ended at Lincoln Center (a city-sanctioned site of "official" culture), a spot most likely chosen for its ironic significance. City efforts at shutting down clubs in no way affected institutions like Lincoln Center, Carnegie Hall, the 92nd Street Y, and so on. Fully licensed and financially endowed, such institutions represented the official face of contemporary culture. Yet places like Le Metro and La Mama Theater, as well as Times Square sex shops, dance halls, and apparently anywhere Lenny Bruce was performing his comedy act, had no such official backing. Even worse in the eyes of city authorities was the fact that these spaces allowed for the promulgation of dissident discourse and behavior.

A different flyer calling for participation in the April 22 march made much out of the fact that the shutdowns were political events based on silencing dissident speech. Announcing "Freedom for the Arts, Torchlight Parade, April 22, 1964" this flyer featured an illustration of a nude Statue of Liberty with her mouth taped shut. Her arm was outstretched in an effort to cover the mouth of a nearby flying angel sporting a large erection.[99] By reading such a document, one can see that the poets and artists of the Lower East Side were using traditional poetic images to distinguish themselves as a significant, culturally rich movement. The erect angel might have elicited associations with Dionysus, the Greek god who is variously depicted as immortal and powerful and irreverent, lusty, and fond of intoxicants and revelry. The figure may also have reminded those who used this flyer of Ginsberg's famous line from "Howl," "Angel-headed hipsters burning for the ancient heavenly connection to the starry dynamo in the machinery of night."[100] Even in their ephemeral flyers, it is clear that the poetic community reached back to traditions that could in some way support and add intellectual, literary, and spiritual seriousness and context to their practices.

The End of Le Metro

By March 1964, the case against Le Metro had been thrown out. "Judge James Camerford . . . dismissed the complaint after a License Department inspector said that he had seen people 'saying words' in LeMetro [*sic*]. An expert described this as simultaneous poetry reading."[101] Legal troubles settled and coffeehouses (and by extension, poetry readings) protected against the coffeehouse license law, Le Metro had become relatively famous. So why did it end? Unfortunately, the growing confluence of poets and "scene makers" at Le Metro, combined with proprietor Moe Margules's growing distaste for the poets crowding his premises and his institution of a much-resented 25¢ minimum for a cup of coffee, led to a violent fight fraught with racial implications. Even before this altercation in the fall of 1965, lines at Le Metro were getting shorter—possibly because the mood inside was turning a little ugly. Margules, a Goldwater Republican, began to put up posters of Republican politicians and engaged in political arguments with poets until the environment became quite heated. Margules remembers that "things were going to break up anyway . . . (there were) fistfights, just pushings & shovings, all this."[102] According to Allen DeLoach in *The East Side Scene,* Le Metro was "a scene that had fallen apart through internal dissension stemming generally from a conflict of social and political beliefs which existed between Moe and Cindy on one side and a small number of poets on the other side, many of whom were 'Umbra' poets . . . The conflict was intense and justly heated. . . . Later attempts to bring about a reconciliation at Café Le Metro only served to continue the readings for a short time without really rectifying the situation."[103] Paul Blackburn did attempt to keep readings at Le Metro after the legendary fight, at least through the end of 1965. In his column "Get the Money," published in the *East Village Other,* Ted Berrigan wrote, "Paul Blackburn, 2nd Avenue's Clyde Beatty, lists Robt Kelly (Dec 1), Kathy Fraser (the 8th), and Jerry Bloedow (15th) as readers at Le Metro in December."[104] However, Margules remembers that "the response was not strong enough, & the onus of attack was too much. After a few months, I can't remember, things stopped."[105]

Precise details of the fight at Le Metro are somewhat vague. The varying interpretations of who hit whom first tends to suggest a *Rashomon*-type event more than anything else. Michel Oren, for example, claims that "Dent was assaulted by an armed guard. . . . The incident, which both Dent and Reed ascribe to Mafia attempts to take over the readings and use them as a front for undercover operations, apparently brought to an end all Lower East Side readings and precipitated the dispersal of the entire scene, black and white."[106] Other poets in attendance insist that Moe Margules attacked Dent, and there are dozens of interpretations of what caused the fight in the first place.

What *is* known is that the fight occurred during a reading being given by the poet Walter Lowenfels and was a result of tension between Margules and the Umbra poets, a predominantly African American group of poets in the Lower East Side who ran their own workshops and published *Umbra* magazine. Moe Margules became involved in an altercation in the rear of the coffee shop with Tom Dent. David Henderson recalls, "A lot of the Umbra poets had gotten on to this Metro thing, and people wanted to read—Ishmael Reed, Lorenzo Thomas, Clarence Major, Lennox Rafael who was writing for the *East Village Other*, Allen Katzman, Trudy Katzman. So anyway, there was a fight at the Metro. The Umbra poets were involved, and Tom Dent was attacked."[107]

In the first issue of the *East Village Other* (published by Allen Katzman), Ishmael Reed wrote a caustic editorial entitled "Poetry Place Protest" (here excerpted) implying that Lowenfels and many other poets involved with Le Metro simply refused to return:

> He is a restless cur wolf inhabited by fleas and moles twitching and rubbing their sticky and moley tentacles in his backside. This constant friction and irritation causes him to blow his wolf cool and leads him to do weird handstands, like going after Archie Shepp with a meat cleaver, or cane whipping Don Harriman or flagellating a gentleman like Tom Dent, former editor of UMBRA Magazine. The Shopkeeper couldn't get past the Dent butler, but these are the arrogant hangups of New York's rude servant community which includes all kinds of mayors and shopkeepers and hairdressers.
>
> After the shopkeeper was diverted from nickel grubbing long enough to indulge in more interesting games like banging Tom Dent around the room in view of Walter Lowenfels who was writing about the nitty-gritty world. . . . The great Walter Lowenfels shut down 'murder incorporated' that night and the shopkeeper was dismayed because he thought that all poets were of the same cut as those who frequented his place—swami pompadours types and anus mongerers. He was in for a surprise! Lowenfels and his followers left as did the moderator Allan Katzman.[108]

The end of Le Metro resulted in a vacuum. From the winter of 1965 through most of 1966, dozens of poets found themselves without an established place to read. However, while it would take almost nine months for the readings at the St. Mark's Poetry Project to begin, poets of the Lower East Side were not completely lost. Many writers continued to perform their work at the Poets

Co-Op (a cooperative housing and performance space on Second Street and the Bowery maintained by Umbra poets and neighborhood anarchists).[109] Other locations featuring familiar Lower East Side groupings included a series at the Atelier East Gallery at 83 East Fourth Street featuring mostly Black Mountain–influenced writers.[110] Additionally, Ted Berrigan ran his own Sunday afternoon reading series at the Folklore Center on Sixth Avenue and Eight Street (featuring poets including Clark Coolidge, Joe Brainard, Tom Clark, and Ed Sanders). Most significant, however, was the work initiated by spring of 1966, when Blackburn organized a Reading Committee—with the help of Rothenberg, Bergé, and others—to begin readings at St. Mark's Church.

The founding of the Poetry Project in the summer of 1966 reinstalled a central location for Lower East Side alternative poets.[111] Additionally, the Poetry Project ushered in an entirely new era of mimeographed magazines. Along with the demise of Le Metro, mimeographed magazines including *Fuck You* and Berrigan's *C: A Journal of Poetry* ceased production, opening up the scene to newer publication ventures. Before we look at the early history of the Poetry Project, a close reading of several of the important mimeographed and bound magazines coming out of the Les Deux Mégots and Le Metro scenes will provide a context for the later publications coming out of the Poetry Project, as it will continue to help us analyze the complex and interrelated gathering of poets in the Lower East Side.

The Aesthetics of the Little

A little magazine's only rationale is its editor's belief that the writers he prints
must be presented as a group. Anything else is just a collation of pages.

WILLIAM CARLOS WILLIAMS

"Just the Extension of the Personal(s)":
Magazines in the Lower East Side Poetic Community

On the Lower East Side throughout the 1960s, much of the poetry that was
read at places including Les Deux Mégots, Le Metro, and the Poetry Project
could best be disseminated through the mimeograph magazine and the small-
circulation, low-cost bound magazine. The mimeograph in particular allowed
for speedy, cheap reproduction. That speediness lent mimeographed materi-
als an urgency allusive of newspaper "extras." Mimeos contained breaking news
of the poetry world, serving as carriers of fresh and vital information. Diane
di Prima recalls that "the last time I saw Charles Olson in Gloucester, one of
the things he talked about was how valuable the Bear had been to him in its
early years because of the fact that he could get new work out that fast. He
was very involved in speed . . . his work, his thoughts, would be in the hands
of a few hundred writers within two or three weeks. It was like writing a let-
ter to a bunch of friends."[1] Hettie Jones, Amiri Baraka's wife at the time, re-
calls that "Roi and Diane—mostly Diane, who owned the mimeograph—
were mailing a sheet called *The Floating Bear,* its purpose to publish new work
faster than the quarterly *Yugen.* Its frequent appearances were ideal for mes-
sages."[2] References to the mimeo's speed, sociability, and even its political
significations are found throughout the correspondence of the poets associ-

ated with the Lower East Side poetic community.³ Exhibiting the growing politicization of many of the poets in response to the Vietnam War, di Prima in 1971 published a note inside the back cover of her militant anarchist poem sequence *Revolutionary Letters* that read, "This is a free book. These are free poems and may be reprinted anywhere by anyone. . . . Power to the people's mimeo machines!"⁴

Poets living on the Lower East Side would take advantage of the mimeo throughout the 1960s, culminating in the Poetry Project's purchase of a nine-hole Gestetner mimeograph machine in 1967. This machine was used by dozens of poet-editors to publish a number of magazines throughout the 1970s and 1980s, up to the publication of the mimeo *The 11ᵗʰ Street Ruse.*⁵ The *Ruse,* which began in 1987, is still (theoretically) alive, though as of 2002 the Lower East Side has not seen a copy of this publication, probably owing to the fact that the machine broke down in September 1997.⁶

Even beyond Dan Saxon's *Poets at Le Metro* series, mimeographed magazines (and, to a slightly lesser extent, the more "professional"-looking small-circulation magazines published in or sympathetic to the Lower East Side community) were closely tied to the reading scenes. In his manuscript "What's New?: An Interior Report on the Socio-literary Uses of the Mimeograph Machine," Paul Blackburn positioned various magazines as centered at Le Metro:

> Aside from the Bear, the richness and variation of the current New York scene might be indicated by the fact that F/U (now announcing its Quaker issue, F/Thee), *C, Intrepid, Yowl,* and *Blue Beat,* all of differing shades, ranges, and intention, work roughly side-by-side out of the same lower East Side coffee-house, Le Metro, which has had so much trouble recently with the City Fathers. Of the five, *C,* a journal of poetry edited by Ted Berrigan, is the first mimeo outlet for "The New York School" (Ashbery, O'Hara, Koch, Denby, Elmslie, Schuyler), plus the young people who started it and their friends.⁷

Such publications served as a kind of metaphorical extended meeting ground for the larger social groupings meeting at Le Metro. Many of the mimeos included community gossip, statements on poetics, "books received" announcements, and announcements of new mimeo publications, as well as poems and correspondence from writers living in other parts of the country. The editors of these publications often commented on the intricate social circumstances of the poets, which tended to emphasize and underscore the very performativity of the poems themselves.⁸ One might, for example, read a poem in a publication that included other "nonliterary" texts such as reports of a fight at a reading or reflections on a loft party. As Paul Blackburn wrote, "These newsletters also serve their audience as such: not just reviews but also recommendations as to what books are on sale at what shops, what new maga-

zines (or newsletters) have started up and their addresses, instructions for rais-
ing rare herbs, or even advertisements (of course, unpaid) for a personalized
blow-job by an infamous movie star. We are not speaking here of the propa-
gation of 'vice,' just the extension of the personal(s)."[9]

This style of publication helped define poetry as living in the mouths of
contemporary people as opposed to distant authors; poetry was presented in
such a way that the reader could easily imagine the poem as an utterance.
Since so much of the poetry associated with the Lower East Side was read out
loud, it was not unusual to find editors interested in enacting—within the
confines of the mimeographed page—the level of sociability inherent in the
real world of the poetry community.

Examining the history of publications also helps to define what being "out-
side" the cultural mainstream actually meant to the poets of the Lower East
Side. Much of the poetry and associated commentary in the mimeos tended
to emphasize and articulate both the poets' allegiances to a historical experi-
mental tradition (Williams, Pound, Stein, and so on) as well as to a height-
ened sense of the poets' fraternity and their marginalized relationship to the
society in which they wrote. This sense of community in the face of a larger,
sometimes hostile culture is visible in the following excerpt from John Wieners's
"Prose Poem":

> We are not alone in our glamour, as we pass the pipe of mariweedge between
> us, dreaming of Mexico and small Italian towns along the Mediterranean coast.

> We exist upon the fringe of the world, small bright fragments that somehow
> burn away the fire's edge. We do not smoke. We scorch, but go on, bearing the
> scars.[10]

One can also look to Ted Berrigan's prose poem "Looking for Chris" for an
overt definition of the poet as outsider:

> I'm on the outside looking in. Those who said they like my poems understand
> this whole thing. It's about Chris. Rubbish! Films run culture through the whole
> back of my head. I have every reason.

> The pressure is (was) from hearing Kenneth Koch read at the Guggenheim,
> pills arriving from a drug manufacturer, starting a tic going down the popula-
> tion in a totem which is growing three times as fast and costs an estimated
> $600.28.[11]

Picking up on Wieners's and Berrigan's sense of social companionship/alien-
ation and economic anxiety, it is more than significant that drug use is re-
ferred to in their poems. While many Lower East Side poets were not crim-
inals by legal definition, many of their poems found in the mimeos satirically

and sometimes seriously promoted and idealized drug use, libertarian or left-ist politics, and general chaos in a way that contemporary poems associated with universities at that time did not. Though many poets wrote of "criminal" activities merely as an aesthetic gesture, the editors and poets associated with the magazines and reading series at Les Deux Mégots and Le Metro were actually made into criminals through a series of obscenity trials. Mimeos including Amiri Baraka and Diane di Prima's *Floating Bear* and Ed Sanders's *Fuck You / a magazine of the arts* were used as evidence by police to arrest those editors and send them to jail on charges of distributing obscenity through the mails.[12] Indeed, "unofficial" poetry appearing in mimeographed form was seen as suspect by the authorities in general. Baraka and di Prima were arrested because jailed poet Harold Carrington "subscribed to *Floating Bear,* which was delivered to him at the jail. Since his jail-house censors read all of his incoming as well as his outgoing mail, they read his copy of the ninth issue of *Floating Bear* before he did, and shortly thereafter Baraka and Diane di Prima were arrested as the editors and publishers of an obscene literary magazine."[13] In the context of the historical reception of poetry, in the 1960s alternative poetry was still considered potentially subversive and dangerous by those outside the cultural environment where it was produced. As Carrington's case indicates, if poetry appeared in an odd (mimeographed) package, it was deemed suspect and examined by prison guards. One is hard-pressed to imagine this happening if prison guards had merely received a "respectable" bound book with a title like *New Poets of England and America.*

Beyond containing material that was too risqué for more established publishing houses, the mimeograph and small-circulation magazine, conceived as a form in itself, was complementary to the general poetics philosophy of many of the poets anthologized in *The New American Poetry* and/or living in the Lower East Side. Alan Golding has pointed out, in reference to Cid Corman's magazine *Origin,* that Charles Olson "thought magazine publication could realize the possibilities of field composition more effectively than could a book, and hence that it reflected his poetics more accurately." Golding then quotes Olson: "'I *like* best, origin, the life & moving of it, the very going on, that a book never, for me, has—quite the openness.' Creeley agreed, commenting to Olson on 'what a mag can have over a book—fragmentia—burst—plunge—spontaneous—THE WHOLE WORKS.'"[14] Magazines and mimeos provided spaces where personal jabs, retorts, poems, smudges, footprints, poetics theory, gossip, and so forth could be included.[15] Such inclusionary strategies lent associations of community to the word *poetry,* a word that might otherwise be interpreted as relating specifically to static texts divorced from or *unrelated to* interpersonal histories and community politics.

An aesthetics of the little becomes visible when we trace the trajectory of the small-circulation magazine as it developed from Margaret Anderson's *The Little Review* and various futurist and dada publications to Eugene Jolas's *transition* in the late 1920s and early 1930s to Corman's *Origin* in the 1950s and, finally, to the explosion of mimeos coming out of the Lower East Side during the 1960s.[16] Felix Pollak has defined some of the aesthetics of the little:

> Little magazines share certain characteristics: they are primarily literary, often experimental, and typically unfettered. Virtually all have a small circulation, and they are usually published, edited, and financed by one person or by a small group of persons who are amateurs—that is to say, people without a profit motive . . . Little magazines can afford to print trash and frequently use this liberty to excess.[17]

As this chapter will show, Pollak's definition applies to all the mimeographed magazines coming out of the Lower East Side during the 1960s. Additionally, another characteristic that Pollak does not mention here is the fact that throughout the twentieth century the "little" often faced stiff opposition from literary and legal establishments—that is, from people in positions of power, including customs officials, police, established professors, professional critics, and the like. For example, Margaret Anderson's *The Little Review* published essays favorable to anarchist martyr Joe Hill just as it published poems and essays by Pound, Yeats, Eliot and sections from Joyce's *Ulysses*. Because of *The Little Review*'s political and "sexual" content, it was seized and burned more than once by customs officials. *The Little Review* also elicited angry letters from offended parents: "I earnestly request you to discontinue sending your impertinent publication to my daughter who had the folly of undiscriminating youth to fall into the diabolical snare by joining the ungodly family of your subscribers."[18] Many of the mimeos coming out of the Lower East Side followed the same kinds of policies and received similar fates. Ed Sanders's *Fuck You / a magazine of the arts* published poetry by W. H. Auden and Beat icons Allen Ginsberg and William Burroughs, alongside editorials calling for a "FUCK-IN Against the Vietnam War."[19] In 1965 New York City police seized Sanders's mimeos, and Sanders was charged with distributing obscene materials through the mail. Partly for these reasons, the little has also been associated with ephemerality; existing for maybe six or seven years at the most, many of the littles closed shop for reasons as mundane as exhaustion and boredom and as significant as a refusal to accommodate to political pressures.

Ephemerality itself became part of the aesthetics of the little: "Little magazines, more than most forms of literary production, often acknowledge, and even make a virtue of, both their own temporariness and the volatility of evaluative standards."[20] Dada and futurist publications certainly provided a "tradition" of ephemerality and even a sense of studied sloppiness to which many of the mimeos coming out of the Lower East Side could look and from which they could receive some measure of vindication for what might otherwise be dismissed as merely amateur. As early as 1914, magazines like Kruchenykh's and Khlebnikov's *Te li le* were "handwritten with decoration by Kulbin and Rozanova, [and] reproduced in color by a primitive gelatine process called hectography."[21] While there is a danger here of romanticizing poverty by asserting that the primitive presentation of these texts was a necessary part of the aesthetics embodied by the work within, it is nevertheless significant that the "do-it-yourself" aesthetic of dada and futurism, which threatened distinctions between "high" and "low" art, managed to survive and find its way into the publishing practices of Lower East Side reading series and related publications. In reference to *Trobar,* a magazine associated with the Deep Image poetic group based in part in and around the Lower East Side and Brooklyn, editor George Economou has explained, "The whole dada, post–World War I attitude was very appealing to us. You know, we don't need to find publishers—we'll just *be* our own publishers. It was a wonderful experience, to have the satisfaction to have picked a bunch of poems, to have written some of your own, and then engage to completion in the physical act of making the book or magazine."[22] Text fragments, rough illustrations, handwritten notes, and gossip made the Lower East Side mimeo publications, in all their variousness, an ongoing entertainment for the cognoscenti. What seemed an air of low-culture referentiality, almost a reverse snobbishness about presentation and a sidelong glimpse at the little magazine of modernist and anarchist assertion, gave a certain funny class to the avant-garde enterprise.[23]

> The interwar little magazine was the matrix of modernist literary monuments, and it is arguably more than coincidence that the experience of discontinuity which typifies periodical reading should also typify the reading experience of the canonical texts of modernism over whose conception and birth the little magazine presided. . . . As the familiar story of Pound's invention of imagism suggests, the literature and poetics of the fragment were produced for and by the little magazine and it was in this poetics (of imagism, of dadaist and surrealist literary collage) that the stylistic techniques of the canonical Anglo-American modernist works . . . originated.[24]

That is, the "experience of discontinuity" inherent in reading the little—the reader can dip into the text by reading fragments or excerpts from longer works and not feel like an essential narrative order is lost or even desired—is particularly amenable to the kinds of texts that modernism, surrealism, and dada produced. The fact that so many of the mimeos coming out of the Lower East Side tended to favor fragmented texts, anonymous and collaborative writing, and (in many cases) politically or socially provocative material combined with basic news on the poetic community suggests the influence of predecessor modernist littles.

Another facet of the "aesthetic of the little" implied by Pollak's use of the phrase "a small group" is the sense that the little is a metaphor for a literary *community* that recognizes the importance of recording events and ideas helpful to its own mythologizing activities. Drawing together a group of writers in the space of a mimeograph magazine or little does not necessarily mean that there is a community *prior to* publication. Rather, it is the gathering of names, and the conscious decision to repeat those names throughout the various issues, that generates the sense of community. Picking up on the job already begun by Anderson's *Little Review,* which had featured excerpts from Joyce's *Ulysses,* Eugene Jolas's *transition* published much of Joyce's *Finnegans Wake* as a "work in progress." *transition* also published "a great deal of Gertrude Stein's work including 'An Elucidation', 'Four Saints in Three Acts', and a re-publication of 'Tender Buttons.' It published portions of Hart Crane's 'The Bridge', early poems and stories by Dylan Thomas, and Samuel Beckett's earliest work."[25] *transition* in this way served to establish further the sense of a modernist community in part initiated by the *Little Review.* James Laughlin added members to the modernist and postmodernist family as editor of *New Directions* and publisher of Pound, Williams, and many other writers. As if to emphasize that his project was a continuation of an overall twentieth-century avant-garde tradition, Laughlin dedicated his series to "the readers, editors, and contributors of *transition* for successfully carrying out the 'Revolution of the Word.'"[26]

Regarding Cid Corman's networking and publishing many of the same writers in *Origin* over and over again, Alan Golding writes:

> The impulse behind Corman's, and indeed Olson's, networking is analyzed in an essay by Paul Goodman that Olson read enthusiastically and recommended, "Advance-Guard Writing, 1900–1950," published, paradoxically, in the rival *Kenyon Review.* Writing around the same time as *Origin* started, Goodman describes one strategy of the twentieth-century poetic avant-garde as "the physical reestablishment of community," a strategy designed to combat writers' sense of alienation from an audience and from themselves. . . . Goodman argues that, in a culture lacking intimate community, "the advance-guard action helps create such community, starting with the artist's primary friends." Among other things, this helps explain Olson's faith in the Black Mountain experiment; and it certainly helps explain the thinking behind *Origin,* which, in the absence of a literal, physical community, established a metaphorical one in its pages.[27]

The "little" is, in theory at least, a way to promote actual friendships— clearly a very different effect of publishing than that of an established publishing house, with its various bureaucratic office structures and departments and its practice of featuring a single author within the pages of a single book. Like their dada, surrealist, and modernist predecessors, mimeograph and small-circulation magazines coming out of the Lower East Side were documents designed for friends as well as vehicles for making new friends. Reva Wolf points out that Baraka and di Prima's *The Floating Bear* "was free . . . and the only way to receive a copy was by knowing a person who worked on its production and thereby could add names to the mailing list. This selective distribution in itself ordained *Floating Bear* as an agent of communication within a circumscribed community."[28] Ed Sanders's magazine *Fuck You / a magazine of the arts* was only available in a select number of stores, hidden behind counters. Knowledge of where to find the magazine was analogous to knowledge of a secret code or handshake necessary for entry into an exclusive if irreverent club. Writers within the pages of the mimeos would also have a big effect on the editorial decisions of the official "editor," suggesting new friends for inclusion and thereby widening the sense of community and shared purpose. Editors from the Lower East Side scene relied on a sense of engaged, dynamic friendship with their readers and contributors as essential to their magazines' identities and survival.[29]

What follows is a history behind some of these magazines and mimeograph publications associated with the poets of the Lower East Side in the years 1960 to 1965, just before the founding of the Poetry Project in 1966. This history shows how the publications were tied into the social world of the reading scenes at Les Deux Mégots and Le Metro, and it illustrates the political and avant-garde stances many poets in the Lower East Side adopted during this crucial era. This review in no way purports to be a comprehensive examination of every magazine coming out of the neighborhood (there were simply too many to list here, and many were interrelated in terms of contributors and editors). However, discussing the following magazines— Ed Sanders's mimeo *Fuck You / a magazine of the arts,* the collaboratively edited magazine *Umbra,* Jerome Rothenberg's *Poems from the Floating World,* George Economou and Robert Kelly's *Trobar,* and Ted Berrigan's *C: A Journal of Poetry*—will provide a relatively clear idea of poetic and political allegiances specific to many of the alternative poets living in the Lower East Side.[30]

"From a Secret Location on the Lower East Side": *Fuck You / a magazine of the arts*

Ed Sanders's *Fuck You / a magazine of the arts,* followed by the legend "EDITED, PUBLISHED & PRINTED BY ED SANDERS AT A SECRET LOCATION IN THE

LOWER EAST SIDE, NEW YORK CITY U.S.A." pushed boundaries; its very title was a radical incongruity that placed the street epithet "fuck you" next to the staid phrase "a magazine of the arts" and thereby declared its challenge to distinctions between high and low art. *Fuck You / a magazine of the arts* instructed readers that poetry could exist as a populist impulse designed to shock, delight, and inform.

Besides threatening the distinctions between high and low, *Fuck You* used literature to question and undermine conservative and legalistic approaches to literary copyright, homosexuality, drug use, intergenerational sex, and the incest taboo. A history of *Fuck You* offers today's poetry readers a carnivalesque and deeply entertaining vision of what a poetry magazine can be and of what it can *do*.

Sex, Politics, Poetry, and the Avant-Garde

The social environment surrounding the poetry scene on the Lower East Side provided Sanders with a home that stood in marked contrast to the comparatively repressive American culture outside the bohemian ghetto. By the 1960s, the Lower East Side was a model for the possibilities offered by sexual liberation. Besides being one of the few areas in North America where mixed-race couples could exist without frequently eliciting excessive hostility, the neighborhood attracted organizations like the Kerista Free Love Society, a commune devoted to the promotion of polygamous relationships.[31] Sanders associated this sexual openness and experimentation with the new poetry of the Lower East Side by positioning the reading series taking place at Les Deux Mégots as a site for the confluence of poetry and sexual experience. Sanders attested to this link between nontraditional sexual mores and oral poetry in gauche references to the café reading series:

Carol Bergé: Sweet poetess whom the entire Editorial Board, you may know, would just love to fuck. Known to lurk about the Les Deux Mégots Coffee House on Mondays, Wednesdays, & Thursdays.[32]

Mary Mayo: fur burger supreme. Poetess. Hustles at the Les Deux Mégots on Mondays & Wednesdays.[33]

Through editorials, poems, and stories, Sanders also referred to the sexual antics taking place among the members of the Lower East Side poetic community and later included such anecdotes in stories including "Siobhan McKenna Group Grope."[34] This story mythologized the gentle orgies of poets who read and socialized at "The House of Nothingness," an appropriate pseudonym for Les Deux Mégots, which took its name from Les Deux Magots, the legendary Parisian café hangout for existentialist philosophers and writers, including Jean-Paul Sartre, author of *Being and Nothingness.*

Additionally, neighborhood organizations like the War Resisters League and Dorothy Day's Catholic Worker, both strong pacifist prolabor groups, were gaining increasing exposure and popularity as the civil rights and antiwar movements became more and more of a social force. Sanders initially typed the stencils for the first issue of *Fuck You* out of the basement office of the Catholic Worker, where Sanders found the paper he printed his material on— bright green and red granatext that was to become *Fuck You*'s signature look.

The historical conditions of the Lower East Side in the early 1960s were crucial both for Sanders's promotion of radical pacifism and for his identity as a sex liberationist. In terms of his social politics, Sanders situated the poetry he published within the context of the political environment characteristic of his place and era. He dedicated each issue of the magazine to "pacifism, unilateral disarmament, national defense thru nonviolent resistance, multilateral indiscriminate apertural conjugation, anarchism, world federalism, civil disobedience, Project Mercury, Peace Eye, the Margaret Sanger institute, obstructers & submarine boarders, and all those groped by J. Edgar Hoover in the silent halls of Congress."[35] In terms of his sexual politics, Sanders also used poetry in tandem with his editorial promotion of marginalized sexual behavior. This is evident from the magazine's long-standing support of "gobble scenes," as one sees in this excerpt from an editorial in *Fuck You:*

> Must we form a Citizens Times Square Gobble Protection Civil Liberties Patrol to protect the personal liberties of the gentle Broadway gobblers!?
> . . . We shall not be free until we can fuck in the streets or anywhere under the rays of Ra, until all gentle AC-DC cadets can suck cock, grope or bugger in total leisure anywhere, until we can smoke our hashish, or snort the energetic freak powders under our own judgement all over the universe![36]

This language suggests the work of poet, actor, and aphorist Taylor Mead, particularly Mead's earlier political statements found in his book *The Anonymous Diary of a New York Youth.* Sanders consistently published Mead throughout *Fuck You*'s history and had advertised Mead's book as "Taylor Mead: STAR of Ron Rice's THE FLOWER THIEF. Poet, thinker, & cocksucker par excellence, author of those banned motherfuckers of books *Excerpts From the Anonymous Diary of a New York Youth.* Get it & he'll cruise yr mind with his hot verbal dick."[37] Sanders's call in *Fuck You* for sexual libertarianism reflects Mead's earlier outrage:

> I can't see the righteousness of these sex laws—I can't see the righteousness at all—trapping yearning loving people on the beach, in cars, in public toilets—

where are you lawmakers locked away in your comfortable houses with your comfortable satiated thoughts and ways unexposed dead—wake up to the world—let my people free![38]

Through editorials, poetry, and the publication of work by Taylor Mead, *Fuck You* promoted queer sex, even though New York was an officially homophobic city. As *Fuck You* celebrated Mead, police raids on gay bars were still taken for granted, and sodomy in New York was criminalized throughout the 1950s and 1960s. It is important to understand how truly shocking such language must have seemed in 1964 to the uninitiated. It was not until 1973 that the American Psychiatric Association eliminated homosexuality from its list of mental illnesses and, in 1980, dropped it from its *Diagnostic and Statistical Manual of Mental Disorders*.[39] By publishing poetry that spoke unflinchingly of homosexual love, *Fuck You* helped provide an environment in which homosexuality could be celebrated during an era when being homosexual could land you in jail.[40]

Fuck You would continue to use poetry as a way to question sexual taboos even further, articulating a very serious if entertaining vision of a libertarian pansexualism. This vision included the publication of poems detailing sexual acts that are still considered abominable, including exaggerated if fictional references to pedophilia. What is a little disconcerting about the following examples is the sense that what is being described might actually have happened, that the staff at *Fuck You* had linked intergenerational sexual relationships and incest to Sanders's overall agenda of "multilateral indiscriminate apertural conjugation":

> the Editorial board was cornholing a young 8 year old boy the other night warming up for a meeting & in walked, sparkle sparkle, Elin Paulson, who blew the lad into a frenzy. The lad then went twat happy and El and he freaked to a 74 scene. That's 69 with the 5 editorial board members watching.[41]

The same issue included a poem by Al Fowler entitled "Caroline: An Exercise for Our Cocksman Leader":

> I saw the hot eyes of my young daughter
> rolling in passion
> her body writhing naked
> groping thru my pants and shorts
> feeling for her daddy's prick
>
> tiny scarlet pussy burning for the lustful
> invasion of my wet, Harvard, unpaternal tongue
> (my slick fingers reaming her ass . . . [42]

Referring to the Fowler poem, Sanders provides us with an editor's note: "Stark paranoia gripped the editor as he typed this stencil. Fuck it." In an interview, Sanders provides some of the reasons for publishing such inflammatory material:

> Well, I thought it was interesting, so in a daring moment I published it. We didn't have an editorial board. I got into some trouble for that. Elin Paulson— there was a jealous spouse. I wrote about it fictionally in "The Editorial Conference" in volume 1 of "Tales of Beatnik Glory"; that's more or less true in the way that came about. Elin's old man went bonkers on me, her mate at the time. There was no actual activity [pedophilia] . . . it was all hot air and it grew out of Ginsberg's many uses of hyperbole in *Howl* and *Kaddish,* so it was an era. Fowler had a fascination with young girls because of experiences he had in the Korean war, so he brought that to play, but there was never any intergenerational or interspecies eros on any level . . . it was like experiments with words rather than experiments in sexuality, at least as far as that is concerned.[43]

In many ways, Sanders's characterization of Fowler's poem as "experiments in words" is typical of the twentieth-century avant-garde. It is no mistake that sexuality and the excretory function, including the visions of oiled rectums and fellating mouths filling the pages of *Fuck You,* have played a major role in twentieth-century alternative arts. We can refer to Marcel Duchamp's submission of a urinal to a 1917 New York City exhibition of the Society of Independent Artists, to Henry Miller's sexually charged *Tropics* series in the 1930s, to the publication of William Burroughs's *Naked Lunch* in 1959, to Karen Finley's smearing her naked body with chocolate and blood and Andrés Serrano's exhibiting photographs of Christian iconographic symbols immersed in urine in the 1980s, and to Chris Ofili's controversial painting *The Holy Virgin Mary,* which was partially composed out of elephant dung, exhibited at the Brooklyn Museum in 1999. Clearly, Sanders was part of a tradition that mocks or challenges the distinctions between high and low through the inclusion of *dirty stuff* into what should be *clean* or free from the historical body. Thus, a mimeo like *Fuck You* served to frame the work within its pages in a manner designed to elicit mass-culture reaction and to affect mass-culture tastes. While descriptions of poet Mary Mayo as a "fur burger supreme" and romanticizations of pedophilia are not particularly sophisticated and interesting, the context in which this language was used—that is, in a magazine featuring some of the strangest and most indelible poetry of contemporary America—clarified that satire was behind such provocations. Readers of *Fuck You* generally understood that Sanders didn't really mean to suggest that women were not much more than meat or that one should rape children. Indeed, Kathleen Fraser, who in 1983 would publish and edit *How(ever)*, a journal for experimental women's poetry, clearly situates Sanders's language in its historical context and points to the inherently liberatory and satirical impulses behind what might otherwise be received as typically sexist or oppressive:

> [Sanders] never seemed "lascivious" or "prurient" but, instead, funny & celebratory—a sort of sexy clown who paraded and satirized the hormonal appetites of his peers, but not in a power-trip way. He was the sort who loved to challenge people's hidden assumptions: he hated hypocrisy and wanted to call its bluff on every level, including sexual social behavior and the masking of language. He was what we now call "in-your-face"—but always with a troublemaking grin. For me—having spent my early formative years in a Midwestern/ Presbyterian culture that encouraged a sort of "in-denial" libidinous tight-rope walk (at least among the girls)—it was a relief to be around his out-front sexual energy and humor.
>
> Ed Sanders was a big splash of cold water. I think it was—& is, still— primarily, this issue of class-inflected sexual masking that Ed refused to go along with. . . . And the brilliance of his attempt was in its playful refusal to be good and pretend. But THAT was him . . . (& that is the role of socially hip, politicized comedians in our culture—like his elders, Lenny Bruce and Mort Sahl). Most people still don't feel "comfortable" hearing his sort of language used in social situations, though they might laugh privately. I'm sometimes in that group. It depends entirely on the character of the speaker & the social context.[44]

Fraser helpfully clarifies for us how *Fuck You* was a space where poetry and fraternity-style humor could coexist, mock, and complicate one another. The "splash of cold water" was Sanders's overt acknowledgment that poets could have prurient thoughts just like everyone else. Such an acknowledgment usefully confronted those in the poetic community of the Lower East Side with their own culpability in their attitude toward women and with potentially hypocritical distinctions between private and public language.

Fraser's link of Sanders's humor to that of comedians Lenny Bruce and Mort Sahl is also helpful when we recognize that despite his ostensibly anti-conventional position, Sanders sought mass-culture interest just as Bruce and Sahl did. One must remember that purportedly antiestablishment figures such as Allen Ginsberg accepted university posts and other "mainstream" positions, including guest spots on the William F. Buckley television interview show, and that artists such as "underground" graffitist Keith Haring opened up commercial establishments (like Haring's Pop Shop) to broaden their audience and make more money.[45] Many members of the so-called avant-garde like and want attention; it helps them distribute their art and message faster. While Sanders, then a student at N.Y.U. majoring in Greek Studies, began *Fuck You* in 1962 by publishing poems written by his close friends and associates, he would go on to become a kind of poetry/rock star. Besides forming the Fugs rock band, Sanders would publish practically all the postwar American poets associated with the avant-garde. Sanders also participated in the highly publicized battle with New York's Department of Licenses over its efforts to shut down Le Metro. Eventually, he made the cover of *Life* magazine.[46] This extremely public role helped Sanders and *Fuck You* gain stature in the literary community. Sanders, however, would make sure to maintain his position on the outside, using his marginal status to promote himself as a populist outlaw.

One of the most effective methods that Sanders used to maintain his marginal status was his consistent deflation of proprietary attitudes toward literary ownership and copyright. Sanders treated literary texts as if they belonged primarily not to the author but to the community, which is why he published such previously suppressed work as Ezra Pound's *Cantos* 110–16:

> I put out one edition of Pound's *Cantos*. Tom Clark and Joe Brainard did that. We got the manuscript from a *very, very* famous poet who—I don't know if I've ever mentioned who it was, I don't think I'm going to. I'll save it for when I write my own book. But a very, very well-known friend of mine turned it over to Tom, who turned it over to me. And we read it. We had heard that Dorothy was holding up the publication of it. At that time even more than now I had an almost microscopic knowledge of all the *Cantos*, and I decided that they were by Pound. The origin was so impeccable, so I did what I did. I know some people got upset with me, in the literary world, just like when I printed W. H. Auden's *Platonic Blow*—it was a magnificent poem, I realized, and again I got it from a source at the Morgan Library, so I know it was real and it's been ascribed to Auden.[47]

As Sanders points out, *Fuck You* had also included Auden's previously unpublished long poem *The Platonic Blow*. This poem, appropriately enough for a magazine called *Fuck You*, described an act of fellatio in explicit detail. Before the poem was "loaned" to Sanders by his source at the Morgan Library, it had been kept under lock and key.[48] *Fuck You* was freeing poems, albeit in a fashion that would earn the wrath of literary executors and conventional publishers. Such acts on Sanders's part ensured that he would be considered a "bad boy," a necessary image for any artist determined to fulfill the avant-garde requirement of staying in trouble through a combination of iconoclastic aesthetic practice and the taking of a radical social/political stance.

Sanders freed poems primarily so they could benefit his immediate community, the poets living on the Lower East Side:

Ted Berrigan and I met at the Phoenix Bookstore. We both used Bob Wilson's mimeograph Gestetner there. Berrigan was doing *C* magazine. I would do my magazine—I did a couple of issues there. Ted and I were peers, we were in the same scene. I used to go over his house all the time, on Ninth Street, on the same block that Charles Olson in the 1940s and Frank O'Hara later on lived on. I would go into the Les Deux Mégots and Le Metro and give *Fuck You* out free. Everybody wanted to be in it.[49]

By 1964, many of the writers associated with *The New American Poetry* (including Frank O'Hara, Paul Blackburn, Amiri Baraka, Denise Levertov, Gilbert Sorrentino, John Wieners, Allen Ginsberg, and Peter Orlovsky) were living or spending a great deal of time on the Lower East Side, being published in *Fuck You,* and reading at least occasionally at Le Metro. Sanders proved determined to help define Le Metro as a scene both by publishing the writers that read there regularly and by becoming involved in the organization and defense of the readings. Sanders's participation in the ensuing legal battles resulted in editorials such as the following one, entitled "A *Fuck You* Position Paper: Resistance Against Goon Squads":

> Shriek! Shriek! The Goon Squads are loose! We are motherfucking tired of the brickout of books, movies, theater groups, dope freaks, Times Square gobble scenes, poetry readings, night club acts, etc. in New York. The Department of Licenses, the freaks in the various prosecutors offices, the nazis, the fascists, et al., have joined psychoses for a Goon Stomp. Poets have been bricked out of their readings—Lenny Bruce puked from MacDougal street—Theaters raided—Actors freaked—Grove Press zapped by creeps! Coffee houses harassed—film makers censored—dreamy eyed loiterers & hustlers seized & humiliated—& even the Times Square dance hall scenes have been stomped! Their motives, particularly those of the prosecutors and the lawyers in the Dept of Licenses, seem to be a) self-aggrandizement, focusing the eyes of the press on themselves in order to groove up politically, b) the whenever-I-hear-the-word-culture-I-want-to-reach-for-my-gun syndrome, & c) the low budget, low payoff scene.[50]

This editorial provides a vision of what *Fuck You* did to promote a libertarian political philosophy and to keep the poetic community aware of issues specific to their scene. Sanders generated a feeling of solidarity among artists of different genres who lived and worked in the same neighborhood, just as he reminded those same artists of their marginalized status by extending that solidarity to Times Square sex workers. Sanders linked these previously disparate and alienated groups of artists and criminals even further as he promoted his vibrant and funny leftist politics. The "Third Anniversary Mad

Motherfucker" issue was "Dedicated also to all those who have been depressed, butchered, or hung up by all these family unit nazis, fascists, war-freaks, department of License creeps, fuzz, jansenists, draft boards, parole boards, judges, academic idiots, & tubthumpers for the Totalitarian Cancer." By this time, the magazine was encyclopedic in its embrace of all movements and publishing practices that threatened conventional morality. While *Fuck You* was still a literary magazine, a "magazine of the arts," it was actively associating political and cultural signs of disaffection with poetry in an effort to include poetry as a social threat as well as to deflate any lingering notions of poetry as stuffy.

In the "Mad Motherfucker" issue, the *Fuck You* "Talk of the Town" page announced the formation of Sanders's band the Fugs.[51] Combining rock and roll with poetry, Sanders anticipated and perhaps even influenced the Poetry Project's link of rock music and poetry. According to the Poetry Project's archived readings list, the Project would go on to feature rock and roll singer Patti Smith reading with Gerard Malanga on February 10, 1971. On April 12, 1972, Patti Smith read with Jim Carroll (who would himself go on to front a popular band). The Poetry Project has maintained strong affiliations with the rock community: at a memorial service on April 12, 1997, for Allen Ginsberg, various generations of rock musicians, including Lou Reed, Patti Smith, Suzanne Vega, and Sonic Youth's Lee Ranaldo, performed.[52]

Sanders's and the Poetry Project's later institutionalization of rock music in a poetry context reminded people of the link between popular music and poetry by reinvigorating the bardic tradition of poetry as song. There was a precedent for this link, of course—the Lower East Side poetic community was certainly familiar with the widely publicized San Francisco Renaissance jazz and poetry readings of the 1950s. However, Sanders made the link between poetry and music even more contemporary and commercial by replacing jazz and poetry with a more populist rock and roll and poetry. Additionally, since many poets on the Lower East Side published and read Paul Blackburn's translations of medieval troubadour poetry, one can theorize that such a poetic community was more philosophically and intellectually ready than most to generate and accept a literal band of poets.

In the context of the distinction between "academic" poets and the more populist poetic community centered on live, often boisterous readings, the Fugs and the later Poetry Project rock and roll/poetry scene insisted that poetry could be fun, sloppy, spirited, and dangerous, as the following article announcing the formation of the Fugs shows:

SHRIEK! SHRIEK! announcing THE FUGS!!!! an unbelievable group of singers featuring Tuli Kupferberg on farto-phone, Brillo Box, finger cymbals, & various percussion instruments; Ed Sanders on organ, sex organ, & Harmonica;

Szabo on Amphetamine Flute & recorder; Ken Weaver on snares & big stomp Buffalo hide drum; & guest stars. Dances, dirty folk spews, rock & roll, poetry, Amphetamine operas, & other freak-beams from their collective existence. These creeps barf from an unbelievable bag. There has never been any thing like the FUGS in the history of western civilization!!⁵³

This promotional editorial, suggesting a link between poetry and "dirty folk spews," invited its readers to reimagine poetry as a collective experience, as opposed to something created and read by an individual to a passive audience. The very atmosphere of a 1960s rock and roll concert, where the expectation of hilarity, ecstasy, and tribal ritual was attached to the reception of the music, was loaned to verse.

Fuck You, Sheep Fucking, and Ginzap

Fuck You was both microscopically local (talking about and publishing the works of the poetic community's main characters) and macroscopically ambitious. It used sexuality (as Duchamp used the significations engendered by the sight of a urinal to attack the tradition of the picture and of painting) to assault the post–World War II academic conception of the poem championed by the New Critics, associate itself with an avant-garde tradition, and at the same time articulate a very real if extremely funny radical sexual politics for the Lower East Side poetic community. One of the tactics Sanders employed to get his message across was to use his relationship with Allen Ginsberg as a sign for those politics.

In 1963, *Fuck You* featured an account by Peter Orlovsky of his masturbating Allen Ginsberg. An editorial note at the end of the Orlovsky masturbation account reads, for anyone doubting the veracity of the piece, "Yes, motherfuck, this IS an authentic document."⁵⁴ Here Sanders established the fact that he knew enough about this famous poetic couple to authenticate their most intimate sexual practices, and he promoted those practices in characteristically humorous if aggressive prose. However, Sanders went beyond using cues such as editorial verification of fact to imply his affiliation with a wide group of politically and socially radical poets. He also wrote poems in part to emphasize the aesthetic allegiances of the Lower East Side and to establish the influence of a poet like Allen Ginsberg on a poet like Ed Sanders. Sanders's "Sheep-Fuck Poem" is a good example of this influence.⁵⁵

While the poem is funny by virtue of (if nothing else) a kind of high rhetorical content affixed to a subject most people would find rather disgusting, the meter and language of this poem and even its subject matter certainly depend on the work of Sanders's poetic predecessor Allen Ginsberg, particularly Ginsberg's poem "Sunflower Sutra." Significantly, Ginsberg's "Sunflower Sutra" contains images that were inspired by the writing of William Blake.[56] Ginsberg has often been quoted describing this formative experience: "I heard Blake's voice pronounce 'Ah Sunflower' and the 'Sick Rose' and experienced an illumination of eternal Consciousness, my own heart identical with the ancient heart of the Universe."[57] As the author of "Songs of Innocence" and "Songs of Experience," Blake wrote poems that contained, besides the archetypes of rose and sunflower, the figure of the lamb:

> Little Lamb, who made thee?
> Dost thou know who made thee?
> Gave thee life & bid thee feed
> By the stream and o'er the mead[58]

As Sanders explained in an interview with Lisa Jarnot, he was aware of Ginsberg's debt to and interest in Blake and was influenced through that relationship: "[Ginsberg's] left behind I believe—someone told me his Blake lectures alone are 3000 typed pages—so his analysis of Blake is quite bright and brilliant."[59] Sanders's poem is an extension of Ginsberg's extension of Blake. Blake's Lamb is found only in "The Songs of Innocence"; Sanders's treatment of the Lamb brings Blake's innocent virgin/child/Jesus Lamb into the realm of sexual, fallen experience. Additionally, language in Sanders's poem, including "the cunt warm / & woman sized / offered by the lamb / which is surely the / lamb of god, the / lamb of the Trembling Flank" is remarkably similar, if absurdly so, to the oratorical flourishes of Ginsberg, who sings in the "Footnote to Howl": "Holy the lone juggernaut! Holy the vast lamb of the middle-class! Holy the crazy shepherds of rebellion!"[60]

Both authors sacralize and magnify everything they touch, and they do so in a remarkably similar tone. Comparing the final lines of "Sheep-Fuck" to the final lines of Ginsberg's "Sunflower Sutra," one finds both authors stringing together a series of nouns in a kind of Whitmanesque catalog. Sanders writes "frenzy morning field / hay hidden / fuck-lamb / day in bloom torrent," and Ginsberg writes "mad locomotive riverbank sunset Frisco hilly tincan evening sitdown vision."[61] The number of consonants in these lines and the mindful use of syllables manage to imbue the poems with an overtly sexual, rushed, gasping quality ending in lines that suggest a kind of orgasmic release followed by postcoital rest. Sanders achieves this effect through the alliteration of the consonants "f" and "h," which when voiced out loud tend to encourage a body's breath to be pushed out, as if panting. Taking these technical points into account, along with the fact that no word in Sanders's lines is longer than two syllables, we are left with a text that aurally reflects the sounds of breath brought on by the rather quick, pistonlike pumping of the speaker into the lamb, ending with the "bloom-torrent": that is, ejaculation, the flowering of orgasm. Ginsberg's text, while not *overtly* sexual, generates the same kind of moments-before-orgasm thrusting sexual effect, though his thrusts are *longer,* since his lines are longer. Ginsberg's poem also ends with the achievement of a bloom or release, in Ginsberg's case a "sitdown vision," a chance to say "ah!" and meditate on all the excitement preceding the final line.

Looking at these poems in light of the real-life social relationships these poets had with each other points to the conditions in which poetry associated with the Lower East Side scene was produced—through influence, mutual admiration, similar reading habits, and a propensity to quote from, imitate, slyly refer to, and model poems in relationship to other poems produced within that community. Poems were in this sense texts *of* that community, serving to articulate in verse the social and literary links among a group of writers.

Ed Sanders, younger than Ginsberg, always looked to Ginsberg's poetry as a model for his own work: "*Howl* . . . seemed like, as a young man, about everything I'd been looking for in terms of a model for writing poetry and combining poetry with your personal life in a way I thought would be appropriate."[62] Sanders, recognizing the Beats in particular as poetic precursors and publishing Ginsberg in *Fuck You* throughout 1962, would get to know Ginsberg personally. By 1963, when the readings at Les Deux Mégots were ending and Le Metro was set to become the next reading forum for Lower East Side poets, Sanders was living just blocks away from Ginsberg on the Lower East Side: "From '63 on, when I formally met him and he took me to a party at Robert Frank's house, I began hanging out with him any time we were around in the same area until he died 34 years later. We had many many capers and adventures and he called all the time and we saw each other now and then. He was part of my life, and part of my family's life, my daughter's life. He was part of the household."[63] Sanders would also end up publishing Ginsberg regularly in *Fuck You,* and would even use *Fuck You* as a kind of "help-wanted" forum for Ginsberg. The following note from an "Ejaculations from the Editor" page shows an Ed Sanders version of a "help-wanted" ad:

PUBLIC NOTICE: In the tradition of Samuel Beckett & Ezra Loomis Pound, who were the secretaries of famous stompers, the one for James Joyce & the other for W. Butler Yeats, we advertise for a sensitive, brilliant, hangup-less, cockful young secretary for Allen Ginsberg, who is running his New York Conspiracy on sheer guts, sperm & mishuganahood. Please! some young Ganymede spurt forward for phone work, letter writing, gobble rehabilitation, raga chanting, note taking, manuscript preparing, & Goon Squad Assault raids. A.G. needs help in directing & coordinating various publishing projects, sex experiments, public campaigns & so forth. Skill in shorthand wd be groovy also, to catch in notes the eternal babble of A. Ginzap. Prospective Boy Thursdays should contact Allen in the lower east side.[64]

Poetry written by Ginsberg, poetry that echoed Ginsberg, poetry that demanded the decriminalization of homosexuality—all placed side by side with job offers for secretarial positions in Ginsberg's office—served to elicit a reading of *Fuck You* as a community newspaper replete with opportunities for advancement. Reva Wolf points to the Lower East Side avant-garde's use of and partial dependence on extraliterary phenomena to add complexity to texts: "The physical presence of the poet at particular venues was important, as was the physical configuration of Sanders's bookstore and like purlieus. These details of environment contributed to the life of poetry off the page."[65] The excerpts from *Fuck You* emphasize how the poets and editors of the Lower East Side themselves (as opposed to cultural commentators, literary critics, or academics) actively worked to insert their social lives into the reception of their poetry, much of which was first read through mimeographed publications including *Fuck You.* That is, Sanders's descriptions of his and Ginsberg's personal experiences, along with notices related to the Fugs, poetry by writers as diverse as W. H. Auden, Ezra Pound, Tuli Kupferberg, and Ted Berrigan, and consistent references to Les Deux Mégots and Le Metro, helped transform poetry into complicated social documents. Poems were not just isolated aesthetic expressions on a page, but necessarily shared and public events. Not knowing the stories and lives behind many of these poems in many ways diluted the potentially satisfying and complex reader response to the texts. Sanders took care of this potential problem by ensuring that readers understood the revolutionary good times the poets of the Lower East Side were having, so that every reading of a poem in *Fuck You* was also a reading of a social scene centered on poetry.

The End of *Fuck You / a magazine of the arts*

Despite the growing popularity and literary seriousness of *Fuck You,* Ed Sanders ceased publication. He had understandable reasons for doing do. In *The East Village Other,* Allan Katzman—one of the regular organizers of readings at Les Deux Mégots and Le Metro—published an article headlined "Poet Arrested on Obscenity." Katzman described how Sanders "was arrested at 5 o'clock Sunday morning, January 2, at his Peace Eye Bookstore and charged with possession of obscene literature and lewd prints. He was released on $500 bail." The article then goes on to point out that the Lower East Side as a neighborhood arts center was being faced *in general* with the kinds of harassment

Sanders faced. The artist Paul Nuchim was arrested on February 9, 1965, on a charge of obscenity "concerning his paintings of vaginas that were hanging in the Yellow Kid Gallery on 10th Street," and Jonas Mekas was arrested for showing Jack Smith's "Flaming Creatures" and Jean Genet's "Le Chant d'amour" at the Bridge Theater on St. Mark's Place.[66]

Not mentioned in the article were a half-dozen other assaults on the arts, such as the Le Metro incidents and the closing of three off-Broadway theaters, including Ellen Stewart's La Mama. In Sanders's case the arresting officer—Sergeant Fetta of the Ninth precinct (located on Fifth Street between First and Second Avenues)—originally came to the Peace Eye on a burglary call. Apparently, someone had broken in and stolen a violin and a drum, but as Fetta was looking through the bookstore, he came across copies of *Fuck You* along with other "obscene" material including personal letters and papers, "one of which was a letter from the Library of Congress asking for a full set of *Fuck You.*"[67]

Sanders recalls going home on the night of January 1, 1966, after the Fugs did a New Year's show at the Bridge Theater. Tuli Kupferberg called him in the early morning to inform him that police were in the bookstore because someone had supposedly broken in. The *Ed Sanders Newsletter* contains Sanders's report on his arrival at the store and his prompt arrest for possession of obscene material:

> I am the only person in the history of American obscenity cases who has had his penis examined during station house questioning. At one point an officer who was typing out my personal history asked me if I had any tattoos or scars. I said no. About a half hour later my arresting officer, Sergeant Fetta, along with another officer came to the room where I was being questioned. They told me to come with them. Fetta said: "OK Sanders, get into that room and take off your clothes." I said: "What's Up?" Fetta said: "I thought you said you didn't have any tattoos." Then I noticed he had a copy of Fuck You / a magazine of the arts, #5, Volume 4, in his hand and he was pointing to the notes on contributors section where usually there are written funny anecdotes about the contributors. In this particular issue I had stated that "Ed Sanders . . . has the ankh symbol tattooed on his penis and the first 53 hieroglyphs of Tut-ankh-Amun's Hymn to the Sun Disc, on his nuts." This upset the officers enough that I had to flash my phallus so that they could check it out.[68]

The New York Civil Liberties Union offered to represent Sanders, who ultimately had a trial before a three-judge panel in July 1966. Sanders's lawyer was "the well known & very energetic Martin Berger," from the N.Y.C.L.U.[69] The N.Y.C.L.U. itself suggested, through its own institutional newsletter, that the "burglary" was a setup to arrest Sanders. The newsletter pointed out that, just after a *Village Voice* interview with Sanders in late 1965, an irate reader appalled at Sanders's attitude and language wrote an outraged letter to Police Commissioner Vincent Broderick. Soon after the letter was received, Sanders was visited by police officers twice in December 1965; then, on the morning of January 2, police entered his bookstore.

Material seized from the Peace Eye by the police was flagged and annotated; that is, the "dirty parts" were all carefully marked, and comments were written on attached notes indicating the levels of disgust appropriate to the given texts. Police planned to use these various documents as evidence in an obscenity trial. Fortunately, Sanders's archivists at the Thomas J. Dodd Research Center at the University of Connecticut have carefully conserved these notations. Regarding a copy of a "fuckpress" catalog Sanders published, police notes read "fuckpress promoting pornography through its subsidiary, The Lady DickHead Advertising Company." The police also isolated and commented on an artwork by Joe Brainard, who had drawn a brightly colored picture of Superman (*sans* head) exposing a large erection. Brainard had attached a text balloon with the words "HI FOLKS!" to the tip of Superman's penis. Police notes on this Brainard piece are bureaucratically dispassionate: "Green colored Headless superman drawing with private parts exposed."

When Sanders was first arrested the N.Y.C.L.U. advised him not to put out any more issues of *Fuck You* pending the court case. The court proceedings dragged on; in the meantime the Fugs became famous. Sanders recalls that he "turned my bookstore over to the hippie community to run as it saw fit, but it sort of mutated into a hippie crash pad there in 1967, and sort of threw away all the books. When you're under attack you have to be very careful, and when somebody like an officer of the N.Y.C.L.U. suggests that you don't publish pending a court case—the fucking thing dragged on for seventeen court dates. The scene at the courthouse? There was Kenneth Koch holding a tennis racket in the front row. He and John Ashbery were my character poetry references. Koch had to be dragooned off the Columbia University tennis court to come down to testify. It was ironic seeing him holding a tennis racket in municipal court."[70]

Sanders was ultimately acquitted of all charges. A press release put out by Sanders headlined "Ed Sanders Wins Obscenity Case" informed readers that "New York City judges Ringel, Sherwin, & Hoffman ruled that Fuck You / a magazine of the arts is not obscene and does not violate the New York State obscenity code (section 1141) and is protected by constitutional guarantees of freedom."[71] Sanders held a party to celebrate his victory and used the occasion to raise some money. The items for sale indicate just how much the Lower East Side poetic community had become institutionalized, albeit in an ironic, self-absorbed, and self-deprecatory manner. Sanders auctioned off a jar that he entitled "73 Pubes in 4 Years." The jar (listed at $200) contained a collection of various poets' pubic hairs that Sanders had been soliciting at parties on and off over the years, including that of Allen Ginsberg and Robert Duncan. Also on sale was a portrait of Ted Berrigan and Padgett by George Schneeman, a John Ashbery matchbook, and a single pubic hair of Philip Whalen (priced at $25). The mythology surrounding these poets that *Fuck You* had in part created through its excessive rhetoric, dada antics, and tireless promotion was paying off—literally.[72]

Although the charges against Sanders were finally dismissed, the eighteen-month-long proceedings, along with Sanders's growing involvement in the antiwar and marijuana-legalization movements, proved to be the death knell for *Fuck You / a magazine of the arts*. Also, Sanders was becoming a rock star. Thanks to the growing popularity of the Fugs, Sanders often found young fans camped out in front of his apartment. He also began receiving bomb threats, and even received a fake bomb in the mail. Sanders simply no longer had the time and energy necessary to continue putting out *Fuck You*. However, Sanders (now living in Woodstock, New York) still maintains a connection to the mimeograph machine that spewed forth over three years worth of *Fuck You*'s: "I have all my printing equipment in my garage. In case things get heavy, I'm ready to go. I don't need electricity. Except I would have to rig a battery-powered generator off my waterfall here to power my Gestetner stencil-cutting machine. I still have it—I'm ready to go."[73]

Umbra and Lower East Side Black Poetics

By the late 1960s, Amiri Baraka changed his political, social, and literary allegiances radically, going so far as to disown the work he had produced in the Lower East Side community. Baraka declined to submit his work to Allen DeLoach's book *The East Side Scene*,[74] stopped socializing with many of his white friends, and ultimately moved to Harlem, where he started the Black Arts Theater. This history is well documented, and, as literary historian Jon Panish notes, many black writers would follow Baraka's lead. By 1965 "many African Americans who lived there began to leave the East Village and their frustrated hopes of an ideal, integrated community behind."[75] The Lower East Side was such a strong influence on Baraka as he was coming to terms with issues of black identity and black nationalism that he felt he had to leave the neighborhood to act on his developing beliefs.

However, racial separatism was by no means a consensus position among young black poets associated with the Lower East Side poetic community. "The name 'Umbra' was a positive assertion of cultural blackness, but it was never totalizing. The Umbra group included some white writers, like Art Berger."[76]

Umbra poets reacted in varying ways following the assassination of Malcolm X and Baraka's subsequent move to Harlem. "The more politically-minded young black poets of this period also seem to have felt an ambivalent attraction to Harlem and responsibility for the black masses there, and they oscillated between the two areas . . . the militant wing of Umbra later went to Harlem with LeRoi Jones to found the Black Arts Repertory Theater/School."[77] This move was by no means total. Poet David Henderson insists, "The downtown poets stayed downtown. Of course, we were nationalists and into the civil rights movement, but we also had a lot of white friends and people of other races. We were just not doctrinaire nationalists."[78] This attitude is defined in the foreword of the first issue of the magazine *Umbra,* which was really a manifesto of sorts for many of the black poets living in the Lower East Side during the first half of the 1960s.[79] While the editors stated that "UMBRA has a definite orientation: 1) the experience of being Negro, especially in America: and 2) that quality of human awareness often termed 'social consciousness'" they also maintained

> no iron-fisted, bigoted policy of preference or exclusion of material. UMBRA will not be a propagandistic, psychopathic or ideological axe-grinder. We will not print trash, no matter how relevantly it deals with race, social issues, or anything else. We are not a self-deemed radical publication; we are as radical as society demands the truth to be. We declare an unequivocal commitment to material of literary integrity and artistic excellence.[80]

After clarifying that *Umbra* was primarily a "literary" magazine as opposed to a "political" one, the foreword continued to position *Umbra* as a group phenomenon: "The magazine grew out of Friday night workshops, meetings and readings on Manhattan's Lower East Side last summer—and out of the need expressed for it at those meetings."[81] Quite a number of poets published in subsequent issues of *Umbra* were to go on and read regularly at Le Metro. According to Lorenzo Thomas, Umbra poets would "hijack the readings at Le Metro and blow them all away—we had lots of energy."[82] The collective nature of editing and workshopping around the magazine found a complement in the scene at Le Metro. "From Richard Wright's time there had been single black writers who had held the public eye as representative of 'the black writer' and who had succeeded each other, but the [Umbra] group rejected this sort of tokenism and began to read eight or ten at a time."[83]

Umbra poets were also visible presences at the earlier Deux Mégots series. Recalling how he first came to Les Deux Mégots, David Henderson describes an event that was to coincide with his first encounter with Umbra poet Calvin Hernton:

I just blundered into the Deux Mégots. I was going to the New School, with these two white guys—one guy was a reporter for the *Daily Telegraph,* and the other guy—Richard—he loved Kazantzakis, and he was a novelist. We would look for places to hang out. At first, I'd hang out in coffee shops in the West Village, trying to see if Ted Joans would come by. And then, somewhere we read about open readings, and went over to the Deux Mégots. But Calvin Hernton came in and just busted the place wide open. It was a very dramatic reading . . . he wore sunglasses and was trained as an actor to some extent, so he could really emote his poem, and so he had a lot of beautiful poems about his southern background, about racism in America. You recall that the civil rights movement was going on at the time, so his poems picked up on that.[84]

The two men introduced themselves, and a literary and social friendship was initiated that was partly responsible for the influence *Umbra* had on the overall political consciousness of the Lower East Side poetic community as well as for the increasing presence of Umbra poets in the Deux Mégots, Le Metro, and Poetry Project reading series and workshops.[85]

At Hernton's invitation, Henderson joined the Umbra workshops. Henderson remembers: "A bunch of black writers living on the Lower East Side, coming from a lot of different directions . . . we were all so happy to meet each other. I remember there were a lot of people—Lloyd Addison named *Umbra* from one of his poems, 'The Umbra and the Aura,' and Paul Brennan published that book in London, and actually at that time *Beyond the Blues* came out, which was a collection of black poetry that Calvin Hernton and Oliver Pitcher were in."[86] Poets in the Umbra workshops began participating in many of the readings centered on the Lower East Side. Henderson recalls, "We just went around, to see what's going on, to *read,* this whole *thirst to read our poems,* you know?"[87]

Lorenzo Thomas conceived of the reading series as a natural extension of basic poetic principles. "The idea was that poetry was something that we lived with every day, and there was nothing esoteric about it—it was a living art. We thought we were continuing the great tradition of poetry. That informs African American poetry as a living language. That's what we were all practicing at the time."[88] As Thomas's comments indicate, Umbra poets consciously adapted the highly visible and orally centered poetry scene of the Lower East Side to their own ideas about poetic form and race consciousness, particularly those ideas that led black poets to associate contemporary poetry readings with African oral traditions. Umbra poets pointed postmodern poetics back to their own experience. They recontextualized a mostly homogeneous white reading scene by "hijacking" it for an African American constituency for whom live readings and a progressive, innovative aesthetics were an essential and culturally specific part of poetic transmission and production.

Baraka's developing ideas about African nationalism and cultural tradition in all likelihood assisted Umbra poets in their co-optation of a live reading scene: "[Baraka insisted] that constant artistic innovation is at the heart of African traditions of expressivity, and that modernity, perhaps postmodernity, is not foreign to but constituent in African and African-American art forms. The strategy, then, was never to 'catch up' with Euro-American modernism but rather to interrogate it, rupture it, and reclaim an unacknowledged black modern that had existed within and as enabling strata."[89] Umbra poets interrogated the Lower East Side scene by inserting racial politics into a formerly racially staid and perhaps disengaged white liberal culture for whom postmodern experimentation could (as the discussion of *Fuck You* shows) threaten social order to some extent as it failed to deal with essential contradictions within its own ranks—contradictions that manifested themselves primarily through the invisibility of black poets both on the pages and stages of the Lower East Side.

Outside *Umbra,* the new poetics associated with the neighborhood, while formally innovative, were not, generally speaking, overtly political. In this sense, the Lower East Side scene had yet to divest itself fully from the ahistorical approach of the New Criticism. This is where the Umbra poets came in. In his discussion of Umbra supporter A. B. Spellman, Aldon Nielsen suggests: "Spellman's generation, whether they were social activists or not, tended to view the political as suitable material for poetic composition. Whether or not they agreed with Auden that poetry 'makes nothing happen,' they viewed the poem as a place where politics could happen, and this may have prepared the way for the dominant view during the Black Arts movement that the chief role of a poem *is* to make something happen."[90] While Umbra poets did assert their commitment to "artistic excellence," one must agree with Eugene Redmond, who stated, "Once one read *Umbra,* however, there was no question of the journal's involvement in the struggle—or of the need for a purely literary black magazine to serve as a forum and laboratory for new aesthetic experiments and analyses."[91]

Much of the content of the poetry published in *Umbra* reflected the conversations being held in the writing workshops taking place at poet Tom Dent's house. Major political figures associated with the civil rights movement would stop by to socialize and organize around specific issues. David Henderson recalls, "The Umbra poets were political to the extent that we were involved in the social struggle and civil rights and injustice. Charlene Hunter would come to the Umbra workshops, James Meredith, Andy Young used to come there, and they were fighting the struggle in the South."[92] Poems in *Umbra* referred overtly and obliquely to the civil rights struggle and to larger international events: The assassination of Congolese Prime Minister Patrice Lumumba and the subsequent political and social conflicts were recurring themes in the magazine, as Lorenzo Thomas's poem "A Tale of Two Cities" (here excerpted) illustrates:[93]

A TALE OF TWO CITIES

"They were like wild animals," said M.
Djoumessi—New York Times, 25 February 1960

   O the wild dancers, the New York
beer-drinkers, running amok at the UN shouting,
  "You've crucified our saintly Lumumba. . . . "

And what about the people's other saints
In Bklyn, do storefront churches worship
     a storefront God?
And elsewhere are there rites? Rights, riots?
How does the mask fit elsewhere on this fraud
     that we call life?
The Times says nights in Cameroun are terrible.
Young intellects, old madmen, philosophers, and
poets, machete the non-believers of their
     political voudon.
Who are their saints, what are their rituals?[94]

This poem is certainly political and internationalist in its references to Brooklyn and Cameroun, as the language Thomas employs is highly allusive of the Lower East Side Beat ethos. Thomas's "O the wild dancers" and the use of the word *saintly* to describe Lumumba both echoes the high rhetoric of Allen Ginsberg's psalmic lines in "Howl" and reminds one of African American blues and church discourse that was as much a part of Ginsberg's source material as it was for Thomas. One can sense tonal and thematic similarities between phrases like Thomas's "O the wild dancers" and "you've crucified our saintly Lumumba" and the martyr-evocative phrases in "Howl," like "angelheaded hipsters" or the famous "best minds of my generation destroyed by madness."[95]

    This combination of a content-based political engagement and Lower East Side alternative rhetoricity and poetics is extended in a later issue of *Umbra*. Ishmael Reed's poem "Patrice" refers to Lumumba and uses the text to implicate Belgian bankers in Lumumba's assassination:

PATRICE

Patrice is   in fields of hemp
    recumbent
Like a Henry Moore.
Where bloated, Belgian brokers
    never tamper.[96]

While both Thomas's and Reed's poems are certainly politically engaged in terms of their basic content, the typography and rhetoric these two poets employed were complementary to Lower East Side poetic conventions. Readers belonging to the interpretive community of the Lower East Side very likely read these texts as both political statements and as aesthetic extensions of an avant-garde impulse. In Reed's poem, the imaginative use of spacing on the page can be related to Olson's theories in "Projective Verse" regarding the possibilities inherent in the typewriter. According to Olson, the typewriter, "due to its rigidity and its space precisions . . . can, for a poet, indicate exactly the breath, the pauses, the suspensions even of syllables, the juxtapositions even of parts of phrases, which he intends":

> If a contemporary poet leaves a space as long as the phrase before it, he means that space to be held, by the breath, an equal length of time. If he suspends a word or syllable at the end of a line (this was most cummings' addition) he means that time to pass that it takes the eye—that hair of time suspended— to pick up the next line. If he wishes a pause so light it hardly separates the words, yet does not want a comma—which is an interruption of the meaning rather than the sounding of the line—follow him when he uses a symbol the typewriter has ready to hand: "What does not change / is the will to change."[97]

In the context of Olson's influence on the poetic community of the Lower East Side, Reed's enormous caesura in "Patrice" is a manifestation of the Olsonian concept of typography's relationship to orality—"the breath, the pauses," the "sounding." The caesura invites the reader to stress and voice the word *is*, which emphasizes the continuing significance of Lumumba to the dramatic speaker; "Patrice *is*" stresses "is-ness," or presence. The caesura then allows for a dramatic pause between the sense of Lumumba's continuing presence and the harsh reality of his "lying in fields of hemp"—that is, lying in his grave. The placement of the word *recumbent* on its own line might lead the reader interested in considering the poem as speech act to place extra emphasis on the syllabic pronunciation of the word—that is, re-cum-bent. The extra stress on the syllables suggests a hortatory speech act, one that is at once allusive of a sermon, an angry and insistent speech (in the sense of the voice's tendency to accentuate syllables when emphatically angry or determined to get a point across), and an elegy. By looking at these words and lines this way, we see that the Umbra poets certainly related Lower East Side poetics to their own innovative practices. We also see, as Aldon Nielsen has recognized, that postmodern poetics and the attendant threat to the closed-form poem are adapted in texts like Reed's to serve a far more insurrectionary function than they otherwise might: "Poets like Baraka and the Umbra group are the connectors here by which a postmodern rebellion against the idea of the poem as icon was joined to an edeology of the social functioning of the poet posited as African-derived tradition and brought into the Black Arts movement."[98]

The political implications inherent in the radical poetic form to which Nielsen refers were a subject of inquiry for Umbra poets. In his essay "Neon Griot: The Functional Role of Poetry Readings in the Black Arts Movement," Lorenzo Thomas suggests that the Black Arts movement commonly associated with Baraka was also a natural extension of *Umbra.* His description of the prosodic practice of the later Black Arts movement in many ways emphasizes the continuing influence of poetics associated with both white and black poets on an increasingly race-conscious group of writers: "While the movement rejected mainstream America's ideology, deeming it inimical to black people, Black Arts poets maintained and developed the prosody they had acquired from Black Mountain and the Beats."[99] In his essay, Thomas continues to measure Black Arts poetry's relationship to Olson as well as to what might seem the more predictable influences of blues, jazz, and church. Thomas also discusses work by Black Arts poets Sonia Sanchez and Johari Amini, depicting their texts as performative scores. The poem as it is printed in Sanchez's case "indicate[s] exactly how Sanchez performed it and how it should be read." Amini's text "instruct[s] and allow[s] the reader to reproduce her breathless, exasperated voice." Thomas goes on to claim that a poem "such as Askia Muhammad Touré's 'Transcendental Vision: Indigo' indicates through its typography a sense of how the poet intends it to sound, and the typographical method used is very similar to that proposed by Olson in his Projective Verse essay."[100]

Note that Thomas writes "very similar," not "following the precepts of." New American poetics were in this sense not the cause of poetry associated with *Umbra,* but a phenomenon analogous and adaptable to independent African American–derived prosody. Formalist questions in this sense were never quite free of their potentially racially determined frames:

> Most of the people at Tom's house were interested in a different kind of poem, formally. They would listen to and read Paul Blackburn, Ezra Pound. Umbra was linking formal experimentation with political dissent. Everyone in Umbra was frighteningly literate. There was a wonderful poem by Ishmael Reed, which

was published in *Liberator* [Nov. 1963], and included a beautiful takeoff on Pound's "Homage to Sextus Propertius." Many readers might not have noticed that, just as half the people who reviewed Ishmael's first novel, *The Freelance Pallbearers,* missed the allusions in that book. They didn't know anything—there was a lot of Jung in there, a lot of what you might call the alternative history of Egypt. All that stuff was in the book but people didn't see it that way. The general reaction was like "Oh, OK, this is like dada in the housing projects." In the end, that was what *Umbra* was about—those politics, along the lines of DuBois, and those experiments in form. If you are a poet, a student of literature, you read *all* poetry. If you don't know French, you read Marcel Duchamp in English, if you do know French like Ron Padgett you read it in French. As far as we were concerned, there was no line or bar or segregation in the library or the poetry reading.[101]

While Thomas does suggest the possibilities for a functional multicultural alternative scene, one should be careful not to uncritically grant the agency of cultural exchange to white avant-gardes.[102] After all, developing ideas about prosody were produced within a milieu that found black arts, African folk-ways, and African American–derived music as major influences. For example, much has been made in any one of dozens of books on "Beat" literature of the connection between jazz and poetry. This link is often discussed in the context of poetics; for example, the similarities between Kerouac's "spontaneous bop prosody," to use his phrase, in his book *Mexico City Blues* and the theoretical underpinnings of a musical improvisatory progression have been noted. Ideas related to improvisation, breath, and phrasing were developed initially by black jazz musicians and used in one form or another by white writers. Additionally, beyond using jazz theory as a source from which to develop new poetics, perhaps one reason that so many white poets attending readings at Les Deux Mégots and Le Metro were attracted to jazz and other aspects of "black culture" was the vaguely perceived historical link between black arts and orality. While later nationalist rhetoric on the part of writers like Amiri Baraka certainly alienated many of the poets of the Lower East Side, nevertheless, complicated and debatable conceptions of "blackness" as especially disposed to utterance continued to form part of the identity of the Lower East Side poetic community. *Umbra* writers themselves made much of black arts' "natural" extension of oral folk traditions. As late as 1990, Calvin Hernton wrote, "The oral culture of the folk is the foundation from which all writing springs. The aesthetics and the concerns of the written literature are contained in the oral, nonliterate foundations of a people."[103] Interpolating blackness into the mostly white scene at Les Deux Mégots and Le Metro helped to establish a general orally based ethos.

While a case can be made for the relatively enlightened state of race rela-tions on the Lower East Side, visible tensions between the Umbra poets and the predominantly white artistic community were often reported—as the af-fairs, lunch dates, and arrests of the Lower East Side poets were reported—through poetry.[104] Lorenzo Thomas's "South Street Blues" (here excerpted), acknowledges the difficulties of an interracial relationship:

> In your
> face a stolen lyric can be read, a medieval tune full
> of eastern Europe, the long nights with dark
> and contemplative men, the midnight pogrom.
> Tune for clarinet and balalaika, violin.
> You don't know why it makes me sing my kind of blues.[105]

Thomas's poem, with its mention of Eastern Europe, pogroms, and bala-laikas, apparently refers to a Jewish woman. While naming such things in a love poem points to a real cultural transgression within the context of white hegemonic culture, nevertheless the woman's relationship to the speaker of the poem is one of marked alienation—the "you don't know why" of the text. Scholar Jon Panish has argued that the social significance of interracial cou-ples during this period on the Lower East Side was problematic. Referring to historian Sally Banes's positive description of interracial couples, Panish states:

> The idea that the existence of interracial heterosexual couples in itself signifies anything progressive about interracial relations in the Village is fallacious. [T]his superficial description neglects the power dynamics that inhered in many of these relationships . . . these interracial heterosexual relationships in the Vil-lage were plagued by many of the same unequal power dynamics that troubled the other social and cultural interactions I have surveyed.[106]

Panish could have focused on David Henderson's poem "The Ofay and the Nigger" to support his pessimistic portrayal of race relations on the Lower East Side. This poem pokes fun at the white hipster and might suggest the un-easiness about white people's appropriation of black culture that Amiri Baraka and later Black Arts writers were to express more strongly:[107]

THE OFAY AND THE NIGGER

> So this ofay and
> this nigger
> they at this party.
> He's bearded—the ofay that is
> (The beard being a symbol
> of Northern Hiptitude) and

has just, quote, "Made the scene,"
unquote.
And the nigger say,
quote,
"Cool, baby," unquote.
The ofay
and
The nigger
say
Quote and unquote
Because they must obey
PARLANCE
      —the god of interracial love,
understanding and Northern Mongrelization.

So this ofay tells
the nigger
how he digs Leadbelly
so much.
And the nigger say,
"Man, that Vaughn Monroe
Really turns me on."
Stroking his beard the
ofay tells the nigger of
his undying love for
that dear, dear Lady Day.
The nigger:
"Man, let me tell you
that Kate Smith is a gas!"
The nigger shifts his eyes————
"You *really* dig her, man?" asks the ofay.
"You better believe it," quoth the nigger.[108]

    This scenario—the white, wannabe-nigger "ofay" attempting to associate himself with the projected "hipness" of the black man—is by now a familiar one. Given the social and literary background of the time, when "Beat" poets were popular and widely imitated, Henderson's poem can serve as a critique of the white dissenter's assumption of easy access to and fellowship with black culture. Reading certain portions of Jack Kerouac's *On the Road,* for example, one can find the "ofay" romanticizing the "black" in the same spirit that a sheltered if well-meaning white person might assert that all African American people are preternaturally adept at playing basketball. Kerouac, through the persona of Sal Paradise, walks "with every muscle aching among the lights of 27th and Welton in the Denver colored section, wishing I were a Negro, feeling that the best the white world had to offer me was not enough ecstasy for me, not enough life, joy, kicks, darkness, music, not enough night."[109] In retrospect, Kerouac's rhapsody suggests that the black person represents vague attitudes about "soul" and not much else. While the Beat poets' cultural disaffiliation from the American mainstream of the 1950s was strengthened by their affiliation with the black underclass, so was Elvis Presley's; that is why white consensus-culture America feared both Presley and Kerouac and why both men were truly subversive figures. However, what goes missing from this equation is precisely what Henderson's poem provides—a model for what *black* America might think about all these white people co-opting its culture.

The "ofay" is a white, middle-class artistically inclined dissenter who observes the black man through "the self-consciously topical prose of Norman Mailer or the breathless panegyrics of Jack Kerouac. . . . Immaculate in poverty, [the black man] lives out the blocked options of a generation of white radical intellectuals."[110] The Beats in many ways *translated* the black "experience," and in particular the black musical experience, for consumption by disaffected white youths. In light of the Beat influence on the white dissenter, it is clear why Henderson focuses on the ofay's apparent appreciation of jazz. By 1963 Allen Ginsberg had returned to the Lower East Side after a well-documented trip to India, and jazz-inflected lines from *Howl,* including, "Holy the groaning saxophone! Holy the bop apocalypse!" were still fresh in the minds of the Lower East side poetic community that looked to Ginsberg as a model poet. Ginsberg's *Howl* and Kerouac's *On the Road* had become guides of a sort for anyone interested in or affecting an oppositional stance. Additionally, post-bop jazz of the early 1960s, characterized by Cecil Taylor's, Ornette Coleman's, and Albert Ayler's free improvisations, confounded and upset traditional music critics as it was embraced by the Lower East Side scene. Possibly it was this aura of mainstream inaccessibility, combined with the continuing popularity of more traditional musicians like Billie Holiday and Leadbelly (who were both nevertheless still *outlaws,* owing to their stints in prison, drug addiction, and so on), that attracted the ofay looking to get in on what it meant to be black— that is, separate from dominant white culture.

Henderson's poem can be read as an outright condemnation of the whole downtown scene, although Henderson is careful to distinguish between the Lower East Side scene and the so-called liberal:

An embarrassing poem now, but at that time it was hot! The point here is that all the people that were living downtown, living in the Lower East Side, they were cool people. That poem is not talking to them . . . they understood jazz, and blues, and they were into black culture and art as much as anyone could be. This is about the liberal at the time . . . you had these people at the time who would mouth platitudes about this and that. In terms of civil rights [they] would say "I feel for their problems, blah blah blah." We met a lot of those types, because we did do a lot of socializing. We would be hired out to go to suburban settings and read our poems out as a group. People would invite us, we'd get all we could drink, blacks and whites, mainly middle-class people, so there was this whole tension with the middle class coming out of the Beat thing, the hippie thing, the black consciousness thing.[111]

While Henderson carefully avoids including the downtown hipster in his condemnation of the liberal bourgeoisie, his tying the "Beat thing" to a middle-class liberality nevertheless shows how commodified and sanitized voices like Ginsberg's and Kerouac's had become. Henderson—and the Umbra writers in general—were thus necessary voices in a poetic community that may otherwise have lacked a volatile, subversive, and self-critiquing mechanism to keep it from becoming too precious, too safe, and too needlessly apolitical regarding matters of race. The Beats, though still literary heroes of the Lower East Side, nevertheless did not extensively engage in issues related to racial politics. Even Ginsberg, who always seemed to be in the right place at the right time, was far more involved in the peace movement, gay liberation struggles, and marijuana-legalization campaigns than he was in the civil rights movement. The Umbra poets filled that gap in the Lower East Side poetic community of the 1960s. After all, texts from that period indicate there would always be a certain tension among the poets associated with *Umbra* based on the very fact that they were in the Lower East Side in the first place. Racial tension and questions about the proper *place* of a black poet—issues that Baraka brought out in the open often belligerently, and that manifested themselves violently at Le Metro—would remain visible in the texts of the *Umbra* poets, as one sees when Henderson asks himself in his poem "Downtown-Boy Uptown": "I stand in my low east window looking down. / Am I in the wrong slum?"[112]

Poems from the Floating World and Trobar

Before *Trobar* there was a magazine called *Chelsea,* founded in late 1957 by the writer Ursule Molinaro, midtown advertising executive and avant-garde literature devotee Venable Herndon (Molinaro's husband), Robert Kelly and his then-wife Joan Kelly (who was known by her friends as Joby), and George Economou. These writers and editors published five issues. After the fifth issue, Robert Kelly, Joan Kelly, and Economou decided that the magazine "wasn't working because we were interested in poetry, and Venable and Ursule seemed more interested in fiction. Not that we had big terrible fights or anything, but there was a kind of tension pulling."[113] The editors decided to have an amicable parting of ways. Molinaro and Herndon planned to maintain editorship of *Chelsea* and agreed to change the name of the magazine from *Chelsea* to the *Chelsea Review*. Robert Kelly, Joan Kelly, and Economou—influenced in part by the earlier publication *Poems from the Floating World* edited by their friend Jerome Rothenberg—agreed to publish only poetry. Both *Trobar* and *Poems from the Floating World* positioned themselves in light of an amorphous if compelling aesthetic theory referred to as the "deep image."[114]

In his book on Clayton Eshleman, Paul Christensen has placed the poetics of the deep image in historical context: "In the late 1950's, Rothenberg and Kelly began reexploring Pound's Imagism for a way around the verse orthodoxy inspired by New Criticism back to the roots of Modernist experiment. Though not a movement in the formal sense, 'deep image' poetry introduced Jungian archetypal psychology into poetry, the most significant innovation to be wrung on Pound's Image since the objectivist movement of the 1930's."[115] Poets associated with the deep image developed their ideas partly in an effort to theorize themselves out of a contemporary conservative poetics and to align themselves with an alternative tradition. Illustrating a conception of "newness" as inimical to "academic" poetry, George Economou said of *Trobar*, "We thought 'this is the new poetry,' not the kind of poetry that you're going to find in the *Partisan Review,* the *Paris Review,* the *Kenyon Review, Sewanee Review,* all those standard magazines of the time."[116] Additionally (as if in homage to Ezra Pound's extensive work in translation and international literary politicking) the editors of *Trobar* and *Poems from the Floating World,* perhaps more than any of the editors of other magazine associated with the Lower East Side at the time, devoted a good portion of their pages to translations.[117] In this light, one can see that the "deep image" was as much a politics of dissent from mainstream poetics and what it suggested as it was an effort to find new uses for the poetic image.

Trobar was christened at a reading series taking place at the Café Cino in the West Village. The word *trobar* is the Provençal counterpart of the French *trouver* (to find). *Trobar* is also the root of *troubadour,* a more familiar word meaning "singer, minstrel"—a poet spreading the word through song. In their poetry, Provençal poets often referred to "my *Trobar,*" meaning "my poetry." Of the link between poets associated with *Trobar* and their medieval counterparts, Economou explains, "*Trobar*—it's literally 'to find,' and it denotes finding the words, as in composing poetry, or finding the right words to fit the melody. That also distinguished the magazine as having European and medieval roots, and also a debt to Pound, who was instrumental in bringing medieval poetry to the attention of readers and writers in the twentieth century."[118] *Trobar* lasted for four years, publishing five issues of the magazine and four books under the *Trobar* imprint.[119]

Typical of Lower East Side publishing practices, pseudonyms were used on the masthead of the magazine. Economou designed the covers under the name "Bernal Nicoya," in an effort to give the magazine an international feel and to indicate that the magazine was professional enough to afford its own designer—which it couldn't. All issues of *Trobar* were typed (with the exception of the first) on an electric typewriter, and printed in the West Village by "a Quaker Marxist who would give us a really good deal. It was photo offset from paper plates. He'd print everything up and we'd go down, pick it up, and have a collating party in our apartment."[120]

Trobar and Jerome Rothenberg's earlier publication, *Poems from the Floating World,* were bound to be read in the context of the general scene at Les Deux Mégots and Le Metro. A glance at the readings list for these series shows *Trobar* editors and contributors including Economou, Robert Kelly, Rochelle Owens, Clayton Eshleman, and Rothenberg reading their poetry or organizing poetry readings at these sites regularly throughout the early to mid-1960s. While these poets avoided coterie classification as deep image poets, nevertheless the consistently published comments and questions referring to the label promoted a reading of *Poems from the Floating World* and *Trobar* as indicative of innovative theoretical developments specific to the Lower East Side poetic community.

One finds Rothenberg characterizing the deep image in his introduction to *Poems from the Floating World* 3:

> From deep within us it comes: the wind that moves through the lost branches, hurts us with a wet cry, as if an ocean were caged in each skull:
>
> There is a sea of connections that floats between men: a place where speech is touch and the welcoming hand restores its silence: an ocean warmed by dark suns.
>
> The *deep image* rises from the shoreless gulf: here the poet reaches down among the lost branches, till a moment of seeing: the poem. Only then does the floating world sink again into its darkness, leaving a white shadow, and the joy of our having been here, together.

Such self-consciously spiritualist language purporting to represent a developing poetic stance suggested that *Poems from the Floating World* and *Tro-*

bar represented an extension of the alternative tradition. These magazines postulated a new poetics for their community that, while indebted to Pound and other familiar figures, nevertheless showed a real effort to expand what avant-garde poets could do in their writing. To emphasize how the deep image project was a new and more diverse enterprise than earlier modernist or New American projects, Jerome Rothenberg wrote to Robert Creeley, "In the next *Floating World,* too, I've tried to include a few 'ancient' texts translated into the native idiom but with the image kept strong or even reinforced: all of this with the feeling that there's other ways into the poem than what we've so far gotten from Pound and Williams: other ways too of music and craft and ultimately that each of us must come to his own 'truth,' etc. from whatever direction: the unique coherence and rightness of each poem."[121]

Rothenberg's representation of a new aesthetic going beyond the familiar modernist inheritance provides an example of the strong impulse among poets in the Lower East Side community to associate themselves with and develop "new" ideas in order to establish themselves as innovators. Rothenberg, Robert Kelly, and Economou would fulfill this mission in part by ensuring that their magazines were international and multicultural in scope.[122] The decision to include Pierre Reverdy's epigraph at the bottom of the contents page in the first issue of *Floating World* showed the magazine's editorial extension of the alternative tradition. Reverdy's text is a surprising blend of Blakean aphorism reminiscent of "The Marriage of Heaven and Hell" along with a Poundian approach to the image:

The image cannot spring from any comparison but from the bringing together of two more or less remote realities . . .

The more distant and legitimate the relation between the two realities brought together, the stronger the image will be . . . the more emotive power and poetic reality it will possess.

One can compare Reverdy's statements (and by extension Rothenberg's editorial philosophy regarding debts owed by deep image poets to predecessor poetics) to Pound's own ideas regarding imagism. Pound describes his poem "In a Station of the Metro" by insisting that "in a poem of this sort one is trying to record the precise instant when a thing outward and objective transforms itself, or darts into a thing inward and subjective."[123] Pound's own "bringing together of two more or less remote realities" was embodied by this poem. Both lines in the two-line poem—"The apparition of these faces in the crowd / Petals on a wet black bough"—represent individual and logically distinct, unconnected "realities." However, the poem manages to reconcile faces in a crowd and petals on a wet black bough without rejecting the poem's potential for historical and literary allusiveness. By yoking distinct images together in text, Pound tacitly invites the reader to transform the images in the poem into sense, emotion, and connection.[124]

Additionally, William Blake's aphoristic sayings in "The Marriage of Heaven and Hell"—a text that in many ways is a primer for the elimination of rational distinctions—are echoed in the writings associated with the deep image. With Blake, conventional moral codes and rules are violently threatened or satirized by the voices of devils eager to erase or question Christian moral strictures. Thus, in Blake we have the shock of a line like "Sooner murder an infant in its cradle than nurse unacted desires."[125] The deep image poets active in the Lower East Side poetic community adapted Blake's theories on—and critique of—the connection between linear time and Cartesian rationalism. One sees these varied connections made in their poetry: Jerome Rothenberg's poem "The Double Vision" makes new a wide variety of literary traditions, including Blake's poetic undermining of time:

> Dawn,
> a yellow line of traffic
> at the bridge:
>
> And
> Rikyuu
> brewing tea
> inside a vanished garden:
>
> Mortal things,
> but real.[126]

In this poem, we sense an attempt to undermine linearity. A contemporary urban scene (the line of traffic) is attached to or associated with a sixteenth-century Japanese scene (the tea master Rikyuu performing a tea ceremony). Both scenes are equally animate. The discrete scenes seem strangely contemporaneous to each other, perhaps because each objective unit in the first stanza has a corresponding objective unit in the second stanza—"Dawn" corresponds with "Rikyuu," "a yellow line of traffic" corresponds with "brewing tea," and "at the bridge" corresponds with "inside a vanished garden." The word *vanished* is especially significant in that it suggests the "apparition" in Pound's "In a Station of the Metro." Both poems contain ghosts—Pound's "apparition" and Rothenberg's "vanished garden"—that serve to blur the reader's sense of "real" time in order to yoke previously distinct and unrelated phenomena together. Both poems also allude to an Orientalist aesthetic—the overt naming of Rikyuu in Rothenberg's case and the Chinese brushstroke–like image "Petals on a wet, black bough" in Pound's. Time leaks in and out of these apparitions, and the subsequent loss of linearity results in a transnational, transcultural, and atemporal connection between things.[127]

Additionally, in much of the poetry associated with the deep image group, the authorial persona does not appear as a primary narrative presence. "Rothenberg, Kelly and others of the group began using archetypal images as the means for generating commentaries, arguments, recollections that led away from self toward the opposite pole of awareness, the 'other.'"[128] This tendency to move away from the "confessional" impulse popularized by academy-approved poets including Sylvia Plath, Robert Lowell, and John Berryman may very well have had as much to do with the historical fact of the myriad readings taking place on the Lower East Side as it did with individual interests in predecessor theoreticians of the poetic image. A redirection of the individual toward the "other" can be seen as a metaphor for the redirection of the isolated poet toward the "other" of a larger poetic community. Many of the poems published in *Poems from the Floating World* and *Trobar* contained a relatively low-profile or nonexistent first-person authorial presence as they directly or indirectly upheld aesthetics associated with orality, performativity, and an ethos of *communitas*. For example, in *Poems from the Floating World*, George Economou translated Takis Sinopoulos's "Ioanna Raving." Sinopoulos's text very likely suggested work associated with the Lower East Side to those readers familiar with the writing and reading practices of the poetic community:

> Constantinos is a door.
> He is a face behind the door.
> He is a door that suddenly slams and crushes your fingers.
> Constantinos is an empty room.
> Scream of peril in an empty room.
> Constantinos is a house, a gloomy house.
> Within him unexplored religions of blood smolder.
> Constantinos is tomorrow tomorrow tomorrow
>   (tomorrow constantly repeated).[129]

Anaphoric use of the words "He" and "Constantinos" was generally typical of much poetry read (aloud and silently) by the Lower East Side poetic community. The use of anaphora as it extended from Whitman to Ginsberg's "Howl" to Joe Brainard's book-length poem "I Remember" (where each prose stanza begins with the phrase "I remember") was a popular practice for the East Side scene. We should consider this in the context of orality. Anaphora is especially suited to invite utterance: from Malcolm X's "Why should white people be running all the stores in our community? Why should white people be running the banks of our community?" to the high oratory of the repetitions in the Psalms and Gospels, we find we want to voice text when we read such repeated words or phrases—we want to read aloud. Thus, the sense of Sinopoulos's poem as a speech act is emphasized through use of anaphora and by the final line "tomorrow constantly repeated," which directs readers to voice the phrase themselves as many times as they want.

The fact that Economou chose to include a poem with a final line functioning as an imperative to *performance*—"tomorrow constantly repeated"—possibly echoed the kinds of performative directions Jackson Mac Low consistently provided for his readers, directions that stressed the oral/aural nature of the texts at hand. The final lines of Mac Low's poem "Leather Costs" (featured in *Poets at Le Metro* 3) feature techniques that are similar to those used in Sinopoulos's text: "Light native cow hides sell year last year / months native cow hides LEATHER COSTS / months native cow hides LEATHER COSTS / (&c / (ad infinitum)."[130] Both Sinopoulos and Mac Low use the refrain and the final directive. In Mac Low's case the directive takes the form of the phrase "&c / (ad infinitum." Mac Low's "ad infinitum" performs the same kind of function as Sinopoulos's phrase "tomorrow constantly repeated" in the sense that agency is handed over to the reader/listener to finish the poem by voicing it. A listener/reader could manifest his or her voice overtly by repeating "Leather Costs" or "tomorrow" out loud, or imaginatively by thinking of the words as voiced in the reader's mind. In these texts, the poem—like the poetry reading—is designed with the reader/listener in mind as a vocal participant in the emergence of the poem.[131]

Poets associated with the deep image linked orality with the idea of poetry as visionary utterance. In "An Exchange" Rothenberg lists (for the benefit of a perhaps skeptical Creeley) the "principles" associated with the deep image:

> The poem is the record of a movement from perception to vision.
>
> Poetic form is the pattern of that movement through space and time.
>
> The deep image is the content of vision emerging in the poem.
>
> The vehicle of movement is freedom.

After naming these principles, Rothenberg asks Creeley, "Would the poem's tension be seen resulting from the almost physical effort to voice it, to make it actual? hence organic to the conceptual impulse, etc.?"[132] That Rothenberg ends a description of a complicated and often obscurely worded theory with a question emphasizing that theory's relationship to voicing a poem helps one see how primary the poetry reading was to poets on the Lower East Side. This is particularly true when we isolate Rothenberg's use of the words *organic* and *actual.* In this scenario, the poem is not finished or real, is not "actual," until it is physically (organically) spoken. Considering this, it is not surprising that Economou—a regular presence at Les Deux Mégots—would choose to translate poetry like Sinopoulos's, which may have evoked the overall aesthetics of the Lower East Side poetic community. Economou was showing, through the Sinopoulos translation, how the oral tradition was manifesting itself as a contemporary international phenomenon, with the Lower East Side serving as one of its spiritual and poetic centers.

From reading poems in *The Floating World* to reading Robert Kelly's short essay "Notes on the Poetry of the Deep Image" in *Trobar* (here excerpted), we see how these two magazines positioned themselves as locations where an ongoing conversation on the significance of the deep image as cosmopolitan and "new" could take place:

> I read FLOATING WORLD as an attempt to plot a series of points, the poems & translations printed, to surround an implicit definition of the powers of the deep image. Rothenberg's first volume, WHITE SUN BLACK SUN (Hawk's Well Press) has just been published . . . the collection is . . . a happening in itself: the appearance of a demand for a new set of concerns in poetry, the appearance of a cogent movement in a new direction.[133]

The discourse that Kelly and others used tended to emphasize their ideas as "new" but at the same time was linked to the poetics of other non-European countries, even if those poetics emanated from a distinctly *non*contemporary era. *Trobar* would go on to feature anonymous poems translated by Rothenberg from the Arabic, as well as the poem "The Return of the Warriors," translated from the Nahuatl.[134]

Publication of Nahuatl poetry in *Trobar* can be related to the magazine's preoccupation with its place in an alternative culture that was busily resuscitating poetry as an oral form through reading series, including those at Les Deux Mégots and Le Metro. "Poem for Warriors" is designed as a communal oral expression of thanks. The following excerpt from the poem illustrates this point as it shows how the pronoun *our* may have been linked by the deep image poets to their own contemporary Lower East Side oral culture:

When the princes
come home
a fog lined with flowers
rises around them

    For which we pray,
    saying:
    Oh giver of life, whose household

this is, our father ruling among us:
the song in your praise will be heard
in Anahuac, and the cup will run over[135]

That the deep image as a theory should rise up in the context of a years-long poetry reading series featuring a relatively stable if growing social group points to a potential motivation for seeking out poems like "The Return of the Warriors" for translation. In "The Return of the Warriors," poetry is utilitarian—it is designed for praise within the context of a community, and this praise is expressed through poetry and song. Discussing the deep image group in the context of Rothenberg's work as an anthologist of international and preliterary poetry in books including *Technicians of the Sacred,* Christensen writes, "The deep image was now to be found among these other cultural and racial groups, the voice of a *collective imagination* which emanated from the discourse of rites, ceremonies, myth narratives, chants. The deep image was thus *a natural mode of speech* for those who had not purged the functions of the unconscious from their waking lives."[136] The theoretical recourse to primitive society and prerational depths of mind among the deep image poets had, in the case of the Lower East Side, the poetry reading as its real-life expression. Here, tribal behavior—group behavior—was demarcated through ritual variously expressed through the open reading, the featured reading, the benefit, and the memorial.

Pointing to a conception of the avant-garde as a primarily populist impulse, Christensen writes that Rothenberg was "convinced that what existed as the folkways and arts of primal society was at the base of 20th century experimentations over openness, spontaneity, the powers of image and chant, randomness and repetition."[137] Rothenberg and other poets articulating the deep image aesthetic connected the kinds of avant-garde poetics associated with poets including Mac Low and Sinopoulos to transnational tribal rituals spanning millennia, redefining the avant-garde from something that was "new" to something that *renewed* forgotten but necessary tribal practices. In light of the avant-garde as tribal, Christensen gracefully ties together the psychological, mythological, historical, and theoretical undercurrents behind the deep image to show how poets publishing *Trobar* and *Poems from the Floating World* imagined the poem as community-building tool:

> The "deep image" implied there is a hidden source of being and ideas within selfhood that had been driven underground to the irrational depths of the mind, whose kinship is primitive society, ancient nature religions, perhaps even the primordial beginnings of human life itself. This is the part of self that had become alienated from other mental functions in modern life; its absence in thought was part of the sickness of contemporary culture.[138]

It is hard to imagine what could be farther from the New Critical conception of the poem as isolated aesthetic object than a representation of the poem as medicine for a spiritually deprived populace and of the poet as healing shaman. Rothenberg would make this populist and mystical vision clearer and clearer as the 1960s wore on. In a later issue of *Trobar,* he wrote that the deep image stemmed "from an impasse in the soul, in which the protective 'reality' & false emblems of the inherited past have drawn a blank. Not as a neurotic outcry either, from the weakness of self-pity, but in the wholeness & fitness of the poet's vision."[139]

The Deep Image and the Academics

Poems from the Floating World and *Trobar* included perhaps the most disparate group of poets—in terms of nationality, culture, and history—than any other magazine related to the Lower East Side scene. The magazines even went beyond their antiacademic relatives by publishing poets Robert Bly and James Wright, who had been published in the Hall/Pack/Simpson anthology. It was possibly owing to Economou's own participation in the academy and in the Lower East Side reading scene that *Trobar* was more diverse in its contributors than other related publications. Economou recalled: "I was one of the few people at that time who was teaching anywhere. I had a Ph.D., and I remember I showed up at a reading one evening with my cheap little briefcase full of student papers which I had to grade at the end of the evening. Joel Oppenheimer said sarcastically, 'Oh, look, there's the professor!' But as it turned out, that's what everybody wanted for themselves!"[140] Economou lived in two worlds—the Lower East Side poetic community and Long Island University. From this vantage point, he used his magazine to reflect the potential for reconciliation between two groups of poets that had, since the time of the anthology wars of the late 1950s and early 1960s, treated each other more as enemies than as fellow bards.

However, Wright and Bly ended up associating themselves with the deep image as a coterie name and a specific aesthetic stance long after the original theoreticians had rejected the phrase as confining. Pierre Joris believes that Robert Kelly, Rothenberg, and other poets associated with *Trobar* and *Poems from the Floating World* should be spoken of as the "insiders" of a short-lived "deep image" quasi-movement:

> "Deep image" as an *appellation* was taken over after the fact (& the brief duration) of the initial burst of thought & writing about that idea by the "academics" like James Wright—& this happened, I believe, via the one outsider momentarily close to the original Deep Image poets, namely Iron John him-

self. The hijacking of the name (which the original conceivers of the trademark had indeed by then if not renounced, at least left behind as not only being of limited use qua poetics but also because of an unease or unwillingness to create a 'movement' with the usual avant-gardish manifestos, etc.) has now gone down in lit-crit so that references in traditional literary histories (if indeed they do mention it) to Deep Image will cite the latter pale imitators.[141]

Joris portrays poets Bly and Wright in familiar ways—while interested in the theories of the deep image, these poets, unlike the "originals," including Rothenberg and Kelly, did not let go of their attachment to the label. Using their more comfortable positions within the world of so-called academic poetry, these writers co-opted the deep image tag that under poets like Rothenberg and Economou was more a tentative community-oriented theory than a definable approach. Then these poets used the deep image appellation to promote their poetry with the added authority that the label contained.[142]

Meanwhile, those responsible for developing the ideas associated with the deep image had, by the mid-1960s, literally moved on. Jerome Rothenberg moved to Europe, Robert Kelly moved to upstate New York to work as a professor at Bard College, and Clayton Eshleman moved to Taiwan. As Christensen puts it, by 1964 "the group had published first and second books, and matured to the point that movements were no longer important."[143] These poets were not interested in anchoring themselves to a recognizable system of aesthetic conventions, deep image or otherwise. The tacit rejection of the very label that Rothenberg, Kelly, and Economou created thus served to maintain poems associated with *Trobar* and *Poems from the Floating World* as temporary sites of resistance. The classifying feat necessary for the academic industry to define a group of poets was made more difficult to accomplish by the lack of a central, definable organizing group principle.

C: A Journal of Poetry

C: A Journal of Poetry was edited by Ted Berrigan and published by Berrigan's friend Lorenz Gude. Berrigan would go on to run the 1965 summer reading series at Le Metro, and his subsequent "involvement with the St. Mark's Poetry Project in New York was crucial to its development."[144] Ending a chapter on Lower East Side magazines with a discussion of *C* is in many ways necessary within the context of a project that aims to demarcate the predominant aesthetics of reading series up to and including the St. Mark's Poetry Project. As Libbie Rifkin points out, "By the time it was phased out in 1966, the [magazine became] one of the dominant organs of the second-generation New York school and a spur to the organizing impulses of the St. Mark's Poetry

Project."[145] Berrigan and *C* were perhaps most responsible for defining what has come to be known as the "Second-Generation New York School." This term alludes to the initial "First-Generation" New York School as it suggests difference from (a generation gap between) "First-Generation" poets Ashbery, Schuyler, Koch, O'Hara, and Guest. As a letter from Berrigan to his wife, Sandy Alper Berrigan, indicates, the differences in aesthetic styles between poetry associated with the First- and Second-Generation New York Schools may have had a lot to do with Berrigan's repeated readings of Donald Allen's *The New American Poetry* and his appreciation for much of the poetry beyond the "New York Poets" section:

> The final literary matter I wanted to talk about was the Grove Press Anthology. Do you have it there? Is that where you read Thank You, and Fresh Air? I guess it must be. I thought I'd tell you some of the writers in the book that I liked most. Robert Creeley's short poems seem very interesting to me. He often says very good things in a very good way. Brother Antoninus writes very good poetry, I think. I like Ginsberg's poem called "A Supermarket in California," and his other things too. I like Gregory Corso some of the time, and some of the poems he has in here, like "Poets Hitchhiking on the Highway" I like a lot. I like Barbara Guest a little, and of course Koch and O'Hara and Ashberry [sic] very much. I like Gary Snyder's work, too. I like some of Michael McClure's work, but like his books better than selected poems from his books. I think that John Wieners is very good, and sometimes I like Ron Loewinsohn, and Dave Meltzer. Personally, I think I can write better than many poets in the book, but I can't write well enough to satisfy myself yet.[146]

As this letter indicates, Berrigan admired many of his contemporaries. This differentiated Berrigan from even a formidable influence like Kenneth Koch who admitted, "In my generation, I really only liked the poetry of John and Jimmy and Frank. I had a very narrow look at it back then. It was even a while before I discovered how much I liked Gary Snyder, whom I really love. It took me a long time."[147] Berrigan's regular participation in and organization of readings at Le Metro and the Poetry Project provided him with a forum where he could meet, socialize with, and in many cases befriend the poets associated with the Allen anthology as well as those younger writers attending who would eventually make a name for themselves as so-called Second-Generation New York School poets. It is likely that such a social situation helped Berrigan reconcile the various loosely defined schools associated with the avant-garde. Indeed, one can tentatively suggest that a study of the similarities and differences between the two New York School generations can be made by reading some of the poems in *C* and by tracing the social connections the editor made during the early to mid-1960s at Le Metro and associated reading series, parties and events taking place on the Lower East Side.

In late 1962 and early 1963, while Ron Padgett was still a student at Columbia University and working as editor of the *Columbia Review* (the university literary magazine), he and the rest of the editorial board considered four poems by Ted Berrigan, which Berrigan lists in a diary entry as "4 poems to Ron for the Columbia Review: Cosmic Apples, Rain Dance, Boom Town, In Memoriam: Charles. Rejected as 'offensive' by Mitch Hall + Jon Cott."[148] Berrigan, however, was a little misinformed at the time. Jon Cott and Mitch Hall actually had nothing to do with the rejection of the poems.[149] In fact, the highest levels of Columbia University's administration worked to suppress Berrigan's poetry. Objections were raised to Berrigan's poem and to a poem by friend and fellow poet David Bearden: Both poems contained "obscene" words including *fuck*. Padgett remembers:

> The four editors—two main editors and two subeditors, as I recall—Jon Cott, Mitchell Hall, myself, and a guy named Richard Tristman—we all agreed that the poems should go in. The magazine had a business manager, which was really a joke position, since there was no business really involved in it. He came in one night and happened to look through the galley proofs of the next issue and he got very upset. Without telling us, he went to the dean of Student Activities, Calvin Lee.[150]

Dean Lee went to the dean of Columbia College, David B. Truman, who, while disliking the poems, felt unqualified to act as censor. Truman then went to Jaques Barzun, one of the most preeminent scholars in literature at the university. "According to Dean Truman, Jaques Barzun felt that the poems were 'absolute trash,' and so Truman notified Calvin Lee that we were not to publish those poems. We objected, crying 'censorship!'"[151] Dean Truman called the four editors into his office and offered them two options: withdraw the poems and publish the issue with the administration's approval or publish the poems and get expelled from school. Padgett recalls, "Those were our choices. Richard Tristman, who was a senior at Columbia and who was very quick on his feet said, 'Actually, there's a third option.' Dean Truman said, 'What's that?' and Tristman responded, 'We could resign, and publish the poems in a venue outside of the university.' Dean Truman said, 'Well, that's an option, if you want to pursue that.'"[152]

The most obvious reason that Columbia University was loath to publish the poems included Berrigan's use of the word *fuck*. However, there had also been a scandal in one of the fraternities about a week before the editors were called in to account for the poems, and as Padgett remembers, "Suddenly the university administration was very sensitized to anything sexual related to the university. Our thing was considered absolutely out of the question."[153] As can be seen in the case of Columbia University, cold war–era Puritanism was still pervasive enough in the early 1960s that word was easily linked with deed. It is interesting to see how poetry managed to maintain a kind of outlaw status by lightly confronting those puritanical impulses. Padgett has said, "There was an edge to it all, because we had just been coming out of an era in which *Lady Chatterley's Lover* by D.H. Lawrence had been banned, and Allen Ginsberg's *Howl,* and James Joyce's *Ulysses* many years earlier, of course. At that point American law and mores were just emerging from a heavy restriction on using four-letter words in literature; even a cabaret performer like Lenny Bruce was busted for some of his routines, and so there was a sense that we were challenging things a little bit."[154] While Sanders's *Fuck You* was the strongest expression of this new realism in its devotion to organizing a "total assault" on conservative culture, *C* in its own lighthearted way staked a localized political position through poetry. As Padgett points out, *C* developed aesthetics (and a resulting politics) designed for the Lower East Side poetic community and associated scenes. "Ted was not trying to take on the law or anything like that, he just wanted to publish poems. Some of that poetry might rub some members of the community the wrong way, but that didn't bother him, because he didn't expect those members of the community to read the magazine anyway. It had a limited circulation . . . you could buy it in the Eighth Street Bookshop, but it wasn't produced for the masses. Children weren't going to read it."[155]

As happens with most cases of literary censorship, Padgett's and Berrigan's work and position in the poetic community were only heightened by the publicity the *Columbia Review* incident received. Berrigan referred to this publicity in his diary: "The Columbia Administration suppressed this issue of the REVIEW when they read the proofs of my poem and Bearden's. Ron went on a TV news show, etc, big deal excitement. Me, I'm busy. Anyway, *they asked me* for a poem. It's all a very shoddy affair and so are all the Review editors except Ron. What his plan is I can't say."[156]

The *New York Post* also found Padgett's predicament newsworthy, as the article "7 Editors Quit Columbia Review in Protest" attests:

> Seven student editors of the Columbia University literary magazine have resigned in protest over administration interference. Mitchell Hall, 20, editor of the *Columbia Review,* said yesterday the campus quarterly dated back "to 1897 or something" and "had never had any trouble about an issue before."
>
> The trouble with the current issue, according to Dean Calvin Lee, is "bad taste." Lee said that ever since a recent editorial in *Spectator,* the student daily newspaper, criticizing irregularities during one Columbia fraternity's "Hell

week," the administration had become unusually sensitive to the content of all student publications.

Lee warned the editors of the Review that publishing the spring issue—which includes three objectionable poems—might result in loss of the magazine's school subsidy and in probation for the editors.

Withdrawing Two Poems

Hall said the editors were told on Friday "that we could take it on faith that powerful people in the university would object to the contents of the issue and use us as fall guys in their anger against student publications in general."

"The important thing," said the self-retired editors, "is to get the issue out, on our terms—including at least the one decent poem of the objectionable three."

They said they had decided to withdraw the other two even before the Dean's office stepped in. But the third, they said, "was definitely a good poem."[157]

After all the excitement, the question about who was going to publish the Berrigan and Bearden poems remained, and that is when a source outside the university offered Padgett the use of its mimeograph machine. "Some sort of other organization, maybe a social action group, offered to let us use their mimeograph machine to publish the issue, which we did. *The Censored Review* came out of that—it sold for twenty-five cents. Eight hundred copies sold out in about five minutes. People were completely disappointed to find nothing scandalous. They were irritated that they had spent this money for a *literary* magazine."[158] Berrigan also mentions the *Censored Review*—the original name for what would become known as *C: A Journal of Poetry:* "Ron + I designed a cover for the Censored Review, using our collaborative poem at my suggestion."[159] The *Columbia Review* issue was put out under its new name, with Berrigan as its magazine editor. With a nod to "C"olumbia University and inspired by the production of the *"C"ensored Review,* Berrigan decided to edit his own magazine: He named his new mimeo *C: A Journal of Poetry.*

C and the Making of the New New York School

Berrigan wrote in his diary, "Finished typing and putting together *C* (#1) a journal of poetry, edited by me, published by Gude—32 pages—17 poems by me."[160] C Press would eventually also put out mimeographed books, edited by Berrigan and Padgett and published by Lorenz & Ellen Gude.[161] The first issue of the magazine came out in May 1963 and featured five poems by Dick Gallup, four poems by Padgett, a remarkably short play and diary by

Joe Brainard, and the seventeen Berrigan poems. All the contributors origi-
nally met in Tulsa, Oklahoma—Berrigan as a college student studying at the
University of Oklahoma under the GI bill, and Padgett, Brainard, and Gallup
as high school students editing the *White Dove Review*.[162]

Berrigan sent the initial copies of *C* to a group of people that in hindsight
reads like a partial Who's Who list of contemporary dada, surrealist, and New
York School artists. One learns that Berrigan

> Got a letter praising my poems in *C* #1 from Frank O'Hara, and a promise of
> poems from him and Bill Berkson. Also ten dollars from Jasper Johns and re-
> quest for *C* from Frank Stella. . . . I have sent out almost 100 copies of *C* my-
> self. I sent copies to all the poets and painters whose addresses I could find in
> the phone book. Kenneth Koch (who praised my poems again) gave me Jane
> Freilicher's address, and Harry Mathews', and John Perreault's, and John Ash-
> bery's. I got Edwin Denby's and Bill Berkson's and Daisy Aldan's and Jasper
> Johns from the phone book and Joe LeSueur. LeRoi Jones and Spellman at the
> 8th Street Bookstore. Anselm Hollo's from Ron and Bill Burroughs' from Ron.
> Barbara Guest's I knew. I sent a copy to Theodore Roethke through Double-
> day and Mike Goldberg through phone book and Larry Rivers at Tibor de Nagy.
> I still haven't gotten addresses of Robt Rauschenberg and Marcel Duchamp—
> I'd also like to send a copy to Man Ray.[163]

The New York School was clearly primary in terms of the people Berri-
gan wanted to reach most. Not only did Berrigan wish to reach the poets,
but he also considered the *painters* to be of major importance. Jane Freilicher,
Larry Rivers, Robert Rauschenberg, and Mike Goldberg were social with
most of the so-called New York School, and Rauschenberg served as an ex-
tra link to the Black Mountain College scene, where he resided for some time.
Duchamp provided Berrigan with the dada connection, and the fact that
Duchamp represented a specifically *New York*–based dada branch was prob-
ably not a coincidence. The link between the New York School poets and
painters has been well documented by Marjorie Perloff, David Lehman and
others, so there is no real need to reiterate how and why painters were such
attractive figures. What is interesting in this case is the way Berrigan wished
to *continue* the tradition of developing professional and social relationships
between poets and painters. Many of *C*'s covers were illustrated by Berrigan's
and Padgett's friend the artist and writer Joe Brainard. Additionally, in a kind
of inadvertent imitation of the social circles that poets like Ashbery and
O'Hara created with painters including Jane Freilicher, Fairfield Porter, Mike
Goldberg, and Larry Rivers (artists who often drew portraits of their New
York School poet friends), Berrigan and Padgett would develop friendships
with contemporary artists including Alex Katz and George Schneeman—who

would in turn create group and individual portraits of many of the Second-Generation New York School.

The fact that Berrigan sent a copy of *C* to Mike Goldberg indicates the extent to which the social world described in poetry played a part in the social decisions being made by the younger poets associated with the Lower East Side scene. In Frank O'Hara's poem "Why I Am Not a Painter," O'Hara details the phenomenology of a visit to Goldberg's studio: "For instance, Mike Goldberg / is starting a painting. I drop in. / 'Sit down and have a drink' he / says. I drink; we drink. I look / up. 'You have SARDINES in it.'"[164] Berrigan had first read this poem in *The New American Poetry*, as this excerpt from a review by Berrigan of O'Hara's *Lunch Poems* attests:

> It's a great book! . . . A book by Frank O'Hara has been long overdue, and it was a foregone conclusion that such a book when finally published would take its place beside HOWL and GASOLINE among the most important documents of contemporary poetry. . . .
>
> In the late fifties I was "beating" it through college in Tulsa, Oklahoma . . . (where) we held our breaths and awaited the Don Allen anthology.
>
> And that's where Frank O'Hara first bumped into me. While romping thru the assorted confessions, obsessions, concessions and blessings of the Allen book I was suddenly given an extremely close reading by O'Hara's poem WHY I AM NOT A PAINTER. For reasons I don't know this poem seemed to straighten all kinds of things out for me, as I immediately explained to Ron Padgett.[165]

A kind of organicism is at work here. In light of Berrigan sending out copies of *C* his connection to the figures he read about in his favored poems can be interpreted as a method for absorbing artistic energies that would transmit themselves, through friendship and association, into Berrigan's own poetry. Reaching Goldberg and O'Hara meant going directly into the world articulated by the O'Hara poem "Why I Am Not a Painter," which "straightened all kinds of things out" for Berrigan. Berrigan's choice to send *C* to Goldberg was an attempt to involve himself in the social world of sophisticated drink and talk and artistic activity described in the New York School poems and to justify his incorporation of many of the typically O'Haraesque type codes—informality, chattiness, a sense of casual erudition—into his own work.

Clearly, Berrigan wanted to participate in and contribute to a literary culture he had respected for several years. However, it is important to recognize that, at the moment of *C*'s production, the New York School world of cocktails, painting, and parties as characterized by the current academic imagination was, in 1964, as yet unincorporated into an organized and easily recognizable sign encompassing a favored scene of poetic production. Libbie Rifkin has argued that Berrigan used *The Sonnets* and *C* to establish both the Second-Generation New York School and Berrigan's position as that school's main spokesperson. Rifkin interprets Berrigan's poetics of citation and collage as prescient careerist strategies aimed at self-canonization.[166] However, how prescient could Berrigan have been if he was indeed building a career on the shaky foundation of a group of writers (O'Hara, Ashbery, and so on) who had yet to secure a significant poetic reputation themselves?

While Rifkin is certainly correct in pointing out that Berrigan was hyper-aware of audience and reception, his poetry and his work as editor might be read more fruitfully as works of microcommunity building that both echoed and complicated the utopian aspects of 1960s counterculture. Rifkin's positioning of Berrigan's work (especially *The Sonnets*) as emanating from a poet who "anticipates an afterlife in the archives and syllabi of secure canonicity" may be partly accurate.[167] However, Berrigan's eagerness to define himself and his peers as heirs to and extensions of the New York School did not perhaps stem *primarily* from his desire to guarantee a future readers' base but from his wish to create and participate in a wholly contemporary alternative community, a wish now certainly established as embodying ideals typical of what one now wistfully refers to as "the '60s." The idea of secure canonicity would probably have seemed ludicrous to Berrigan, since the writers he most respected were entirely dismissed by the academic establishment throughout the 1960s and early 1970s. The idea of a localized and literary microcommunity of which he could play a starring role, however, would have seemed highly desirable to Berrigan as a poet whose tastes ran to a mostly ignored group of writers.

Perhaps Berrigan's primary career move was to promote a group and a participatory ethos and to serve as comic ringleader for poets involved in developing new modes of writing. At least before the late 1960s—before government and corporate funding of formerly "marginal" artistic production—such promotion was always performed with self-conscious irony owing to the understanding that, in poetry (particularly experimental poetry), there was little cultural capital and absolutely *no* material returns for work expended. Thus, Berrigan constantly qualifies his assertion of group dynamics, thereby exhibiting his understanding that canonicity beyond his small chosen circle was implausible: "I used the sonnet sequence to be my big jump into poetry and stardom, *as it were*" and "I used to tell people they could join [the New York School] for five dollars."[168] The possibility of future widespread recognition was certainly a desired but unlikely, and humorous, possibility.

For Berrigan, New York School work was to be absorbed, recycled, and made new, even as the company he kept in his poetry (through intertextual references to primary New York School figures) ended up serving him well as references on his poetic curriculum vitae. The possibility of absorbing artistic energies is illustrated in a diary entry in which Berrigan records the effects of O'Hara's physical voice on his own artistic output: "This Sunday night (tonight) I went to the poetry reading by O'Hara and Koch at the New School. Koch was good but read old stuff. O'Hara was marvelous! He read from *2nd Avenue* and his 'odes'—which inspired me to rush home and write *Ode to Joe Brainard*."[169] For Berrigan the poetry reading was not simply an incidental opportunity to socialize and advance as an established writer but an inherently valuable form for receiving and creating poetry. Poetry as a heard thing was a necessary component for Berrigan, who said of his own book *The Sonnets,* "Well, *The Sonnets* as a book is to be heard rather than simply to be read off the page—should be being heard at the same time—for I am speaking all the lines, it is my voice and where it's coming from is—is—I am literally standing up in front of an audience and reading the sonnet sequence . . . there was a performance element in it then."[170]

"My Own Line of Descent Is Beatnik cum Frank O'Hara"

While poets associated with the First-Generation New York School were not regular figures at Le Metro, nevertheless, Berrigan, Padgett, and others read their poems as paradigms illustrating the intersection of poetry, orality, and social life. Since Frank O'Hara's shorter poems often recorded lunch dates, dinners, and parties, Berrigan developed a taste for cosmopolitan gatherings and old world–style rhetoric. "I had a marvelous dinner Friday evening with Edwin Denby and Rudy Burckhardt and Yvonne and Frank Lima and Tony Towle—and an Italian poet. Later we (Tony and I and Edwin) went to Denby's and talked about John Ashbery whom we'd been talking about all evening and Denby told us stories about John Ashbery and James Schuyler and O'Hara and De Kooning saying 'John' and 'Jimmy' and Frank and Bill so easily that I soon fell into it too. Edwin Denby is a fine example of a gentleman."[171] However, Berrigan showed a propensity to combine his rhetoric of casual sophistication with a more romantic, Beat-identified language. Regarding a picture of Allen Ginsberg featured in *Time* magazine, Berrigan wrote:

TIME magazine has written the worst article I have ever seen anywhere on poetry. It is horribly banal, patronizing, dishonest, and completely wrong. I never thought that even TIME could be so stupid, so evil. But at least they published a couple of good pictures. Here's one of a fellow un-goy of yours, which is fine. Does this look like the anti-Christ? Like a horrible beatnik? Or like a good person, a young, sincere, serious, slightly bemused poetic fellow?[172]

In a later letter to his wife, Sandy, Berrigan wrote:

> And more news, good things, something to make me feel good, something for
> me to brag about to you; Frank O'Hara sent me a card today in answer to the
> letter I sent him. Isn't that good that he answered? I told him I would under-
> stand if he didn't. Here's what he wrote:
>
> *Dear Ted Berrigan:*
> *Boy you certainly know how to cheer a person up. Thank you very much for your*
> *letter and for the poems which I like a lot especially Traditional Manner, Biogra-*
> *phers, and Words of Love. Forgive this card, I thought perhaps you could give me a*
> *call at work during the weekdays (CI 5–8900) and we could meet for a drink or*
> *something. Also do you want to meet K. Koch? He's great. Anyhow, if you want the*
> *poems back before we arrange to meet, let me know and I'll mail them. Otherwise*
> *I'll give them back when I see you.*
>
> I'm really thrilled very much. It's like having Picasso tell Joe [Brainard] he likes
> his work. I'll write and tell you what we talk about and all the rest when we
> meet.[173]

As the two letters indicate, a kind of reconciliation takes place here be-
tween New York School sophistication and Beat anger and social engagement.
The voice of rage over *Time* magazine is assuaged by the voice of pleasure
over the upcoming treat of a cocktail with Frank. Additionally, it is significant
that Berrigan in his review of *Lunch Poems* placed O'Hara's book alongside
those of Beat poets Ginsberg and Gregory Corso, describing these texts as "the
most important documents of contemporary poetry." One can argue that what
characterized the difference between the "First-" and "Second-"Generation
New York School poets was the Second Generation's occasional use of typi-
cally Beat writing practices, including a slightly more rough-edged approach
and (particularly in Berrigan's case) a greater tendency to disclose personal
information that emphasized the speaker's use of illegal drugs or other stereo-
typical dissolute activities.

In his personal notes, we see how attached Berrigan was to notions of the
poet as Beat-dissident. Berrigan often drew on typical Beat icons and associ-
ations of criminality in an effort to portray himself as a kind of *poet maudit*
along the lines of Rimbaud and Gregory Corso:

> This year, in this season, I am "sick" because among other things I scorn their
> new God of analysis. But they know better. It is not analysis I scorn, but the
> analysts. I would love to be analyzed by Freud, or Otto Rank, or Carl Jung, or
> Wilhelm Reich, or even Alfred Whitehead or Bernard Shaw or Walt Whitman
> or Allan [sic] Ginsberg, or Sandy Alper Berrigan but I am not about to be an-

alyzed by [conventional psychoanalysts] whose home and swimming pool are symbols of the very things which I need to repudiate *for myself* so I can be like Freud or Whitman or the rest. Did Freud have a swimming pool? Or a practice in Miami? Did Whitman, or does Carl Jung?[174]

Poe, Baudelaire, Henry Miller, Tom Wolfe, Whitman, Celine, Arthur Rimbaud! A drunk, a psychopath, a pornographer, a baby, a homosexual, a criminal, a satanic madman! Lock them all up, they're raving nuts. If we don't put them behind some kind of bars they might murder us all, rape the blessed virgin, blow up the white house, embarrass everyone, make a disturbance, or write Annabel Lee and Flowers of Evil and Tropic of Capricorn and Look Homeward Angel, and Leaves of Grass and Journey to the end of Night, and Illuminations! . . . Better lock up Socrates, he's inciting all the kids to quit work, mock great men, be beatniks; and Jesus, that sonofabitch keeps telling everybody to quit work, too, and give away all their possessions, and don't worry about it! And Buddha, that bastard wants everyone to beg! That's o.k., but who does he expect to feed all those people? I mean, some of us have to put our shoulder to the wheel, and be responsible, and why should we feed people who don't work. Why don't Buddha and Jesus and Socrates get a job? And why doesn't Jesus shave his goddam beard off? What is he, a beatnik? Beatniks! God damn, they're everywhere! Never work! Take pills! Make fun of America! Ginsberg! Miller! Whitman! Poe! They should all be put in the Jackson Memorial Hospital so that the world can be safe.[175]

In many ways, these letters lend some credence to Charles Bernstein's formulation that Ted Berrigan's work "can most usefully be read not as a document of a life in writing but, inversely, as an *appropriation* of a life *by* writing."[176] In his writing as in his "real life," Berrigan showed a consistent use of appropriation, cutup, and pastiche, whether it was in his poems or his personal correspondence. Reading through these texts, we lose a sense of Berrigan as a stable individual voice—instead, he becomes a figure absorbed in and by other people's writing. In the first letter, the line "this year, in this season, I am sick because I scorn their new God of analysis" alludes to Rimbaud's "A Season in Hell," its high drama echoing lines from Rimbaud's poem like "I detest my native land. The best thing is a drunken sleep, stretched out on some strip of shore."[177] In the second letter, the line "some of us have to put our shoulder to the wheel" was probably a self-conscious echo of Ginsberg's famous poem "America," which ends with the line "America I'm putting my queer shoulder to the wheel."[178] Berrigan fondly referred to these kinds of poetic appropriations and variations as a weakness—"I am in love with poetry. Every way I turn / this, my weakness, smites me."[179] His poetry and personal correspondence consistently reflected this "weakness," in that the concept of an individual voice is replaced by a refashioning of the authorial role from one of origination to one of quotation and cutup. As Charles Bernstein put it, Berrigan rejects "the psychological 'I' as the locus of the poem's meaning" in order to transform himself into an astonishing recycling center for a variety of prewritten and often dissident voices.[180]

Berrigan employed editorial policies that would in many ways build on his own collagist aesthetic by publishing poems that reflected, through veiled allusion, poets from the New York and Beat schools. In the first issue of *C,* Berrigan included his own "Poem in the Traditional Manner," which had previously been published in John Ashbery and Harry Mathews's Paris-based magazine *Locus Solus* 5.[181] *Locus Solus* was probably a familiar sight to many poets on the Lower East Side; throughout its run, it published poems by Frank O'Hara, Anselm Hollo, and John Wieners, to name just a few writers. However, what made *Locus Solus* 5 particularly different compared to other magazines coming out of the Lower East Side (besides its rather professional appearance) was the preponderance of writers who were associated with the First-Generation New York School crowd.[182] Berrigan's "Poem in the Traditional Manner" stood out somewhat in this context. While the poem fit that part of the New York School aesthetic characterized by whimsicality and use of wry, oddly dated language, the text also paid homage to Beat poet Gregory Corso and thus served as an example of how Berrigan was a kind of bridge between New York School sophistication and Beat shenanigans.

The final stanza of "Traditional Manner"—"Of my darling, my darling, my pipe and my slippers, / Something there is is benzedrine in bed: / And so, so Asiatic, Richard Gallup / Goes home, and gets his gat, and plugs his dad"— would have recalled for those readers in the Lower East Side poetic community Corso's own poem "Birthplace Revisited," which Berrigan is certain to have read in Allen's anthology. The final lines of "Birthplace Revisited—"I am with raincoat; cigarette in mouth, / hat over eye, hand on gat"—in all likelihood influenced Berrigan's own choice of the word *gat* (a street name for a low-quality handgun). Berrigan's allusion to Corso's poem can be read as an insinuation of the typical Beat tough-guy pose exhibited through figures Corso, Kerouac, and Neal Cassady into a "New York School"–style poem. Since all the male poets of the "First-Generation" New York School were homosexual except for Kenneth Koch, such a macho pose indicates another quantitative difference between the two generations. Berrigan was "straight" in both his life and his poetry. His use of iconic male signs, including references to guns and heterosexual sex, in his writing bolstered his sexuality and differentiated him from the campy homotextualities (John Shoptaw's term) of writers like O'Hara, Schuyler, and Kenward Elmslie.[183]

Throughout *C*'s history, Berrigan would refer rather consistently to the integration of Beat and New York aesthetics. In *C* 1, no. 7, Berrigan published Padgett's poem "I'd Give You My Seat If I Were Here." A year later, Berrigan cited this poem in *Kulchur* magazine in his review of Padgett's book *In Advance of the Broken Arm*. The review manages to illustrate the effect of the "original" New York School on the younger poets even as it conflates influences of the surrealists and the Beats:

> Sometime during writing the phonograph must have started playing, if not in the room, then in his head, because the one certain thing I can understand in that poem is that the line "Tonight she's in her grave at the bottom of the sea" is from a folk song named "The Sweet Kumadee" of which Ron has a version by Woody Guthrie (I have a better version by Ewan MacColl and Peggy Seeger). Actually, speaking of points of fact about the poem, my suspicion is that the last line is plagiarized from John Ashbery's poem, "And You Know."
>
> Ron . . . has perhaps been influenced by some Elizabethans (e.g. Herrick), the French Dadaists and Surrealists (especially Apollinaire & Reverdy) and maybe John Betjeman; but it is more likely that the gentle electricity of his lines is a result of his teen-age "Jack Kerouac & Allen Ginsberg Period."[184]

Here "electricity" is attributed to the Beats. One can turn back to Kerouac's passage in *On the Road* where Sal Paradise is walking "with every muscle aching among the lights of 27th and Welton in the Denver colored section, wishing I were a Negro, feeling that the best the white world had to offer me was not enough ecstasy for me"—to get the idea that to Berrigan the word *electricity* was synonymous with the rhapsodic rhetoric of the Beats. Berrigan suggests that Padgett's poem "I'd Give You My Seat If I Were Here" *quietly* alludes to this kind of Beat ethos. While the first line of Padgett's poem is delicate—"The shadows these flowers are making on each other"—the second line brings in the word *wild:* "The wild and sleepy eyes they make."[185] This line plays off the phrase "making eyes"; two people who were coyly and flirtatiously looking at each other are said to be making eyes. This coyness is balanced by associations of Beat excessiveness brought in through the use of the word *wild* to complicate and add a little grittiness to the tones bequeathed to Padgett by poets like Koch and O'Hara.[186]

Collaboration, Appropriation, and Anonymity in the Second-Generation New York School

As Berrigan points out in his review of Padgett's book, Padgett's "electricity" is a *gentle* electricity—one tempered by the surrealist-tinged language of Continental New York–School influences, including Apollinaire and Reverdy. In his early poetry (published throughout *C*'s history), Padgett occasionally refers to and incorporates iconic Beat language while remaining faithful to the inheritance of the New York School. Padgett, like Berrigan, also used the word *gat*. His poem "Ash Tarzan "(included in *C* 1, no. 2) ends with the line "Untune that gat, the day was fair."[187] However, to confuse matters further, "Ash Tarzan," while credited to Padgett, is not listed in *C*'s table of contents. Instead, where the reader would expect to see the titles of individual poems, there is simply "Ron Padgett . . . Two poems from the Poem Machine." According to Padgett, "the Poem Machine was Ted and me, and we invented all these different methods for writing poems together. There was no physical object involved."[188] That is, either Berrigan or Padgett could have written the line ending including the word *gat*. Appropriation and collaboration, in the tradition of the relatively contemporary cutups of Burroughs and Gysin, to the collaborative work of Eluard and Peret, to the classical work of Aeschylus, was being resuscitated by the new New York School.[189] Padgett has said of appropriation:

> It was fun, yeah. It was a little bit naughty, yes, but also it was making art. There were all the precedents for it, which we were fully aware of at the time, so it wasn't as if we were being *real* naughty. It did challenge that notion of the solitary author sweating it out. Using other people's lines means you have a bigger toolbox to work with. It doesn't mean you're going to make better or worse art. You just have more possibilities.[190]

One finds texts throughout *C* magazine that in their own rough way fit into a tradition that used poetry to threaten preconceptions of individual authorship and preformulated generic distinctions. The consistent intertextual references by Second-Generation New York School poets to poems written by First-Generation poets are so preponderant that a single poem by Frank O'Hara found itself recycled in literally dozens of other texts. Echoes of O'Hara's "The Day Lady Died" pop up again and again both in *C* and in documents associated with the poets regularly published in the magazine. Lines four through eight of Berrigan's "Sonnet II" published in *C* 1, no. 1, essentially impersonate O'Hara's poem. The first stanza of Berrigan's poem—

> It's 8:30 P.M. in New York and I've been running around all day
> old come-all-ye's streel into the streets. Yes, it is now,
> How much longer shall I be able to inhabit the Divine
> and the day is bright gray turning green
> feminine marvelous and tough[191]

—is similar in tone and rhythm to the first stanza of O'Hara's poem:

> It is 12:20 in New York a Friday
> three days after Bastille Day, yes
> it is 1959 and I go get a shoeshine
> because I will get off the 4:19 in Easthampton
> at 7:15 and then go straight to dinner
> and I don't know the people who will feed me.[192]

The word *yes* is employed by both poets as a conceit to acknowledge time—in Berrigan's case a witty and even more willfully contemporary "Yes, it is *now*" in relation to O'Hara's "yes / it is 1959." Berrigan's poem, while clearly imitating O'Hara's, also alluded to other poems associated with the New York School. The line "How much longer shall I be able to inhabit the Divine" is identical (except the final word) to the title of one of John Ashbery's poems, "How Much Longer Will I Be Able to Inhabit the Divine Sepulcher . . ." While Reva Wolf does not talk about Ashbery's poem in light of Berrigan's "Sonnet II," she makes a valuable point regarding issues of appropriation between the First- and Second-Generation New York Schools:

> Berrigan adored the idea of composing verse by piecing together lines of poems by other writers. He loved to think about the multiple potential implications—artistic, legal, and those regarding identity—of the act of copying words. It is obvious that to write candidly about his 'borrowings' gave him great pleasure and amusement. For instance, in 'Personal Poem #7,' (a title adapted from O'Hara's writing), he recorded that he 'Made lists of lines to / steal' after reading Ashbery's poem "How Much Longer Will I Be Able to Inhabit the Divine Sepulcher?"[193]

Ashbery himself probably provided Berrigan with the justification necessary for such a practice. The collaborative issue of *Locus Solus* included John Ashbery's "To a Waterfowl." The poem was in cento form. "The word *cento* comes from the Latin word meaning 'patchwork,' as in 'patchwork quilt.' The cento is a poem made entirely of pieces from poems by other authors."[194] O'Hara's poem was echoed not only in poetry but in correspondence. A letter to Bill Berkson from Gerard Malanga is written in the style of "The Day Lady Died":

> Dear Bill, hello. It is Wednesday 9:05 P.M. in New York and yes
> it is 1963 and Frank is reading poems about lunch and how
> beautiful the twentieth century can be
>
> it is probably 1:05 A.M. in Paris
> I'm writing to you to say that I've gone mad thinking

I'm somewhere between Rudolph Valentino and James Dean

        which is why I don't

quite make it as a lover[195]

As these variations on O'Hara's poems suggest, borrowing became a definable practice among poets associated with the Second-Generation New York School who would go on in 1966 and 1967 to become dominant organizers of and participants in the Poetry Project. Some have argued that Second-Generation New York School poets are, by nature of their overt debt to New York School poets O'Hara, Ashbery, and Koch, minor poets overshadowed by or unable to reject successfully the overbearing paternal role that First-Generation poets apparently represented to Second-Generation poets. Critic Geoffrey Ward writes:

> O'Hara is simply inescapable for that generation. To go all out for a comic poetry as Padgett has done has meant committing himself to something hugely enjoyable that sidesteps confrontation with the larger themes of experience and with poets to whose greater abilities his work has openly capitulated. Padgett and Berrigan were made as poets by their reading of and contact with Frank O'Hara. It can't now be known—at least in Berrigan's case—whether an alternative, perhaps more powerful poetry that they might have written wasn't blighted out of existence by O'Hara's dominance.[196]

Ward, however, is perhaps being a little unfair in asserting that all Padgett's work is "comic"; a truly comic work does not automatically elide seriousness, nor is it somehow "beneath" wholly serious work. Ward seems to be focusing here on content, an approach that tends to avoid the very real formal innovations that Padgett and Berrigan developed, such as "false" translations, anonymous collaborations, inventive uses of typography, treating the list poem and catalog poem far more ambitiously as forms than had been done previously (for example, Joe Brainard's *I Remember*), and so on. One is left feeling a little uneasy by Ward's use of the phrase "a more powerful poetry," for it is precisely this notion of poetry as a dramatic, serious, and intensely personal and passionate pursuit that the Second-Generation poets were complicating through their wit, their intertextual sociability, and their formalist play. Wit was a method used by both generations of poets to carry on what David Lehman has characterized as "a pointed literary attack on the poetics of the New Criticism and the values of TS Eliot . . . [t]he fun in Koch's poetry, the hysteria as well as the joy, was simultaneously affirmative and escapist."[197] While the Second-Generation New York School poets were certainly imitative of the First Generation in general and of Frank O'Hara in particular, their collaborations and their continuing challenge to a poetics of sense and closure suggest that the Second Generation was extending a tradition as opposed to merely aping one.

We can suggest that Berrigan's and Padgett's roles in the reading series at Le Metro had an effect on *C*; Berrigan made sure to adopt and refer to many of the same modernist predecessors the Lower East Side community had claimed as its own. In *C* 1, no. 2, the table of contents included an excerpt from Richard Elleman's biography of James Joyce that probably would have reminded readers from the Lower East Side poetic community of John Cage's and Merce Cunningham's chance operations (and by extension Jackson Mac Low's work using chance-determined texts):

> Once or twice he dictated a bit of *Finnegans Wake* to Beckett, though dictation did not work very well for him; in the middle of one such session there was a knock at the door which Beckett didn't hear. Joyce said, "Come in," and Beckett wrote it down. Afterwards he read back what he had written and Joyce said, "What's that 'come in'?" 'Yes, you said that' said Beckett. Joyce thought for a moment, then said, "Let it stand."[198]

Berrigan's acknowledgment on the front cover of his magazine of a modernist predecessor was a decision typical of the Lower East Side scene at the time. Linking one's own project to high modernism served to bestow a certain historical validity to the contemporary alternative project. Additionally, *Finnegans Wake* was originally published in bits and pieces in at least five different "littles," including Ford Madox Ford's *transatlantic review*, Adrienne Monnier's *Le Navire d'Argent,* and Eugene Jolas's *transition.* While there is no easy way of ascertaining whether Berrigan knew of the publishing history behind *Finnegans Wake,* it is at the very least a notable coincidence that a new little—in this case Berrigan's mimeographed *C* magazine—should indirectly point back to the littles that in many ways went through the same kinds of financial and aesthetic challenges that Berrigan would face as editor of an avant-garde periodical. Finally, this excerpt from Joyce's biography serves to emphasize the value that Berrigan as an editor placed on chance as an ingredient in composition; it is as if Berrigan was overtly and idealistically linking his uses of chance, along with its distant cousin appropriation, to a history in literature that went beyond the mid-century avant-garde.

Randomness, repetition, anonymity, and chance also had a visual counterpart to Berrigan, Padgett, and other poets published in *C.* Andy Warhol's influence became more evident as the abstract expressionist painting of De Kooning and Jackson Pollock favored by the First-Generation New York School and championed in the 1950s made room for the pop aesthetic developed by Warhol and advocated by poets of the Second Generation. Berrigan published poems including Padgett's "SONNET to Andy Warhol" which Reva Wolf has already linked to Warhol's movie *Sleep,* in which the camera simply trained its eye on the sleeping figure of poet John Giorno. *Sleep* was echoed in poetry by Padgett:

SONNET to Andy Warhol

Zzzzzzzzzzzzzzzzzzzzzzzzz
zzzzzzzzzzzzzzzzzzzzzzzzzz
zzzzzzzzzzzzzzzzzzzzzzzzzz
zzzzzzzzzzzzzzzzzzzzzzzzzz
zzzzzzzzzzzzzzzzzzzzzzzzzz
zzzzzzzzzzzzzzzzzzzzzzzzzz
zzzzzzzzzzzzzzzzzzzzzzzzzz
zzzzzzzzzzzzzzzzzzzzzzzzzz
zzzzzzzzzzzzzzzzzzzzzzzzzz
zzzzzzzzzzzzzzzzzzzzzzzzzz
zzzzzzzzzzzzzzzzzzzzzzzzzz
zzzzzzzzzzzzzzzzzzzzzzzzzz
zzzzzzzzzzzzzzzzzzzzzzzzzz
zzzzzzzzzzzzzzzzzzzzzzzzz

Padgett's "SONNET to Andy Warhol" advances the practice of creating works that tend toward a nearly invisible author figure. Besides calling a series of "zzz"'s a sonnet and thereby having some fun at the expense of poetry traditionalists, the poet as a biographical "I" representing the poem is comically extinguished by the surfeit of "z"'s. Like Warhol's mechanical reproductions of everyday objects and images, this reproduction of a single letter emphasizes process and surface, thereby denying symbolic significance to a sacral word or image. Repeating the final letter of the alphabet, while serving the functional purpose of imitating the sound of someone snoring, also can suggest (in a more serious way, which Padgett himself has denied) a whimsical frustration over the restriction inherent in the alphabet's twenty-six letters.[199] For a poet for whom public readings were a major opportunity to develop and promote new work, the end of the alphabet might be burlesqued in "SONNET" to suggest a frustration with phonetic finiteness suggested by the letter *z.*

The practice of minimizing authorial presence—as one sees in Padgett's "SONNET" and as implied through the consistent use of fake names, collaborative authorship, and other forms of authorial appropriation and blurring of identities—was taken to increasingly extreme levels in poems published throughout *C*'s various issues. After some time, anonymity itself was lampooned, as one sees in the following text by John Perreault included in *C:*

Some guy I used to know named John Perreault
is writing a book about all the people he knows
named John Perreault.
In order to protect himself he is using
the pseudonym "John Perreault"[200]

C in Poetry Readings of the Lower East Side

The following excerpts from Berrigan's diary illustrate the growing social re-
lationships between Berrigan and members of the older New York School, as
well as the convergence with the Andy Warhol crowd and poets reading reg-
ularly at Le Metro. As an editor, Berrigan was assisting in the formation of a
group that was to grow during the Poetry Project's first five years. Every poet
mentioned in these excerpts found their way into the pages of *C* and (except
for O'Hara, who died in 1966) behind the microphone of the Poetry Project:

> Tuesday, May 1963:
>
> Went with Sandy and baby and Johnny [Stanton] to the Frank O'Hara read-
> ing tonight which was a little disappointing except for the last poem HOTEL
> TRANSYLVANIE.
>
> Talked to Malanga and Tim [Baum] and [Jim] Brodey there, and Tony Towle
> introduced himself to me. Talked also to John Wieners briefly—and met Andy
> Warhol. The literary scene is faintly nauseating—and O'Hara seemed to think
> so too.
>
> Tuesday, August 6th, 1963:
>
> Read my poems at Le Metro last night—stupefying everyone except Tim Baum
> and Dick Gallup. Also read Dick's SOME FEATHERS
>
> Gerry Malanga took my poem TO THE BEAUTIFUL PRINCESS for the Wagner
> Literary Review. Ah Sweet Success! (and all that).
> Andy Warhol said he'd do a cover for C 4.

After *C* 1, no. 4, (featuring the work of Edwin Denby), *C* magazine began to
include a more heterogeneous group of writers—a scenario similar to specific
issues of many of the mimeographed magazines coming out of the Lower East
Side community.[201] Typically for these magazines, the first issues contained
work produced mainly by close friends of the editors. With the sponsorship
and encouragement of a patron/poet like Kenneth Koch or Allen Ginsberg,
these initial issues served to attract "big-name" poets, thus guaranteeing these
otherwise fleeting publications a place in the alternative canon.

C 1, no. 5 included poetry by Lorenzo Thomas. Thanks to Thomas, *C* could claim to contain a political consciousness that would otherwise be seen as lacking; a sense of political engagement (apart from some of Frank O'Hara poems) was not part of the overall poetics among writers of the First Generation.[202] From Thomas's poem "Political Science," the racial consciousness of the *Umbra* group works its way into the pep and verve of the new New York School:

> Now could I read Browning,
>   "Home
> Thoughts from abroad
>   & it still lucid, cool streams descend
> for every corpulent jew.
>
>
>   My fingers" (accentuated
>   my eyes heavy-lidded
>   and my fingers thick. They magnetize
>
>
>   silver to christianize
>   my palm,
> This is a set of affairs
>   like warm adventures in darkest africa "Afric-ay
>
>
>   Ah, forty years ago.
>
>
> entire geography history a jumbled a yellow in fireside[203]

Thomas's poem successfully avoids the shrillness and didacticism associated with propagandistic political poetry, maintaining a coolness and lightness of tone. The surrealistic jumble of the final line—"entire geography history a jumbled a yellow in fireside"— claims the authority to speak for history while creating hiccuplike sounds that lead to a fracturing of linear sense. Thomas has said, "Berrigan idolized Frank O'Hara—I did too, I had sort of like an altar to him. Amiri was also indebted to Frank, and vice versa."[204] In many ways, "Political Science" attests to this influence: O'Hara more than any other poet associated with the New York School inserted political subtexts into his poetry as he maintained surface lightness. Poems like his "Personal Poem," where we hear that "Leroi comes in / and tells me Miles Davis was clubbed 12 / times last night outside BIRDLAND by a cop" or his poem "For the Chinese New Year and for Bill Berkson" with the elegiac line "whither Lumumba whither oh whither Gauguin" could have served as potential models for Thomas's poetry.[205] That is, O'Hara was relatively interested in racial politics as they manifested themselves in his social circle, and he included them as topics in his writing. Thomas's work picked up on this trait of O'Hara's and broadened it by at times emphasizing the racial themes in his texts. Thomas's Olsonian use of the page combined with a content that directly refers to race marks it—and by association *C* itself—as a complication of New York School–style poetry rather than a mere mimicry of that style.

C, like the public reading environment at Le Metro of which it was a part, was useful as a staging ground for experiments performed within a collaborative context. Berrigan "conceived [the magazine] as a periodical workshop for the development of group poetics."[206] "Group poetics" in *C*'s case signifies both collaboration and purportedly original texts written by an individual author. In Berrigan's case *C* served as a forum for his ever-increasing sonnet sequence. Each sonnet echoed, varied, or alluded to individual lines from other poems, particularly those of O'Hara and Ashbery. Such an approach to writing or "building" a poem can be seen as collaborative even if only one person is putting the lines together. Berrigan conceived of "collaboration as an encounter between any number of different writings, set in motion but not controlled by a single writer."[207] In this sense, Berrigan's tactics for building his sonnets suggests the poetry reading, where a multiplicity of voices converges for an event centered on poetry. Like the poetry reading, Berrigan's sonnets were highly social: "writers, friends and readers were the same figures appearing at different moments on the poem's turning wheel."[208] This sociability tended to redistribute authorship to a variety of given voices. Despite his stereotypical Bohemian reputation, Berrigan wrote himself into the role not necessarily of "poet" in its individualist sense but of a poem-administrator collaging a variety of carefully chosen "found" texts to produce new work.

In an environment where the utterance of poetry often led to hugs, laughter, clapping, and new social connections within the context of a multifunction poetry reading, Berrigan's collagist poetry was not so much appropriate for the occasion as it was emanating out of the occasion. While Rifkin does not mention the poetry reading per se, her chapter on Berrigan in *Career Moves* nevertheless captures a historical moment where a proto-hippie ethos of sharing and a theoretical disdain of personal ownership found a poetic parallel in Berrigan's poetry: "His poetry is so roomy, so full of other poets' names and lines, that it emerges as a kind of free-love alternative to traditional figurations of literary family as necessarily nuclear, claustrophobic, and oedipal."[209] The scene at Le Metro, where every Monday writers from across the avant-garde spectrum met at open readings that at least temporarily suspended hierarchies associated with professionalism, must have had an impact on Berrigan's sense of what it meant to be a poet. After all, everyone attending a reading at Le Metro could be published in *Poets at Le Metro* and represented as part of a scene. It is a small step from such anarchic democracy to the textual parallels visible in Berrigan's poetry, poetry in which the names, verses, and utterances of the poets and friends closest to his interests and life were weaved in and made part of an overall dialogic text.

Berrigan was happy to be invited to the Berkeley Poetry Conference of 1965. He was particularly pleased that Robert Duncan wrote a poem at the conference entitled "At the Poetry Conference: Berkeley after the New York Style." Duncan used this poem to point out the eccentric valences of avant-garde poetry, which he described as "a Black Mountain / Berrigan imitation North Carolina / Lovely needed poem for O'Hara." Rifkin notes, "The timing was perfect for Berrigan's combination of individual bravura and imitative reverence. With its poetic of citation and collage, *The Sonnets* enacted on the level of rhetoric the self-canonizing maneuvers that were taking place at the conference's readings, panel discussions, and, most of all, cocktail parties. Berrigan wrote himself into the institution of the avant-garde by anticipating the moment when the institutions around poetry fold back into poetry itself."[210] *C* and *The Sonnets* provided Berrigan with a forum where he could refresh and recycle a babble of highly attractive voices representative of the New York School, Black Mountain, and Beat milieus. Additionally, by consistently publishing, editing, and borrowing lines from Ashbery, O'Hara, Schuyler, and Koch, Berrigan established his own social role in the actual lives of these poets, particularly since his job as editor of *C* meant that he would be in frequent correspondence with First-Generation New York School poets.

The work published in *C* and in other mimeos reflected a poet's day-to-day social world in a way that glossy bound magazines could not, partly because these magazines could not be produced as fast as the mimeos. Thus *C* was a kind of progressive autobiography charting the growth of a circle of friends. By 1963, Kenneth Koch was a sponsor, friend, and fan of Berrigan and Padgett, and *C* continued to gain new subscriptions and growing attention from visual artists and literati on the Lower East Side and beyond. A letter from Kenneth Koch shows how he singled out Berrigan and Padgett for praise:

> Dear Ted:
> Thanks for *C* 2. I think its very good. I especially like your "Words for Love" and Ron's "Homage to Max Jacob." What's so nice, and unusual, about the issue is that the language is interesting all the time. When will *C* 3 be gotten together and come out? I do want to send you something.[211]

Koch, along with Ashbery, Barbara Guest, Kenward Elmslie, Schuyler, and all the other poets associated with the First-Generation New York School, eventually submitted their poems to *C,* and (along with their younger peers Padgett, Berrigan, Ceravolo, and Thomas) would determine the overall tone of the magazine until its final issue. Ultimately, Berrigan's and Padgett's regular attendance and participation at Le Metro and the Poetry Project, combined with their close friendship with Poetry Project director Anne Waldman, had an enormous effect on the programming at St. Mark's. To understand the early history of the Poetry Project, then, it is time to turn our attention to *how* the Poetry Project was founded out of the demise of Le Metro and out of federal government subsidies, and how it was in many ways responsible for the emergence of First-Generation New York School poets as oral readers via the support of figures including Berrigan, Padgett, and Anne Waldman.

4

The Poetry Project at St. Mark's Church

St. Mark's Church and the "Political" Avant-Garde

Peter Stuyvesant, the Dutch governor of what was then known as New Amsterdam, founded St. Mark's Church, officially called St. Mark's-in-the-Bouwerie. The original chapel was built in 1660. Stuyvesant's land holdings extended from what is now Broadway to the East River and Fifth Street to Seventeenth Street. This property was known as Stuyvesant's "Bouwerie," derived from the Dutch word meaning "cultivated farm" or "gentleman's estate."[1] After the original chapel deteriorated, the present structure was built on the same site in 1799.

As the Lower East Side began to attract large numbers of European immigrants in the first half of the twentieth century, and as artists and writers began the slow migration eastward from the West Village in the 1950s, the church became known as an iconoclastic parish that valued its artistic constituency. Artists, dancers, and poets including W. H. Auden (who lived on St. Mark's Place near First Avenue) were members of the church, and the administration developed a number of professional artistic programs designed to engage the interest of local young artists. Even in the church's role in the relatively liberal Episcopalian establishment, St. Mark's was seen as unorthodox, particularly when Michael Allen became pastor in 1959. To Auden's chagrin, under Allen's leadership St. Mark's Church abandoned the traditional

123

Latinate *Book of Common Prayer* in favor of an English-language liturgy. Auden at first tried to tolerate this change, and he spent some time helping Allen with the new wording of the services. However, Auden "soon came to hate the change, and began to declare that the church should instead go back to Latin. . . . He himself ceased going to St. Mark's, and began to attend a Greek Orthodox church a few blocks away."[2] Allen also brought in a relatively radical perspective on the role that artists could play in the church; according to church administrator Steve Facey, "Michael Allen understood prophetically in the early 1960s the cultural and political ferment that we were going through. He opened the door up to artists, particularly to the poets who were being closed out of Le Metro coffee shop, and the reason he opened up the place to artists was because he felt they were among the few people in society that were really doing theology. When he was drafting me to be the administrator, he wanted to create a climate that would really foster the development of these arts projects."[3]

The social environment of the Lower East Side, particularly from 1966 to 1968, paralleled and influenced the radical climate that Facey refers to. "Thousands of newcomers—mostly white, middle-class, well-educated men and women in their late teens and twenties—descended on the neighborhood, transforming unrenovated tenement rooms into 'pads' for drug parties and 'love-ins.' During the months of May and June 1967, it was estimated that two thousand hippies moved into the tenements adjacent to Tompkins Square Park."[4] New publications arrived to document the changes. The *East Village Other,* a countercultural weekly that covered the neighborhood's political and artistic renaissance and regularly attacked church, military, police, and governmental icons representative of the "Establishment," began publication in October 1965. Geared mostly to the newly arriving, predominantly white hippie subculture, the *East Village Other* included articles by armed revolutionaries, idealized drug dealers, and poets.

Artistic production on the Lower East Side expanded beyond literature, jazz, and the visual arts. New music, including acid rock and the drone-influenced sounds of the Velvet Underground, became part of the neighborhood's soundtrack.[5] Pop artist Andy Warhol rented the Polish National Social Hall at 23 St. Mark's Place and transformed it into the Electric Circus. At the Electric Circus, Warhol debuted the multimedia Plastic Exploding Inevitable, where poet Gerard Malanga and "superstar" Edie Sedgwick danced on stage to the music of the Velvet Underground as psychedelic light shows played throughout the space. In early 1968, Bill Graham opened the Fillmore East, a performance space on Second Avenue where musicians including Janis Joplin, the Who, the Kinks, the Grateful Dead, and Jefferson Airplane could all be heard.[6] As a result of all this activity, the neighborhood's makeup visibly changed. "[Between 1966 and 1967] the novelty of the hippie phenomenon kept apartments and storefronts leased and rent levels increased. Rent for apartments adjacent to St. Mark's Place doubled, in part due to new leases from frequent turnover as new hippies replaced those who left . . . the neighborhood's countercultural atmosphere attracted copywriters, editorial workers, fashion designers, and commercial artists, among others."[7]

All these phenomena helped give the Poetry Project and St. Mark's Church as a whole the reputation as a radical space. An article in *The East Village Other* defined St. Mark's as an institution that could offer a real alternative to traditional authoritarian organizations:

> Artists may wonder what a church has to do with the free, open spirit of Art, which dictates its own laws of experiment, investigation, and analysis. But the spirit of St. Mark's is precisely the spirit of Art. It is dedicated to open experiment, honest investigation, and analysis of the world it lives in. It challenges the Establishment and quests after its own truth—independent of rules and laws. It waits to be either illuminated, or to luminate.
>
> "Its Christ is not the Christ of little old ladies in white Sunday hats," said a parishioner, "but the vigorous Christ of rebellion against the vested hierarchy, the Christ of Challenge and of violence, who sweated and bled and understood the smell of sin, Christ the man who perhaps pissed in his pants when they drove in the nails . . . "
>
> St. Mark's-in-the-Bouwerie is physically old, but it's spiritually young. It awaits the painters, the writers, the photographers, pornographers, poets, and musicians who care to use its facilities towards their own ends. It is perhaps the very spirit of the Lower East Side.[8]

Beyond using the church's facilities "towards their own ends," artists and poets socialized and worked with church administrators. As a junior high school student, Anne Waldman grew to know Michael Allen when he was working as assistant to the rector. When Waldman eventually became director of the Poetry Project, she served on the church vestry (the governance board of the church) working as a liaison to the Arts projects.[9] Many poets and artists echoed and supported the Reverend Michael Allen's activism against the Vietnam War, and Waldman, Bernadette Mayer, and other writers formed friendships with the Reverend David Garcia, who eventually succeeded Allen after his departure.[10]

Additionally, by 1966 the church had already established Theater Genesis, which produced around thirty new plays, two of which were produced off-Broadway. Playwright Sam Shepard was associated with the early St. Mark's theater projects and would go on to tour productions in Copenhagen and Paris that were initiated at the church. A film program was also established in 1965 called PROJECTION that was used to justify the creation of the Millennium Film Workshop (a project running concurrently with the Poetry Project). PROJECTION, made up of a group of young avant-garde filmmakers who met once a week for closed showings of their films followed by discussion, became the core of much of the filmmaking going on in the East Village.[11]

As Anne Waldman recalls, the church, for decades before the formation of the Poetry Project, had been a center for alternative arts and lectures, featuring summer jazz concerts as well as appearances by Frank Lloyd Wright, Harry Houdini, and other figures.[12] In this context, the church was a natural site for new organized poetry readings. Before the Poetry Project officially began, poets including Anselm Hollo, Ree Dragonette (featuring her jazz-poetry series), and Jackson Mac Low had all read at St. Mark's Church. "Reading on April 28, 1966, was John Ashbery, just back from Paris, intro by Ted Berrigan."[13] Anticipating the by-now legendary mass readings taking place at St. Mark's every New Year's Day, St. Mark's organized a benefit featuring fifty poets for the *East Side Review* on March 10, 1966 (about three months after the readings at Le Metro had ended). Those writers included most of the Le Metro regulars as well as poets including W. H. Auden, Stanley Kunitz, John Ashbery, and James Wright.

Adding to the Lower East Side's growing reputation as a site for the antiwar movement, St. Mark's also provided a forum for an increasingly politicized and radicalized group of poets responding to the expansion of military activity in Vietnam. In April 1966 (five months before the official beginning of the Poetry Project), a benefit reading for the Committee for Non-Violence was held in the parish hall.[14] A tape of the event indicates that a rather anarchic spirit prevailed. One can hear someone getting forcibly ejected from the parish, interrupting Allen Ginsberg's reading of his poem "Wichita Vortex Sutra." The emcee yelled to the unwanted audience member in a tone approaching hysteria, "Move away from the door! Now come on now, no arguing. I want you to leave!" Ginsberg, taking on the persona of the person getting ejected, responded, "Awright" in a theatrically sheepish tone. The audience began laughing, only to have Ginsberg say, "Actually, it might be better to calm the scene—*dharani* to remove all disasters." Ginsberg then began playing hand cymbals and chanting. This took a few minutes, after which the church hall was completely silent. Breaking the silence, Ginsberg quietly explained, "Used in Zen Buddhist ritual as a mantra or magic formula prayer for the removal of disaster," and then started to read "Wichita Vortex Sutra" with a marked increase in enthusiasm: "*The Biggest Little Town in Kansas / Macpherson* / Red sun setting flat plains west streaked / with gauzy veils, chimney mist spread / around christmas-tree-bulbed refineries."

This particular reading was clearly well attended. At one point the emcee exhorted the crowd, "For your own comfort and safety, will somebody please open the rear door that leads to the yard, please. Will you ask the people at the door not to enter, and that the hall is already overcrowded!" Audience chatter could be heard over his pleas, indicating that attention was not necessarily focused on the proscenium. Directly after Ginsberg's reading, Ginsberg's lover and fellow poet Peter Orlovsky came on to the stage—the common poetic community practice of putting Ginsberg and Orlovsky on succeeding pages in magazines including *Fuck You* was echoed by presenting the poets in sequential order at live poetry readings. As if to emphasize the familial relationship between Orlovsky and Ginsberg, Orlovsky chose to read a text that described an incident when Orlovsky was buggered by Ginsberg as Orlovsky was typing: "He takes his cock out of my ass gently, a ball of shit falls out on the pillow, looms like shape of chicken heart, Allen thought it was cum, but no. He puts it on white paper and carries it. He gets behind me and wipes my ass with underpants." The audience laughed uproariously at each intimate revelation.

The scatological and the sexual, traditional tropes for a communally minded avant-garde, were themes that popped up consistently at this antiwar benefit. Ed Sanders's presence at the reading received perhaps the greatest applause, possibly because the audience was familiar with his long-standing role as sex liberationist, poet, antiwar protester, and troublemaker. The first thing Sanders did when he got on stage was to yell out, "OK, pants down!" After a few seconds, Sanders peevishly asked the audience, "This is a church, isn't it, is this a church?" Someone yelled back, "Yes, it is a church!" Then Sanders said, "Pants up, church," which elicited a host of whistling, laughter, and hooting from the audience. Introducing his "Gobble-Gang Poems," Sanders explained how he worked in a cigar store in Times Square for five years. "I got to know this bull-dyke, who ran a gobble-gang. I was peace-freaking at the time and I managed to convert her towards a peace-position, pacifist cluster. The lady's name is Conzuela."

This confluence of "gobble-gangs" and politically charged rhetoric, poetry, and sexually explicit descriptions of homosexual sodomy indicates that the potential impact of poetry on the individual depended in part on the highly social context of a live audience's reaction to a poet's work. Even as it is heard on the displaced environment of the cassette tape, audience response at the benefit reading for the Committee for Non-Violence often affected the voicing of a given poem. Laughter in St. Mark's parish hall begat an increase in volume on the part of the poet, audience heckling elicited poet's coyness, and so on, all of which affected the reception of a poem. Considering that this particular reading was organized to promote pacifism as a response to the Vietnam War, the *kind* of avant-garde aesthetic such a reading was promoting reached back to and adapted the early twentieth-century avant-garde's anti-militaristic, antibourgeois, and absurdist elements. This is not to say that the poets so far mentioned were in any way privileging overtly political content in their work. In fact, many poets reading at the Poetry Project (particularly those poets affiliated with the New York School) rejected overtly political language as somewhat confining. Manifestoes were thought of as unnecessary in staging a political position; as Kenneth Koch has said, "I remember being always willing to read my poetry for what I thought was a good cause, whether or not my poetry spoke about the cause. And it usually didn't. That's about it. I was happy to read against the war. If people wanted me to read something about roller-coasters to show that poets were against the war I would always do it."[15]

In the face of the Vietnam War, showcasing a poetry of buggery, drug use, and other illegal acts to support the Committee for Non-Violence personalized poetics and politics for those who might otherwise have interpreted the war through a more typical political rhetoric. In line with Renato Poggioli's definition of the role of humor in the avant-garde, this kind of poetic environment used the derogatory images of the fart, cum, anus, and blow job "not only as a vehicle for caricature and grotesque representation, but also as an instrument to disfigure, or transfigure, the object so as to produce a radical metamorphosis. . . . The very humor of the avant-garde is not so much a free creation of the *vis comica* as a secretion of bile, a case of black humor, an attack of spleen or hypochondria."[16] Anger was still possible in this environment. Recognizing that "everybody's shit stinks"—as Sanders and so many other poets associated with St. Mark's made clear—was a funny *and* serious tactic for destabilizing figures associated with the puritanical military-industrial complex.

As an example of how writers in the Lower East Side enriched political rhetoric through their poetry and through participation in poetry readings, one can look to Ginsberg's poem "Who Will Take Over the Universe?" This poem is an archetypal instance of a poet's associating what Bakhtin in his work on Rabelais called "the material lower bodily stratum" with contemporary political figures in order to "produce a radical metamorphosis" of those figures. Lines like "Che Guevara has a big cock / Castro's balls are pink / The Ghost of John F. Dulles hangs / over America like dirty linen" and "Dust flows out of his asshole / his hands are full of bacteria" in a later reference to Dulles do not depend on more familiar political rhetoric like "U.S. out of Vietnam!"[17] Rather, the poem—like so many of the poems read at St. Mark's Church in April 1966—incorporates the genital and excretory functions of the body into poetry to provide an audience with an entertaining and still-subversive politicized experience. The poetry that was read for the Committee for Non-Violence was not "art for art's sake" detached from daily life. Most obviously, this was owing to the simple fact that the poetry read that day was for a leftist, dissident cause. More interesting, however, the poetry of the poetic community in the Lower East Side shifted the role of critique from that which was hortatory and obvious to that which was funny, unsettling, shocking, and new.

St. Mark's Church and the Strange New World of Federal Funding for the Arts

Many of the poetry events at St. Mark's before the Poetry Project was formed occurred thanks to the labors of Paul Blackburn. By January 1966 (just after the fight between Tom Dent and Margules at Le Metro), Blackburn, Carol Bergé, Carol Rubinstein, Allen Planz, Jerome Rothenberg, Paul Plummer, and Diane Wakoski formed a "Poetry Committee." These individuals, most of whom made up the essential core of the Deux Mégots and Le Metro poetry reading series, were largely responsible for ensuring that the Lower East Side poetic tradition would find a new home at St. Mark's Church.[18] However, St. Mark's was not a wealthy church—it needed money to maintain its services, and Michael Allen knew that he would have to begin looking for alternative sources of funding if the arts programs were to survive. What happened at St. Mark's in May 1966 (just months after the end of the Le Metro readings) in many ways characterizes the by-now familiar method in which nonprofit creative institutions adapt language to meet the criteria of a grant. St. Mark's Church decided to accept nearly $200,000 in federal government money earmarked for the socialization of juvenile delinquents.

According to information gathered in Bob Holman's unpublished oral history of the Poetry Project, the grant from the federal government to the church was based in part on the fact that the Health, Education, and Welfare Office of Juvenile Delinquency and Development had money it needed to get rid of by the end of the fiscal year. Israel Garver, a man working in the department at the time, was responsible for allocating these funds, so he called his friend Harry Silverstein (then a professor of sociology at the New School) to ask if Silverstein could think of programs that needed the funds. Silverstein's first instinct was to suggest that the funds go to the Judson Church on Washington Square, which already offered a variety of highly successful arts programs. The New School in turn would lend its support, provide the administrative structure for the program, and receive salaries for doing so. However, Howard Moody, the rector at Judson Church, was unsure about accepting government funds, and asked the Judson's theater director Al Carmines what he thought. Carmines's answer was unequivocal: "We don't need sociologists running around in an arts program."[19]

Silverstein then went to St. Mark's Church and suggested to the Reverend

Michael Allen that he apply for the funds. Allen's response was the opposite of Carmine's: "Silverstein's plan sounded unbelievable, but here he was. Nobody knew who he was, but here he was."[20] Within a week, the New School, in collaboration with St. Mark's Church, wrote a grant proposal that would eventually elicit the necessary money to fund the first few years of the Poetry Project (along with the Theatre Genesis theater project and the Millennium film project).

The actual grant was submitted to the Office of Juvenile Delinquency and Youth Development, which was part of the Department of Health, Education, and Welfare in Washington, D.C. The Reverend Michael Allen was named project director, Harry Silverstein (the sociologist from the New School) was the co-director, and Bernard Rosenberg (who had received his Ph.D. in sociology from the New School in 1949) was named research associate.[21] According to the grant, Allen's duties entailed responsibility for the overall planning and implementation of the creative arts program as well as "recruitment of all personnel for the creating of its program" and "the direct supervision of the program directors and their assistants." Silverstein was responsible for the direction and organization of the evaluation and assessment process: "[Silverstein] will engage in the participant-observation process and develop a field journal describing the various characteristics of the youth subculture. He will be responsible for the construction of all evaluation techniques including the format of the depth interviews. He will conduct all depth interviews and will be responsible for their evaluation and analysis." Rosenberg was enjoined to assist the co-director in constructing evaluation techniques and "depth interviews" of the people attending project functions and to assist in analyzing and evaluating these interviews and other reports.

The official "Name or Title of Project" was "Creative Arts for Alienated Youth." As if to emphasize to the government that the money really was going to fund a sociological experiment designed to socialize deviant youth,[22] the name and address of the applicant agency on the grant form was the "Center for New York City Affairs, New School for Social Research, 70 Fifth Avenue, New York, 10011." The "Official Authorized to Sign Application for agency" was Dr. Robert M. MacIver, the chancellor for the New School for Social Research. In other words, the church was not listed as the primary administrative body—instead, the New School, populated by officially accredited professors, would oversee the project. This stress on the New School's role in the administration of the projects translated into higher salaries for Harry Silverstein and his New School associates. Silverstein received a full-time salary of $16,000, and the Reverend Michael Allen a "one-third-time" salary of $3,000. Since the grant proposal listed "three major components: (1) Theater Programs; (2) Film-making Program; and (3) Poetry and Writing Workshop," the three program directors were to receive $12,000 and the assistant program directors $5,720. Altogether, the church received $197,586. The grant was designed to last from July 1, 1966, to June 30, 1967. However, the grant was extended to two years, and the New School's role was eliminated in the second year because of administrative difficulties.[23]

Silverstein did in fact publish a report in 1971 that he submitted to the Office of Juvenile Delinquency and Youth Development, though by that time the Poetry Project had found other sources of funding to keep it alive. Silverstein put a spin on the projects by acknowledging that the "youths and artists," while doing whatever they wanted to, learned a great deal about art in the process thanks to the hands-off approach of the government funders:

> Many youths and artists feared the intrusion of government, university or church at those points where creative work extended into and encroached on social and political sensibilities. Despite the fearfulness of many participants about the potentialities of censorship, the program proceeded by establishing that the sole criteria of artistic restriction would be based on aesthetic objectives—a form of control that is intrinsic to art.[24]

This language and attitude certainly reflect the truth on the part of poets wary of government intrusion into the poetry scene. However, in the context of what the projects were "supposed" to be according to the original grant application, Silverstein's definition is somewhat debatable. Joel Sloman, the first assistant director of the Project, recognized this aspect of the grant early on:

> The Poetry Project is a "project" because it began as a project supported by the Department of Health, Education, and Welfare (Office of Juvenile Delinquency and Youth Development), directed, in part, by a couple of sociologists. Though we were theoretically trying to lure "alienated youth" back into the "mainstream culture," hardly any of the artists associated with the Project treated it as anything other than a pretext to support a money-poor artistic community. All of the people I can recall who participated in workshops and programs in poetry, theater, and film pretty much fell into the category of "aspiring artist," many of whom, today, would be in some sort of university program.[25]

The "Summary of Proposed Project" section of the grant inadvertently serves to emphasize Sloman's point. Here the proposal sold itself primarily on the possibility that the projects would inspire wholesome, legal behavior on the part of a constituency that was supposedly angry, drugged out, and threatening to social order—that is, the grant offered a method for drawing youth back into the mainstream: "The arts program is geared towards deflecting trouble-prone and deviant youth from potentially self and socially destructive activities while at the same time enabling them to develop their individual potentialities through creative expression." However, these "trouble-prone and deviant youth" were far more complicated and ambitious than the parameters of the grant suggested. Dozens of poets associated with the Project were actively writing and publishing, starting up new presses, and becoming increasingly involved in social activism. Additionally, these same poets found in St. Mark's a place where, as poet Bernadette Mayer recalls, poets simply "wanted to meet other people who were interested in poetry, and there were very few places you could go. Plus everybody at the church was incredibly cute back then."[26] Owing to the fact that people associated with the Poetry Project during the early years sponsored parties featuring free LSD punch, broadcast an illegal pirate radio station run by poet John Giorno, and basically used the church as an institutionalized gathering place, the social engineering envisaged by the government plan for the St. Mark's Projects did not work out as expected, nor did it correspond to the rather hopeful language Silverstein used in his follow-up report.

Admittedly, the first page of the grant proposal does not mention juvenile delinquents. In fact, it stresses the "bohemian" nature of the "East Village": "In part, by virtue of close proximity with Greenwich Village (bordering on the west) with its artistic and intellectual history dating back more than a century, a new community of artists has grown adding another special social characteristic indigenous to this area." However, Silverstein goes on in the second page somehow to characterize the predominantly white, mostly middle-class group of poets (part of the "subculture of the uncommitted") from all around the country as akin to "juvenile delinquents":

> This unique movement is comprised of individuals chronologically youthful, primarily those in the age span from fourteen through the early twenties, many of whom have taken permanent residence in the East Village. . . . Their participation in community life is little if any. They are loosely bound together by a subcultural mystique which bears to some extent the externals of intellectualism, humanitarianism and artistic creativity but whose form and substance are amorphous and unstructured. Eligibility and participation in this "subculture of the beat" as it is sometimes known, is in part through a linguistic system which often typifies subcultural groupings.

It is likely that poets including Ed Sanders, Carol Bergé, Paul Blackburn, Ron Padgett, and Ted Berrigan would have been slightly perturbed to be told that an official line claiming they had no prior "participation in community life" somehow made possible their very participation in Poetry Project activities. However, this fictional dissolution and lack of "participation" among the well-known and lesser-known poets, artists, and hippies of the Lower East Side were stratagems employed by the grant writer in his attempt to get the money. While Silverstein was not necessarily referring to the individual poets just mentioned, he nevertheless manipulated and recast notions typical of the Lower East Side poetic community—notions that "avant-garde" art was dangerous, strange, asocial, and somehow criminal—in order to characterize the community as "disaffected" despite the fact that the community in question did in fact have an intellectual (if socially libertarian) tradition.

The grant positioned the projects to help "disaffected" young poets and artists *and* actual Lower East Side kids, who were characterized as "youths indigenous to a poverty community." However, the Poetry Project did not reach out to the minority ethnic children who were natives of the Lower East Side. This is not meant as an attack on the poets working within the Poetry Project; indeed, a number of poets did reach out to the community and to the programs the church itself initiated despite the Poetry Project's disaffiliation from its purported mission.[27] For example, Anne Waldman recalls participating in the Young Lords Committee to Free Carlos Feliciano as well as working in the Black Panthers Soup Kitchen.[28] Nevertheless, the Poetry Project's main function at first appeared to be helping many predominantly young white poets find a foothold in New York's literary world, as poet and novelist Michael Stephens remembers:

> Every Monday night I went to the Open Reading at Saint Mark's run by Paul Blackburn, often reading new poems of my own. Wednesday evenings I attended the regular poetry reading. Other days I attended writing workshops at the Old Courthouse on Second Avenue and Second Street. Joel [Oppenheimer] was my main source of workshops. But I often attended classes given by his assistants Anne Waldman, Joel Sloman, and Sam Abrams, once or twice I went to workshops by Ted Berrigan, and even a playwriting workshop offered by Sam Shepard. . . . [The Poetry Project] certainly was the centerpiece of my week, not only the source of my creative energies, but also the locus of my grim, meager social world. I would not have been exposed to so many fine and different writers in so short a period of time. Also, I probably would have drunk myself to death or killed myself with drugs if I did not have these readings and workshops to attend nearly every day of the week. In that sense, maybe the pastor was right. The workshops did keep me from becoming a self-destructive brick-throwing, gun-toting, bomb-blasting maniac or, at least, it slowed down that process in my brain.[29]

While Stephens does point to the possibility of the projects serving as a kind of socializing anesthesia, we must recognize that the effects of such a program on writers like Stephens were more incidental than calculated. The poets organizing the reading series at Les Deux Mégots, Le Metro, and the Poetry Project were primarily concerned with promoting an alternative orally based poetics, as opposed to using poetry in the context of social engineering, public-school pedagogy, and community self-improvement. Silverstein—and the church administration as a whole—were willing to fudge the impetus for petitioning for the project funds. Of course, the fact that these funds initiated what is now a reading series that has existed for more than thirty years is in itself a cause for rejoicing. What is not cause for rejoicing are the perhaps somewhat cynical manipulations on the part of the grant writers to acquire the funds in the first place, manipulations that depended on the presence of silent though real impoverished youth in the Lower East Side so that the *true* constituency— the poets and artists of the neighborhood—could benefit.

Literary Politics and the Inception of the Poetry Project

In the grant application to the U.S. Department of Health, Education and Welfare, Silverstein wrote:

> Under the direction of a respected and accomplished poet and his assistant, the program will consist of poetry readings of accomplished poets, which represent clarified thought about the community and its goals, a weekly workshop with free readings, criticism and discussion, and more individualized attempts to make contact with youth who are inclined to find expression through the written and spoken word. The programs are concerned with effectively moving potentially trouble-prone youth whose interests may center around a lifestyle of drug use or other deviant activities, to a more creative and productive existence.

In a letter to Charles Olson announcing his decision to accept the job as director of the Poetry Project, Joel Oppenheimer wrote:

> dear charles: yo' boy has made it, it says in the papers. i've done that fatal thing and allowed myself to move out of the nice world of the print shop and into the cruel world of our art. i'm running a poetry project on gov't money (HEW) out of st marks in the bouwerie—sort of an extension of the reading programs there. there is also a small budget for putting out a poetry magazine 'of high quality'. so what i'm doing here i don't know—but i had to find out.[30]

And finally, in a letter to Denise Levertov expressing misgivings about working as assistant director of the Poetry Project, Joel Sloman wrote:

> Many artists will be against the program simply because of the gov't money, not to mention other doubts, and the artistic community will be split. I think that the only solution for the program is that it be overtly anti-government, anti-social, etc., not merely open-minded . . . People's minds are really chang-

ing now. The air has danger and excitement in it. People are beginning to think up elaborate excuses to do more radical, dangerous, exciting things.[31]

Because of their experience in a reading environment characterized by the excitement and anarchic spirit of Le Metro and Les Deux Mégots, it must have seemed odd to the poets of the Lower East Side to have their scene characterized in the language of establishment culture. Thanks in large part to the unpaid labor of Paul Blackburn and the Poetry Committee, poets in the community had finally found a relatively stable home at St. Mark's Church.[32] However, a scene that had been contained and under their control was unavoidably affected by a system that demanded hierarchies, rules, bureaucratic structures, and at least a semblance of accountability. Most significant, the grant mechanisms resulted in administrative decisions on the part of church authorities that left many poets associated with the earlier reading series rather upset, especially in terms of the politics of literary factionalism.

The decision to choose Joel Oppenheimer as the first director of the Poetry Project was a case in point. Oppenheimer was hired in the summer of 1966, while Paul Blackburn was at the Aspen Writers Conference in Colorado. In this excerpt from a letter to Blackburn, Oppenheimer breaks the news of his appointment as he anticipates objections to be raised from poets including Carol Bergé:

> the earth is shaking: the gov't came through with a three-prong grant to st marks for poetry theater and film, and i am running the poetry end. i don't need to tell you, but you may need to tell carol and her ilk, that i did not solicit the office, etc., etc., etc. on the other hand don't tell carol—let her think i am as much involved in politics as she is.

> what it looks like the grant means is: 1) expansion of the reading set-up, i.e., the open and selected readings going much as before, plus a beefed up prime-time reading series clearly competitive with the y and the gug;

> of course, i want and need you for help in this stuff, but more than that i need someone who can get to assholes like carol, and ask them if they want things like this to happen, or if they would rather blow the whole thing up to satisfy their own vanities.[33]

Paul Blackburn dealt with the appointment with characteristic grace and generosity. In a postcard to Oppenheimer, Blackburn wrote, "Dear Joel, heard the good news of yr Komisariat" and then asked Oppenheimer to send him a manuscript for potential publication: "Do you have an extra book or 2 up to 96 pp.? I've found a great Philippine publisher crazy enuf to want to do American poets for there and here and I want to make recommendations, discreetly etc. I have that 5 Spot tape of you and Sanders couple yrs back and am spreading yr fame into Far Ouest etc."[34]

By this time, however, members of the Poetry Committee who had administrated several readings at St. Mark's during the early part of 1966 discovered that someone outside their immediate circle had been chosen to direct the new project. Sara Blackburn (Paul Blackburn's wife at the time) retains a deep resentment over the co-optation of a poetry scene that resulted in decisions that seemed to have no bearing on Blackburn's real role in the creation of a poetic community:

> It became officialized, and Joel Oppenheimer was hired for money. I remember the incredible. . . . I couldn't believe it. I couldn't believe it. Joel was one of the people who always had expressed contempt toward the concept of open readings. It was a matter of tremendous grief to me. I remember I never talked about it with Paul, whose heart I think was really broken, but who nevertheless kept persisting, kept being part of the scene, kept being available, kept recording the readings. I wanted to kill everybody. Paul had created this incredible world, and suddenly someone else was being *hired* to preside over it, as if it were a new undertaking. I am usually someone who is very eager to reconcile differences, but in terms of the whole St. Mark's incident, I've always carried a big grudge on Paul's behalf. Paul never exhibited any anger about it, but probably had more to drink than usual.[35]

Poet Carol Bergé was also furious and wrote letters to a variety of people, including the Reverend Michael Allen demanding to know why Blackburn had been bypassed as director.[36] She sensed that decisions that historically had been made among a group of poets were now being made by a church hierarchy. In fact, the decision-making process of the poetry scene in the Lower East Side was radically altered owing to the grant attached to the projects at St. Mark's Church and the administrative mechanisms it entailed.[37] Now, beginning in the summer of 1966, an Episcopalian reverend and a sociologist from the New School would determine who would run the most vital and securely funded alternative poetry reading series in the Lower East Side.

Many poets associated with the Lower East Side to this day feel that the directorship should have initially been extended to Paul Blackburn. Anne Waldman, official director of the Poetry Project from 1968 to 1978, stated that "the job should have been offered to Paul—he should have been asked first."[38] George Economou, a close personal friend of Blackburn's, remembers:

> Paul Blackburn started the readings at St. Mark's before the official "project" opened. Paul was really the leader in that. There was kind of a committee that I and Bergé and others were on, but Paul really did all the work. He set up the

contacts, we helped with some things, but the thing that happened was when the St. Mark's readings became so successful, there was this idea to go for a federal grant. I remember the shock when it was announced that Joel Oppenheimer was going to be the director. Paul was deeply hurt, but he wouldn't say that he was. His then-wife Sara was furious. She thought Paul had really been screwed.[39]

Even Oppenheimer was relatively uneasy about being chosen director in place of Paul Blackburn. He theorized that the church's decision to hire him may have had more to do with its desire to move beyond the familiar social circles of the Deux Mégots and Le Metro inner circle than it did with his administrative ability: "I might not have been the right person for it, but if it had come out of the Poetry Committee it would have stayed very parochial. I was everybody's second choice: second best womanizer, second best lush."[40] Another possible reason for choosing Oppenheimer over Blackburn may have been something as simple as timing. In Bob Holman's "History of the Poetry Project," Jerome Rothenberg suggests that because the grant came about so suddenly in the middle of the summer, and because the deadline was looming, the church had to make a quick decision. With Blackburn and most members of the committee away for the summer, Reverend Allen contacted Oppenheimer, and the decision went through rather hurriedly.

Whether one or a combination of those reasons led to the decision, Oppenheimer was chosen to direct the Poetry Project despite Blackburn's active role as organizer of the Lower East Side reading scenes. This meant that the justification for the continued existence of the original Poetry Committee was going to be disputed, especially since Blackburn was a particularly active member of the committee. Ultimately, there was a quiet dispersal of the committee—people no longer wanted to be associated with it, particularly since poets on the committee itself were being invited to read at the church anyway. Beyond his role as a leading reading-series organizer, Blackburn's position as gatekeeper and collector of donations for the poets was no longer needed in this more professional environment. "The Committee would find itself a quasi-official advisory board to the new Poetry Project. George Economou would join it in the fall (of 1966), only to discover The Committee was 'pretty much a figurehead.' Ted Berrigan turned down an invitation because he felt those hired to run baby Project needed room to establish their own policies. . . . So the Committee just sort of faded away."[41]

Joel Oppenheimer's Year at the Poetry Project

Bergé was perhaps a bit hasty in condemning Oppenheimer and Sloman, at least when it came to what the Project (under Oppenheimer and later Anne

Waldman) could do for poetry and politics. "Although Joel was not one of the inner Metro family, he lived in the neighborhood and participated in its activities, including at least one of the group readings on April 7, 1964, at New York University, protesting the cabaret license laws."[42] As the first director of the Poetry Project, Oppenheimer certainly maintained an alternative, nonacademic environment for the poetry community of the Lower East Side and tended to suspect coterie divisions as arbitrary and counterproductive. In a letter to Charles Olson written in 1958 (as Donald Allen was editing *The New American Poetry*) Oppenheimer complained "the shit of it, sucking around don allen and the grove press, and i find, from him, i ain/t a new york poet, that/s o/hara and his boys. isn't that nice. i live here, work here, write here, and where will he get a label?"[43] Oppenheimer developed his critique of Allen's classifications (as a glance at the reading list for the first year of the Poetry Project shows) through his work as reading series organizer. While there would be no so-called academic poets reading at the Project during the first few years, the series was certainly inclusive of the whole alternative scene.

Additionally, in the various news articles covering the grant, the Poetry Project was described, in language typical of characterizations of the Lower East Side at the time, as generating a kind of antiestablishment dissident aura:

> At St. Mark's in the Bouwerie, the 167–year-old Episcopal church where Peter Stuyvesant lies buried, rebellious young artists from Manhattan's lower East Side are staging plays and reciting poems which might make staid elders blanch. . . .
>
> Before the federal funds were approved, [the Reverend Michael] Allen made it clear to the federal agency that some of the plays his group produced might be hard to swallow. There could be anti-Administration plays, or works that might be considered obscene.
>
> "But these kids are not going to accept dictation from us," he said. "We've either got to take them as they are, or let them drift away somewhere else. . . .
>
> Joel Oppenheimer, poet and playwright who heads the poetry division, was asked if he thought Peter Stuyvesant ever turned over in his grave because of the goings on upstairs.
>
> "Look," said Oppenheimer, "Stuyvesant was the grooviest cat of his day. If his ghost is doing anything, it's sitting up in the rafters, applauding."[44]

Dissident politics and alternative poetics were conflated in St. Mark's Church, and the church was thereby positioned as antiestablishment. Oppenheimer helped create this phenomenon, as one sees in a letter to Olson in which he emphasizes his vision of the Poetry Project as a real alternative to the established, aesthetically more conservative reading series located uptown: "i hope to have a live group of young 'uns cooking here, and the hope is we'll be able to set up a reading series that is in every way competitive with those at the y and the gug."[45] The language Oppenheimer uses here is the typical rhetoric of contrast—there are two kinds of poetry, that of the "established" places like the 92nd Street Y and the Guggenheim Museum, and that of the rougher, edgier places (the Poetry Project at St. Mark's was destined to become one of the latter).

Part of the funds granted to the Poetry Project was earmarked for poetry workshops. These workshops were free and took place at the Old Courthouse on Second Street near Second Avenue that also housed the Millennium Film Workshop. The first year of the workshops found Seymour Krim, Alan Kapelner, and Ishmael Reed teaching prose, Oppenheimer, Ted Berrigan, Sloman and Sam Abrams teaching poetry, and Sam Shepard and Murray Mednick teaching playwriting.[46] Oppenheimer positioned his classes as sites for collaboration and as forums where writers new to the neighborhood could meet their peers and possibly stake a claim as poets invited to read at the Poetry Project itself. One did not have to be a poet to participate in the workshops, a fact that (according to Oppenheimer) confused government officials who actually sat in on some of his workshops to chart the progress of the Project:

> We were worried about government involvement of course. They sat in on one of my workshops, and the next day we had lunch together. The guy next to me said, "I was terribly interested, Mr. Oppenheimer, because yours is the first out-screening program we've ever funded" and he went on like this for a long time, and finally I said to him, "I have to tell you, I don't know what out-screening is." What he meant was, I opened the workshop to anyone, and if they were bored or destructive to the rest of the group, they were gently invited out. . . . I [asked the government official] "Well how are other people doing it?" "All the other programs, you have to apply and show," he said. I said, "Well you know, it's a poetry-writing thing. Who's supposed to judge? And if you're coming in to see if you can write poetry, what do you show to show whether you can find out?" I think they were a little confused by that, and we were a little scared of them.[47]

Of Oppenheimer's workshop in the late fall of 1966, Joel Sloman (who also taught a workshop as part of the Poetry Project) remembers:

> Workshops were loose and democratic, poets reading their work and hearing comments about it from all or any of the participants, who were very miscellaneous. Two older participants I remember were Ruth Krauss, whose Steinian plays were being produced by the Judson Theater at the time, and Jean Boudin, whose husband was a lawyer who, I believe, represented Cuban interests in the States, and whose daughter, Kathy, became a notorious radical later on. There were also at least a couple of serious young seminarians—not

exactly the lost dropouts the Project was envisioned as serving. As a workshop instructor, Joel didn't talk about poetry from a theoretical point of view. He was interested in the nitty-gritty. I had a hard time articulating my point of view, in part because I was in transition as a poet and wasn't quite sure how to talk about the work I intuitively admired. Once, as a joke, Sam Abrams, who lived across the street from St. Mark's, put a notice in the *Village Voice* saying that my next workshop would discuss "Sex and Poetry in the Sixties." As a result, we got our largest turnout ever . . . it might say something about the mood of the times.[48]

In an undated cover letter Oppenheimer sent to Goddard College in Vermont about a potential position as a professor, Oppenheimer wrote, "The format of the workshops is best described as organic, by which I mean that the discussion stems directly from the students' work." However, this rather staid description belied what was really a more free-for-all environment where a rather machismo sexual politics and a sense of a poetic lineage were dispensed with equal energy. Former student Michael Stephens describes Oppenheimer's first workshop: "A workshop with Joel: here are some words frequently uttered by him: cock, cunt, fuck, shit, asshole, and, perhaps his all-time favorite image—as witness his *Women Poems*—tits. . . . The more cynical on Second Avenue called us 'the third generation Black Mountain poets.'"[49]

Oppenheimer was clearly an active participant in macho theatrics. Indeed, Waldman's growing influence at the Poetry Project would attract more women poets and bring a welcome infusion of feminist consciousness into the scene, counterbalancing Oppenheimer's tendencies to see life through a macho lens. With the sudden (and well-funded) influx of young poets into the workshops and the then-free readings at the Poetry Project, St. Mark's Church saw both a continuation and expansion of the Lower East Side poetic community as well as the emergence of a far more politicized constituency, one that tied politics to the growth of the avant-garde. Women poets were becoming more visible in a way that began to mitigate the overall macho tone set by many male poets and the earlier strangely minor presence of women poets in earlier publications (as opposed to actual readings) associated with the Lower East Side.

Responding to a question about his role at the Berkeley Poetry Conference, Ted Berrigan provided a picture of the prevailing attitudes toward women poets before the inception of the Poetry Project: "I had this totally competitive eye on Ed Sanders and John Sinclair, he used to come read at the Metro sometimes, and I knew him. I did not know who this Lenore Kandell was, but I figured since she was a girl she couldn't be too good. I mean at that time, it was that way, just to be straight about it. She was just a girl, she wasn't somebody specific. . . . I didn't know of any young and exciting women poets and I knew a few who were coming to the Metro but none of them were very exciting."[50] In contrast to this predominantly male scene, Anne Waldman writes of the Poetry Project, "Out of a total of forty authors in the Allen anthology, only four were women. I took this as a personal challenge. The new poetic community must invite women's writing. . . . Such collective energy resulted in a new downtown scene, an especially welcome facet of which was its inclusion of young women writers."[51] Future issues of the St. Mark's–based mimeographed magazine *The World* included a higher percentage of women writers in comparison to Dan Saxon's *Poets at Les Deux Mégots/Le Metro* series, including Waldman herself, Marilyn Hacker, Ruth Krauss, and others. Certainly by the early to mid-1970s the Poetry Project featured readings by a wide variety of innovative women poets, including Alice Notley, Bernadette Mayer, and Joanne Kyger. Finally, Bernadette Mayer's workshops at the Poetry Project held throughout the 1970s have achieved near-mythic status in the alternative poetry community. Mayer's widely published writing exercises, as well as the fact that such so-called language-school writers including Charles Bernstein, Hannah Weiner, and Nick Piombino were early participants in her workshops, had much to do with this phenomenon.

The early years of the Poetry Project helped transform the church into a kind of center for boisterous if peaceful partisan activity. According to an archived readings list kept at the Poetry Project, during 1967 and 1968 benefit readings were held for the National Organization for Women, the predominantly African American Sun Arts Festival, the Benefit for the Catonsville 9, and the "Recently Arrested Andrei Codrescu."[52] The Codrescu benefit repudiated the official line that the projects as a whole were designed to socialize troublesome youngsters. In a letter to Margaret Randall, Codrescu recalled, "The cops are fully stretched. I got busted on a phony charge of possession of grass, acid, guns and pipes. I got out after spending all my money and nerves."[53] The fact that the Poetry Project, using government money, assisted Codrescu in raising legal fees to fight these charges ("phony" or not) indicates that the Lower East Side poetic community would not reject their community allegiances to conform to an institutionalized set of expectations.

Considering the political and cultural transformations taking place on the Lower East Side as a whole, it is no coincidence that during its first two years the Poetry Project would become known as an arena of real political dissent. Independent of specific poetic communities, activists both within and outside the Lower East Side scene had already set up poetry as complementary to the antiwar movement. Flyers and related ephemera found within various archives testify to the historical phenomenon that linked poems, music, and a by-now dated hippie rhetoric in an effort to establish a sense of a unified movement. One typical flier advertised an antiwar demonstration on December 23, 1967, to benefit the "Veterans and Reservists to End the War in Vietnam" march, which began at Washington Square Park and wended its way up to Times Square. The flier billed the event as a "Peace Illumination Walk" and contained phrases framing various psychedelic prints including "Wear yr firs—Giant Monotonic Hum," "Joy—Celebration—Joy," "Magic Love Environment," and so on (note the contraction "yr," a typically Poundian device widely used in the Lower East Side poetic community). The same flier pointed out that entertainment would include "the Fugs, Gilbert Sorrentino, Jackson Mac Low, Denise Levertov, Allen Ginsberg, Joel Oppenheimer, and the Hare Krishna Chanters." Clayton Eshleman recalls that by the late 1960s alternative poetry was so tied to the antiwar movement that the nascent Poetry in the Schools organization run by Betty Kray (who organized readings at the 92nd Street Y) instituted a rule that "there was to be no discussion of the war in the classrooms, and no 'war poetry.'"[54] Apparently, Kray feared that poets would contaminate the minds of young students with antigovernment propaganda disguised as prosody.

Other events that combined 1960s radicalism with alternative poetry included the Three Penny Poetry Reading that Clayton Eshleman coorganized at the Fillmore East around the same period. Andrei Voznesensky was reading at the "uptown" 92nd Street Y, so Eshleman and other poets asked him to read downtown at the Fillmore East to call attention to the Lower East Side poetic community and, more important, to provide a unified voice against the Vietnam War. Admission was three cents (allusive of Brecht's Three Penny Opera), and two to three thousand people attended. Eshleman remembers:

About 20 Americans read with Voznesensky; I was the master of ceremonies, wearing a white raw silk suit! At the beginning of the reading, the poet Piero Heliczer came up to me and said: I want to read. I told him . . . there was no way to include people not on the program. This pissed him off and he retreated backstage and proceeded to get drunk during the long, long reading. Jackson Mac Low was the last reader. He was standing on the stage holding up a filthy, tattered American flag he had found in the gutter that day, proclaiming, when Heliczer rushed out with a bucket and tossed its contents into, he intended, the audience. However, most of it—water and piss—went into the faces and cameras of the Shirley Clarke camera crew, in the orchestra pit, filming the reading.[55]

To augment these one-time events, Eshleman, David Antin, and others would also rent flatbed trucks and megaphones and drive to areas including suburban Queens, the entrance to the Metropolitan Museum, and the upper-class shopping district along Fifth Avenue in Manhattan to demonstrate against the war. Eshleman recalls, "We had huge blowups of horribly wounded Vietnamese children, and we read poems, and passed along war information; also handing out stapled leaflets with poems and statements. People tried to crawl up on the flatbed and beat us up, or pull us off etc."[56]

Clearly, the antiwar movement and related culturally leftist phenomena did not lack for models linking poetry to dissent. The Poetry Project in particular, thanks to its institutional stability, became a center for politically radical events tied specifically to the oral presentation of poetry. This was due in large part to the poets that read at the Project and the younger crowd (many of them strangers to the earlier reading series) who were drawn to the Project's promise of free poetry, free parties, and a sense of community. However, Oppenheimer and Sloman were also responsible for encouraging the conception of the Project as a radical space. Both director and assistant director recognized the sticky position they were in as political leftists and radicals receiving their livelihood from a government program aimed at pacifying juvenile delinquents, and they proved determined not to let the grant taint their convictions. From the very beginning, Oppenheimer stated his unease with the source of the Poetry Project funds. On June 22, 1967, near the end of his career at the Poetry Project, Oppenheimer participated in a panel discussion in Warrenton, Virginia, on "The Arts in an Age of Affluence." At this panel, the economist John Kenneth Galbraith insisted that, "Artists have always functioned best under the most lavish handouts of the state." Oppenheimer, on the other hand, "questioned whether the Government, foundations or business would be willing to take risks in the arts for the sake of the arts rather than for sociological or other purposes."[57] The "sociological" government role as it pertained to the Poetry Project was somewhat troublesome to Oppenheimer.

Oppenheimer and Sloman: Significant Models for Alienated Youth?

According to the language of the grant, the directors of the projects at St. Mark's Church were supposed to "represent significant role-models for alienated youth. The assistant program directors will be youth who are still members of the 'uncommitted' group but who have also begun their own creative work. They represent a strategic bridge through which the program will be able to reach out to alienated youth of the community." At least when it came to the relationship between Sloman and Oppenheimer, the notion that Oppenheimer was a "significant role model for alienated youth" was in some ways true, particularly when it came to Oppenheimer's growing commitment to the anti–Vietnam War movement. Months before the Poetry Project began, and before Oppenheimer was to be hired as director, his "active opposition to the Vietnam War gained national attention on 21 February 1966, when he appeared in front-page articles in the *New York Times* and other newspapers. A police officer had tried to sing 'God Bless America' at a 'Read-in For Peace' anti-war rally, and 'Joel Oppenheimer, a poet with tangled, shoulder-length hair' told the policeman, 'Get off. . . . What do you think we're here for. We've been hearing that song too long,' while the crowd shouted its opposition to the policeman."[58]

Joel Sloman was already heavily involved in the antiwar movement himself—in fact, he would leave the Poetry Project in the fall of 1967, first to go to Cambridge, Massachusetts, and later to Cuba.[59] However, the contact that led Sloman to Oppenheimer and then to the Poetry Project was typical in terms of the social circles of the Lower East Side poetic community. Sloman, having won the 92nd Street Y's "Discovery" Award, was invited to give a reading at the Y on April 16, 1966. Paul Blackburn introduced the reading, and Sloman was fortunate to have Ted Wilentz—the owner of the Eighth Street Bookshop and friend and publisher to poets including Amiri Baraka and Ted Berrigan—in the audience. Sloman remembers, "At that time, I had begun to get involved in anti-war politics and was writing some more-or-less political poetry. Wilentz liked the politics in my poetry and mentioned me to Joel Oppenheimer, when Joel was asking people to suggest young poets as possible assistant directors at St. Mark's."[60] Partially by virtue of Sloman's relatively radical politics, he was hired as first assistant director to the Poetry Project.[61] While Sloman was not a familiar presence in the Lower East Side poetic community, he was not a stranger to it either. His ties to that community, as tenuous as they may have appeared to some, initially placed him in the same kind of position Anne Waldman, Lewis Warsh, and other younger poets were in—as part of a new generation of writers associated with the Lower East Side.

Sloman had a Brooklyn working-class background. His father was a cutter in the New York fashion industry and his mother a secretary for various Manhattan businesses. Sloman attended City College of New York, where he was active in the college literary magazine, *Promethean*. While Sloman was at CCNY, he became acquainted with Lewis Warsh, whose poems he published in the magazine. By 1963, Sloman remembers being, if not an active participant, then an enthusiastic onlooker of the downtown scene. Sloman flunked out of college by the winter of 1963, moved to Avenue B on the Lower East Side, and got a job as a typist for the Linguaphone company, which had offices in Rockefeller Center. He met Denise Levertov at a poetry reading at CCNY in March 1963. "I traveled part of the way downtown with her on the subway, where I showed her poems of mine that were in *Promethean*. Then I wrote her an adolescent letter and enclosed some more recent poems. She wrote back to tell me that the letter was ordinary, but she liked the poems."[62] Just as Levertov promoted the earlier Deux Mégots scene, she would prove to be an important and influential supporter for Sloman—she published him in the *Nation,* and persuaded Norton to publish his first book, *Virgil's Machines,* in 1966. The Norton publication was Sloman's "official" ticket to the position of assistant director, since part of the grant parameters demanded that the assistant to the director had to have a professional publication to his or her credit that would help in promoting the assistant as a true role model.[63]

Sloman was offered the position of assistant director of the Poetry Project just after he quit his job at Linguaphone. However, he had serious reservations about accepting it. In a letter to Levertov, he wrote, "My life has been ridiculous, now it's becoming interesting, and there are some real disgusting turns of events. About three weeks ago, I got a call from Joel Oppenheimer, offering me this job which three other guys also were asked about, relating to a government grant that found its way to St. Marks Church through the New School, for a Poetry-Theater-Movie program." After describing the basic idea behind the grant, what Sloman called "the premise of the program," he suggests that, "The complications are really political . . . this program might be just tainted enough by the sociological 'evaluation of the youth population' in the area to destroy it on a purely political level."[64]

Sloman's letter to Levertov was, in hindsight, prophecy. By late February 1967, those "complications" associated with accepting government money in the midst of a highly unpopular war would take on a very real political meaning, particularly for Oppenheimer. Ken Jacobs, the director of the Millennium Film Workshop, which was to film what the Poetry Project was to poetry, was fired by the Reverend Michael Allen and Harry Silverstein for overspending his budget. Allen appeared determined to make the projects accountable to the government funding sources and felt that Jacobs and his staff had no intention of following any guidelines. Allen insisted, "When the filmmakers set up their project, we didn't realize that what they were saying was 'We're going to rip off the government & you too.'"[65] While it is difficult to determine whether Jacobs did in fact act in bad conscience in regards to how the government funds were used, he certainly promoted an attitude of disrespect and dissent in terms of the Millennium Film Workshop's relationship to the grant sources. In the first issue of the *East Village Other,* Jacobs placed an ad that read "Turds on American dollars. Only true passion gives you access to the facilities at the Millennium Workshop. See Ken J. or Stan K."[66]

On March 1, 1967, the Reverend Michael Allen, Joel Oppenheimer, and Ralph Cook (director of Theater Genesis, the theater project) held a meeting at the headquarters of the Millennium Workshop at Second Avenue and Second Street to defend the decision to discharge Jacobs. Their stated reasons, especially within the context of the purported mission of the grant, was met by derision on the part of the alternative press and those Lower East Side residents who had by that time aligned themselves with Jacobs. It is clear from reading periodicals at that time, including the *East Village Other,* the *Village Voice,* and even the *New York Times,* that many people associated with the "alternative" scene in the Lower East Side were fully aware of the language and purported purpose behind the government grants to St. Mark's Church. These residents of the Lower East Side were determined to express their view that anyone conforming to the stipulations of a government grant was automatically politically suspect. A lengthy *Village Voice* article (here excerpted) used language that seemed lifted directly from the grant—phrases like "uncommitted," "subculture of the beat," and "disengaged" are consistently employed to provide an ironic contrast to a negative portrayal of Oppenheimer and Allen:

> A confrontation between members of the "subculture of the beat," alienated from a Federal project called "Creative Arts for Alienated Youth," and a pillar of the Episcopal Church occurred last Thursday night in the project's headquarters—a former night court—at Second Avenue and 2nd Street.
>
> A hundred hippies and East Village others filed into a large white room marked "Social Court." The bag was to ask the hip Reverend Michael Allen . . . why he fired Ken Jacobs, director of its film workshop.
>
> For six hours, the baby-faced reverend turned one pink cheek and then another—and estranged the alienated. In this he was ably assisted by program directors Joel Oppenheimer and Ralph Cook.
>
> Oppenheimer, a dead ringer for Leon Trotsky, criticized Jacobs because he would not play Washington's game. "It's a peculiar way for a peacenik poet to talk," said one of the disengaged. "Do you suppose he's with the CIA?"
>
> "We applied for a particular grant under a particular program," Oppenheimer said. "We acceded to that. Despite the fact that we are dealing with a pretty dirty organization—the U.S. Government—there are ways to play this game. Ken had his own ideas . . . "
>
> Interviewed at the church, Reverend Michael Allen was unwilling to clarify his reasons for firing Ken Jacobs, but he was anxious to dispel rumors, circulated by the alienated, that his project salary is $30,000. The reverend's take is $3,250 of Federal funds—a modest sum compared to the $26,300 skimmed off by the New School for administration and the $120,650 eaten up by staff salaries. The total amount of the grant is $188,543—and it seems to have alienated all sides.[67]

Instead of characterizing the grant monies as a happy if slightly absurd miracle for the poets and artists of the Lower East Side, the *Voice* writer and the people she describes clearly look on the funds with a certain amount of contempt. Oppenheimer in particular is demonized, simply because he acknowledges that accepting the grant forces people working within the projects to behave in certain ways. This meeting reflected the mood at the time on the Lower East Side—anything to do with the government is suspect, and anyone who works against the government is good, especially if he or she takes advantage of government largesse. In the article Oppenheimer appeared to be playing up to this belief somewhat, by describing the U.S. government as a "dirty organization." However, his attempts to align himself with the crowd's dissenting spirit got him nowhere. Using Oppenheimer's status as poet against him, the "disaffiliated" accused him of complicity in a government conspiracy against Ken Jacobs. Significantly, poetry was treated by this audience as something that ideally should be in a dissident position to dominant culture, as indicated by the phrase "that's a peculiar way for a peacenik poet to talk." On the Lower East Side, poets were supposed to cause trouble, not stand in solidarity with church and government representatives opposed to a countercultural martyr like Ken Jacobs.

Using an argument that would currently (and ironically) be welcomed by any conservative opponent of the National Endowment for the Arts, an article on the Jacobs debacle from the *East Village Other* insisted that government had no role in organizing arts programs, as it implicated Oppenheimer as a government stooge: "It's about time the Government realized that artists workshops and projects should be run by artists. Politicians manipulate people . . . artists manipulate things. Artists workshops should therefore be autonomous and democratic. And by democratic I don't mean the ego driven paternalism of appointed representation but the cooperative activity that comes through delegated administration."[68] Clearly, the author of this article is referring to Oppenheimer through the phrase "appointed representation," since he was in fact appointed by Michael Allen, who accepted government funds to run the projects. The article then continued by denigrating Allen: "If the Rev. Michael Allen as administrator of the project, could not, as he says, communicate with Ken Jacobs over the subject of the purchasing of equipment for the Workshop, it must be because he lacks the technical competence that is vital for the administration for this kind of project." The mood at the time, at least according to the two major alternative newspapers, favored artists over all—whatever Jacobs said is assumed correct, whatever the government (and government appointees) said is defined as suspicious and ignorant. "If [the students at the Millennium Film Workshop] had any doubts about their relationship with the system before the firing of Ken Jacobs, their Director, their doubts have now been doubly reinforced."[69]

The Jacobs incident was used to provoke an overall critique of both the

Millennium Film Workshop and the Poetry Project. Owing to the popular readings taking place in St. Mark's Church, the Poetry Project served as a forum for people unhappy with the way things were being handled. On the night of a reading by Denise Levertov on March 9, 1967, leaflets were handed out containing a list of highly charged questions including inquiries into staff and director salaries, fees for guest teachers and lecturers, whether stipulations of the grants had been reached, and reported personality conflicts between the Reverend Allen and Ken Jacobs. While the language of the leaflet maintained a respectful attitude toward the poetry reading itself—"THIS IS NOT A PICKETING OR BOYCOTTING OF TONIGHT'S READING. THIS IS A DISSEMINATION OF INFORMATION ABOUT THE PROJECTS AT ST. MARKS CHURCH. PLEASE ATTEND THE READING HERE TONIGHT"—it asked for "a public investigation at this time to determine whether there has been mismanagement of this federally sponsored Arts Project, while a further grant is considered."

However, the Jacobs incident ended with Jacobs's dismissal intact. Jacobs left the Millennium Film Project and revitalized it under independent auspices a year later. Oppenheimer's reputation after this was somewhat tarnished, but his relationship with his young assistant Joel Sloman—who was active in antiwar politics—in many ways helped him recuperate some of his prestige as a "peacenik poet." Oppenheimer remembers of Sloman: "He made me pay more attention to the outside. He convinced me that you could bitch about the Vietnam War in a poem."[70] Sloman recalls that about a month after the Jacobs fiasco, at a major demonstration in Central Park in the spring of 1967, he was in charge of a flatbed truck that had an enormous painting by James Rosenquist as its backdrop, the subject of which was a woman's hand sprinkling salt on a soldier's military medals. Many poets (including Oppenheimer) who were associated with the Poetry Project were either assisting, performing, or in attendance at the demonstration. While Sloman's truck got stuck in a ditch in Central Park, poets managed to read their work from there and from a nearby truck. This event marked one of the few times that Oppenheimer read his poems in a political context—as the recently appointed director of the Poetry Project, it is significant that he became more overtly politically active *after* receiving a relatively high-profile, government-funded position. Sloman remembers that Oppenheimer "was very shy about making political statements, though we all felt he was on the right side. Simply put, many people felt that by taking advantage of government money they had to do something to prove to themselves that they weren't being bought."[71] Oppenheimer, an employee of a federal government he distrusted, was himself distrusted because of his behavior during the Jacobs incident. His actions afterward tended to emphasize his political radicalism more emphatically than ever before.

The Genre of Silence

What, then, according to the grant, was *supposed* to be published out of the Project, and what in fact did get published? Given the political complications surrounding the acquisition of the grant and the dismissal of Ken Jacobs, the story of *The Genre of Silence,* the first publication associated with the Poetry Project, is tied as much to the partisan leanings of Oppenheimer as it is to the production of "quality literature."[72] In terms of the "Poetry and Writing Program," the grant guidelines stated that there was supposed to be a "Publication of Journal 3 times yearly @ $2725 each publication—$8175. Each journal is estimated as 6 × 9 inches in size containing 96 pages. Each Journal will be composed of approximately ¼ poetry, ¼ art and ½ essay." This is not what happened.

What did happen was that Oppenheimer made sure to produce something the grant guidelines clearly did not have in mind. The introduction to the magazine (excerpted here) served to make fun of the government functionaries who expected poets to act in conformity with specified guidelines:

> Some thirty years ago, Isaac Babel in addressing a congress of fellow writers said that since he could not write the way they wanted him to, he was now the master of "the genre of silence." It seemed to the editor of this magazine that the title, THE GENRE OF SILENCE, would therefore be appropriate for a journal financed by a government grant.
>
> The title became more pertinent when we in the Poetry Project at St. Mark's Church In-the-Bowery began to realize that no real purpose would be served by a glossy little magazine and that, in fact, we would serve ourselves and our hoped-for public much better by concentrating on a mimeographed magazine already in publication called THE WORLD.
>
> This then will be the first and last issue of THE GENRE OF SILENCE. The editor hopes that it is indeed to some extent a presentation of things they don't want us to write and also a measure of where good writing is today. It is not easy to produce a magazine in these circumstances i.e. when you are not sure why the money is being given at all. The tendency is to cop out to either side. One falls back then on the old and valid concept of the poet as gadfly and lets him bite where he will.[73]

To underscore Oppenheimer's independence from the grant guideline's requirements for the magazine's content, practically the entire journal was made up of poetry. There was no essay. While there was photography (thus fulfilling the "art" criterion), most of it documented Angry Arts Week, a citywide anti–Vietnam War event in which artists, poets, and dancers performed in opposition to government policy.[74] Joel Sloman's text was the first poem included in the magazine, and it served to underscore Oppenheimer's irreverent attitude toward the government funders. Entitled "Suggested Titles for St. Mark's Literary Journal," Sloman's list poem contains potential titles for a theoretical unnamed literary magazine. Sloman's text was probably read by those in the Lower East Side poetic community as referring specifically to the context of *The Genre of Silence* and the strange environment the Poetry Project found itself in as a beneficiary of government largesse in the midst of an unpopular war. Almost every title in Sloman's poem is a badly disguised mockery of the government funders. "Suggested Titles" include the lines "Rub It In," "Your Taxes Magazine," "Avant-garde Slice of the Pie," "Love Thy Kill Ratio," "American Grant," "Corporate Profits," "Napalm is Jellied Gasoline," "Vietnam Butter," "Slaughter," "Genocide Magazine," "The American American American," "Dropout," and "Sex (Any)."[75] Oppenheimer himself published an uncharacteristically political poem that was a (somewhat painfully) obvious critique of government policy in Vietnam. Called "Poem in Defense of Children," the text included lines like "it is not my business \ that another child burn so \ mine shall live. it is not \ your business. it is nobody's \ business. \\ or put it this way. \ that woman in black pajamas \ with babe at breast is evil and \ abominable, while my wife with \ my child's lips sucking at her \ is a holy thing."[76]

Emphasizing the poets' refusal to adapt their publications to governmental criteria, *The Genre of Silence* began and ended as a generally strong attack on government policy in Vietnam as well as a more personal and localized thumb-nose at the government's stated requirements for publications coming out of the Poetry Project. In the introduction to the photographic series on Angry Arts Week, Sam Abrams wrote a text that somewhat elliptically called for American artists to "revolt" against the machine of the Establishment: "The fact of anger, that finally only this is left, is at least, direct . . . the dreadful prediction has come to pass and, in particular photographs of children, mutilated melted beyond, far beyond the monster of bosch . . . the whole machine care less, even the pretence, the hypocrisy that enabled us day by day, not to believe, melted away, that we must, with our arts, even in revolt, technique in disgust, at what we, men, american, have, are, can, will."[77] The final images in *The Genre of Silence* were not poems—rather, they were pictures of poets, artists, and assorted other protesters holding up placards with photographs of napalmed babies emblazoned on them.

The Genre of Silence was in many ways a harbinger of Oppenheimer's increasing inability to fulfill the administrative requirements attendant to his job. Ron Padgett remembers that the "[*Genre of Silence*] is dated June, 1967, & I don't even know if that's when it actually appeared. There were some incredible hassles with its printing—vast amounts of money spent, and it appeared incredibly late."[78] Out of this bureaucratic inefficiency, Anne Waldman, who was originally hired by the project as a secretary, found herself taking on increasing amounts of administrative responsibility because of Oppenheimer's negligence. By April 1967, Sloman had already left for Cambridge, Massachusetts, and Waldman was named assistant director. By the end of that summer, Oppenheimer left, and Waldman became director—a position she would hold for the next ten years.[79] Lyman Gilmore writes that, "In August [of 1967], Joel Oppenheimer left St. Mark's; he simply drifted away from a job whose administrative duties, which had not been of interest to him from the beginning, had become even more demanding as the time approached for the government grant to be renewed. Also, his drinking and immersion in the social life of the Lion's Head had begun to take precedence over his project activities. Anne Waldman was in full command, as both Joel and she acknowledged."[80] In an even franker assessment of Oppenheimer's handling of the Poetry Project, Oppenheimer's student Michael Stephens wrote: "He was perhaps the least efficient of administrators. Besides the politics of it, some wondered how a man who had not drawn a sober breath in years was going to operate a poetry center with a several hundred thousand dollar budget."[81]

Waldman proved to be well suited to handling the Poetry Project, as her ten-year tenure and continuing involvement with the Poetry Project suggests. Most important, Waldman was able to reconcile her own creative output as a writer with the humility and "shmoozing" skills necessary in an arts administrator. In the dawning age of government funding for the arts, Waldman was to prove capable of getting money to keep the Poetry Project alive.

Anne Waldman, *The World*, and the Early Years at the Poetry Project

Although the meeting ground of the Lower East Side Group was Tulsa, Oklahoma, it currently centers itself around St. Mark's Church in the Bowery, and is united by regularly scheduled readings there, several more-or-less self-serving publications (of which *The World* is the most prominent), "Dial-a-Poem" and other frivolities, and most especially by a worship of the Gospel According to Frank O'Hara.

DAVID LEHMAN, THE WHOLE SCHOOL

The New York School in *The World*

Anne Waldman was in many ways a natural choice to inherit the director position at the Poetry Project. Born in 1945, brought up in Greenwich Village, and associated with St. Mark's Church since her early teens, Waldman was part of an intergenerational bohemian milieu that would inform the choices she made as arts director. Her mother, Frances LeFevre, had been involved with the Utopian Delphi Ideal community with her Greek father-in-law, Anghelos Sikelianos (the poet), and her American mother-in-law, choreographer Eval Palmer Sikelianou. Anne Waldman was also introduced to Buddhism in a Quaker high school and had received teachings from a Buddhist lama in 1963. Thus Waldman was introduced to a notion of a "sangha," or community, that was to resonate in her directorship of the Poetry Project.[1] Additionally, Waldman had already worked as editor of a poetry magazine during her student days at Bennington College, where she edited *Silo* magazine and where she became increasingly familiar with and attached to New York School–affiliated poetry. In the summer of 1965, Waldman attended the legendary Berkeley Poetry Festival, where she met poet Lewis Warsh (whom she would marry and with whom she would edit and publish *Angel Hair* magazine).

It is especially necessary to bear in mind Waldman's work as editor when looking at the first few years of the Poetry Project. Such a history, while taking *The Genre of Silence* into consideration as the first "official" publication coming out of St. Mark's, would be incomplete if it didn't include the early history of the (initially) mimeographed magazine *The World* and the social environment that surrounded its production. A history of this mimeo is also a history of Waldman's increasing influence on the reading series and a record of the growing influence that poets associated with the New York School had on the poetry read, written, and celebrated at the church. This is not to say that the St. Mark's Poetry Project *remains* a New York School bunker where no one else is allowed reading space, nor is it to say that *only* New York School "types" read during Waldman's tenure. Again, it must be emphasized that practically all the poets associated with the Lower East Side poetic community read fairly regularly throughout the first three years of the Poetry Project. The real difference here is that the New York School grew considerably in its influence on younger writers once the Poetry Project began.

In her introduction to *Out of This World,* Waldman wrote, "The New York School shaped the 'local environment' through literary and art magazines, readings, opening, and parties and provided, in a sense, the matrix for The Poetry Project."[2] A number of writers who have read at the Poetry Project over the past thirty years also conceive of the Poetry Project as a New York School phenomenon. While many poets included in the Poetry Project anthology *Out of This World* did not write any "contributors' notes," forty-four writers who did contribute notes emphasize Ted Berrigan and/or the New York Schools as shaping their conceptions of what the Poetry Project meant to them. Poet Dennis Cooper writes, "When I was first getting serious as a teenaged writer in Los Angeles, most of my favorite poets were involved with St. Mark's in one way or another: Ashbery, Schuyler, Elmslie, O'Hara . . . just to start. To me the 'New York School' was holy, and St. Mark's was literally its heart, its church."[3]

New York School aesthetics, defined by Waldman in her introduction as "subtle, witty, urban, visual,"[4] became so attractive to younger poets coming into the Lower East Side poetic community that writing practices associated with the New York School, including collaborative writing, appropriation, incorporation of visual images with text, and use of surrealist and dada disjunction turned up again and again in *The World*. There were also at least half a dozen other small presses operating and mimeos being published concurrently with *The World* that featured poets associated with the Poetry Project: Waldman and Warsh's *Angel Hair* (which was a beautifully printed letterpress publication, as opposed to a mimeo), Clayton Eshleman's *Caterpillar*, Aram Saroyan's *Lines,* Bernadette Mayer and Vito Hannibal Acconci's *o to 9,* Larry Fagin's *Adventures in Poetry* magazine and press, and others.[5] In many ways, these magazines were more professionally organized and run than the early issues of *The World;* another book could be written about the history of those publications and their aesthetic stances.[6] The main reason I have chosen to write here about *The World* is that it represented—through its institutional and editorial affiliations to the Poetry Project—the most direct link to St. Mark's and the scene that was developing there. *The World* also proved to be the longest lasting of the mimeograph publications. As of 2002, *The World* was in its thirty-sixth year.

Sloman edited the first issue of *The World* in the winter of 1966 to 1967, mailing mimeographed stencils to contributors and asking them to type up their own work. Any question about how the influence of the New York School became so overt with the newer writing of the younger poets is essentially answered by Sloman, who recalls, "*The World* was more of an expression of my will and values than anything else I did at the Project. This was true in rather straightforward, simple ways. I wanted the journal to be pretty much what it became, and what Anne was better able to accomplish. That is, in addition to naming it, I intended *The World* to be a successor to Ted Berrigan's and Ron Padgett's *C* magazine, whose format I copied."[7] *C* clearly promoted and extended the role of the New York School and essentially created a second generation of New York School poets based primarily on the figures of Berrigan, Padgett, Dick Gallup, and Joe Brainard.[8] This second generation was itself extended (both through publication in *C* and the inception of the Poetry Project and *The World*) to writers including Jim Brodey, Lewis Warsh, Joe Ceravolo, and Gerard Malanga, many of whom had taken classes with Kenneth Koch at the New School and at Columbia and who would prove to be regular readers at St. Mark's Church.[9]

The readings starting during the fall of 1966 and, up to Oppenheimer's departure in the summer of 1967, continued the Lower East Side poetic community tradition by featuring writers including Bérge, Blackburn, and Rothenberg. However, by late 1967, one could detect a real change in the correlation between who read at the Project and who got published through the Project in *The World*. Issues 1 to 3 included relatively little work from the poets associated with the Poetry Committee and the earlier Le Metro reading series, despite the fact that these poets read regularly at the Poetry Project throughout Oppenheimer's short tenure as director. This was a radical departure from earlier publishing practices, at least when compared to Don Katzman's *Poets at Les Deux Mégots* and *Poets at Le Metro* series. That is, where those earlier publications included basically everyone who read on a given night, *The World* showed much greater editorial influence in terms of whom was in and who was out of the magazine. The familiar faces associated with Le Metro that were in *The World* tended to be made up almost entirely of those in the New York School lineage—Berrigan, Brodey, Malanga, and so on. Additionally, because of the implementation of free writing workshops, many of the writers featured in the early issues of *The World* were students who had no previous contact with the Lower East Side poetic community.

Much of the change initiated by *The World* had to do with the new social circles being developed in the Lower East Side poetic community as well as basic changes within the Poetry Project administration. Starting in the summer of 1967, the Poetry Project was now essentially in Waldman's hands. Waldman, Lewis Warsh, and Oppenheimer edited *The World* volume 3, but after that issue Waldman and Warsh edited the magazine. Earlier Lower East Side poetic community writing practices were still evident in *The World*—for example, the first issue features a page with the poem "Zen You" by Joel Oppenheimer at the top with the poem "The Reject Paper" by Anne Waldman directly underneath it. This practice of placing poems on the page to reflect the social relationships between the poets has already been discussed, though the administrative joke in this case is new. That is, Anne Waldman, as secretary of the Poetry Project at that time, was purportedly under Oppenheimer on the bureaucratic scale. However, even in the first issue, the social world surrounding Waldman and Warsh's apartment at 33 St. Mark's Place and its relationship to the Poetry Project just two blocks away is articulated in a kind of insider's code, and tends to have a far greater presence in the magazine than any other interrelated systems of friendships and literary allegiances.

In *The World* volume 1, the collaborative practices of the New York School, made somewhat famous on an underground scale in the special collaborative issue of *Locus Solus,* were extended in a poem entitled "I Wrote the Word *Love* and You Wrote the Word *Why?*"[10] The text is attributed to Gerard Malanga, Lewis Warsh, and Anne Waldman, so no individual line can be positively attributed to any one poet. It is possible, however, that anyone familiar with this social world may have been able to make educated guesses. For example, the line "and the angel hair in the dream is a dream" was likely written by Waldman, since her high school friend Jonathan Cott had written a poem containing the line "Angel Hair sleeps with a boy in his head." Waldman credits this line with inspiring her and Warsh to name their magazine *Angel Hair.* Another line from the poem, "'Today not much happened' is written in the diary notebook," may have been written by Warsh; his journal entries, written in a characteristically flat, reportage-like tone, were well known among his friends and were published in books including his *Part of My History.* Finally, the line "This is the line 'Benedetta repeats the landscape'" possibly originated from Malanga. Malanga had written a series of poems dedicated to Benedetta Barzini, a woman with whom he was in love at the time. The first edition of the Benedetta poems—*3 Poems for Benedetta Barzini*—was published by Warsh and Waldman's Angel Hair Press.

It is significant, however, that these guesses are by no means definitive. Collaboration in *The World* often led to a sense of authorship approximating anonymity—no one could *really* be sure of who wrote what line. Anne Waldman has said, "There was a wonderful sense of anonymity in the early years of publishing *The World,* which is why I'm so drawn to Balinese culture, where they do not have a word for art, and where you go to performances and you don't have programs, you don't see everybody's bio; it's much more integrated."[11] Ownership of words was no longer the provenance of an individual author. Instead, language was a shared material produced and administered by a community of writers. Collaborations could be literal collaborations, with a group of poets sitting in the same room and writing a book or poem together. They could also take the form of intertextual collage, with a poem incorporating, alluding to, and depending on other literary texts as source material.

In an environment where Ted Berrigan was a major influence on many younger writers, the number of collagist texts serves as partial evidence of Berrigan's influence on the scene at the Poetry Project. This influence had dada as its inheritance,[12] along with the accompanying sense that dada art could be fun, nonsensical, irrational, and social—a perfect set of values for the relatively anarchic scene typical of the early years of the Poetry Project.[13] Dada had formerly achieved narrative disjunction and surprise by collaging words and images. "Collage encouraged the notion that words and other foreign elements in the visual arts represented a transformation of traditional art practices. The very use of collage obscured the primacy of meaning behind these fragments of language. What was celebrated by the critics was the innovation of adding disparate elements to a created object, producing a composite in this fusion."[14] Dadaist collage was broadened by the writing practices of the Second-Generation New York School, in that collaging prepublished text into other text through direct quotation or heavy-handed allusion (as opposed to collaging text into a visual image) tended to blur even further the question of what words were supposed to do and who they belonged to. That is, a word collaged into a picture could at least be discussed within the context of visual representation and aesthetics. Collaging "original" text into another purportedly "original" text disrupts even this tenuous painterly convention, since a collaged text does not provide one with the luxury of imagining a word as an aesthetic object against or correlating to a visual field. Rather, the words in a collaged text of an individual author are displaced so much that no one author really owns any particular line. While collaborative and collagist texts in *The World* may not have obscured the primacy of *meaning* behind fragments as much as the dada and surrealist word/images, they certainly obscured the primacy of authorship. As Larry Fagin puts it, "There was less concern for product than there was for process. It was the sheer joy of the activity. Thumbing your nose at formality. With collaboration, if it's between two writers, the result is something that neither person would have (or could have) written on his/her own. Sometimes it was just trading lines, but you'd still wind up with a third voice. A third sound."[15]

A kind of metaphorical collaboration was attainable through intertextual references. One sees this kind of conflation of collage and collaboration in *The World* in a text by Jim Brodey entitled "A Poem & Prose." At once picking up on the chattiness of his mentor and lover Frank O'Hara and his friend Ted Berrigan, along with the diaristic approach of Lewis Warsh, Brodey uses this piece to record one day on the Lower East Side.[16] Frank O'Hara, who died in the summer of 1966, is at first rather obliquely referred to both through the "I do this, I do that" style of writing and through the presence of a pack of Gauloises cigarettes—a familiar icon in O'Hara's poem "The Day Lady Died." This reference served to indicate Brodey's knowledge of the texts necessary to establish his position in what was quickly becoming a Second-Generation New York School.[17]

In "The Day Lady Died," O'Hara writes that he asks "for a carton of Gauloises and a carton / of Picayunes, and a NEW YORK POST with her face on it," with "her" referring to Billie Holiday.[18] In his poem Brodey writes: "Open a new fresh pack of cigarettes from the icebox (Gauloises) and lay back on bed and pretend to read (actually scan through) The Nature of the Universe by Fred Hoyle and read that 'Immortality is nothing but information' and sigh."[19] Brodey's O'Hara-esque mode is continued through a breezy introduction of the speaker's friends, one of whom—Ted Berrigan—was already long associated with O'Hara: "Call up Ted and Sandy says he's on his way home and think about taking that bath, but Sandy says that will take too long, so I forget it all." Then, the O'Hara-esque reading of this text gets complicated through the inclusion of a typically Beat commodity, as Jack Kerouac suddenly pokes his head into the easygoing piece: "I go to backroom and make immediate choice of a pair of pants to wear, I choose 'The Book of Dreams' Kerouac Special Airo-Spacer and go downstairs and over through streets again which are not much like dreams to Ted's on Second Street."

In the context of Berrigan's role as someone who combined a kind of rhapsodic, street-oriented Beat identity with a New York School world of casual, humorous sophistication, Brodey's reference to Kerouac in the midst of a typical "I do this / I do that" narrative serves to reemphasize Berrigan's role as a "Beat/New York School" figure.[20] That is, bringing up Berrigan, only then to bring up Kerouac, establishes the lineage between those two writers, and it does so in a style typical of Berrigan's *other* major influence—O'Hara and the New York School. This is especially appropriate when considering that O'Hara himself augured the connections between New York School urbanity and the somewhat wilder, more romantically tinged Beat aesthetic. O'Hara had, from the mid 1950s, supported the work of poets including Gregory Corso and John Wieners, and Allen Ginsberg has said of O'Hara, "I was amazed he was so open and wasn't just caught in a narrow New York Manhattan Museum of Modern Art artworld cocktail ballet scene."[21] Berrigan and writers like Brodey developed the possibility for combining the "Beat" ethos with the "artworld cocktail ballet scene," as Berrigan recognized: "They were all sophisticated sons-of-bitches, all these [New York School] Harvard-educated poets who knew very well very talented painters and we were a little bit more barbarian and yet we had the advantage of having seen things that their sophistication had produced."[22]

Most of the middle section of Brodey's prose poem centers on the Berrigan family, though Ted himself is absent. In Berrigan's absence, Brodey goes out "thinking up marvelous Poesy . . . I think of myself as sidekick gunslinger-type goofy poetbuddy of their bearded oldman." This line of inflated rhetoric is typical of Kerouac, down to the appropriation of western icons and the benzedrine-allusive language of "goofy poetbuddy."[23] Finally, near the end of the poem, Brodey combines both the figures of O'Hara and Kerouac in the lines "I go down Avenue B & figure on going over to see X, the secret king of the International Pothead's Conspiracy, but I don't I run into Harry who yells and we go to eat. And we eat and we eat. And we talk of things still to be done before we are famous and have to smile and even probably grunt a lot to keep America on its toes."[24] The Kerouac influence rests on the image of "Harry" and the speaker eating and speaking. A banal act is transformed into extravagant legend through the assumed (if self-consciously exaggerated) power of the speaker's ability to "keep America on its toes." Lines and images like these are found throughout Kerouac's work, particularly in *On the Road,* in which a simple road trip offers the speaker "girls, visions, everything; somewhere along the line the pearl would be handed to me."[25] Yet O'Hara's influence on Brodey, as it would in the work of Berrigan, helps temper such theatrics. Where O'Hara writes, "I get a little Verlaine / for Patsy with drawings by Bonnard although I do / think of Hesiod, trans. Richmond Lattimore or / Brendan Behan's new play or *Le Balcon* or *Les Nègres* / of Genet, but I don't, I stick with Verlaine," Brodey writes, "but I don't I run into Harry who yells and we go to eat," perhaps to imbue O'Hara-style casualness into what could turn into an embarrassingly faux-rhapsodic Beat text.[26]

Texts like Brodey's were typical in the context of Lower East Side alternative publishing practices. In many mimeos social lives were alluded to so often that texts in the mimeos served (perhaps unintentionally or unconsciously) as a way for the reader to gauge how deeply connected he or she was to the scene being referred to. By the time *The World* 3 came out, the social world centered on Warsh and Waldman's apartment at 33 St. Mark's Place had taken over at least the publishing end of St. Mark's Poetry Project. Paul Blackburn was only occasionally published in the early issues of *The World* (and figures like Bergé, Sherman, and other lesser-known writers associated with Les Deux Mégots and Le Metro were not published at all). While Blackburn was the first poet to read under the auspices of the Poetry Project in September 1966, he read only occasionally at St. Mark's until his death in 1971.[27]

There is something sorrowful about Blackburn's gradual movement away from the poetry limelight on the Lower East Side. Blackburn was certainly a pivotal figure standing between the national New American Poetry and the Lower East Side scene. Nevertheless, despite Blackburn's work developing an inclusive reading community, the Second-Generation New York School was clearly in the ascendant. Lewis Warsh remembers Blackburn's status among this younger crowd:

> The Poetry Project, by its second year, became a center for New York School poetry. Les Deux Mégots and Le Metro were different. That was a different mesh—like Black Mountain coming out of a street scene. Creeley wasn't around, but his work dominated, along with Oppenheimer's and Blackburn's. The Poetry Project was interested in expanding the frame. And with it the social coordinates changed as well. I remember Paul coming to one of the early parties at 33 St. Mark's and looking around bewildered, a bit lonely and vulnerable. The crowd was very different from the Metro or Deux Mégots and it had all happened very quickly. Blackburn was a hero of mine and I felt bad—so we ended up talking a bit that night. No doubt he should have been the Poetry Project's first director—at least logically that made sense—but sometimes the thing that doesn't make sense is the right way to go.[28]

Blackburn—the man perhaps most responsible for developing a vibrant poetic community on the Lower East Side and possibly the last writer who could be situated within the high modernist tradition—physically gave way to the New York School–dominated era of the Poetry Project. As the texts typical of the earlier, Black Mountain–centered Lower East Side poetic community slowly vanished from *The World,* so too did the very presence of those poets diminish, owing to the younger writers who were quickly supplanting them both in publications and in downtown social life. At the memorial reading for Paul Blackburn on October 13, 1971, no one associated with the New York School is listed as having read in Blackburn's honor, though Anne Waldman did say that "Paul Blackburn was in many ways the father of the Poetry Project that we've had here for the last five years, and it was largely due to his energies and faith and love and his feeling about the whole thing that the scene got started, and thank you Paul, for that." Oppenheimer, speaking at the memorial, sounded like a representative of the old guard as he said, "I would like to read the poem I wrote for Carlos [Blackburn's son] when he was born, which in fact was read here two years ago. I don't know what relevance it has. I think what I'm saying is there have been too many good men dying."[29]

"Where It's At": The Scene at 33 St. Mark's Place

Warsh and Waldman's apartment on St. Mark's Place proved to be a center for the new New York School and the relationship of that coterie to the Poetry Project. One of the reasons that 33 St. Mark's was so exciting, especially in terms of the Poetry Project, *The World,* and the New York School, was the mix of poets, painters, and other artists that had (by the end of 1967) established this site as a center of a poetic and wider artistic community. The fact that Ted Berrigan was a regular presence at both the Warsh/Waldman home and the Poetry Project proved extremely attractive to poets influenced by *The Sonnets* and other works. The notion of a "Second-Generation" New York School was, unlike the almost arbitrary "New York Poets" characterization found in Donald Allen's anthology, consciously nurtured and developed by Berrigan and his peers and admirers. As Berrigan said, "Because like with me and my friends, it was across almost—it's funny to say—generations, but when you get a difference of eight, ten, fifteen years in age across people . . . I mean, I'm eight years older than my closest friends, Ron Padgett and Dick Gallup . . . And then the next people we got to know are about six years younger than they are . . . Anne Waldman and people like that."[30]

Besides serving as a social center, 33 St. Mark's was the site for the production of collaborative texts, many of which appeared in *The World.* Poet and editor Larry Fagin has exhibited home movies of the scene at 33 St. Mark's that show writers Tom Clark, Ted Berrigan, Michael Brownstein, Waldman, Warsh and others writing collaborative pieces within a festive atmosphere of marijuana, music, and laughter. The apartment on St. Mark's, however, was not just for poets. This scene reflected, in its own way, the social scene of the earlier New York School.[31] As Warsh remembers it, the apartment on St. Mark's Place encouraged an environment where painters including George Schneeman, musicians from the Velvet Underground, Andy Warhol, and the ever-present Ted Berrigan would meet:

A big part of the social life at the project was taking place in Anne's and my apartment. We were also editing *Angel Hair Magazine* and Angel Hair Books, and because our apartment was so central, we began having parties, certainly after every reading. And when we started doing this, we really didn't know very many poets. After we published the second issue of *Angel Hair,* Ted Berrigan started coming over every night. And then gradually other people started coming over. It's hard to believe now, because nobody was working, nobody had jobs. Our apartment became the central stopping-off point, and we were open to that happening. Literally every night we had people coming in.[32]

Perhaps one of the reasons that New York School poetry was so attractive to younger poets growing up in the mid-to-late 1960s was that much of it did in fact incorporate reportage of social events like parties and lunch dates; one can look to Frank O'Hara's "Adieu to Norman, Bon Jour to Joan and Jean-Paul" as an example of such writing. This poem, beginning with the lines "It is 12:10 in New York and I am wondering / if I will finish this in time to meet Norman for lunch / ah lunch! I think I am going crazy / what with my terrible hangover and the weekend coming up / at excitement-prone Kenneth Koch's" indicates the level to which a poetics of sociability had come to define O'Hara's (and, to a somewhat lesser extent, Schuyler's, Koch's, Guest's, and Ashbery's) voices.[33] The acts of collaboration typical of the social life at 33 St. Mark's were in this sense natural extensions of such a poetics.

One of the first glimpses that Ron Padgett and many other Second-Generation poets had of historical examples of collaboration was issue 2 of *Locus Solus*. Entitled "A Special Issue of Collaborations" and edited by Kenneth Koch, *Locus Solus* 2 featured collaborations by Abraham Cowley and Richard Crashaw and by Samuel Taylor Coleridge and Robert Southey and "Surrealist Proverbs" (translated by Koch) by Paul Eluard and Benjamin Peret. Second-Generation poets often referred to this issue in conversation and correspondence. Partly as a result of *Locus Solus* 2, the festive atmosphere of 33 St. Mark's was both a continuation of a collaborative literary tradition and a facet of the social experiments in community typical of 1960s counterculture. Of *Locus Solus* 2 as a document appropriate for the historical occasion, Padgett says:

> There were all sorts of freewheeling ideas about community in the air—communes, the abolition of all private property, shared ownership. Ted and I had actually written some collaborations together when I was still in high school in Tulsa. I think we created the fictitious poet Harlan Dangerfield then, as the author of some poems we wrote at Dick Gallup's house one summer afternoon as a way of spoofing a literary editor who had rejected my poems. Those were our first collaborations. When the second issue of *Locus Solus,* edited by Kenneth Koch, came out a few years later, it gave a big impetus to our writing collaborations. Not only was that magazine wonderful in itself, it provided historical precedents. The collaborative spirit that Kenneth fostered in that issue energized me and Ted to do more collaborations. And then Ted became the unofficial gray eminence of the Poetry Project, and as an informal teacher and father figure, he had a tremendous influence on many of the young poets and some of the older poets around the Project. Suddenly a lot of people were writing collaborations.[34]

The World certainly reflected the environment that Padgett refers to by including literally dozens of collaborative works in its early issues. The fact that *The World* extended the mimeograph revolution initiated by Baraka, di Prima, Sanders, and the Deux Mégots/Le Metro scenes certainly influenced the content included in the magazine; the mimeograph machine itself generated notions of community that, when related to the younger poets at the Poetry Project, was tied to ideas of collaboration in literary, social, and political matters. This use of a machine that is interpreted by people as a sign representing real social connections taking place within a low-cost, bohemian environment is especially evident in *The World* 3. In this issue, edited by Warsh, Waldman, and Oppenheimer, the low-technology social significations of the mimeograph come into play in the editors' decision to include ephemeral collaborations. The mimeograph, a machine designed to generate quickly produced, cheap, easily expendable material, was used by poets active in the Poetry Project to circulate texts that were themselves fleeting and expendable records of parties, conversations, and play. Lewis Warsh remembers:

> In the apartment at St. Mark's Place we'd sit around all night writing collaborations. Then a few weeks later these works would suddenly appear in print. A lot of my own poems were pretty dumb, but I published them anyway. Type the stencil, run it off, staple it together, and then it's out there. A lot of the anti-intellectual epithets aimed at the Poetry Project had to do with the surface mindlessness of these collaborations. The idea of writing poems that didn't have to be good was one thing—but actually publishing them in a magazine where a lot of other poets wanted to publish—was really nervy, and pissed people off. Who cared?[35]

One can assume that Warsh's mention of the other "poets [who] wanted to publish" in *The World* included those in the former Black Mountain–influenced Deux Mégots crowd, who must have been doubly frustrated to be frozen out of what used to be their publishing territory while witnessing what they considered to be drivel take over the Lower East Side–centered mimeographed page. Again, though, it must be remembered that the Lower East Side poetic community was changing, as Blackburn's awkward presence at Warsh's party indicated previously. Since Berrigan himself became close personal friends with Waldman and Warsh, it was just a matter of time before the older "Second-Generation" New York School figures and those based at the apartment at 33 St. Mark's Place dominated the pages of *The World* at the cost of removing earlier reading-series organizers from the community magazine.

Berrigan, acting in a way as connector and conciliator, slowly brought the world of what had by this point been defined as the core Second-Generation

New York School into Waldman and Warsh's home.[36] The third issue of *The World* records this phenomenon, as one sees in the collaborative poem "80th Congress" written by Second-Generation "elders" Berrigan and Dick Gallup. This fourteen-line poem (here excerpted) blesses the Warsh/Waldman home as a central location in the Lower East Side poetic community, using sixties hipster lingo to centralize the home as "where it's at":

It's 2 A.M. at Lewis & Anne's, which is where it's at
On Saint Mark's Place, hash & Angel Hairs on our mind
Love is in our heart (what else?) dope & Peter Schjeldahl
Who is new and valid (in a blinding snow storm) . . .

Yes, it is now, 1967, & we've been killing time (with life)
But at Anne & Lewis's we lived it up
Anne makes a lovely snow-soda, while Lewis's watchamacallit warms up this
Happy New Year's straight blue haze.[37]

That this poem is written in a form approximating a sonnet would probably have encouraged in-the-know readers to associate the significance of Berrigan's book *The Sonnets* with the social world of Waldman and Warsh. The submerged presence of Berrigan's *Sonnets* in a poem that partially serves as a review of a new "scene" underscores the value that Berrigan and Gallup placed on 33 St. Mark's. Additionally, the fact that the poem is a collaboration (a time-honored practice signifying knowledge of First-Generation New York School writing procedures and allegiances) lends yet another authorizing note to 33 St. Mark's. Fortunately for Peter Schjeldahl, himself a newcomer to the scene, Berrigan and Gallup also use the poem to validate him: "Peter Schjeldahl / Who is new and valid." The poem "80th Congress" announces another poet accepted into the coterie by virtue of the (if not particularly serious) approval of the New York School Second-Generation elders.[38]

The social scene at 33 St. Mark's emanates from the poems in the third issue of *The World*, which, besides "80th Congress," includes six collaborations. New names in this issue of *The World* include Ted Greenwald, Jonathan Cott, Andy Warhol–associate Rene Ricard, and Tom Clark, who had arrived on the Lower East Side from England in 1967. Clark had been editing the established *Paris Review* since November 1963, and he had also been editing and producing mimeographed magazines while still in England. His entry into the world at 33 St. Mark's found him editing more mimeos, and later he was guest editor of *The World*. Clark would also ensure that the Second Generation received mainstream exposure through the *Paris Review:* poems in *The Paris Review* 41 were almost entirely written by poets associated with the New York Schools.[39]

Five poems by Tom Clark were included in this issue of *The World*, along with one collaboration with poet (and future art critic) Peter Schjeldahl entitled "Easter." This poem shows the younger poets' slightly irreverent attitude toward poets of "schools" other than the New York School. Written in a typically chatty mode while employing lively juxtapositions of images—"Tonight she's spunky / to outstrip the flame / 'Kowabunga!' she says, / 'I outstrip the flame!'" and "Wait a minute, snot-nose, / I want you to read this dictionary / of names of famous perverts"—the poem also pokes fun at the growing "fad" of Eastern religion: "Eastern religion is great, / therefore I smell / Great, being an Eastern religion."[40] Reading this line in the context of the Lower East Side poetic community, it is not too far-fetched to posit that these writers may have been indirectly referring to Allen Ginsberg's growing public persona as Eastern religion's wacky American statesman. Ginsberg was already appearing at poetry readings playing Tibetan Buddhist–style finger cymbals, and thousands of Americans in the late 1960s were adopting and adapting Eastern modes of spiritual practice. Ginsberg's practice of course had its origins in the earlier Beat-affiliated writers' commitment to various forms of Buddhism—Gary Snyder's widely known devoted practice of Zen Buddhism in Japan, for instance, or Jack Kerouac's more iconoclastic references to Buddhism found in his book *The Dharma Bums*. What Clark and Schjeldahl do in this poem is use New York School–style breeziness to poke fun at the counterculture's growing fascination with Eastern spirituality.

This attitude on the part of New York School poets toward figures emblematic of an increasingly Westernized Buddhism was at times manifested in public at readings taking place in the Poetry Project. Referring to a Gary Snyder reading, Anne Waldman wrote in a letter to Bernadette Mayer: "I've been to NY, heard Gary Snyder who really packed them in—got a sort of religious revival feeling in the Church—I really dug it tho most of the so-called NY school a bit 'aloof.'"[41] Bringing down sacred cows was a favorite pastime of many poets associated with the New York Schools; this critical attitude toward populist Western adoption of ancient Buddhist practice was in hindsight a rather refreshing response to what in many cases (Snyder *not* included) was really an Orientalist fetishism of religion.

"Don't Take Yourself Too Seriously"

These poets did not stop at poking fun at "Eastern religion." It is essential to emphasize that the social world as described, defined, created, and administrated through the production of poems was always lightened by the ironic insistence of poets associated with the New York Schools and the Poetry Project reading series never to take things too seriously. This attitude came out in both the poetry published in *The World* and in the poets' skeptical attitudes toward the government grant's far-fetched stipulations calling for socialization of "alienated" and "deviant" youth. Joel Sloman remembers feeling a real conflict between his sense of political commitment on the one hand and his attraction to New York School aesthetics on the other: "At the time I joined the Project, I was something of a New York School wannabe. I was most interested in assimilating the work of poets like Ashbery, Berrigan, O'Hara, Padgett, and many others. This aligned me with some poets in the community more than with others. Because I also was active in a still relatively small antiwar movement that had naive and/or ideological notions about art, and because the artists I most admired were avant-garde, I often felt alienated from both worlds. I thought that I didn't know how to be both, but more truthfully I didn't know how to be either."[42] This sense of the New York School actually representing prescribed formal elements characterized by a light, ludic touch is echoed by Anne Waldman in her introduction to *Out of This World:* "The aesthetic sensibilities of the so-called New York School held a particular attraction for younger poets. It didn't complain or call attention to itself."[43] As Lewis Warsh put it, "The New York School—part of the characteristic was 'don't take yourself too seriously.'"[44]

Treating subject matter and one's place in the literary pantheon with an inordinate amount of reverence or seriousness would unavoidably alter and damage the irreverent mystique characteristic of much of the New York School poets, particularly those associated with the Second Generation. Alice Notley, the poet and wife of Ted Berrigan, remembers, "We never used words like 'avant-garde' or 'experimental' in those days, except to make fun of using such words, though I did say 'academic' sometimes. Where people now tend to say mainstream. I always assumed we were the future mainstream."[45] As Notley's comments indicate, even characterizing an avant-garde project as avant-garde was in a sense reaching for a kind of professional, calculated status that ideally should not be solicited.

This attitude is evident in the Tom Clark/Peter Schjeldahl take on Eastern religion, as well as in Warsh's poem "French Windows," included in the third issue of *The World* and dedicated to Tom Clark. Warsh managed to include politics in the poem while avoiding sermonizing tones and typical narrative applications. "French Windows" ends with the lines "That is why coffee / is famous for the architecture / on which someone pees, though it is only a dog / in a factory who will someday manage one." While the poem closes with a critique of the factory (and by extension of its function within capitalist modes of production) through the negative figure of the manager "dog," it nevertheless is not the kind of poem that would be read at a union meeting to rally the workers. In the New York School tradition of surface wordplay and destabilization of conventional meaning, earlier lines threaten *any* language that might be used for clearly stated political ends: "Never / leave a simplified form to / abbreviate off that sleek burr in / a jockey's first thought to pee on you, / for it is spacious and survives the day."[46] These lines don't make any conventional sense, but this lack of sense may be in reaction to the language of partisan politics, which is often employed to make totalizing universal claims. Such uses of language are suspect in the aesthetic of the New York Schools. Using scatological nonsense in a poem is a paradoxically political act; it imperils political language by suggesting a kind of individualistic liberty inherent in an asocial babble. Such liberty might otherwise be unavailable within a language-system purporting to be laying down facts along the lines of "Workers of the world, unite, you have nothing to lose but your chains!" or "The Soviet Union is an evil empire."[47]

However, as Warsh shows, idealism is not thrown out the window in this poetry—one is still a "dog" if one's goal is to manage a factory. The poet can still treat subject matter seriously—just not too seriously. Such an attitude had a precedent, as so much Second-Generation New York School poetry did, in Frank O'Hara's poetry. As Geoffrey Ward has recognized, the final section of O'Hara's poem "In Memory of My Feelings" alludes to the line "love of the hero corrupts into worship of his statue" found in Emerson's essay "The American Scholar." In O'Hara's poem, the hero is presented as a rather clumsy figure: "The hero, trying to unhitch his parachute, / stumbles over me. It is our last embrace."[48] While Ward rightfully points out that, "the nature of love, the image of the hero, and the representation of both through sculpture and statuary were to recur prominently in the series of odes O'Hara was to write over the coming period," one might take this further and suggest that O'Hara is actually critiquing a style of poetry.[49] The hero here is really a stand-in for the Sturm und Drang of literary bombast and Dylan Thomas–like "Welsh spit."[50] Excessive love of this "hero" results in artifice, gauche decoration, and excessive rhetoric, so O'Hara and other New York School poets must reject him. After all, too much love of the hero leads to idealizing a figure who, by virtue of his predictably sonorous striving toward great poetic heights, trips over his own parachute.

The Immediate Community

The glut of collaborative work in the early issues of *The World,* as well as an overall resistance to seriousness, would be paralleled in the readings going on at the Poetry Project itself. These aesthetics often resulted in poets' referring to speed in composition as a virtue. At the benefit reading for Andrei Codrescu on March 4, 1968, Ted Berrigan introduced his poem "Waterloo Sunset" by saying, "It's a collaboration with another poet, Ron Padgett. It was written last night." Even relatively "serious" writers like Clayton Eshleman fixed on the virtue of the quickly produced poem as something attractive and worthy of disclosure to an audience.[51] At the same benefit reading, Eshleman introduced a poem beginning with the line "Was sympathetic" by explaining "the fourth piece I wrote about 5:30 this evening. It's untitled." Much of this blithe attitude toward the act of composition can probably be traced back to Frank O'Hara's by-then well-known composition of his "Poem (Lana Turner Has Collapsed!)." David Lehman has described how O'Hara, on a ferry on his way to read in Staten Island on a shared bill with Robert Lowell (whose poetry O'Hara disliked intensely), quickly penned his poem. "On the way to the Staten Island Ferry, O'Hara bought the *New York Post* and on the choppy half-hour ride he wrote an instant meditation on the tabloid revelation that Hollywood actress Lana Turner had collapsed . . . O'Hara read the poem that afternoon, making it clear that he had written it in transit. The audience loved it; Lowell looked put out."[52] Such a story, retold by Berrigan and others so often that it became legend, possibly—if partially—accounts for the consistent referrals that poets at St. Mark's Church made to the relatively short time it took them to write poems. This was a potentially refreshing model for any audience member attached to notions of poetic production as tied to stereotypes of the poet as agonized, misunderstood, and solitary muse-inspired genius. Celebrating speed in production made a value out of immediacy, spontaneity, and risk. It made poetry fun.

Another factor besides the famous O'Hara anecdote that could explain the positive conception of speed and improvisation in composition—and one that could account for less obvious figures like Eshleman—may very well have been the omnipresence of the mimeograph machine. "Mimeographs brought low-quality publishing within everyone's reach. The means to produce broadsides was at hand everywhere, and the tide of social change brought the motivation. As in earlier periods, they functioned as material signs of community and of a variety of social, political, and cultural commitments, a way of forging connections that would encourage people to think of themselves as part of larger movements."[53] One can theorize that in an environment where the mimeograph machine allowed poets to write a poem one evening and have it disseminated to hundreds of people just weeks later (and, in Larry Fagin's case in editing *Adventures in Poetry,* the following day), quickness would become a kind of ideal for poets.[54] Anne Waldman recalls that production of *The World* involved "Long hours late at night in the office minding the machines. Then we'd have a collation party the next day with the heavy-duty stapler. . . . The magazine was always too big, messy, uneven, democratic, inclusive, raw, and even boring at times. . . . The impulse was always toward the *immediate* community, so it covers most of the so-called New York School plus what comes after, with a bow toward Black Mountain, the Beats, San Francisco Renaissance, and the New York Scene."[55]

Like group conversations, mimeograph magazines generated a sense of collaboration and participation. *The World* in particular, through its consistent publication of collaborations that referred readers to a specific place populated by a specific group of contemporaries laughing, shrieking, and trading off lines, reminded people that poetry was designed to be heard and even produced within a context of community. Thus, the mimeograph magazine was imbued with a social aura and an attendant "oral aura."[56] Michael Davidson writes, "If the little magazine revolution of the 1960s was fueled by a neoromantic poetics of testimony and protest, it was enabled by photographic processes that returned the poem to its producer in a most palpable way. Thus, the immediacy advocated in the poetics of the period was materialized via forms of photomechanical reproduction and printing."[57] Davidson's use of the term *neoromantic* is particularly significant. Speed in composition suggests a sense of wanting to be without mediation; lack of mediation was central to romanticism. One should also consider that poets like Berrigan were, if not individually, at least chronologically part of a generation raised on instant products such as TV dinners. Additionally, these poets were writing as popular music, including the Doors' song "The End" (climaxing with the phrase "We want it all and we want it . . . NOW!"), was being widely distributed. Such apparently peripheral phenomena may have added to the emphasis on immediacy in this poetic community.

A sense of immediacy, speed, and improvisation resonated against the background of the readings themselves, in that performance made physical the moment of transmission from author to audience far more than solitary reading could. In the many readings he gave at the Project during its first three years, Ted Berrigan reminded people at St. Mark's of the aural and oral nature of poetry over and over again. At the Codrescu benefit, for example, Berrigan introduced his poem "Tamborine Life" by saying, "It's not really addressed to an audience, but it's meant to be *listened to* by an audience." While it is useful to focus on the significance of the mimeograph magazine and its relation to community and orality, in terms of *aurality* Michael Davidson has helpfully theorized on the significance of the tape recorder as a signifying agent of community. Berrigan was sure to know that his comments were being recorded, which suggests that he was probably aware that anything he said that was recorded was eventually going to be listened to. The presence of the tape recorder in the parish hall (at points there were two—Blackburn's and the "official" church tape recorder) helped transform the poetry reading into a performative act as opposed to a discrete reading of a written text. Oral presence was in a sense emphasized at the Poetry Project over the absence implied by writing. That is, by virtue of the tape recorder's very act of recording or aurally inscribing a text, the poem being read now had an aural counterpart as permanent (albeit not as widely distributed) as its written echo.[58] As mimeographed magazines came out of a kind of avant-garde publishing history, the tape recorder(s) in the Poetry Project can also be read as suggestive of a rich symbolic history:

> Ginsberg's generation included a loosely knit group of poets living in New York's lower east side during the 1950s and 1960s for whom the tape recorder became an increasingly important element in composition. Paul Blackburn, LeRoi Jones (Amiri Baraka), Jerome Rothenberg, David Antin, Armand Schwerner, Robert Kelly, and Jackson Mac Low linked tape recording to European avant-garde experimentation. Within the group could be found an interest in projectivist and "deep image" theories, applications of John Cage's chance operations, religious and ritual uses of the voice, Russian Futurist and Dadaist theater. The tape recorder participated actively in all of these areas . . . Blackburn's omniscient tape recorder was more than a vehicle for retrieval; it became a dimension of his material text, as immediate as pen and paper had been for previous generations. It was a device for testing the page and its notation against the voice and, in some cases, for generating new materials that would be incorporated into the poem. And because it was invariably on stage with the poet, the tape recorder became synonymous with the body of the performer.[59]

As the tape recorder became synonymous with the physical body, so the mimeograph machine and the mimeographed page engendered a sense of physicality and utterance based on the highly social environment in which these technologies were applied. Both poets and editors associated with *The World* and the majority of poets reading at St. Mark's during its first three years assumed either that the audience knew the poet and vice versa or that the ideal audience would use the mimeographed magazine as a kind of tacit invitation to participate in or imagine a local poetic community.[60]

At the Poetry Project itself, comments made in introduction or directly before or after the reading of a given poem tended to boost the communitarian potential of the public reading and the poem. For example, on November 8, 1967, Ted Berrigan introduced Anne Waldman and Jim Brodey by saying, "Hello mother. Hello everybody. Welcome to the poetry readings at St. Mark's Church. The magazine of the Poetry Project *The World* is on sale for fifty cents on this table over here where this man with the cowboy hat is sitting, and there's a bowl to put the money in. I'm not sure what kind of remarks I should make to introduce these readers since I think most of you know one or the other or both." After this familial introduction, Waldman began the reading with her "Poem in New York," which tended to underscore Berrigan's introduction by emphasizing her sense of *place*—the Lower East Side of Manhattan—as well as the community inhabiting that space: "Here, I can be myself, taking the whole day to get up. / Sleeping even through it, or / else walking around it / Inside and out. / Friends come in over the edges / Filling out the middle, which is about twelve midnight."[61]

Sometimes the kinds of collaborative activity recorded in *The World* took place during a reading itself. A John Wieners reading on January 3, 1968, introduced by Allen Ginsberg, elicited audience suggestions on how to reword a certain line and essentially turned into an impromptu poetry workshop. The reading began with Ginsberg's announcement of Amiri Baraka's conviction "by an all-white jury of possession of revolvers, which he announced in an interview in Evergreen Review that he did not possess." After what sounds like some scattered indignant clapping and whistling, Wieners was introduced. Wieners began the reading with a poem that began: "Have you forgotten, am I forgotten." As he continued, Wieners ended up stumbling over the words *possibility probability.* After a short, uncomfortable pause, Wieners began to theorize on all the different permutations of the line: "Should it be 'the probability of making love permitted performance prohibited by possibility'?" After a few seconds, Ginsberg is heard suggesting, "The possibility permits but the probability prohibits." Then someone in the audience is heard referring to Edward Albee, which immediately encouraged another audience member to yell out, "Who's afraid of Virginia Woolf?" Wieners proceeded to carry on an erudite conversation on line, Albee, and all kinds of other rather digressive topics with the audience. After about three minutes, another audience member is heard offering a variation on the "possibility" line. For some reason, this encouraged Wieners to raise his voice: "Now the probable is more our concern . . . everyone has the possibility, it's the probable that opens before us potentiality!" Wieners then began talking about the erotic practices of kings. As if to bring Wieners back to the reading, someone stated, "Our friend's friend LeRoi Jones has something to say about the play called 'The Toilet,' now this is sort of tied in." Wieners responded with the elliptical statement, "'The Toilet' that Mr. Jones created comes too late to those school-chums," and then went back to reading his poem.

The ability of the audience to participate in and affect the outcome of a reading would find a particularly radical manifestation a week after the Wieners reading, when Kenneth Koch read at the Poetry Project on January 10, 1968. Continuing the tradition of glamorizing speedy composition, Koch introduced his second poem by saying, "This is just a little poem I wrote when I was thinking about this reading. It's called 'To My Audience.'" Koch has stated, "On the whole subject of poetry readings, I must admit I'm kind of skeptical, because I'm not sure that much has ever happened because of poetry readings."[62] The first lines of "To My Audience," designed specifically for this particular reading, wittily allude to Koch's skepticism by portraying the St. Mark's audience as surrealist cartoonlike creatures: "My audience of camel dung and fig newtons, / My audience of hats, and how shall I address my audience / of new york green frock bats. Are you sure there is an audience / I won't go in if there's no audience." However, at the end of the line "morpheus sleeps, mercury or Murphy," Koch's reading was suddenly interrupted by the poet Allen Van Newkirk yelling out "Stop!" followed immediately by the sound of two reports of a pistol.[63] According to Lewis Warsh (who was sitting in the front row at the time), Newkirk had quietly walked from the rear exit of the parish hall up to the front of the stage, pulled out a pistol, and fired two blanks directly at Koch.[64] As heard on the cassette tape of this reading, there was a large thumping sound immediately after the shots. Ron Padgett (also in the front row) remembers:

> A tall, somewhat scraggly white man, in his mid-to-late twenties and wearing a Dostoevskyan overcoat, emerged from the door behind the podium and took a few steps towards Kenneth, on Kenneth's left side, and he aimed a small revolver at Kenneth and from close range fired several shots. It was quite loud and stunning. Kenneth cringed and lurched. The audience jumped. I jumped too, but I kept my eye on Kenneth and saw that he was not shot. Around this time there were a lot of Happenings, and other unusual art events with pranks set up to fool the audience, so you never knew. But it was very unlikely that Kenneth was going to set up a thing like this. When I saw that Kenneth wasn't in fact hurt, and I realized that this must be some kind of stunt, I was mightily relieved. Meanwhile, the assailant walked down the center aisle toward a cohort who was distributing leaflets from the back—it turned out to be Andrei Codrescu, who had recently arrived in this country. The two were told to leave—by Ted Berrigan, I think—and they did, shouting slogans.[65]

This being January 1968, one can understand why Koch momentarily believed that the assassination attempt might have been authentic. This was the decade of the Kennedy assassinations, the Malcolm X and Martin Luther King assassinations, and (just to name a small number of cities) the Detroit, Los Angeles, and Newark, New Jersey, riots. Additionally, Amiri Baraka had just been convicted (as Ginsberg had announced a week earlier) of illegal possession of firearms. "During the Newark ghetto revolt of 1967, Baraka was injured, arrested by the police, and indicted for unlawfully carrying firearms. An all-white jury convicted him, and after the judge read Baraka's poem 'Black People!' to the court, the poet was sentenced to 2–2½ years in jail without parole."[66]

John Wieners at Simon's Rock Poetry Festival,
1970. Photo © by Gerard Malanga.

Back room at Café Le Metro, 1964. *Left to right:*
Gerard Malanga, Harry Fainlight, Kate Heliczer,
Allen Ginsberg, Pierro Heliczer, Peter Orlovsky
(wearing cap), and Harry Smith. Photo © by
Archives Malanga.

(Judy Linn; photo)

....Reading... February 10... 8:30... 1971
Gerard Malanga: POETRY.
patti smith: WORK ▬
St. Marks Church-on-the- Bowery... 2nd Ave. + 10th St.

Flyer for poetry reading by Gerard Malanga and
Patti Smith at St. Mark's Church, New York City,
February 10, 1971. Photo © by Archives Malanga.

Ted Berrigan clowning around with John Ashbery in
front of the St. Regis Hotel, New York City, 1971.
Photo © by Gerard Malanga.

Ron Padgett screen test, 1965. From *Screen Tests,*
a collaboration by Andy Warhol and Gerard
Malanga. Film enlargement © by Gerard Malanga.

Anne Waldman reading at St. Mark's Church, 1970.
Photo © by Gerard Malanga.

Anne Waldman and Lewis Warsh in the courtyard
of St. Mark's Church, New York City, 1969. Photo
© by Gerard Malanga.

Ted Berrigan, outside the Gem Spa, corner of
Second Avenue and St. Mark's Place, New York
City, 1971. Photo © by Gerard Malanga.

Poetry reading, Wagner College, February 9, 1962.
Left to right: Robert Lowell, Robert Harson, Willard
Maas (moderator), Frank O'Hara, and Gerard
Malanga. Photo © by Archives Malanga.

Bernadette Mayer *(left)* and Anne Waldman, Bard
College, 1970. Photo © by Gerard Malanga.

Bolinas, 1969. *Left to right:* Bill Berkson, Lewis
Warsh, Joanne Kyger, and Andrei Codrescu.
Photo © Archives Warsh, photographer unknown.

Jim Carroll, Bolinas, 1969.
Photo © Lewis Warsh.

On the tape, Koch sounds a little shaken as he states, "That was a benefit shooting." This comment elicited what seems like relieved laughter from the audience, and Koch resumed reading his poem, beginning with the line "mercury or murphy is creeping up to him, yes it's murphy." However, Koch's voice indicates that he was still rather upset by this incident. He stopped his reading to say in a sardonic tone, "Poetry is revolution." Then Koch is heard to sigh, "Well," as he looked at one of the fliers Newkirk and his cohorts were circulating throughout the parish hall. After some period of silence, Koch stated, "Well, now, I don't want the congregation to get upset by these hijinks. These young people have a very fine cause that they're working for, and this seems to be about LeRoi. Now, I don't think the judge should have put LeRoi in jail because he wrote a poem.[67] If that's the point these people wanted to make they could have made it in a better way it seems to me. So why don't you stop interrupting the reading." At this point Newkirk heckled Koch again, to which Koch responded by shouting, "Scram!" In response to Koch, Newkirk shouted, "Fuck you!" Unfortunately, the tape did not capture what Newkirk said right after this, except for a sentence ending with "surrealist with a gun, get out of here, fuck you!" Koch again yelled out, "Get out!" The heckler then intoned, "Revolution—the only solution!" Some audience members could be heard laughing rather contemptuously in response to the slogan. Koch himself said, "Grow up!" and then, in an indignant if amused tone, muttered "revolution." Someone else from the audience suggested that Koch "start at the beginning." Koch quickly said, "I never should have said 'my audience of camel dung!'" which elicited a torrent of laughter and clapping. Koch then followed up on this quip with, "I thought the one place you had sanctuary from all this was a church." Someone in the audience could be heard shouting out "Wrong!" to which Koch then said "Wrong? Oh, are you part of the revolution too?" Finally, Koch is heard asking Lewis Warsh, "Lewis, is there any chance of there not being any more shootings and things?" Then "I think I better read 'The Pleasures of Peace,' I was going to read it later (laughter, clapping). Well, yeah I'm changing the order of readings." What follows is what, even on a cassette tape, is a truly compelling reading of Koch's long poem. Lines including "Now I must devote my days to the Pleasures of Peace / to my contemporaries I'll leave the horrors of war / they can do them better than I" take on an added resonance given the environment, as does the whimsical "One single piece of pink mint chewing gum contains more pleasures / Than the whole rude gallery of war."[68]

There is good reason to pay attention to those playful, adamantly nonserious early issues of *The World* alongside anecdotes of readings taking place at the Poetry Project during its early years, even if those issues of *The World* never really published poems considered part of the "canon," alternative or otherwise. In many ways, *The Genre of Silence* was the deluxe counter to what was to become *The World,* and that is why *The Genre* was doomed in the context of the Poetry Project's early, problematic relationship to the government that was funding it. Owing to its expense, its glossy cover, and its superficial conformity to government requirements that the magazine be a "quality" object, *The Genre*'s rich presentation, while corroborating the value of the poems in *The Genre* as "real" (that is, designed to be published seriously in book form), did not correspond to the far more irreverent, anarchic spirit of the New York School–infatuated poets frequenting the Project. The period from 1967 to 1968 was a historical moment: *The World,* like the increasingly complicated grants structure that supported it in its later years, would itself become far more professional in both appearance and content, but the inception of the Poetry Project demanded a sloppier project, as the readings themselves created a space for audience participation, collaborative back-and-forth, disclosure of coterie politics, symbolic assassination attempts, and so on. After all, the Poetry Project did in this case have the money to put out a glossier product, and reading series organizers could certainly have organized readings in a more traditional and distanced way. However, the editors and organizers at the Poetry Project chose not to adapt to or create a more professional environment.

This choice is significant. *The World* worked as a magazine that in many ways served as a metaphor for the risk-taking group of poets who were associating sixties values of community and experimentation to their poetry scene. As Lewis Warsh remembers it, "The Fillmore East, on Seventh Street and Second Avenue, was just down the street from the church, and Max's Kansas City was a few blocks north. Andy Warhol was around, David Amram, a whole constellation of people. The Velvet Underground came to 33 St. Mark's one night to listen to the master of their first record for the first time."[69] Like the mimeographed broadsides that Sullivan discusses, *The World* was not always made to last. In this respect, the meaning of the early issues of *The World* was more directly tied to the moment of their publication and distribution in the context of the immediate community formed by the reading series.

The Scene at the Poetry Project Changes

As 1967 turned into 1968, the Poetry Project achieved a social glamour and status foreign to predecessor reading series. On some nights, limousines were seen pulling up to the church and discharging Upper East Side socialites curious about the "scene." Additionally, poets reading consistently in the Poetry Project found themselves anthologized in a book whose editor had no real social ties to the Lower East Side poetic community; Paul Carroll's anthology *The Young American Poets,* introduced by the established poet and writer James Dickey, announced to the literary world that there was a new group of poets, many of them from the Lower East Side, that deserved to be taken seriously.[70] While there had of course been poetry anthologies after *The New American Poetry,* the most significant volume (in terms of its inclusion of Lower East Side poets) was editorially ahistorical. Robert Kelly's and Paris Leary's *A Controversy of Poets* featured familiar alternative names, though it made much out of an editorial vision that idealistically valued the "poem itself" as opposed to the poem and its attendant coterie associations and sociohistorical context.[71] Carroll's book capitalized on what was quickly becoming poetry's relationship to radical chic, going so far as to print a picture of Diane Wakoski holding a gun aimed squarely at the viewer.[72] Reviews of the anthology spoke of it as a natural successor to the Allen anthology, even though the poems in the book were especially varied; formalist texts by poets including Mark Strand and David Mus shared pages with far more "experimental" texts like the patterned concrete verse of Richard Kostelanetz and the serial poetry of Clark Coolidge.[73]

However, the book was predominantly alternative, defined primarily by writers associated with the Lower East Side poetic community, despite the fact that the editor was a poet who lived almost his entire life in Chicago. One review of the Carroll anthology isolated the "New Yorkers" as particularly noteworthy:

> A majority of the more interesting things here are by the New Yorkers, the Lower East Side Mother-"C"-Angel Hair group. Ted Berrigan is the Ginsberg of this group, Gerard Malanga the Lord Byron and so on.
>
> The New York poets seem to be nourished by a reservoir of attributes including, mainly, wild, improbable juxtaposition, diction that turns corners sharply, put-ons, very mock ingenuousness and urbane faggotry.[74]

The reviewer then goes on to describe pithily the writing styles of poets like Berrigan, Berkson, Padgett, and MacAdams emphasizing their debt to Frank O'Hara and praising them with words and phrases including "uncanny inanities," "cool and supple," "elegant," "limpid and soft-spoken," and others suggestive of a queer, urban aesthetic. It is significant that these writers managed to appeal to reviewers and editors beyond the immediate environs of the Poetry Project and the Lower East Side. The sympathetic aesthetic practices of Lower East Side poets as a "group" were becoming more attractive to literary cultures outside New York City. As a result, their publication opportunities became more established, more familiar, less underground, and less throwaway. Mimeographed magazines were a 1960s and early 1970s phenomenon—the

Carroll book was in many ways a precursor to the end of this phenomenon, in the sense of the book's being a nationally distributed anthology that theoretically minimized the significance of place in relationship to poetry. Indeed, by 1968, poets including Ted Berrigan and Andrei Codrescu had temporarily or permanently left the neighborhood. However, an offshoot of the Lower East Side poetic community had taken hold by the fall of 1969. Ironically, this community was cultivated in a resolutely pastoral environment: the small California coast town of Bolinas.

The New York School in Bolinas and Beyond

Lewis Warsh remembers first visiting Bolinas in the summer of 1968, where Tom Clark and his wife, Angelica, were already living. Warsh and Waldman's marriage ended in 1969, so Warsh decided to return to this small town an hour north of San Francisco. There Warsh became romantically involved with the poet Joanne Kyger and developed his friendships with poets Tom Clark and Ebbe Borregaard. By Christmas of 1969, "Bill Berkson came to visit, then Ted Berrigan and Alice Notley—we all spent New Year's Eve together, the last night of the sixties. Then they left, and Joanne and I began living together in a house near Agate Beach. It was a very dark house. Bolinas was beautiful, but I had a hard time living in a place where going into a room and trying to do some work was considered an antisocial impulse. There was a lot of pressure just to hang out and smoke dope all day."[75]

Bill Berkson showed up for his second visit in a car with Jim Carroll, Jayne Nodland, and Devereaux Carson, all of whom stayed a few weeks before returning to New York. In the summer of 1970, Berkson decided to rejoin this burgeoning community and ended up staying in Bolinas for twenty years. The move these poets made to more idyllic environments was part of the overall transformation of the hippie movement from an engaged, urban phenomenon to more rurally based experiments in community. The hippie population of the Lower East Side especially added to this transition. "By 1969, the spatial core of hippie culture was no longer the city but the countryside as hippie communities and communes popped up across upstate New York and Vermont and, on the West Coast, in Northern California, Oregon, and Washington."[76]

The scene at Bolinas, while rural and far more laid back than the one on the Lower East Side, quickly became an extension of the New York–based alternative poetic community. Lewis MacAdams and Aram Saroyan established homes there, Joe Brainard arrived for an extended visit, and Robert Creeley and Bobby Louise Hawkins arrived in the summer of 1970. The Bolinas scene was significant enough for Lawrence Ferlinghetti to publish a City Lights anthology entitled *On the Mesa: An Anthology of Bolinas Writing*. It should be noted that the anthology organized a group of writers who for the most part had arrived in Bolinas less than a year after the original 1969 Woodstock Festival. Woodstock had engendered a collectivist and pseudoagrarian spirit that was distributed widely through national media. This spirit was later to find its most popular expression in Crosby, Stills, and Nash's song "Woodstock," with its chorus "and we've got to get ourselves back to the garden." The Bolinas anthology, then, with its suggestions of a community-based rural retreat, was very much a part of the consciousness specific to 1960s hippie culture. The editorial statement on the back cover of *On the Mesa* served partly as a testament to the late 1960s "back-to-the-garden" movement, which, roughly speaking, celebrated individuality through the ethos of "doing your own thing" as it established nonconformists into a group:

> This is a gathering of poets & writers & artists living on or around the mesa in Bolinas, California. Not so much a school of poets as a meeting of those who happen to be at this geographical location at this point in wobbly time, several divergent movements in American poetry of the past 20 years (Black Mountain, San Francisco Beat, 'New York School' of poets) have come together with new Western and mystic elements at the unpaved crossroads of Bolinas.

The Bolinas anthology served as further evidence, along with the Carroll anthology, that the scene that in many ways was centered on the Lower East Side was not simply a hermetic, underground, and localized literary movement (though that is certainly what it *once* was) but a gathering of poets who could be situated and promoted as writing in a lineage originally named in the Donald Allen anthology. The fact that David Meltzer, Robert Creeley, Ebbe Borregaard, and Joanne Kyger now shared the same pages and lived in the same community as their younger cohorts, including Bill Berkson and Lewis Warsh, pointed to the by-now transnational and transgenerational significance of the Lower East Side poetic community in relationship to the postmodern American avant-garde.

Additionally, many poems in *On the Mesa* continued the typical Lower East Side practice of using poems as social and occasional documents: Joanne Kyger's "A Testimony for Ebbe and Angela on their Wedding November 29, 1970," for example, or Tom Clark's poem "The Book of Love" with the epigraph "for Joanne Kyger." Creeley's "Bolinas and Me . . . " (here excerpted) described the town of Bolinas while naming figures like Joanne Kyger associated with the scene:

The sea, the drive
along the coast in L.A.

I remember Joanne. I
want to. She's

lovely, one says.
So she is. So

are you too.
Or one. Have

done with it.
You see that

line of rocks out there?
Water, waves, two

dead sea lions,
says Peter.[77]

This act of naming echoed the mythologizing use of names popular-
ized by O'Hara.[78] The practice of naming names—like in O'Hara's "I am
wondering / if I will finish this in time to meet Norman for lunch" or in Cree-
ley's "I remember Joanne"—elevated the everyday of social discourse to the
status of poetry. Writing those names imbued them with traces of permanence
engendered by the very act of publication. However, at the same time this el-
evation demystified poetry (or at least those notions of poetry as a "higher
art" with an attendant high rhetoric) by including chatty disclosure of per-
sonal news typical of O'Hara or the strangely minimal notation of a mem-
ory found in Creeley's line "I remember Joanne."

In this way poetry was used to establish community. Naming names in
the context of Bolinas affirmed the existence of an environment where cross-
references could be made between individuals on a first-name basis. Neverthe-
less, while "I remember Joanne" is an exclusive statement designed for in-the-
know readers, the phrase also opens the poem up to sociability. That is, a line
like "I remember Joanne" can suggest to the uninitiated reader that the best
tactic for reading is to imagine a kind of tacit participation in a poetic com-
munity. One is invited to imagine and remember one's own Joanne.

The dispersal of poets to various parts of the country both led to a dis-
semination of New York School–style poetics in other regions of the United
States and opened up the Poetry Project to other groups of poets.[79] In the
summer of 1968, Ted Berrigan promoted the New York School through his
job as a writing workshop instructor at the Writer's Workshop of the Uni-

versity of Iowa in Iowa City, where he joined a faculty including poet Anselm Hollo. Berrigan then went to Ann Arbor in 1969. From there he returned to the University of Iowa, and then from Iowa he went to teach in Chicago where, according to Ron Padgett, "He made a huge impact there on a whole generation of poets, many of whom followed him to New York."[80]

Berrigan's influence is visible in (among many others) the writing of Slovenian poet Tomaž Šalamun, who attended the University of Iowa at the invitation of the International Writing Program. Šalamun, a former political prisoner under Marshall Tito who had written mostly surrealist-style texts, ended up writing in a new style that appears partly influenced by his experience taking classes with Berrigan. Šalamun's texts include list poems, poems with chatty diction, and poems with dates on them, including "1/1/73," which featured lines reminiscent of the final section of Kenneth Koch's "Fresh Air." Where "Fresh Air" used the refrain "Goodbye" in lines like "Goodbye, Helen! Goodbye, fumes! Goodbye, abstracted dried-up boys! Goodbye, dead trees! Goodbye, skunks!"[81] Šalamun's "1/1/73" (here excerpted) replaced the refrain "Goodbye" with the phrase "Good morning" and also made great use of exclamation points—a syntactical conceit allusive of Koch's and O'Hara's (and Berrigan's) extravagant use of the exclamation point as generative of poetic whimsy: "Good morning, sun! / Good morning, New Year! / Good morning, all friends on earth, / all enemies, and the meager, good morning! / Good morning, Marushka, when you wake up, / good morning, Ana, kitten! / Hi, Ron!"[82] Additionally, the scene at Bolinas (with its Lower East Side nuances) spread somewhat starting in January 1971. On Union Street in the North Beach neighborhood of San Francisco, Lewis Warsh took over the "Intersection" reading series that Andrei Codrescu had been running. This series lasted about six months and was in many ways a temporary West Coast version of the Poetry Project; Robert Creeley and Ted Berrigan shared a bill, Joe Brainard and Joanne Kyger read together, Philip Whalen read with Allen Ginsberg, and so on.[83]

In light of the Lower East Side scene becoming more accessible to poets outside New York City, one sees that 1968 and 1969 brought perhaps the first noticeable social shift in the Poetry Project—or at least a shift strong enough for a small group of people to begin the highly debatable round of assertions that the Poetry Project could start looking back on its "good ol' days." This shift can roughly be ascribed to several significant departures of particular individuals, the resulting end of the social scene at 33 St. Mark's, and—in a larger historical context—social changes in the Lower East Side neighborhood and in the general counterculture.

On an interpersonal level, Lewis Warsh and Anne Waldman's separation had larger social repercussions, though Angel Hair Press continued: "Something changed in the scene when Anne and I broke up. I moved to California for a while, and I sense that the salon atmosphere in the apartment didn't continue. It's inevitable that things change—relationships, friendships, and the world itself, which during those days was a kind of mirror to a lot of what we were writing about."[84] In the neighborhood as a whole, a certain innocence associated with the hippie movement was lost when, in October 1967, an African American hippie and a Black Nationalist were accused of raping and murdering eighteen-year-old white hippies Linda Fitzpatrick and James Hutchinson in the basement boiler room of a tenement building at 19 Avenue B. "Following the murders, the representations that had characterized the East Village as liberated from the ghetto of the Lower East Side were quickly discarded. They were replaced by a discourse of urban decline. . . . As a reporter wrote, there was a 'sudden realization that the East Village was a slum.'"[85]

Poets noted the changing mood on the Lower East Side as they witnessed the Summer of Love fading away. Andrei Codrescu wrote of this time:

> I left New York one month ago because my novel was done and because the ugly tensions on the street took hallucinatory forms. Bikers without bikes, chain-people and dead hippies at each other's throats . . . The Saint Marks Freak Corner is stuffed with fury. I hope it explodes soon (New York, I mean). Besides, poetically, the city is disintegrating. And it's not for the summer only. Ted Berrigan left for good. He's in Iowa, residing. Tom Clark bought a house in California. Diane di Prima runs a communal thing in S.F. Carol Bergé is going to France or maybe to Honolulu. Allen Van Newkirk is gone. Sam Abrams is going to Cuba, maybe he's there already.[86]

Codrescu shows how urban tensions took hold of the popular imagination, in turn leading many poets to respond as part of the counterculture—choosing to drop out and move to more rural environments or to become more politically committed. Poet Ted Greenwald has stated, "I've always felt that at this time, 69–70, certain people had been really hot with their work & had kind of come to a dead end & had to figure out what to do next. The energy was different in the late 60's. The War. Everything wasn't happening at once & things tended to be more political. Cambodia. Politics. Not who was the next editor."[87] By 1970, with the advent of the Weather Underground and the accidental bombing of the Underground headquarters on Eleventh Street in Greenwich Village, Anne Waldman would write: "N.Y. is crazy. The 11th St. incident is really strange & creepy. I know one of those girls—Kathy Boudin—who escaped. I knew her when I was a little girl & now not so well tho I know her parents & see her mother a lot (she writes poetry). Our generation. And the other bombings! Spoke to folks in NY who say it's a state of emergency . . . I wonder. Seems like it was bound to happen sooner or later. Blow it up."[88]

On a national political level, Richard Nixon was elected president despite the increasing unpopularity of the Vietnam War, and the F.B.I. was making increasing inroads into revolutionary organizations, including the Black Panthers and Students for a Democratic Society through the notorious Counter Intelligence Program or "COINTELPRO." The antiwar movement was under violent attack from federal, state, and local law-enforcement officers, as the police riots at the Democratic Convention in Chicago in 1968 proved most overtly. Former pacifists began to talk of the necessity of armed struggle and formed militaristic cells including the Weather Underground. The kinds of fun, collaborative activity (theatrical dada performances, days-long readings, Happenings, demonstrations, and other events typical of the Poetry Project) that the hippie/yippie counterculture had used as a weapon against the Establishment were failing, at least politically, as witnessed by the increasing escalation of the war, the continued criminalization of drugs, and the inability of the political left to find a viable antiwar presidential candidate.

However, the "change" Warsh refers to and the fracturing of the counterculture should in no way be taken to imply that the Poetry Project suddenly became a dull bureaucratic structure. In fact, after the initial government grant ran out in 1968, Anne Waldman found herself in control of an organization that looked as if it were facing extinction. As early as January 1968, there was talk that the Poetry Project was not going to survive past its initial grant. In a letter to Gerard Malanga, Waldman wrote,

> Lewis has been working for Thomas Y Crowell publishers for 3 weeks now—A bit difficult to readjust to working schedule & also makes severe changes in our own home-life—Can't have all night sessions as before, but the change is good—we're trying to save money, become more organized etc. But poets shouldn't have to go through this—I'm so lucky with my job and the readings, workshops, magazine have been so much improved over last year—In the last few weeks, John A., Robert Creeley have read—This Wednesday, John Wieners, and next, Kenneth Koch—The future of The Poetry Project is a bit dim at this point, but perhaps we can secure funds from a private foundation, since the gov't can no longer support it—But can't worry about this now.[89]

In the midst of this economic uncertainty, Waldman continued to run a highly successful reading series and to administrate the free poetry workshops. The reading lists from that era do not look demonstrably different from those related to the first two years of the Project, since even the poets who had moved out of New York City returned for visits and to read at the Poetry Project. In fact, from around 1969 to 1970, the Poetry Project became even more radical in spirit as it weaned itself from the federal government fund. "The money was gone, so were some of the restrictions. The Project got smaller, or maybe just more concentrated. The room that had been taken up by fed funds & ultra-scam was now wall-to-wall poets & poverty, breathing energy, pencils sharpened, nothing but wits about them, vital."[90] Money no longer came from a benevolent if despised federal government. Instead, cash had to be cobbled together from a variety of sources, as church administrator Steve Facey (whom Larry Fagin has referred to as "the great hero of St. Mark's Church") recalls:

> I came in November of 1967 to pick up the last seven or eight months on that program, to administer the arts program and the parish. The task was to generate an institutional structure for the arts projects to flourish there. I went out to find money to sustain them. That was contemporaneous with the New York State Council on the Arts. Michael Allen and I met with John Hightower, because the federal grant ended on June 30 of 1968. We got some money then from N.Y.S.C.A., and from the Kaplan Fund. The Rockefeller Brothers funded us; I think even Lifesavers Candy gave us money.[91]

Waldman remembers, "If anything people were getting stronger, more confident as writers, committed to the scene as a result of the interactions with one another, the exchange through readings, collaborations, magazines & the second gen. was breaking into larger press."[92] By "larger press," Waldman is referring to the growing literary stature of Second-Generation New York School poets. Certainly by 1970, many of the writers who were published in *The World* and earlier mimeographed magazines had developed professional relationships with corporate publishers. These publishers had sent editors to Poetry Project readings to scout out the "new talent." Berrigan's *The Sonnets* was published by Grove Press; Padgett's *Great Balls of Fire* was published by Holt, Rinehart; Clark Coolidge's *Space,* Dick Gallup's *Where I Hang My Hat,* Tom Clark's *Stones* and *Air,* and Lewis MacAdams's *The Poetry Room* were all published by Harper & Row; Padgett and David Shapiro's *An Anthology of New York Poets* was published by Random House;[93] and Anne Waldman's *Baby Breakdown* and *The World Anthology* were published by Bobbs-Merrill. Mimeograph magazines had not exactly died, though they were no longer necessary for Second-Generation New York School figures in simply ensuring distribution of texts. While the Poetry Project itself continued to feature mass political readings and to encourage new writers to participate in its programs, the social scene surrounding the Poetry Project was altered by these personal events.[94]

The apartment at 33 St. Mark's Place was no longer the center of the Poetry

Project scene. There were no more regular parties, and one couldn't just decide to spend the night there anymore. With Ted Berrigan's departure came the end of a specific social dynamic that had Berrigan serving as éminence grise to a younger generation of poets.[95] Berrigan's wife—the poet Alice Notley—remembers that Berrigan himself felt the Poetry Project had hit its first bump by 1970: "Ted talked about the Poetry Project all the time. He was extraordinarily enthusiastic about it, but also had this attitude by 1970 that it was over the hill and should close up and leave the field to a new outfit. He always talked as if its best years were its first years, when it was loose and didn't have a lot of rules."[96]

The Poetry Project in many ways used poetry to reflect and comment on these new personal and political commitments and events—for example, readings for the Chicago 7, the Berkeley Defense League, and other politically motivated gatherings—that underscored the changes going on in the culture at large. However, political commitment on the part of these poets resulted in some comparatively conservative responses from figures including the Reverend Michael Allen. A benefit reading in January 1970 for the Ron Gold Defense Fund resulted in a measure of chaos that was to determine behavior at future mass readings.[97] This thirty-hour marathon event involved dozens of Lower East Side residents sleeping in the church. When it was all over, the Reverend Michael Allen discovered extensive damage throughout the church. Pews were damaged, the church organ had been vandalized, and the rugs had been ruined. This discovery resulted in the end of what was slowly becoming a tradition—the large, chaotic, anarchistic, and sometimes days-long poetry event.

Radio Free Poetry

One of the main contributors to the bacchanalia at the Ron Gold benefit reading was the poet John Giorno. Giorno was primarily responsible for organizing poetry-based performances that tended toward highly theatrical, technologically innovative controlled chaos; these events were staged in an effort to fight what he believed were the unnecessarily boring aspects of the traditional poetry reading.[98] Giorno had already achieved some notoriety for his "Dial-A-Poem" experiments based at the Architectural League of New York townhouse on Sixty-fourth Street and Madison Avenue, where Giorno set up about twelve different telephone lines that broadcast twelve different prerecorded poems. One would call the "Dial-A-Poem" telephone number and listen to a randomly selected text. Through "Dial-A-Poem," Giorno made the simple discovery that if he drew media publicity to an arts project, he would receive a lot of attention. The *New York Times* wrote a story about "Dial-A-

Poem," and as a result, the phones rang incessantly. Officials from the telephone company warned Giorno that if "Dial-A-Poem" continued they were going to disconnect all the telephone lines. Recognizing that he had to adapt his technology, Giorno began to think about wireless transmission of poetry. The year after his "Dial-A-Poem" experiments, Giorno recalls that "the Jewish Museum had a major show called 'Software.' The piece I had there was a small radio transmitter which circulated signals via a simple plug which you stuck into an electrical socket. The signal was transmitted within the three stories of the Museum through electrical wires in the building. Everyone in the lobby was handed transistor radios. I called it 'Radio Free Poetry.'"[99]

By 1968, Giorno had developed a system that would allow him to broadcast poems over an area covering approximately a thousand square feet. At this point, Giorno decided to aim higher:

> I figured out that if I broadcast Radio Free Poetry from the bell tower of the Poetry Project, one could reach a big swathe of around ten blocks. And of course one was very fearless in those days. There was a guy who wrote about the station in the *Village Voice*, and he let people know that I was going to transmit a show from the church. It was for a benefit for Ron Gold. At three o'clock the afternoon of the Gold benefit, the FCC arrived and asked me, "Are you John Giorno?" I said, "Yes, I am." Then one guy said, "I just want you to know that if you continue with this and start broadcasting, we will arrest you." The last thing I wanted to do was go to jail, but I had] already broadcast it that morning. I did it that afternoon anyway, just to do it. It was the sixties, after all.[100]

Giorno also used an unconventional light show at the Ron Gold reading: "I had this light column. It was about ten feet tall, it was a double column, and there was a series of lights alternating red, blue, and yellow. The lights were designed in such a way as to analyze the light content of sound. Pitch was in color—red the high end, blue the low end. Brightness was volume. As the sound tapes I made were played, the pitch was registered in the color. This was the precursor of disco lights."[101] Giorno enhanced the visual spectacle by engaging the attendees' olfactory senses with a strong perfume that he sprinkled throughout the church. Various fog machines were also in operation, and Giorno and his assistants manipulated spotlights that circled high-intensity beams throughout the crowd. During the last three minutes of his performance, Giorno remembers

> [these firemen] coming through the fog with their rubber hats and rubber coats! They could tell it wasn't smoke, but they had these big poles with hooks— everyone was trying to explain to these men that it was a poetry performance, and I was yelling "FOG MACHINE! FOG MACHINE!" Then all of a sudden the

two or three minutes were over, and these cops and firemen were all just standing around. At this particular reading I had provided LSD punch for those that wanted it. We made this punch, so one had this big pitcher full of LSD punch to the right of the altar, and everyone would stand around it with his or her paper cups. One did that, and one also gave out a couple of hundred joints around—the idea was to entertain and relax, rather than have everyone sit around on a hard chair looking at some poet.[102]

This performance, while entertaining and wildly popular with the attendees, apparently did not sit well with the Reverend Michael Allen. In a letter to Bernadette Mayer, Anne Waldman wrote:

> What I had come to NYC for was this giant meeting at the Church to air the hostilities over the last 30 hour marathon benefit freak-out & try to save the new one coming up (Jan 24 for John Sinclair) which only I could do somehow. The Rev. Michael Allen completely went berserk loco over recent organ, rug, pew damage & bad scene confrontation with John Giorno over FCC creeps coming with summons to warn John he couldn't broadcast guerrilla radio etc. & Michael signing it saying No we won't do it & John going ahead and doing it of course. Meeting is so unreal, Michael Allen screaming and swearing and the word "fuck" a million times & me just out of the snow (country) & stoned & people shouting at each other & saying amazing things etc . . . Whole outcome is yes, we'll have benefit but I have to supervise carefully, no giant all-night sleep-in etc.[103]

After the Ron Gold benefit, the radical community could no longer treat the church as its personal crash pad and home base. Of course, this social shift in the Poetry Project scene was by no means the "end" of the Poetry Project, nor did it in any way mark a reversal of the Poetry Project's commitment to present and encourage experimental and innovative writing from poets associated with the Lower East Side poetic community. If anything, the New York School found new adherents who read and participated in Poetry Project workshops throughout the 1970s. Ted Berrigan has pointed to the possibility that his departure in some ways opened up the reading scene at the Poetry Project to newer groups of writers: "My leaving was just the first of many departures. We'd come full scale, & most of us had been 8 years in New York. It was time to do something else for a while. Things just began to splinter."[104] The fact that this study in a sense "ends" with the departure of Ted Berrigan can only serve to indicate, in the context of a still-functioning Poetry Project, that the church reading series was a dynamic institution able to adapt to changing circumstances.

Berrigan's departure marked (until his return in the late 1970s) the end of a Berrigan-centered scene as well as a change in the highly social scene at 33 St. Mark's. One party was over; reading series assistant organizer Harris Schiff simply stated in response to a question about Berrigan's departure, "When Ted left to go to Iowa we felt a big drop off. Without Ted I didn't feel so clear about things."[105] However, this does not mean that there were no more parties to look forward to. Ending a history of Lower East Side reading series at around 1970 is a somewhat arbitrary decision, arrived at primarily out of convenience. In many ways, this book is an invitation to future writers to explore the effects that the still-running Poetry Project reading series had on significant poetic social phenomena of the 1970s, 1980s, and 1990s, including the "Third-Generation" New York School through figures including poet and author Eileen Myles and poets Tim Dlugos, David Trinidad, and others and the Jack Kerouac School of Disembodied Poetics at Naropa College in Boulder, Colorado, founded in 1975 by Anne Waldman and Allen Ginsberg. The remainder of this book will consider "language" poets and the Nuyorican Poets Café as they stand in relationship to the Poetry Project. My hope is that these chapters serve as more a postscript than a conclusion, since the history of the Poetry Project itself is still unfolding.

Bernadette Mayer and "Language" in the Poetry Project

I didn't know Ted Berrigan that well—I wasn't part of his clique. Certainly some of the people around him were hostile to what we were trying to do. A lot of that was couched strictly in terms of anti-intellectualism. There wasn't much interest in creating another alternative way of writing, or sense of what's reading all about, or reconfiguring of literary history. But people were amiable enough, and reasonably friendly as long as you weren't disrespectful toward the elders, and those were writers I generally liked. People like myself, Hannah Weiner, Peter Seaton, Nick Piombino, and Jackson Mac Low provided an alternative poetics space for what the St. Mark's crowd had already been doing. $L = A = N = G = U = A = G = E$ wasn't New York based—we weren't focused on just the community and the small-press scene in this town.

BRUCE ANDREWS, INTERVIEW BY AUTHOR

"Incapacity and Awkwardness and Fragmentation"

By the early 1970s, things were changing at the Poetry Project. The Reverend Michael Allen left New York City in 1970 for a position as dean of the Berkeley Divinity School in New Haven, Connecticut. With Allen's departure, the Project was now being led by a new generation of reading series organizers and administrators, including Larry Fagin and Steve Facey. New York School aesthetics were at this point familiar to the vast majority of poets living on the Lower East Side. First-Generation poets had all published books with mainstream publishers. While poets like Padgett and Berrigan never achieved the kind of mainstream success accorded to poets like Richard Howard or Robert Pinsky, they nevertheless were no longer as strongly associated with the avant-garde—if by "avant-garde" one refers to its manifestation as an underground, ephemeral phenomenon. In 1973, Ted Berrigan would even have some of his sonnets included in the *Norton Anthology of Modern Poetry,* albeit with a "disparaging headnote."[1] The Project, while strongly maintaining its ties to poets associated with the New York School, was also ready for some new poetics.

Richard Kostelanetz writes, "Whenever the current state of an art is generally perceived as decadent or expired, then a new avant-garde is destined to arise."[2] With the relative establishment of Second-Generation New York School writers through their national publications and their subsequent geographical dispersal, a new avant-garde of sorts did arise out of the Poetry Project. This new phase at the Poetry Project was influenced in some ways by Bernadette Mayer's work in earlier publications and by her poetry workshops, which were held at the church from 1971 through 1974 and intermittently throughout the subsequent two decades. The workshops served as forums where poets including Charles Bernstein, Hannah Weiner, and Nick Piombino—all writers associated with the "language school"—socialized and theorized with one another. Bernadette Mayer's workshops provided an environment where a new alternative approach could be developed in marked contrast to the roughly defined if preponderant and clubby Poetry Project scene.

The content of these workshops was to play a part in the theoretical and critical work promoted in the later 1970s through magazines including $L = A = N = G = U = A = G = E$.[3] Mayer, perhaps more than any other poet associated with the Lower East Side, brought to the Poetry Project an outside discourse of critical thinking that earlier writers had cockily rejected as being "too serious." Even in the context of two decades of experimental writing characteristic of the scene, Mayer's reading lists for her workshops and her own literary output in the 1970s were generally more overtly intellectually ambitious and "serious" than what had preceded her. Mayer developed what she called "A Reading List to be Added To" and encouraged all her students to read as many books on the enormous and evolving list as they could. Mayer divided the list into various sections including "On Reading" (featuring books including Barthes's *The Pleasure of the Text,* Whitehead's *Modes of Thought,* and Wittgenstein's *Philosophical Investigations*); "Prose and Poetry and Prose Poetry" (Motherwell's *The Dada Painters and Poets,* Dante's *La Vita Nuova*); and "Children's Books" (The *Curious George* books, *The Complete Works of Roald Dahl,* Paula Danzinger's *The Cat Ate My Gymsuit*). Mayer also included photocopies of charts showing the evolution of the English language, Hebrew alphabet tables, and selections from Raymond Queneau's *Exercises in Style.* Mayer generally encouraged her students to think of the act of literary production far more critically than they might otherwise have done.

Mayer's work as an editor and poet also provided a model for the more critically minded and theoretically determined writing associated with the language-writing phenomenon. Mayer's ongoing experiments in procedural verse techniques, initiated in 1967 in her and Vito Acconci's magazine *0 to 9,* proved a new model in marked contrast to the generally friendlier, chattier, and more conventionally accessible (if socially exclusive) texts in *The World*. Mayer consciously viewed these experiments as determining a new territory for writers on the Lower East Side. "*o to 9* manifested a 'resistance' to 'New York writing'; and it appears that the cloistered sociality of 'New York writing' may have been one of [the] spurs to this resistance. In [an interview with Lisa Jarnot], [Mayer] says 'Ted and Ron would do these collaborations and send them to *o to 9* and we would never publish them,' going on to say 'I guess it was because of their style or something.'"[4]

Mayer's early poetry readings also deviated, if not departed, from the norm at the Poetry Project. A particularly radical example of Mayer's consistent interrogation of the authorial public persona is seen in her work with Ed Bowes and Clark Coolidge. For one film, Bowes (using a handheld camera) chased Coolidge and Mayer around Coolidge's home in the Berkshires as they read from the Yale volume of Gertrude Stein's work. The tape was eventually shown at the Poetry Project for an event billed as a poetry reading featuring Clark Coolidge and Bernadette Mayer (listed as occurring on February 24, 1971). The audience, expecting to see the two poets, instead witnessed the film, where the poets themselves were rarely visible and were not reading from their own work. Thus, in one neat performative move, Mayer and Coolidge rejected the primacy of authorial presence, threatened the stability of authorship by reading from Stein's work without citing her, challenged the audience's attention span and flouted their expectations, and generally moved away from a model of the poetry reading as one that offered compressed insight into a text into one in favor of performativity and process. At later readings, Coolidge further disrupted expectations of sociability attendant to poetry readings, going so far as to read all of his book *Polaroid* at the Paula Cooper Gallery (an event that went on for more than two hours, and that Coolidge recalls frustrated and antagonized quite a few of the audience members).

Thus, Mayer proved to be an alternative to the "alternative" defined by Second-Generation New York School writers, and she offered a set of new literary and evaluative standards that moved toward a more overtly theoretical poetics of multiple referentiality[5] and syntactical rupture that was generally suspicious of the poem as an emotive or expressivist composition.[6] Such an approach was highly attractive to emerging writers based in New York, many of whom were put off by what they viewed as the exclusive nature of the Second-Generation New York School social world and the relatively unambitious work that such a culture produced.[7] Charles Bernstein recalls sensing that something at St. Mark's had to be shaken up, and that he and his peers— a number of whom met each other at Bernadette Mayer's workshops—might be able to have a part in reinvigorating an avant-garde spirit at the church:[8]

In the 1970s, St. Mark's certainly had a very strong social hierarchy. It wasn't completely obvious, and it was less so than the visual arts world, which made it seem more democratic, certainly. But it still seemed not as open as I would have liked to have seen. The things I was very interested in when I was editing and organizing events was to open things up beyond the local and sometimes clubby qualities that sometimes developed. I think that what I'm saying about the poetry readings at St. Mark's, which is more important to me than terms like *theory*, is this idea of how you would know something, what you would judge something based on, apart from who you knew and what scene you were part of. That would naturally involve some insistence on nonlocality—on national and international—not to say historical—publications. That is very much against the grain of a certain kind of St. Mark's neighborhood aesthetic. It seemed ludicrous to me that people would hold on to a kind of bohemian identity associated with slogans like "I never go above Fourteenth Street." Lifestyle as a basis for poetry always seemed to be problematic for me, and it was always and already co-opted. Everything gets co-opted, but you want to create some dialectic so that there's a possibility for oppositional or adversarial activity.[9]

Consistently questioning and revising literary inheritance as well as critiquing the role social formations played in determining and defining reception became perhaps some of the most valuable and insurrectionary functions language writers played throughout their (ongoing) history. As the 1970s progressed, the primacy of New York School poets within the alternative poetic community was threatened by some language writers. Referring to Charles Bernstein's work in editing a poetry anthology, Ann Vickery writes, "Bernstein was hesitant about including [Mayer's] more recent work which he felt was oriented more towards the New York school. It was envisaged that L=A=N=G=U=A=G=E would distinguish a poetics separate to the New York school."[10] Such stances were often underscored by literary and linguistic theories (often kept at arm's length by many New York School–associated poets), particularly those of poststructuralist thinkers. California-based poet Ron Silliman wrote to Mayer: "[What] I'm specifically hoping to get at . . . in the collection (the title of which is 'The Dwelling Place' from Roland Barthes' 'the Word is "the dwelling place"' in *Writing Degree Zero*) is diminished referentiality, via either the kind of formal speech-oriented poems of Mike Palmer's, wherein the meanings cancel out, Coolidge's work, Grenier's sort of minimalism, or the kind of visuals Lee Dejasu's work contains."[11] Mayer takes credit for promoting much of this extraliterary reading material among specifically New York–based writers who would come to be organized under the "language school" label: "The language thing happened because I was teaching all the things they wanted to know. Wittgenstein, Lacan, all the things they needed to know. In my workshops, when I first began to teach them, a lot of the language poets came. That's another wrinkle. Charles Bernstein, Bruce Andrews, and Nick Piombino, Peter Seaton, were all in my workshops."[12]

While the poets associated with language writing did not deny their New York School inheritance, they tended to place more significance on the longer, more fractured and "experimental" pieces. Charles Bernstein isolates several instances of New York School texts that were especially amenable to language writers' interest in multiple referentiality: "Koch's 'When the Sun tries to Go On,' or Ceravolo's 'Fits of Dawn'—I was looking for a certain kind of work, and these poems fit that bill. Also, of course, Ashbery's *The Tennis Court Oath*. These fit a certain kind of interest. I'm really interested in incapacity and awkwardness and fragmentation as an experiential dimension of the poem less than the fact of confusion as a theoretical concept, or even as a lifestyle."[13] Language writers set up a kind of dialectical tension between the two dominant New York School "styles": the New York School of the "I do this, I do that" tendency that influenced many Second-Generation New York School writers to write similar and at times derivative homages and the New York School of the longer, more disjunctive works mentioned by Bernstein, which had yet to find a considerable number of ambitious poets willing to expand on and complicate.

Additionally, literary style was associated with lifestyle. Where Second-Generation New York School writers tended toward a more typically bohemian social nexus, language writers proved less easy to pin down within what might be imagined as an avant-garde "poet's life." Variously working as medical writers, community activists, and—as the 1970s progressed into the 1980s—university-level professors, language writers have more generally rejected the bohemian lifestyle, regarding it as, in Bernstein's words, "already co-opted." They chose instead to elide completely the easily recognizable "antiestablishment" stance in favor of working in more geographically and psychically diffuse areas.

Both aesthetics and lifestyle helped language writers differentiate themselves from the earlier New York–based avant-garde, even as many poets took advantage of the scene at St. Mark's to develop and transmit their poetics:

An effect of $L = A = N = G = U = A = G = E$ (even if unintentionally) was to widen the divisions between poetic communities in New York. . . . Visiting New York in late 1978, Kit Robinson witnessed a territorial struggle between East Side poets and Language writers, which included some boycotting of readings (although he escaped unscathed). Bernstein believed that there was a dangerous but very real "groupism" occurring. He would write to Silliman on New Year's eve of 1979, "Circles seem to close tighter & tighter, corral the wagons, in an ever diminishing ability to imagine oneself in some corner other than the one one's been painted into."[14]

Other poets associated with the Second-Generation New York School found language writers unnecessarily obscure, academic, and didactic. This attitude toward language poetry, which very often slipped into outright anti-intellectualism, was to find its most hilarious if ferocious expression in Tom Clark's essay "Stalin as Linguist," which was printed in various versions in the magazine *Poetry Flash* as well as *The Partisan Review:* "[The language school writers] are as long on critical theory as they are (relatively, and I think also absolutely) short on poems. Their criticism is mostly written in a pretentious intellectual *argot* that sounds a little like an assistant professor who took a wrong turn on the way to the Derrida Cookout and ended up at the poetry reading."[15]

Nevertheless, such opposition was necessary if there was to be progress within the Poetry Project scene, which had by the early 1970s served as a base for the production of an enormous number of poems through various mimeographed magazines while remaining uninterested in providing a clear, self-critiquing mechanism that would continue to interrogate the process whereby poetry—and poetic communities—was produced. Language writers were determined as much to write innovative poetry as they were to examine how poetic reception was defined by the various circulating discourses of politics, both on a coterie and a geopolitical level. In this sense, language writers introduced a far more inquisitive and theoretically determined conversation into a community that had perhaps become complicit and complacent in the face of its own nascent and self-enclosed mythology.[16]

However, while language writers introduced a kind of division and at times unwelcome progression into the Poetry Project and certainly among the alternative poetry scene at large, the Project nevertheless played a part in determining the theoretical impulses specific to this group. Writing workshop exercises that Mayer developed specifically for her classes during the early 1970s at the Poetry Project are similar in content and tone to statements made in the magazine $L = A = N = G = U = A = G = E$. This is not to say that poets published in $L = A = N = G = U = A = G = E$ were all somehow in debt to Mayer. Apart from those poets living in New York, many language writers did not have significant relationships with Mayer. Rather, the point here is that Mayer and the scene in and around the Poetry Project were *partly* responsible for putting these ideas "in the air," as it were, of the poetic community.[17]

The consistently evolving set of writing prompts that Mayer called "Experiments" and distributed to Bernstein and others are as suggestive of New York School style irreverence as they are of an increasingly fashionable post-structuralism. Mayer's "Experiments" included "Attempt to eliminate all connotation from a piece of writing & vice versa" and "Work your ass off to change the language & dont ever get famous."[18] While language that encouraged its readers to eliminate all connotation from a piece of writing and to "work your ass off to change the language" could have suggested a poststructuralist approach to language, the phrase "dont ever get famous" may very well have been influenced by Frank O'Hara's earlier and widely known statement in *The New American Poetry:* "I don't think of fame or posterity (as Keats so grandly and genuinely did), nor do I care about clarifying experiences for anyone or bettering (other than accidentally) anyone's state or social relation, nor am I for any particular technical development in the American language simply because I find it necessary."[19] Mayer was in a rather tough balancing act here; fascinated by the possibilities for linguistic innovation, she nevertheless maintained a connection to writing as expressivist, microsocial, and personal. However, Mayer's students at the Poetry Project ended up focusing much more on the theoretical impact of her (and their) ideas, and used their writing to extend this philosophical and linguistic inquiry initiated in some measure by the Mayer workshops and earlier publications associated with her.

Threatening and questioning the supposedly inherent connotative and monologic impulses in language was of primary importance to writers including Bernstein, Andrews, and Silliman. Language writers were influenced in part by Mayer's "Experiments" list, particularly those sections of the list that whimsically challenge the primacy of the individual author and emphasize the materiality of speech and instability of meaning: "Rewrite someone else's writing. Experiment with theft and plagiarism . . . Get someone to write for you, pretending they are you."[20] Silliman's text "For L = A = N = G = U = A = G = E" in many ways parallels Mayer's "rules" for writing as published in her ever-evolving "Experiments" list, and shows the extent to which language writers adapted theory in the late 1970s to serve as aesthetic gestures:

> Word's a sentence before it's a word—I write sentences—When words are, meaning soon follows—Where words join, writing is—One's writing is one writing—Not all letters are equal—2 phrases yield an angle—Eye settles in the middle of word, left of center—Reference is a compass—Each day—Performance seeks vaudeville—Composition as investigation—Collage is a false democracy—Spelling's choices—Line defined by its closure: the function is nostalgic—Nothing without necessity—By hand—Individuals do not exist—Keep mind from sliding—Structure is metaphor, content permission, syntax force—Don't imitate yourself—we learned the language—Aesthetic consistency = voice—How does a work end?[21]

Silliman's text shows the extent to which writing associated with the language school became self-reflexive and highly self-conscious of itself as writing. Both tentative—"How does a work end?"—and humorously arrogant in its manifesto-like imperatives, these phrases revolve around interrogating the process of composition itself. Silliman overtly raises questions that had been raised suggestively by predecessor poetry including the anonymous, collagist, and collaborative work found in mimeograph magazines like *The World;* Bernadette Mayer's and Vito Acconci's *o to 9;* and Mayer's workshop magazine *Unnatural Acts* (discussed below). Many language writers, who suggested in various articles that their poetics were developed out of an intellectual inquiry into what it meant to be part of a community, were able to look back on the communal model articulated in these and other predecessor magazines, even if, like Silliman, they lived outside New York City.[22] Additionally, in the context of specifically New York–based writers like Bernstein and Andrews coming together at the Poetry Project, one can theorize that favoring a communal vision and critiquing representational literature may have been partly influenced by the collaborative atmosphere of the Poetry Project. While this scene promoted personalities like Ted Berrigan, it also depreciated the value of authorial and individual presence through acts of collaboration and political organization.[23]

That poets published in *L = A = N = G = U = A = G = E* were often committed left-wing activists was somewhat predictable, considering both the cultural fact of their presence on university campuses during the 1960s as well as the more localized environment at places including St. Mark's Church during the early 1970s. "In the terms used by the Language group, the new stress is on the poetic demystifying, unveiling and *sharing* of meaning, in contrast to a view of language that has to do with ideological closure, fixed meaning as the expression of power relations, and communication as a mere 'exchange of prepackaged commodities.'"[24] When one considers that this "sharing of meaning" and rejection of "ideological closure" had partial origins within the radical political and social milieu of the Poetry Project and the late 1960s and early 1970s increasingly militant counterculture, we see how some language writers might have conceived of their poetics as a critique of conservative, capitalistic social and linguistic order.

Bruce Andrews epitomizes this possibility in his essay "Writing Social Work and Political Practice" published in *The L=A=N=G=U=A=G=E Book,* where he discusses the subversive possibilities for an "alternative structuralist view" in poetics:

> More radically, the poetics would be those of *subversion:* an anti-systemic detonation of settled relations, an anarchic liberation of energy flows. Such flows, like libidinal discharges, are thought to exist underneath & independent from the system of language. . . . The coherence between signifier & signified is con-

ventional, after all—rather than skate past this fact, writing can rebel against it by breaking down that coherence, by negating the system itself. Result: an experimentalism of diminished or obliterated reference. . . . So: a spectrum stretching from "stylistic display" work to a more disruptive political work— within the mostly self-contained linguistic system, of the sign.[25]

Note here the language of eroticism combined with the language of avant-gardism; we have the orgasmic "detonation" and "liberation of energy flows . . . like libidinal discharges" in relation to subversion, "experimentalism," and a rejection of the "conventional."[26] This was both a highly social and sexual vision of poetry and a politically charged revelation. Bearing in mind that Andrews was part of the poetic community at the Poetry Project,[27] we can tentatively point to the sexy and political atmosphere of the Poetry Project itself as one of a number of possible sources for Andrew's ideas on what poetry could do within the context of a community. Poets in many ways resanctified St. Mark's Church as a contemporary tribal space and used that space to en-act organized challenges to the dominant political culture through events like read-ins against the war and drug-bust release funds. Despite having some se-rious misgivings over what he felt was an unnecessarily exclusive scene, An-drews maintained: "Nevertheless, if you were looking for readings or some kind of social scene in the poetry world that wasn't connected to mainstream academic life or workshop kind of bullshit, you had St. Mark's."[28]

Many language writers focused on the poetry reading itself as a crucial site for poetic reception and dissemination. The poetry reading was used to pro-mote a new trend in antirepresentation; writers including Bernstein, Andrews, Piombino, and Silliman eschewed social realism, as a glance through their writ-ing makes clear. Even a relatively conventional poetics of observation visible in Silliman's long poem "What" (here excerpted) indicates the pleasure that some language poets took in letting the materiality of speech itself disrupt realism:

The scudding wind
pushes the brim of my hat.
The ridges in the red rock
ripple, the dust atop
a lighter yellow. Tongue touches teeth
to form an "L." Each line
breaks at the point
where anxiety peaks.
This can be spelled
double "e." Thees
can be spilled. . . . Hard "S,"
breath pours over tongue's flesh.[29]

This section of "What" suggests that realism as a mimetic concept is bound to collapse with the welcome indeterminacy of the temporal breath. *Speaking* the poem distributes it, thereby fracturing it into the mouths and tongues—and subsequent overflow of interpretations—in which the text finds itself. This section of the poem/story disintegrates into erotics of sound and voice; the poetic line "breaks" out of anxiety, only to be suffused by the pleasures of associative spelling and connotative slippage. The realism of a walk in the wind is happily subsumed in a poetics of utterance. The speaker call forth breath, which materializes and decontextualizes speech and language "over tongue's flesh." Charles Bernstein places this kind of text firmly within the context of live readings:

> I would say that because of the complex prosodies being enacted by something like Silliman's poem, which don't have an obvious way to read them, the poem becomes a sounding board. Readings are crucial sites for testing the sound. If you think as I do that the poetry reading is as crucial as the book in terms of the enactment and transmission of the work, of course it allows for certain kinds of acoustic exploration to take place that wouldn't if the reading took place silently. Silliman's poem evokes a scene of reading out loud to yourself—the actual sound gets in the way of a certain sort of transparent image. This kind of poem prevents the production of transparent meaning via the material production of sound.[30]

An aesthetic of dislocative utterance suggested by Bernstein had already been defined in part by Roland Barthes. Barthes (whose writings Mayer assigned to her workshop students) played an important role in that period in helping language poets conceive of writing as an essentially performative enactment of the instability of the relationship between signifier and signified. In "The Death of the Author," Barthes wrote, "*Writing* can no longer designate an operation of recording, of observation, of representation, of 'painting' (as the Classics used to say), but instead what the linguists, following Oxfordian philosophy, call a performative, a rare verbal form . . . in which the speech-act has no other content (no other statement) than the act by which it is uttered: something like the *I declare* of kings or the *I sing* of the earliest poets."[31] Recognizing (as many of the language writers felt one should) that stable referentiality was itself a construct enabled poets to break rules and threaten social order through performance; we have as examples Ron Silliman reading his poems out loud on various forms of public transportation in San Francisco and the more discrete readings held at the Poetry Project and related spaces in the late 1970s and 1980s.[32] This was not, however, the kind of performativity associated with a figure like Charles Olson, whose personality and poetry were conflated so much that Olson as an individual became practically deified. Rather, the performativity of language poets suggested an attempt to enact a new avant-garde, one that was far more interested in "the social rules and context of utterance, along lines indicated by Structuralism and Speech Act theory," as opposed to "an expressivist aesthetics derived from Romanticism which characterized earlier avant-garde formations such as the New York or Black Mountain groupings."[33]

The reason that a purportedly late 1970s and 1980s movement like "language poetry" is being discussed here is only to suggest that language poetics (as defined through literally thousands of essays, manifestoes, and e-mails found in texts like *The L = A= N = G = U = A = G = E Book* and on the Buffalo Poetics List, www.wings.buffalo.edu/epc/poetics/)[34] owe a partial historical debt to events that occurred in the poetic community of the Lower East Side in the late 1960s and early 1970s. The profusion of commentary related to what was to become known as the "language school" points to that school's self-conscious extension of an avant-gardist stance. As Paul Mann writes, "The avant-garde is completely immersed in a wide range of apparently ancillary phenomena—reviewing, exhibition, appraisal, reproduction, academic analysis, gossip, retrospection—all conceived within and as an economy, a system or field of circulation and exchange that is itself a function of a larger cultural economy. Art exhibits an active relation to the discursive economy, a will to discourse that is its most general if not its most basic commitment."[35] As we will now see, the language writers' tendency to produce this abundance of rhetoric associated with the production of poems was partly influenced not only by the social scene at the church but also by Bernadette Mayer's work editing the magazines *o to 9* and *Unnatural Acts.*

0 to 9 and *Unnatural Acts*

Bruce Andrews summed up the essential role that journals such as *o to 9* played among the language writers:

As a graduate student in Baltimore, the only way I could connect with anyone was to submit work to magazines. I remember getting ahold of the Paul Carroll anthology—I was starting to write, extending radical modernist traditions that I was able to track down through the century, but I had no idea there were people my age doing this. I noticed things like Stein, or *The Tennis Court Oath,* but I was missing out on the magazines. I remember getting ahold of *o to 9,* I remember getting ahold of the *Paris Review* when it was edited by Tom Clark— the *Review* was publishing people like *o to 9* editor Vito Acconci, and Clark Coolidge. I would send poems to the *Paris Review* every couple of months. I remember I got a letter back from Ron Padgett, who was working for Clark in the New York office of the *Paris Review*. He wrote, "Dear Mr. Andrews, this is to let you know that the *Paris Review* isn't the only magazine in the world." He sent me addresses for some other magazines. That was where I started. Then, finally, sometime around 1970, Padgett wrote, "This latest batch we really liked, and I'm sending them on to the big boss." And they published a piece of mine in 1970, a year after I started writing. I sent stuff to *The World* in the early 1970s, I sent stuff to editor Acconci right when *o to 9* ended. I got Berrigan's address and sent him some work, maybe in 1971. He wrote me back a nice note saying, "These poems are great. You should do what Ron and I did. Publish a little magazine, publish all your friends, and get rich and famous." I had a sense of there being this activity. The only kind of angle into the small press poetry world was the radical fringe of what was going on at St. Mark's, some loose formulation of experimental poetry which at that point would include concrete, visual, conceptual or sound work.[36]

By editing *o to 9* with her brother-in-law (performance artist, filmmaker, and writer Vito Hannibal Acconci) and extending the theoretical impulses of the magazine into her workshops, Bernadette Mayer helped to promote a kind of theoretical inquiry that had been relegated to the background by New York School poets loathe to appear too "serious" (and academic). Additionally, Mayer actively supported work and study in genres outside poetry. Ed Friedman, an early participant in Mayer's workshops and current director of the Poetry Project, remembers, "The scene became more 'open' in a certain way. Bernadette perceived herself as *not* part of the church scene, or at least she didn't see her writing that way. On the other hand, she always talked about Ron and Ted being great poets. She recognized though that there was an interest in having a more critical, theoretical tone in poetry. One workshop I remember read Einstein's autobiography."[37]

The performativity in and of poetry, as well as what Friedman refers to as "a more critical, theoretical tone in poetry" now associated with much language writing, is especially visible in *o to 9*.[38] In an environment where avant-garde poetry readings and performance-oriented "Happenings" occurred throughout the Lower East Side, *o to 9* consistently presented relatively abstract texts within a context of highly social performativity. Like *Trobar* and *Poems from the Floating World* before it, the second issue of *o to 9* performed a kind of literary archaeology, recovering tribal texts that tended to conform to the magazine's overall ethos of fragment and ellipses, while at the same time pointing back to these texts' function as part of an oral tradition. The August 1967 issue of *o to 9*, for example, included anonymous "Eskimo Songs" (here excerpted):

Though I walked on the ice down there,
Though I walked on the ice down there,
It did not seem like real ice.

Such a text was bound to be read in sympathy with the Gertrude Stein piece "IN," published in the same issue (here excerpted):

Was is ice
Was is ice
Was is ice
Was is ice
Elastic. Elastic in layed.[39]

Here we have a magazine that carefully positioned one fragmented text— "though I walked on the ice down there"—alongside another fragmented text from high modernist Stein—"was is ice / was is ice." Thus, one reads Stein (a crucial literary predecessor figure for many poets published in $L = A = N = G = U = A = G = E$) in relation to a poem from the Eskimo oral tradition. Both texts point to each other, the Eskimo song suggesting Stein through repetition and use of the word *ice* and vice versa. By virtue of the elements these texts share, Stein asks to be read within the context of the performative and the anonymous characterized by the Eskimo songs.

Mayer would extend these performative and anonymous elements in poetry in her workshops during the 1970s, particularly in her administration of the magazine *Unnatural Acts*. As Ed Friedman remembers it, one workshop devoted itself entirely to producing the magazine:

Towards the end of Bernadette's first workshop at the Poetry Project, which ran from Fall 1971 through Spring 1972, we came up with the writing method which produced *Unnatural Acts*. We were interested in collaboration and *process*. When I say process, I mean that we were intending to be less precious about the actual product or outcome of writing experiments, and therefore, leaving more room for writing to be a present-time document of the writer's mind while writing. What we came up with was a way to compress the collaboration process; we decided to have everyone in the workshop writing in the same place for an extended time period. Everyone anonymously contributed a piece of writing, which someone else in the group used as the basis for composing a new work. The "originals" were then discarded and the afternoon proceeded with everyone continuing to write works inspired by the reworkings of reworkings of reworkings. We decided to publish the results as *Unnatural Acts;* since no one could really claim complete ownership of any of the individual works, none of the pieces were credited to a particular writer. The following fall (1972) we repeated the experiment, inviting John Giorno, Anne Waldman, Joe Ceravalo and others to participate. One of the funny things that happened was that we got a set of pieces written in Giorno's "repetition style," only I don't think John wrote any of them. We published the results as *Unnatural Acts* 2.[40]

The trends referred to by Friedman initiated in part through *Unnatural Acts* were certainly carried over by later language writers; in *Content's Dream,* Charles Bernstein challenges the assumption that writing is a "natural" expression of a writer: "'Natural: the very word should be struck from the language.'" Bernstein goes on to suggest that "naturalness" is artifice: "Personal subject matter & a flowing syntax, whatever those descriptions mean to a particular writer, are the key to the natural look."[41]

As Friedman's earlier comments suggest, *Unnatural Acts*—like later work associated with $L = A = N = G = U = A = G = E$—challenged the conventional view of writing as expression naturally unique to a solitary individual. This was done in an effort to undermine normative and essentialist assumptions about what made a writer a writer and about what it meant to "own" one's own writing. *Unnatural Acts* set up a situation in which authorial identity was jeopardized by a communal quasi-Marxist writing model. The second issue used its cover to advertise slogans and fragments that clearly stated the participants' overall political and theoretical affiliations. Language like "WHERE NO PIECE THAT IS WORKED ON IS OWNED—*PROPERTY IS ROBBERY,*" "*FIRST* the word / you will speak it / and then me / it will share our power" and "*WHY SO MUCH DIALOGUE*" indicated the participants' conception of the valences between writing, politics, and community. The texts inside this issue also continually refer to the process of composition and the political atmosphere surrounding that process. The magazine featured poems with lines including "the fascists are taking over everywhere (nov. 11) & they do not know what they are doing & there's no heroin for heroin addicts" and "I'll take out the I's: / just the grass, green grass, tall grass."[42] Such lines worked in tandem with the stated goals of *Unnatural Acts* participants, particularly those in the editorial statements included on the cover that emphasized the texts as a "collaborative writing experiment" destabilizing author / ity through their removal or "taking out" of the monologic "I."

This is not to say that there were never any tensions between the desire to participate in a collaborative experiment and the desire to make a name for one's self as an individual author. Mayer remembers:

When Ed Friedman and I were doing this magazine which we did for three issues, *Unnatural Acts,* the idea was that it was going to be just collaborations. So we used to write in one eight-hour period, and we'd invite all these other people to come write with us. I remember the second time we did it, it was hard to get people to do it, because they didn't want to lose their identity. Someone came up to me the second time we did this and said to me "Is anyone going to know what part I wrote?" I said, "No, I don't think so." That was a big problem for this writer. Times were changing in the 1970s, that's for sure. There weren't so many communes around, which was in a weird way tied into poetry and this growing resistance on the part of poets to participate in a communal, anonymous-type activity.[43]

Although there was still a fair amount of idealism, the historical fact that a certain era was coming to a close had its effect on the production of *Unnatural Acts:* There was to be only one more issue. The need among poets of the Lower East Side to connect a text to a single author remained strong. Writers in the Mayer workshop and the later language school have not, in the most fundamental sense, rejected author/ity by disassociating themselves from their texts by using pseudonyms or other strategies. Nevertheless, we can see the poetry—and the associated social environment—of the language school as part of the legacy of the Mayer workshops and related publications.

Bob Holman, the Poetry Project, and the Nuyorican Poets Cafe

"I Learned That Poetry Could Be about Community Here"

A POETRY SLAM INVOLVES A GROUP OF POETS READING THEIR WORK TO AN AUDI-
ence—members of this audience then score the poet's poem and perform-
ance, and the winner receives some kind of symbolic or cash prize.[1] In his in-
troduction to *Aloud: Voices from the Nuyorican Cafe,* Cafe founder Miguel
Algarín writes that slams in the early 1990s at the Nuyorican started with

> our host, Bob Holman, reading his Disclaimer: "We disdain / competition and
> its ally war / and are fighting for our lives / and the spinning / of poetry's co-
> coon of action / in your dailiness. We refuse / to meld the contradictions but /
> will always walk the razor / for your love. 'The best poet / always loses.'" Judges,
> who have been selected whimsically from the audience, are introduced with
> such "qualifications" as being born in Brooklyn or having never been to a Slam
> before. These judges will rate the poem from zero ("a poem that should never
> have been written")—to ten ("mutual simultaneous orgasm") using the "Dewey
> decimal rating system" to avoid ties and "the dreaded Sudden-Death Haiku
> Improv overtime round." Here we are in the realm of literate humor, with no
> discerning of "high" and "low," all in the service of bringing a new audience
> to poetry via a form of entertainment meant to tune up fresh ears to a use of
> language as art that has been considered dead by many.[2]

To end this study with a brief discussion of the role the Poetry Project has
played in influencing the so-called spoken word or poetry slam movement
is, in a sense, to ask for trouble. Generally speaking, the audience at a Poetry
Project reading is composed mainly of middle-class white intellectuals. Con-

trast this to the Nuyorican Poets Café audience, which Christopher Beach rightly characterizes as including "middle-class whites from Queens and Bensonhurst, Latinos from the Lower East Side, blacks from uptown, and visitors who have come to this mecca of slam poetry from Chicago, Los Angeles, Boston, or Dublin."[3] The poetry performed at the slams reflects this diversity. Slam poetry is a multicultural poetry; a glance through the anthology *Aloud: Voices from Nuyorican Poets Cafe* shows a far larger number of poets of color participating in the social scene at the Nuyorican than the Poetry Project has ever had. Much of the poetry produced for slams is primarily performative and immediately accessible. This poetry is perhaps more indebted to such varied influences as the traditional rhyming couplets found in contemporary rap and hip-hop, 1970s punk, comedy club performances, and the vivid spectacle of late 1980s performance art than it is to any modernist inheritance. Nevertheless, poets reading at the Nuyorican petition their predominantly urban audience—often with extravagant and personal presentations—to participate and listen to a poetry and performance–centered event. Writers who were initially associated with the Nuyorican, including the novelist Paul Beatty (whose book of poems *Big Bank Take Little Bank* was "blurbed" by Allen Ginsberg) and Edwin Torres (whose work combines Puerto Rican inflected language with Futurist experimentation), have by now broken through the boundaries between the Poetry Project and the Nuyorican by merging experimental form with a hip, urban populist presentation.

Holman's "invocation" to *Aloud* declares the book's challenge to distinctions between popular and high art and isolates rap as the conductor joining the two: "This book dares state the obvious—RAP IS POETRY—and its spoken essence is central to the popularization of poetry. Rap is taking place, aloud, as a new poetic form, with ancient griot roots."[4] Nuyorican Poets Cafe regular Reg E. Gaines's popular poem "Please Don't Take My Air Jordans" complements Holman's proclamation. The poem could easily work as an "old-school" style rap, in that it serves a pedagogical role expressed here via a heavily rhythmic, rhymed critique of urban consumer and fashion culture:

> my air jordans cost a hundred with tax
> my suede starters jacket says raiders on the back
> I'm stylin . . . smilin . . . lookin real mean cuz
> it ain't about bein heard just bein seen

Here Gaines presents the reader with a persona whose obvious function is to send a clear message against shallow materialism. Later on in the poem, Gaines adds pathos to the picture by emphasizing the persona's lack of critical insight and his victim status as pawn of the multinational fashion industry.

and the reason i have to look real fly
well to tell ya the truth man i don't know why
i guess it makes me feel special inside
when I'm wearin fresh gear i don't have to hide

but i really must get some new gear soon
or my ego will pop like a ten cent balloon.[5]

In contrast to the kind of hip-hop aesthetic of Gaines's text (and echoed in many of the poems included in *Aloud*),[6] Marcella Durand notes, "There are still persistent problems [at the Poetry Project], such as the lack of non-white women editing and publishing through the Project . . . this goes for non-white men as well."[7] Additionally, the Poetry Project has remained relatively noncommercial—that is, though the Project continues to survive partially off of corporate funding, one would not find banners for Pepsi or Microsoft on the Poetry Project proscenium. Poetry slams, however, have been underwritten by a variety of multinational corporations. Just a few examples include Nike's sponsorship of a poetry event (ironic in the context of Gaines's poem) in which poems were read during the Winter Olympics in Japan, Borders Bookstore's sponsorship of Youth Slams in San Francisco and New York for the organization Writers Corps, and MTV's broadcast of "spoken word" features including "Spoken Word Unplugged" and "Fightin' Wordz."

This kind of corporate participation in poetry invites a certain amount of controversy. Poetry "purists" have accused slam participants of commercializing and thereby minimizing the value of poetry. In an essay published in *Harpers,* Jonathan Dee wrote that the work of poet Emily XYZ, who participated in the Winter Olympics event, "has no content—which is to say, no connection between the language you use and your actual conviction." Dee went on to claim that XYZ would be known essentially as "the poet from the Nike television commercial. . . . As for what her work concerns, the question is moot, since she has demonstrated that the content of her work is arbitrary; that is, it's for sale."[8] However, while Dee complains about corporate investment in poetry, poetry associated with slams has reached thousands of people. Commercial sponsorship and distribution has resulted in nothing less than a spoken word phenomenon; the first national poetry slam held in San Francisco in 1990 featured three teams. In Chicago in 2000, the tenth anniversary national poetry slam featured forty-eight teams from around the country, all of them gathering to perform and celebrate their versions of poetry.

Many people are responsible for initiating and promoting the spoken word phenomenon whose epicenter was the Nuyorican Poets Cafe on East Third

Street between Avenues B and C. Miguel Algarín, the founder of the Nuyo-
rican, has provided a space for slams for more than a decade, along with pre-
senting original drama and music from poets and writers including Amiri
Baraka, Ishmael Reed, Steve Cannon, and Ntozake Shange. Bob Holman,
however, was perhaps the most visible promoter of poetry slams. Holman wit-
nessed the original poetry slams run by Marc Smith in Chicago's Green Mill
bar and coffee shop. Impressed by what he understood to be a truly oral,
community-based poetry tradition, Holman suggested to Algarín that the
Nuyorican Poets Cafe begin its own poetry slam nights. Algarín agreed, and
subsequent years found slam nights at the Nuyorican attracting hundreds of
people from the Lower East Side community, students from local colleges and
high schools, and representatives from recording labels and the theater com-
munity. Press attention followed; Holman has been a guest on TV shows in-
cluding *Charlie Rose,* Ted Koppel's *Nightline, Today, The Tonight Show,* and
Good Morning America, and he acted as poetry slam emcee in the motion pic-
ture *Slam.* He has also been featured in a myriad of newspaper and magazine
articles, most of which present Holman as one of the primary organizers of
a populist and multicultural poetry movement.

It is at this interstice—of Holman and the Nuyorican Poets Café—that
we recognize how the Poetry Project indirectly contributed to the environ-
ment surrounding poetry slams. Asked where and how he was influenced to
promote a series of live readings at the Nuyorican Poets Café and elsewhere,
Holman responded: "I remember when Jim Brodey did *Howl* in five languages
at the Poetry Project. They were read simultaneously—unrehearsed, just to
do it. The performance dynamic at the church has been nurtured and im-
portant and was what allowed me to go down to the Nuyorican Poets Cafe
and start my thing there."[9] The public and collaborative nature of poetry read-
ings at St. Mark's in which Holman actively participated as contributor, as-
sistant director, and performer provided him with a model that he extended
to the more populist, multiethnic, and ultimately more commercial slam scene
at the Nuyorican:

> The Nuyorican Poets Cafe opened in 1974 or '75—it was a little bar on Sixth
> Street between A and B. In 1980, it moved to the building on Third Street and
> closed in '82. It opened up again in 1989. I wanted to start a club—I had been
> traveling around, getting into the rap-is-poetry modality. I credit the Project
> with getting me into this mind-frame. That's where I was—I learned that poetry
> could be about community here. How? The workshops were free. The maga-
> zines were printed by people walking around a table. The horrors of institu-
> tionalization were made human by Allen Ginsberg saying, "There should be
> more parties! Decisions are really made at parties!" Ted [Berrigan] was an ab-

solute model both of some kind of ultimate hippie Jabba the Hut and also some totally learned intellect. That was our world, and we were allowed to have it. There was no concern about pushing it out into populism, but in fact that's the essence of what we were doing.[10]

The Poetry Project inspired Holman to articulate his belief that poetry "could be about community," and Holman extended this lesson to his promotion of poets reading at the Nuyorican Poets Cafe and elsewhere. Whereas language poets have adapted the performative aspects inherent in the Poetry Project to their own ends while maintaining an active role in publishing, slam poets have tended more toward performativity as an end in itself.

As Beach points out, "What the spoken word phenomenon has convincingly demonstrated is that the published anthology is no longer the privileged forum for presenting the work of these poets, as it is for mainstream academic poets."[11] For many of the poets active in poetry slams, writing that exhibits a clear (and often conventionally narrative) social engagement in the local community takes precedence over the articulation of and experimentation with more theoretical approaches to poetry characteristic of language writers. Holman distinguishes between the language writer's performance and the slam poets' performance: "When [Ron Silliman's] *Tjanting* is chanted on BART, it is done as an art event. When Pedro Pietri reads his poems on a sidewalk, it is their natural locale. When Pedro reads, or Willie [Perdomo] reads, it's going to be part of the world. When you hear Pedro read, you can see in the audience how he gets over. That's not in the concern of the language poets. They're doing it because the art carries it in that direction. Pedro and Willie do it because that's what they have to say; it's the natural way to say it."[12] We can see in Holman's response a kind of tension regarding the different kinds of performative impulses characteristic of the Poetry Project. In many ways, Holman's promotion of populist reading events goes back to the Poetry Project's role in the late 1960s in presenting multigenre poetry events at which the community party was in many ways inherently connected to the poem. Currently, the Poetry Project does not engage in these kinds of affairs; most Wednesday-night readings are comparatively staid events where the poet for the most part reads as the audience quietly (with perhaps the occasional shout, giggle, or yell) listens. Friday nights at the Nuyorican are entirely different. Audience and performer call-and-response are the norm, alcohol flows, cigarette smoke fills the air, and so on. Additionally, the crowd is far more heterogeneous in terms of age and race at the Nuyorican than at St Mark's. If one's standards rest solely on promoting the idea of poetry to a diverse group of people, the Nuyorican is clearly ahead of other reading series—including the series at the Poetry Project.

Yet the Poetry Project is not invisible as an influence in this equation. Holman's participation in and organization of readings at the Poetry Project have helped him to justify the poetry in the slams *as poetry* despite the lack of traditional publishing venues for slam poetry. That is, slam poets were not publishing during the early 1990s—they were performing. Yet they referred to themselves primarily as poets as opposed to performers. This dynamic echoes the earlier Poetry Project environment, where an entire community could define itself as poets based primarily on the sheer volume of live poetry readings and despite actual publication credits.

Maria Damon offers a particularly interesting connection between the orality of slammers and the orality of the medieval troubadours: "The question of whether to publish arises for slammers and oral poets. Like Nagy's medieval trouvères (discoverers) their work ends when something is definitively cast in print; and there's a reasonable desire to forestall closure on a creative process: invention and reinvention, improvisation, performance, competition, and other interactive modes."[13] Like the discourse used to promote and justify the earlier poetic community based on the Lower East Side, Damon's writing evokes tradition—the troubadour poets—to lend some historical weight to what otherwise might be dismissed as mere fad. Here poetry is especially valued as it is composed on the tongue, affected and changed by performance, and created for community consumption as opposed to published for alienated solitary reading. One could disregard Damon's connection between slam poetry and troubadour poetry as wishful thinking. However, in the context of the Lower East Side poetic community of which the Nuyorican Poets Cafe is the latest and most popular manifestation, one can see the Nuyorican as yet another extension of an oddly populist spoken-word movement that began in 1962, on East Seventh Street, at Les Deux Mégots coffee shop.

Notes

Introduction

1. Allen Ginsberg, foreword to *Out of This World: An Anthology of the St. Mark's Poetry Project, 1966–1991,* ed. Anne Waldman (New York: Crown Publishers, 1991), xxvii.

2. Pierre Bourdieu, *The Rules of Art: Genesis and Structure of the Literary Field* (Palo Alto, Calif.: Stanford University Press, 1992), 290.

3. Bourdieu, *Rules of Art,* 237.

4. Paul Chevigny, *Gigs: Jazz and the Cabaret Laws in New York City* (New York: Routledge, 1991), 59.

5. "According to the [cabaret] ordinance, a cabaret license was required for:

   any room, place or space in the city in which any musical entertainment, singing, dancing or other similar amusement is permitted in connection with the restaurant business or the business of directly or indirectly selling the public food or drink.

   . . . The ordinance must have been largely directed at the black music and dance that was performed in the Harlem clubs, as well as the social mixing of races that was part of 'running wild,' because in 1926 [when the cabaret ordinance was drafted], the 'jazz' about which the aldermen complained was being played mostly in Harlem"; see Chevigny, *Gigs,* 56–57.

6. John Ashbery, interview by author, in Ashbery's home, New York, February 22, 1999.

Chapter 1: Community through Poetry

1. Steve Watson, *Strange Bedfellows: The First American Avant-Garde* (New York: Abbeville Press, 1991), 7–9, my italics.

2. Christopher Mele, *Selling the Lower East Side: Culture, Real Estate, and Resistance in New York City* (Minneapolis: University of Minnesota Press, 2000), 142.

3. Mele, *Selling the Lower East Side,* 142–43.

4. Mele, *Selling the Lower East Side,* 143.

5. For a history of the real estate industry's role on the Lower East Side during the first half of the twentieth century, see Mele, *Selling the Lower East Side,* chaps. 1–3.

6. Mele, *Selling the Lower East Side,* 283.

7. Amiri Baraka, *The Autobiography of LeRoi Jones/Amiri Baraka* (New York: Freundlich Books, 1984), 232–34.

8. According to Stuart D. Hobbs in *The End of the American Avant-Garde* (New York: New York University Press, 1997), in 1960,

   only four out of forty-four contributors to Donald M. Allen's *New American Poets* [sic] had held full or part-time academic employment. . . . But when Allen reissued his anthology twenty-years [sic] later as *The Postmoderns,* the status of the contributors had changed. More than half of the writers, including Allen Ginsberg, John Ashberry [sic], Robert Creeley, and William Everson, held posts as university faculty. By the 1960s, more than 40 percent of the contributors to little magazines held academic positions, and by the 1970s the number rose to 60 percent and more. (136)

   Poets associated with the reading series in the Lower East Side from Les Deux Mégots to the Poetry Project who ended up as full- or part-time professors included Allen Ginsberg, Allen DeLoach, John Ashbery, Joel Oppenheimer, Carol Bergé, George Economou, Kenneth Koch, Jerry Bloedow, Anne Waldman, Pierre Joris, Ron Padgett, Jerome Rothenberg, Charles Bernstein, and Bruce Andrews, to name just a few. This is not to say that *all* these positions opened up in the 1960s; rather, the decade of the 1960s saw literary renegades beginning to be accepted into formerly rigid institutional settings.

9. Kirby Congdon to Ed Sanders, August 27, 1962, Ed Sanders Archive, Thomas J. Dodd Research Center, University of Connecticut, Storrs. The poet Clark Coolidge, who would go on to participate in the Lower East Side scene, was working at the Brown Library during this period, helping Roger Stoddard (the head of Special Collections) gather material from alternative literary journals.

10. For a description of poetry and its role in the student movement during the late 1960s, see James D. Sullivan, *On the Walls and in the Streets: American Poetry Broadsides from the 1960s* (Chicago: University of Illinois Press, 1997).

11. The resulting social exchanges between poets in Donald Allen's seminal anthology *The New American Poetry* (New York: Grove Press, 1960) and those poets associated with the Lower East Side scene at Les Deux Mégots and Le Metro extended the avant-garde and oppositional significations of the poets in the Allen anthology, allowing those poets in the book to hold on to their status as outsiders and dissenters despite growing acceptance in the academic and cultural mainstream throughout the 1960s. Alan Golding has noted, "[*The New American Poetry's*] tone and contents assailed the walls of the academically established canon, eventually broke them down, and Charles Olson, Robert Creeley, and such were admitted. But when these poets became tentatively canonized, their combative rhetoric was assimilated by the cultural institution it assailed

and lost much of its point. As numerous theorists of the avant-garde argue, this is the likely fate of any extracanonical group or individual seeking the acknowledgment of serious attention"; see Alan Golding's *From Outlaw to Classic: Canons in American Poetry* (Madison: University of Wisconsin Press, 1995), 32. This is true: Ginsberg and others eventually acquired teaching positions (albeit temporary ones) in various universities, and even before they achieved such mainstream success their faces could be seen in *Time* magazine and the *Herald Tribune.* However, one might disagree with Golding's contention that the oppositional rhetoric of the *New American* poets "lost much of its point" simply by virtue of poets acquiring university teaching posts. Golding is perhaps not acknowledging that readers continued to assign avant-garde credentials to Professors Olson, Ginsberg, Creeley, and others; that is, Golding does not mention the possibility that how a text is received by a community determines its role in culture and that interpretive communities drawn to the avant-garde may be inclined to attribute avant-garde status to certain writers, even if they happen to be academics. The Lower East Side scene was precisely this interpretive community that guaranteed, through association, an extended avant-garde status for the poets in the Allen anthology. The continuing affiliation between poets reading at Les Deux Mégots, Le Metro, and the Poetry Project and the poets in the Allen anthology, combined with the newer faces' lack of access to academic posts, maintained avant-garde status for the latter despite the growing absorption of the *New American* poets into the cultural mainstream. For some particularly excellent treatments of the importance of this book to postwar avant-garde formations, see Alan Golding's *From Outlaw to Classic* and the first chapter of John Lowney's *The American Avant-Garde Tradition: William Carlos Williams, Postmodern Poetry, and the Politics of Cultural Memory* (Lewisburg, Pa.: Bucknell University Press; Cranbury, N.J.: Associated University Presses, 1997).

12. Johanna Drucker noted in an essay exploring the links between typography and visual arts, "The aesthetic arenas in which visual experimentation takes on a developed form in the first half of the century include Italian Futurism, Russian Futurism, German and Swiss Dada, English Vorticism, Dutch De Stijl, Anglo-American modernism, and, to a lesser degree, French modern poetry and visual arts associated with Cubism and then Surrealism. In other words, there was a visual component to almost every area of modern poetry"; see her "Visual Performance of the Poetic Text," in *Close Listening,* ed. Charles Bernstein (New York: Oxford University Press, 1998), 132. Drucker's list is a canonical list of the avant-garde, and the poets associated with the Lower East Side scene looked to those movements as predecessors.

13. Richard Kostelanetz, ed., *The Avant-Garde Tradition in Literature* (Buffalo, N.Y.: Prometheus Books, 1982), 406.

14. John Giorno, "I'm Tired of Being Scared," in *An Anthology of New York Poets,* ed. Ron Padgett and David Shapiro (New York: Vintage, 1970), 267.

15. There is a kind of parallelism here between typographical experimentalism, new technologies, and performativity as it played out both in the aforementioned literary movements and in the Lower East Side poetic community. The Italian futurist Filippo Marinetti, for example, developed visual poems that he performed, often with groups of other poets and artists. Marinetti went so far as to imagine aerial poems performed by airplane and stuntmen; as quoted in Michael Kirby and Victoria Nes Kirby, *Futurist Performance: With Manifestoes and Playlists Translated from the Italian by Victoria Nes Kirby* (New York: Dutton, 1971), 221:

As soon as freedom of the air is restored, we Futurist aviators will perform in the Milan sky daytime and nocturnal representations of aerial theatre with dialogue flights, pantomime, dance, and great poems of aerial *paroliberi,* composed by the Futurist poets Marinetti, Buzzi, Corra, Settimelli, Folgore, etc. Above innumerable spread-out spectators, painted airplanes will dance during the day and at night they will compose mobile constellations and fantastic dances, invested with lights of electric projections.

Giorno, as further discussion will show regarding his use of light and radio technology, especially extended these kinds of futurist and dada methods of performance as they were attached to poetry.

16. Of his first meeting with Bob Moog, Giorno remembers, "Once, in 1966, Rauschenberg did something called Experiments in Art and Technology (E.A.T.). He coupled artists with Bell Labs engineers. At that point in 1966 Rauschenberg and I were lovers. I was a young kid, a poet, and I worked as the cameraman. A guy came out to Bob's house, called Bob Moog"; John Giorno, interview by author, in Giorno's home, New York, February 25, 1999.

17. Giorno, interview.

18. Of Dick Higgins, Jackson Mac Low writes, "Dick wrote, composed, and made artworks throughout his childhood, and in the later '50's became publicly active as an artist in many media and 'intermedia.' (In the 60's he initiated the use of that term for works falling between media categories or within several.)" See Jackson Mac Low, "Dick Higgins, 1938–1998," *Poetry Project Newsletter* 174 (1999): 6.

19. Pierre Joris adds, "There is also the whole psychedelic underground press typography of the late sixties—enabled by first versions of word-processing. (I remember when editing CORPUS on the lower east side in 1970, getting IBM to loan us its first word-processing computer—a huge machine filled half the room!—but the fun we had shaping text around visual objects etcetera. . . .)"; e-mail to the author, March 19, 1999.

20. In his introduction to *New American Poetry,* Donald Allen had stated that all the poets he had anthologized were "[f]ollowing the practice and precepts of Ezra Pound and William Carlos Williams" (ii).

21. John Lowney writes in *American Avant-Garde Tradition,*

Williams's appeal to experimental poets as diverse as Louis Zukofsky, George Oppen, Charles Olson, and Robert Creeley, Allen Ginsberg, Frank O'Hara, Diane Wakoski, and Denise Levertov can be attributed to his Americanist avant-garde rhetorical stance. His sustained opposition to the elitist assumptions of high modernism, especially to its insistence on preserving the autonomy of art in a canonical tradition, became increasingly relevant as the academic hegemony of the New Criticism appeared to foreclose any links between poetry and politics. The Black Mountain poets, the New York poets, the San Francisco poets, and the earlier generation of objectivist poets, among others, cited Williams's poetic theory and practice in their polemical writings to challenge New Critical doctrine, which, with its aestheticist separation of poetry from history, was seen to be complicit with the dominant cold-war ideology. (19)

22. Paul Blackburn to Charles Olson, December 8, 1950, Charles Olson Archive, Thomas J. Dodd Research Center, University of Connecticut, Storrs.

23. Ezra Pound to Paul Blackburn, September 20, 1950, Paul Blackburn Papers, Mandeville Special Collections Library, University of California, San Diego. Pound con-

tinued, "Excellent that the PB shd / be learning his purrfession. Now to save time, and spare grampaw 'splanations, but with view getting necessary texts into print / wd / PB and Dudek between 'em report on age, sex, colour, creed, religion etc. of the following bkshops."

24. Pound to Blackburn, July 4, 1950, Paul Blackburn Papers, Mandeville Special Collections Library, University of California, San Diego.

25. Opening the book of Pound's letters practically at random, I found the following from Pound's letter to William Bird, #199: "Re Studio. If Hem don't want it, can yr. friends find 2000 fr. recompense? . . . Mail from friends will reach me with 48 hour delay. As this wd. be inconvenient for 3 Mts. Press, I confide to you that my address is now: *Albergo Monte Allegro, Rapallo*"; see *The Letters of Ezra Pound, 1907–1941*, ed. D. D. Paige (New York: Harcourt, Brace, 1950), 189.

26. Quoted in Lee Bartlett, *Talking Poetry: Conversations in the Workshop with Contemporary Poets* (Albuquerque: University of New Mexico Press, 1987), 157.

27. Ted Berrigan, "Sonnet LVIII," *C: A Journal of Poetry* 1, no. 3 (1963).

28. Ron Padgett, interview by author, Teachers and Writers Collaborative, New York City, December 12, 1997.

29. George Economou, telephone interview by author, March 10, 1998.

30. By 1961, quite a few of the poets anthologized in *The New American Poetry,* including Paul Blackburn, Ray Bremser, LeRoi Jones (now Amiri Baraka), Denise Levertov, Gilbert Sorrentino, Frank O'Hara, Allen Ginsberg, Joel Oppenheimer, Peter Orlovsky, Gregory Corso, Larry Eigner, Kenneth Koch, and John Wieners, were living or at least socializing on the Lower East Side and surrounding neighborhoods. Many of these poets were also reading regularly at Les Deux Mégots and (starting in early 1963) Le Metro, and at related spaces including the Five Spot on Cooper Square and in various art galleries throughout Manhattan. Beyond this group, the majority of poets in the Allen anthology were associating on some level with poets on the Lower East Side. Associations could take the form of basic correspondence as well as publication in mimeographed magazines coming out of the Lower East Side, including Amiri Baraka and Diane di Prima's *The Floating Bear,* George Economou and Robert Kelly's *Trobar,* and Ed Sanders's *Fuck You / a magazine of the arts.* Ron Padgett, active at Le Metro and the Poetry Project, recalls, "The Allen anthology was a confirmation of all I was reading and thinking about, and it made a huge statement about *another* tradition in American poetry that was neglected by the public at large, by universities, by critics. But the Pack anthology . . . I remember reading it and thinking 'that has nothing to do with me'"; Ron Padgett, interview by author, Teachers and Writers Collaborative, New York City, March 24, 1998.

31. Referring to Columbia professor and "academic" literary critic Lionel Trilling, Frank O'Hara wrote in his "Personal Poem," "We don't like Lionel Trilling we decide, we like Don Allen"; see Frank O'Hara, "Personal Poem," *The Collected Poems of Frank O'Hara,* ed. Donald Allen (Berkeley and Los Angeles: University of California Press, 1995), 335. "Personal Poem" serves in part to record a lunchtime conversation between O'Hara and Baraka (the "we" of the poem), both of whom were anthologized by Donald Allen—a good reason to "like" Donald Allen, by anyone's standards. Lionel Trilling and his wife, Diana, were held in some suspicion by downtown poets, since

Diana Trilling had written a critique of a reading that Allen Ginsberg and Gregory Corso gave at Columbia University.

32. Cecil Helmley, "Within a Budding Grove," *Hudson Review* 13, no. 4 (1960–61): 631.

33. Amiri Baraka, untitled article responding to Cecil Helmley's review of *The New American Poetry, The Floating Bear* 2 (1961).

34. Felice Flanery Lewis, *Literature, Obscenity, and the Law* (Carbondale: Southern Illinois University Press, 1976), 197.

35. Lawrence Ferlinghetti, "Horn on Howl," *Evergreen Review* 1, no. 4 (1957): 145–47. Ferlinghetti was also included in Allen's *New American Poetry.*

36. *Evergreen Review* 1, no. 2 (1957). This issue reprinted (from the original City Lights edition put out by Ferlinghetti) all of Ginsberg's poem "Howl." Not surprisingly, Donald Allen would go on to reprint the vast majority of these writers in his anthology. The editorial blurb included on the back of this issue emphasized the avant-garde and socially radical nature of the poets and poetry between the covers, describing the San Francisco scene as composed of "a vigorous new generation of writers, painters and musicians in the Bay Area . . . revolting against the sterility of American 'academicians.'" Here one sees a machismo and generative language; indeed, the alternative poetry scene in San Francisco and its later manifestation on the Lower East Side often tended to unselfconsciously use male-centered language to inject a sense of pioneering vitality into their mostly male ranks. Sperm imagery abounds in this culture; the American avant-garde here is a "vigorous" and fertile avant-garde, boldly exploring new aesthetic frontiers, in contradistinction to effete academics. This often sexualized depiction of an alternative poetry scene in distinction to an academic scene would stay in place for a remarkably long time. By the early 1970s, women poets finally came to the forefront at the Poetry Project and related spaces, and as a result male-centered sexualized rhetoric was interrogated and, in some cases, transformed. See chapter 5 for an extended discussion on the renaissance of women poets in the alternative poetry scene.

37. A letter from John Wieners to Paul Blackburn provides a definition of a poetic community that sets up the "San Francisco Renaissance" as a social precursor to the Lower East Side scene: "I imagine what moves me here is the scene one can make. That all eyes are on you, that all is public, and of no value to them, unless in community, readings, books, posters, that I am swept into this"; Wieners to Blackburn, April 4, 1958, Paul Blackburn Papers, Mandeville Special Collections Library, University of California, San Diego. The emphasis on the social world and its relation to poetry certainly anticipated the later poetic community in the Lower East Side, as poets including Ginsberg and Wieners moved to or read regularly in the neighborhood and joined the Deux Mégots and Metro regulars as part of what was becoming a developing oral tradition.

38. Michael Davidson, *The San Francisco Renaissance: Poetics and Community at Mid-Century* (New York: Cambridge University Press, 1989), 20. In the "San Francisco Renaissance" issue of the *Evergreen Review,* Ferlinghetti would also refer disparagingly to the New Critical hegemony: "[In an article published May 19, 1957, in the *San Francisco Chronicle*], I said I thought ["Howl"] to be 'the most significant single long poem to be published in this country since World War II, perhaps since T. S. Eliot's

Four Quartets.' To which many added 'Alas.' Fair enough, considering the barren, polished poetry and well-mannered verse which had dominated many of the major poetry publications during the past decade or so"; see "Horn on Howl," 146.

39. Kenneth Rexroth, "San Francisco Letter," *Evergreen Review* 1, no. 2 (1957): 12.

40. Quoted in Hazard Adams, *Critical Theory Since Plato* (New York: Harcourt Brace Jovanovich, 1992), 865.

41. Of the reading scene at North Beach, Kenneth Rexroth wrote in the *Evergreen Review* 2, no. 6 (1958): "Don Allen called me up and asked me to say something about the poetry and jazz programs Lawrence [Ferlinghetti] and I have been doing at the Cellar. First, they have been startlingly successful. The first night there were about four hundred people trying to get into a club that holds seventy-five. We had to call the Fire Marshal to clear the hallway. Just as a show it was a wowser. . . . I hope some record company takes us up soon. It should make not just a very popular twelve-inch disc, but it might well start a craze like swallowing gold fish or pee wee golf" (14).

42. Christopher Beach, *Poetic Culture: Contemporary American Poetry Between Community and Institution* (Evanston, Ill.: Northwestern University Press, 1999), 94.

43. Rexroth, *Evergreen Review,* 6–7.

44. Lorenzo Thomas, "Alea's Children: The Avant-Garde on the Lower East Side, 1960–1970," *African American Review* 27, no. 4 (1993): 573.

45. Quoted in Michel Oren, "The Umbra Poets' Workshop, 1962–1965," in *Belief vs. Theory in Black American Literary Criticism,* Studies in Black American Literature, vol. 2, ed. Joe Weixlmann and Charles J. Fontenot (Greenwood, Fla.: Penkeville Publishing, 1986), 189.

46. "The New Critics may have represented a literary conservatism, but it was as much their social and cultural philosophy—particularly in its southern agrarian manifestation—that a poet like Rexroth found so offensive"; see Davidson, *San Francisco Renaissance,* 18.

47. Davidson, *San Francisco Renaissance,* 18. Hostility toward the academic played itself out in a variety of ways. In the early 1960s there was "a 'cold war' (Eric Torgersen's term) between two competing anthologies: the 'cooked' *New Poets of England and America* (1957) edited by Donald Hall, Robert Pack, and Louis Simpson, and the 'raw' *New American Poetry*"; Golding, *From Outlaw to Classic,* 28. For Hall, Pack, and Simpson, *new* simply meant young poets writing new poems, whereas Donald Allen's *New American Poetry* presented itself (particularly by the statements on poetics in the back of the book) as a forum for a contemporary avant-garde. For further analysis of the "anthology wars" and the role of the New Criticism, see Jed Rasula, *The American Poetry Wax Museum: Reality Effects, 1940–1990* (Urbana, Ill.: National Council of Teachers of English, 1996), 68–98, 223–47.

48. Charles Rembrar, *The End of Obscenity* (New York: Random House, 1968), 59.

49. Rembrar, *End of Obscenity,* 60.

50. Rembrar, *End of Obscenity,* 65.

51. Ironically, the same Jacques Barzun would go on in 1964 to aid in the censorship of some Ted Berrigan poems from Columbia University's *Columbia Review.* Ron Pad-

gett (interview by author, Teachers and Writers Collaborative, New York City, March 3, 1998) remembers,

> [Dean of Student Activities] Calvin Lee got very nervous because he didn't know what to do [about whether to allow the publication of the Berrigan poems], so he went to the dean of Columbia College, David B. Truman. Dean Truman looked at the material in question and got upset, but he didn't feel he could act on his own, so he went to Jaques Barzun, one of the most preeminent scholars in literature in the university. According to Dean Truman, Jaques Barzun felt that the poems were "absolute trash," and so Truman notified Calvin Lee that we were not to publish them. We objected, crying, "Censorship!"

52. Rembrar, *End of Obscenity,* 90–91.

53. Rembrar, *End of Obscenity,* 91.

54. Rembrar, in *End of Obscenity,* details Grove's problems with censorship, including the reaction to the publication of Henry Miller's *Tropic of Cancer.* See also Lewis's *Literature, Obscenity, and Law.*

55. Jed Rasula, in his discussion of Helen Vendler's *The Harvard Book of Contemporary American Poetry,* refers to a reviewer's comment that "even before we crack the cover, we sense an uneasy alliance between taste and institutional weight"; see *American Poetry Wax Museum,* 333.
      We can apply this to Grove Press, in that Grove was developing a kind of *anti-institutional* institution through its publishing practices—such an institution, generated visually by the Grove imprint covers, created an "alliance" between an "alternative" literary taste and sensibility and an "alternative" publishing institution.

56. Richard H. Kuh, *Foolish Figleaves? Pornography in and out of Court* (New York: Macmillan, 1967), 141.

57. Amiri Baraka was put on trial in 1961 for sending obscenity through the mails— obscenity in this case being determined by the publication of sections of Baraka's "The Eighth Ditch" and William Burroughs's "Roosevelt at the Inauguration" included in Baraka's and Diane di Prima's mimeographed magazine *The Floating Bear.* He was quoted at his trial stating that writing "should be regarded as pornographic only if it is intended to arouse" and that the work in question had "some old Anglo-Saxon words . . . but they were necessary for the literary effect"; see "A Poet Laments Time Lost in a Courthouse," *New York Post,* October 19, 1961, 27.

58. "Legalize Poetry," *East Village Other* 2, no. 5 (1967): 15.

59. Bernadette Mayer, interview by Lisa Jarnot, *Poetry Project Newsletter* 168 (February/March 1998), 6–7.

60. Lee Lockwood, "Still Radical After All Those Years," *Mother Jones* (September/October 1993); available at www.motherjones.com/mother_jones/5093/lockwood.html.

61. David Henderson, interview by Lisa Jarnot, *Poetry Project Newsletter* 163 (December/January 1996–97): 6, my italics. Additionally, Anne Waldman, who grew up in Little Italy just southwest of the East Village, wrote in her *Autobiography* (Detroit: Gale Research, 1993), 272, "We were weird. All the kids were getting weird. The times were weird, contradictory. If you didn't have a focus or path you could even get twisted. Reflecting on this period now I appreciate how rich and unique it was as

an early ground for a developing sense of alternative community. Realities of racism, anti-abortion, economic social inequities, other poisons permeated the urban atmosphere."

62. Hettie Jones, *How I Became Hettie Jones* (New York: Grove, 1997), 74.

63. James Schuyler to Gerard Malanga, November 28, 1971, Gerard Malanga Archive, Harry Ransom Center, University of Texas, Austin.

64. Quotation from Mele, *Selling the Lower East Side,* 26. Mele, while not addressing the formation of poetic communities per se, does refer to some of the poets under discussion in this study and discusses the effects that middle-class dissidents had on real estate in the Lower East Side during the 1960s. Mele's history of the Lower East Side is a fascinating companion to this work, in that it raises thorny issues of class, white privilege, and the uneasy relationship between artists and real estate developers that are pertinent to questions of the Lower East Side poetic community overall. Mele shows, in *Selling the Lower East Side,* 26, how the Lower East Side was treated as a semiotic field that alternative groupings mined to add substance to their dissent:

> Subcultures, whose identity, social practices, and rituals intentionally embraced and espoused cultural difference, ranging from the bohemians in the 1920s, the beats in the 1950s, the punks in the 1970s, to the queer subculture in the 1980s, found the East Village reputation propitious to the expression of alternative lifestyles. These groups expressed their opposition to bourgeois society by rejecting familiar and comfortable surroundings and taking up residence among the "undesirables" in the urban "abyss." . . .
>
> The Lower East Side emerged as a preferred *site* for subcultures and avant-garde movements in New York City primarily because the struggles between insiders (ethnic and racial working class) and outsiders (white, middle and upper classes) became a *source* of inspiration and expression of a critique of capitalist culture and, in particular, of a bourgeois lifestyle.

65. John Gruen, *The New Bohemia: The Combine Generation* (New York: Shorecrest, 1966), 8.

66. Ted Berrigan, "Sonnet XLI," *The Sonnets* (New York: United Artists, 1982), 41, and "Sonnet XXXVIII," 38. In an interview with Anne Waldman and Jim Cohn, Berrigan stated, "I'm this American. . . . I believe in guys that wear coonskin caps and fringe jackets and go traipsing around America, the migrant teacher circuit, just like the frontier scouts"; quoted in *Talking in Tranquility: Interviews with Ted Berrigan,* ed. Stephen Ratcliffe and Leslie Scalapino (Bolinas, Calif.: Avenue B; Oakland, Calif.: O Books, 1991), 135.

67. George Economou, "Crazy Eyed Cowboys," in *The East Side Scene,* ed. Allen De-Loach (New York: Buffalo University Press, 1968), 81.

68. While Ed Dorn was not a member of the Lower East Side poetic community per se, his books *Gunslinger* and *Hands Up!* (whose titles and content were influenced by cowboy rhetoric) would prove highly influential. Again, fashion extended cowboy iconicity. Poet Michael Stephens remembers seeing Joel Oppenheimer for the first time: "When he walked off the airplane at the Ithaca airport and stepped onto the tarmac, Joel was, at least to my inflamed teenage imagination, every inch a poet. He was tall and frazzled, a bit drunk; bearded, cowboy-hatted, also cowboy-booted, and

shearling coated"; see Michael Stephens, "Poetry Project Days (Meditations on the Oppenheimer that Was)," *Talisman* 20 (Winter 1999/2000): 95.

69. Charles Olson, "Projective Verse," in *Selected Writings* (New York: New Directions Press, 1966), 16–23.

70. At the Vancouver Poetry Conference of 1963, Carol Bergé reported, "During one of the early Seminar sessions, one morning last week, Allen Ginsberg blithely and accurately and instantly tacked a label to the four poets leading the talks that morning: he himself as a 'beatnik,' Duncan as the 'nasty aesthetician,' Creeley as the 'maker of exquisite little poems,' and Olson as the 'father figure of us all.' Much delight and laughter at this assessment: so accurate"; see *The Vancouver Report* (New York: Fuck You Press, 1963).

Joel Oppenheimer said of Olson, "He handled me the way I wish my father had handled me," and Fielding Dawson (a regular reader at Les Deux Mégots, Le Metro, and the Poetry Project) described Olson as "my other father"; quoted in Tom Clark, *Charles Olson: The Allegory of a Poet's Life* (New York: Norton, 1991), 210. Dawson, at the memorial reading for Olson held at the Poetry Project in 1970, stated, "We became [Olson's] sheep, and his animals, and his children. He absolutely accepted his role as father." Olson was the father figure not just to many of the poets in the Allen anthology but also to many of the younger male poets reading at Les Deux Mégots, Le Metro, and the Poetry Project, who themselves tended to look at the poets in the Allen anthology as slightly older, more successful peers.

When Olson died, a memorial reading for him took place at the Poetry Project on February 4, 1970. Poets who read at the memorial included Lower East Side reading series regulars, including Sanders, Berrigan, John Wieners, Gerard Malanga, Fielding Dawson, Clayton Eshleman, Ray Bremser, Diane Wakoski, and Blackburn. The language poets used in eulogizing Olson at this event both echoed a typical antiacademic rhetoric and emphasized Olson's role as father figure. Ed Sanders insisted, "Time and time again, you read lines that would spew puke upon the dogma of a Catholic funeral. These poems are just incredible, their importance. He makes all these creeps who win the National Book Award sound like idiots"; from the memorial reading for Charles Olson, St. Mark's Poetry Project, New York, February 4, 1970 (sound recording), Paul Blackburn Papers, Mandeville Special Collections Library, University of California, San Diego.

Additionally, Alan Golding has noted a "mini-tradition" of revisionist anthologies coming out of the Allen anthology. Placing Eliot Weinberger's 1993 anthology *American Poetry Since 1950: Innovators and Outsiders* (New York: Marsilio Publishers) firmly within that tradition, Golding points out: "As with Allen again, though less directly, Olson is central to Weinberger's view of the period. A manuscript page from *The Maximus Poems* makes up Weinberger's frontispiece, while his 1950 starting date is 'the date of the magazine appearance of Charles Olson's *The Kingfishers,* the first major work by a new writer in the postwar American poetry renaissance'"; *From Outlaw to Classic,* 32.

71. Aldon Nielson, *Black Chant: Languages of African-American Postmodernism* (New York: Cambridge University Press, 1997), 161. Amiri Baraka, then LeRoi Jones, edited *Yugen* with his then-wife, Hettie Jones. In his autobiography, Baraka states that "Projective Verse" was "a bible" for him; see *The Autobiography of LeRoi Jones/Amiri Baraka* (New York: Freundlich Books, 1984), 282.

72. Albert Ellis, "Introduction," *Femora* 2 (1964). The cover of this particular issue was a bright pink card stock with an illustration of six naked women of relatively plump stature standing around looking at themselves.

73. Paul Blackburn, interview by David Ossman, WBAI, New York, 1960 (sound recording), Paul Blackburn Papers, Mandeville Special Collections Library, University of California, San Diego.

74. Rachel Blau DuPlessis, "Manifests," *Diacritics* 26, nos. 3–4 (1996): 46.

75. For an extended analysis of the heterosexism implicit in Olson's work, see Michael Davidson, "Compulsory Homosociality: Charles Olson, Jack Spicer, and the Gender of Poetics," in *Cruising the Performative,* ed. Sue-Ellen Chaser, Philip Brett, and Susan Leigh Foster (Bloomington: Indiana University Press, 1995), 198, 202–3, 207.

76. Bob Holman, "History of the Poetry Project," Poetry Project Archives, St. Mark's Church, New York, 1978.

77. Sara Blackburn, interview by author, in Blackburn's home, New York, August 8, 2000.

78. Susan Howe, "Since a Dialogue We Are," *In Relation* 10 (1989): 16–23.

79. Edward Foster, *Understanding the Black Mountain Poets* (Columbia: University of South Carolina Press, 1994), 39.

80. Baraka, *Autobiography of Amiri Baraka,* 282.

81. Gay male poets associated with the New York Schools include John Ashbery, Frank O'Hara, James Schuyler, Kenward Elmslie, Joe Brainard, and others.

82. John Shoptaw, *On the Outside Looking Out: John Ashbery's Poetry* (Cambridge, Mass.: Harvard University Press, 1994), 47–48.

83. Olson, *Selected Writings,* 161.

84. Suspicion of mythic archetypes in poetry would be extended to figures associated with the Second Generation New York School. In a letter to Clayton Eshleman, poet and artist Vito Acconci, who edited the magazine *o to 9* with Bernadette Mayer, wrote what he termed "corrections" to some accusations Eshleman had made to him in an earlier letter; see Vito Acconci to Clayton Eshleman, March 26, 1969, Clayton Eshleman Archives, Elmer Holmes Bobst Library, Fales Library, New York University:

    Corrections:
    "You very elaborately tell me you don't like to think. Or imagine much." No. Rather: I (not elaborately, but pretty sketchily I admit, but it was only a start) told you that I don't like to be forced to kneel before what sets itself up as "myth," "legend," etc. (Further: when someone announces something as myth, he doesn't ask for thinking, he asks for nodding.)

85. Kenneth Koch, interview by author, in Koch's home, New York, October 12, 1998.

86. Kenneth Koch, "Fresh Air," in *New American Poetry,* ed. Allen, 230.

87. Koch, "Fresh Air," 232–33.

88. Michael Davidson, "'Skewed by Design': From Act to Speech Act in Language Writing," *Aerial* 8 (1995): 241.

89. Olson, "Projective Verse," 390.

Chapter 2: Oral Poetics on the Lower East Side

1. Amiri Baraka, "Poetry Christmas," interview by David Ossman, WBAI, New York, n.d. (sound recording), Paul Blackburn Papers, MSS 4, Mandeville Special Collections Library, University of California, San Diego.

2. One should note that Olson's "field poetics" helped produce a highly *visual* poetry, one in which page layout was self-consciously manipulated to generate a sense of vibrancy and orality.

3. In an interview by David Ossman, WBAI, New York, 1960 (sound recording), Paul Blackburn Papers, Mandeville Special Collections Library, University of California, San Diego, Blackburn has said of the San Francisco scene, natural speech rhythms, and their relationship to form,

   What goes into the poems, especially in the last ten years, is very much a matter of speech rhythms, and of natural, rather than forced rhythms. That is why very often a poem will seem to have no obvious structure whatsoever in terms of what's conventionally thought of as quatrains or three lines, six lines, eight lines. It just doesn't work out that simply, because the rhythms that you're starting with and that you have to resolve are very often irregular themselves, because they are the way we speak. It started from there—ten years ago, Olson, Creeley, Corman, myself, and then the people at Black Mountain picked up from Corman. That would include Max Finstein, Joel Oppenheimer, although they're still writing small things rather than long speech rhythms. Apparently the things came to some kind of explosion with the San Francisco Renaissance, where an awful lot of the people who came out of that—the so-called Beat poets—are writing very much with speech rhythms but tremendously long lines, tremendously powerful lines in terms of the buildup of emotions.

4. Quoted in Allen Ginsberg, *Allen Verbatim: Lectures on Poetry, Politics, Consciousness,* ed. Gordon Ball (New York: McGraw-Hill, 1974), 134.

5. Kenneth Koch, interview by author, in Koch's home, New York, October 12, 1998. Koch adds,

   I was the one who had the most enthusiasm for the jazz-poetry nights. I read about three times. One night I read, and Larry was sitting with some painters, among them Mark Rothko. I read my poems, and Larry said, "What do you think?" Rothko replied, "Why don't these poets make any sense?" For the last two readings I had, Larry got Mal Waldron and his trio. These guys sort of objected to the setup. It was mainly funny stuff I read. I read my short plays: *Bertha,* a ten-minute play about the queen of Norway who's getting kind of old and bored so she decides that she'll conquer Norway again and liven things up. Larry said the jazz musicians were very serious, but he guaranteed them that they'd get their soul back after they stopped accompanying me. I had a lot of fun doing that, and I thought I'd achieve instant fame. After the second time I did it, Larry told me, "There's a guy in the back that wants to talk to you." He offered me a job as a master of ceremonies at a downtown gay nightclub. I said, "No, I don't think I can handle that." The last night I read, Billie Holiday came, because Mal was her accompanist. Billie was there at the bar. Mal introduced me to her, and she said to me, "Man, your stuff is just crazy!" I hoped that meant "good." That night the audience prevailed upon Billie to sing—it was the night Frank O'Hara would write about in his poem "The Day Lady Died." She almost had no voice—it was like a very good old wine that almost tastes like water.

   Of the Five Spot, Jon Panish writes in *The Color of Jazz: Race and Representation in Postwar American Culture* (Jackson: University Press of Mississippi, 1997),

The Bowery bar called the Five Spot became a central Village location members of almost every artistic avant garde frequented between the mid-1950's and the mid-1960's. Characterizing the Five Spot as a "nerve center" where "the arts became democratized," Greenwich Village historian Terry Miller says that "a new underground formed here, and painters, writers, and jazz musicians joined forces to stage an assault on the very definitions of art, music theater, and literature." (27)

It is likely that poets on the Lower East Side were inspired to participate in the jazz-poetry nights at the Five Spot by Jack Kerouac's reading (with Philip Lamantia, Howard Hart, and David Amram) at the Brata Gallery on Tenth Street in December 1957, an event that Clark Coolidge has informed me is generally acknowledged to be the first (Beat) reading of poetry with jazz. Also, poets may have been inspired by witnessing Rexroth himself since in April of 1958 Rexroth brought the San Francisco Renaissance to the neighborhood by performing his poetry to jazz accompaniment at the Five Spot café itself.

6. Michael Magee, "Emancipating Pragmatism: Emerson, Jazz, and Experimental Writing" (Ph.D. diss., University of Pennsylvania, 1999), 257–58.

7. Sascha Feinstein, *Jazz Poetry: From the 1920s to the Present* (Westport, Conn.: Greenwood Press, 1997), 93.

8. Sascha Feinstein has explored the links between white avant-garde's poetic form as it was influenced by jazz. See his fifth chapter, "Chasin' the Bird," in *Jazz Poetry*, for an exploration on how bebop determined poetic phrasing.

9. Feinstein, *Jazz Poetry*, 96.

10. Charles Olson, "Projective Verse," in *Selected Writings* (New York: New Directions Press, 1966), 22.

11. Evidence for Blackburn's effects on the Lower East Side poetic community are manifold; poet after poet pointed to Blackburn as contemporary exemplar of what it meant to construct a "new" oral tradition in a poetic community. George Economou says of Blackburn, in "Some Notes Towards Finding a View of the New Oral Poetry," *boundary 2*, no. 3 (1975): 653–63:

   A lot of people were responsible for developing the poetry-reading tradition from 1960–1970 in New York City, but I think that Blackburn only was a seminal figure. I cannot think of many series or programs in that period that he didn't help in some way; in my memories of the places he keeps coming up, advising, organizing, reading, inspiring, providing a model, starting and running a program. Certainly, many people deserve credit for their parts in this history. Yet when I survey that aspect of my own past right down to the present, I find Blackburn at the center of it—running the readings at the Café Le Metro, then setting up a great series at St. Mark's Church (only to be inexplicably passed over for the position of director when the church received a grant from the government—though he went right on supporting the Poetry Project there).

12. Peter Middleton, "The Contemporary Poetry Reading," in *Close Listening: Poetry and the Performed Word*, ed. Charles Bernstein (New York: Oxford University Press, 1998), 268.

13. Laura Kendrick, *The Game of Love: Troubadour Wordplay* (Berkeley and Los Angeles: University of California Press, 1988), 31.

14. Quoted in Middleton, "Contemporary Poetry Reading," 263–64.

15. "Contemporary Poetry," with Paul Blackburn, WBAI, New York, n.d. (sound recording), Paul Blackburn Papers, Mandeville Special Collections Library, University of California, San Diego. Wieners actually asked Ted Berrigan if he could borrow Berrigan's glasses, as the tape and a diary entry of Berrigan's referring to this reading indicate.

16. John Wieners, poetry reading, Le Metro, New York, September 11, 1963 (sound recording), Paul Blackburn Papers, Mandeville Special Collections Library, University of California, San Diego.

17. Blackburn, interview by Ossman.

18. Middleton, "Contemporary Poetry Reading," 273.

19. Bourdieu, *Rules of Art,* 164–65.

20. Ed Sanders, interview with Lisa Jarnot, *Poetry Project Newsletter* 166 (October/November 1997: 20.

21. Jackson Mac Low, poetry reading, St. Mark's Poetry Project, New York, February 14, 1968 (sound recording), Paul Blackburn Papers, Mandeville Special Collections Library, University of California, San Diego.

22. Michael Kirby and Victoria Nes Kirby, *Futurist Performance: With Manifestoes and Playscripts Translated from the Italian by Victoria Nes Kirby* (New York: Dutton, 1971), 7.

23. Mac Low himself has explored the move from a model of poetic reception as conditioned by solitary reading to one of poetic reception as one that is fully determined by often collaborative performance. In a series of questions he asks himself in the introduction to his *Representative Works,* Mac Low wonders with regard to the shift his work took in the 1950s: "Why did I begin at that time composing poems, musical works, group performance works ('simultaneities'), and plays by means of chance operations? Why did I begin to view *performance* as central and texts as primarily notations for performance (if only by a silent reader)?" See Jackson Mac Low, *Representative Works: 1938–1985* (New York: Roof Books, 1986), xvi.

24. For a description of this reading, see *Wholly Communion,* ed. Alexis Lykiard (New York: Grove Press, 1965).

25. *Village Voice,* June 1, 1961, classified section.

26. All the poets who read regularly at the Tenth Street Coffeehouse, including Jackson Mac Low, David Antin, Robert Kelly, Jerome Rothenberg, Diane Wakoski, Don and Allan Katzman, Jack Marshall, Ree Dragonette, Howard Ant, George Economou, Diane Wakoski, and Rochelle Owens, simply shifted to Les Deux Mégots when Micky Ruskin opened it up. For a condensed chronological history of the Tenth Street–Deux Mégots–Le Metro reading series, see the introduction to Allen DeLoach's *The East Side Scene* (Buffalo: University Press, State University of New York at Buffalo, 1968).

27. Information on the Paris café scene was found in Noël Riley Fitch, *Literary Cafés of Paris* (Washington, D.C.: Starrhill Press, 1989). It should be noted that *mégots* means "cigarette butts," while *magots* refers to Chinese porcelain figures. This misspelling

was not meant ironically on the part of Deux Mégots owner Mickey Ruskin but was in fact a simple error, as an interview with Carol Bergé makes clear: "Why did Mickey call it Mégots instead of Magots? It means cigarette butts, but Mickey wasn't qualified enough to know that. He had no French at all"; quoted in Ronald Sukenick's *Down and In: Life in the Underground* (New York: Beech Tree Books, 1987), 147.

28. Quoted in Sukenick, *Down and In,* 148.

29. Allen DeLoach, ed., *The East Side Scene* (New York: Buffalo University Press, 1968), vi.

30. Howard Ant, Introduction to *Seventh Street: Poems from Les Deux Mégots,* ed. Allen Katzman, Don Katzman, and Robert Lima (New York: Hesperidian Press, 1962), ii.

31. Poets including Louis Zukofsky, Ed Dorn, Joel Oppenheimer, Muriel Rukeyser, Jackson Mac Low, Denise Levertov, Paul Blackburn, and LeRoi Jones (Amiri Baraka) read on the solo nights at Tenth Street or Les Deux Mégots.

32. Jackson Mac Low, "The New York Coffeehouse Poetry Reading Scene in New York, 1960–1967," in *Light Years,* an anthology of memoirs about the coffeehouse readings in New York from 1959 through the 1960s, ed. Carol Bergé (unpublished), 4–5. David Henderson adds, "Here's the story of St. Mark's. St. Mark's came out of The Deux Mégots, right? Then The Deux Mégots readings went to Le Metro, which was . . . Le Metro now is called the Telephone. And Le Metro was a downstairs café and they had the open readings there"; see David Henderson, interview by Lisa Jarnot, *Poetry Project Newsletter* 163 (December / January 1996–97): 5–9. Jerry Bloedow recalls, "Poetry was in extremely bad shape at that time. It was all coming out of colleges, it was all Breadloaf, and you paid money to get your poetry published, and so forth. So when people like Howard Ant and Ree Dragonette set up the readings (at the Tenth Street) it was really a terrific thing, and it grew and now it's over at St. Mark's"; from Jerry Bloedow, interview by author, New York University, April 29, 1998.

33. Ron Padgett, interview by author, Teachers and Writers Collaborative, New York City, March 24, 1998. Of rexograph, which is similar to mimeograph, Ron Padgett says, "Rexograph sheets produced a kind of purple print. Like mimeo, rexograph uses a master sheet to print from called the spirit master—a wonderful name. You could write on them or draw on them, but you couldn't get a very clear or crisp image. I think with rexograph the disadvantage was that the print run would be rather short because the spirit master would begin to disintegrate after a while. Mimeograph you could run off five or six hundred copies before the spirit master would get all screwed up."

34. For a parallel idea about the poem's shape as generative of its meaning, especially in the context of abstract expressionism, one can look to Brad Gooch's book *City Poet: The Life and Times of Frank O'Hara* (New York: Knopf, 1993). Gooch discusses Frank O'Hara's poem "Easter" and states that O'Hara "finally managed an 'action poem' in which his form was as free as the canvases of the 'action painters,' a term coined by Harold Rosenberg in *Art News* in 1952 to describe the effort of the Abstract Expressionists to turn the action of painting into its own end" (225). See also chapters 1–3 of Marjorie Perloff's *Frank O'Hara: Poet Among Painters* (New York: G. Braziller, 1977) for an extended discussion of the sympathies between abstract expressionism and contemporary poetry.

35. Johanna Drucker, in "Visual Performance of the Poetic Text," in *Close Listening*, ed. Bernstein, writes,

> A visual performance of a poetic work on a page or canvas, as a projection or sculpture, installation or score, also has the qualities of an enactment, of a staged and realized event in which the material means are an integral feature of the work. The specific quality of presence in such a work depends upon visual means—typefaces, format, spatial distribution of the elements on the page or through the book, physical form, or space. Such a material, visual performance of a poetic work has no necessary temporal, spatial, or social relation to the author or artist. Written work is always at a remove from the writer, cast into an autonomous form, not dependent of the presence of the author as a performance. (131)

36. Jerome Rothenberg's introduction to his and David Guss's anthology, *The Book, Spiritual Instrument* (New York: Granary Books, 1996), illustrates his concern with book as content and book as object:

> What Guss and I set out to do, then, was to assemble a number of such rhymings: historical & contemporary instances from cultures (both literate & oral) that offered alternative visions of the book, set side by side with Mallarméan & post-Mallarméan experiments with what Karl Young . . . speaks of below as "bookforms." . . . With an eye toward deeply rooted works & practices that could (re)illuminate our present workings, we left room for instances of traditional or early written art: paleolithic calendar notations, Egyptian & Mayan hieroglyphs, recastings of Bible & other Jewish bookworks, Old Norse runes, & Navajo pictographs (to name a few that come immediately to mind). . . . I could focus on the written alongside—& drawing from—the oral, & with a strong awareness of how central the book was in that highly charged, sometimes over-determined context. (8)

37. From Alan Golding, *From Outlaw to Classic: Canons in American Poetry* (Madison: University of Wisconsin Press, 1995), 133.

38. Jerome Rothenberg, a regular participant at Deux Mégots and Le Metro, developed rich theories on oral, primitivist, and medieval poetics, as one sees in later magazines like Rothenberg's *Alcheringa* and his essays written over the last four decades on oral poetries and "ethnopoetics."

39. Kendrick, *Game of Love*, 31.

40. Allen Katzman, "Poem for the Poet," *Poems Collected at Les Deux Mégots* 2 (1963). In 1965 Allen Katzman (twin brother of Don Katzman) went on to edit the newspaper *East Village Other*, which provided a forum for many of the radical political voices of the 1960s.

41. Bloedow, interview.

42. At the Vancouver Poetry Conference, Vancouver, British Columbia, August 5, 1963, (sound recording), Paul Blackburn Papers, SPL 203, Mandeville Special Collections Library, University of California, San Diego, Allen Ginsberg situated the practice of cut-up as an inherently political act:

> I adopted Burroughs's message to cut my way out of holy anxiety and paranoia and counterparanoia that was going on. I took Kennedy's statement and I took Khrushchev's statement, and I put them together and cut them up with a razor and then mixed them up like confetti. When I retyped the whole thing up I had a real clear picture of what the Cuban situation was. Mainly I cut myself out of the whole society and I cut myself in the sense that

it gave me an objectivity and a lack of anxiety and a realization of how much these guys were coming on from obsession.

43. David Henderson, interview by author, Café Limbo, New York City, April 8, 1998.

44. Max's Kansas City was a restaurant/bar that poets, musicians, and artists including Ginsberg, Corso, members of the Velvet Underground, and Andy Warhol frequented. Joel Oppenheimer is credited with coming up with the name for Max's as well as the logo, which was "Steak, Lobster, and Chick Peas." Paul Blackburn ran a reading series at Max's in 1969–1970.

45. Carol Bergé, "An Informal Timetable of Coffee-House Activities in New York," in *Magazine-2* (New York: Crank Books, 1965).

46. Nelson Barr, *Fuck You / a magazine of the arts* 3, no. 5 (May 1963). "A Bouquet of Fuck-You's" was a regular column, written by Nelson Barr, which served to colorfully criticize anything in the neighborhood that provoked the ire of the poets associated with *Fuck You.*

47. Joe Brainard, (New York: Full Court Press, 1975), 112.

48. Paul Blackburn to Flossie Williams, June 21, 1963, Paul Blackburn Papers, MSS 4, Mandeville Special Collections Library, University of California, San Diego. In her obituary of Williams, Stephanie Gervis wrote, "Younger poets, poets at least a generation behind Williams when he died Monday morning at the age of 79, poets like Paul Blackburn, Robert Creeley, Gil Sorrentino, Joel Oppenheimer, thought of him (and his old friend Ezra Pound) as—in Blackburn's words—'where we all start from, like, our fathers'"; see Gervis, "William Carlos Williams (1883–1963)," *Village Voice,* March 7, 1963, 1.

49. St. Mark's Poetry Project continued the practice of having weekly open readings every Monday, though this has since been amended to one open reading on the first Monday of every month. Additionally, the Project continues to feature individual poets every Wednesday (usually two poets). This practice indicates some organizational debt to the Le Metro predecessors.

50. Bloedow, interview.

51. Bob Holman, "History of the Poetry Project," 1978, Poetry Project Archives, St. Mark's Church, New York, 9.

52. Padgett, interview, March 24, 1998.

53. Ed Sanders, telephone interview by author, April 15, 1998.

54. Before the reading series at Le Metro, one could find ads for the coffee shop in the *Village Voice* promising a perfect environment for a romantic pre- or post-theater date—the theater in this case being not Broadway but "alternative" Lower East Side theaters like the Living Theater and La Mama.

55. Blackburn is seen by many of the poets at that time as the primary figure and "organizing spirit" at the Le Metro readings. As Ed Sanders put it in an interview (April 15, 1998):

Blackburn had a sainted position in the poetic community. He was the one who took the care and time to tape-record many of the readings and to play them. I would visit his house, and Paul would pull out his archived reel-to-reel tapes and pop them on to his tape recorder and play. He exalted in this process, this concept of café readings, and more importantly to me than the squabbles as to who ran what and who made decisions and who made decisions as to who would get featured readings or not is the struggle in the summer of 1964 against the Department of Licenses.

56. Brodey was anthologized in *An Anthology of New York Poets,* ed. Ron Padgett and David Shapiro (New York: Random House, 1970).

57. Quoted in Holman, "History of the Poetry Project," 13.

58. Brodey wasn't the only one who pointed out Blackburn's vague aversion to the New York School. In an interview with Barry Alpert, Ted Berrigan states, "Paul Blackburn . . . thought of himself as very open but had a natural aversion to people who seemed like they were from some elegant minority: the way that Frank O'Hara and Kenneth Koch and John Ashbery must have seemed to him. To me they didn't seem . . . it seemed that poets were some sort of minority anyway"; see Barry Alpert, "Interview with Ted Berrigan," in *Talking in Tranquility,* ed. Stephen Ratcliffe and Leslie Scalapino (Bolinas, Calif.: Avenue B; Oakland, Calif.: O Books, 1991), 48.

59. Holman, "History of the Poetry Project," 11. See chapter 3 for an extended discussion of the connections Berrigan made between Beat and New York School aesthetics.

60. Ron Padgett, "Judging the Judges," *Columbia Spectator,* April 24, 1964, Ted Berrigan Papers, Rare Book and Manuscript Library, Columbia University, New York.

61. Padgett, interview, March 24, 1998.

62. O'Hara worked for the Museum of Modern Art, Kenneth Koch worked as a professor at Columbia University, and James Schuyler and John Ashbery both served as contributing writers and editors for *Art News.*

63. Padgett interview, March 24, 1998. Gregory Corso's contribution to an issue of *Poets at Le Metro* is surely an example of what Padgett meant when he discussed "poem pictures" and their place in the *Poets at Le Metro* series. Corso entitled his piece "The Rebel"; it is an illustration of nine little birds placed horizontally on the page. All the birds are facing left except for one bird, fourth from left, facing right with a question mark above its head. Gregory Corso, "The Rebel," *Poets at Le Metro* 5 (1963).

64. Lorenzo Thomas, telephone interview by author, September 6, 1998.

65. Christopher Mele, *Selling the Lower East Side: Culture, Real Estate, and Resistance in New York City* (Minneapolis: University of Minnesota Press, 2000), 154.

66. "Prior to 1964 there was no place popularly known as the East Village. By 1965, the place-name was used pervasively by hippie locals and owners of commercial establishments, newspaper and magazine writers and editors, and landlords. *East Village* referred exclusively to the area's hippie community and not to the communities of older white ethnics and Puerto Rican families, who were nonetheless the predominant residents"; see Mele, *Selling the Lower East Side,* 160.

67. Ed Sanders, "Poem Describing the Cover of the Next Issue of *Fuck You,* Issue 5 Volume 5," *Poets at Le Metro* 8 (1963).

68. Holman, "History of the Poetry Project," 9.

69. Ted Berrigan, diary entry, September 13, 1963, Ted Berrigan Papers, Rare Book and Manuscript Library, Columbia University, New York.

70. Ted Berrigan, untitled poem, *Poets at Le Metro* 7 (1963).

71. John Ashbery, "Last Month," *The Mooring of Starting Out: The First Five Books of Poetry* (Hopewell, N.J.: Ecco Press, 1997), 168.

72. Ted Berrigan, "Homage to James Brodey," *Poets at Le Metro* 8 (1963). Jim Brodey was a student of Frank O'Hara's at the New School. See Gooch, *City Poet.*

73. The O'Hara poem contains the same kind of gee-whiz enthusiastic use of exclamation points and lighthearted tone, as well as a primary figure who is a Hollywood icon: "LANA TURNER HAS COLLAPSED! / there is no snow in Hollywood / there is no rain in California / I have been to lots of parties / and acted perfectly disgraceful / but I never actually collapsed / oh Lana Turner we love you get up"; see *The Collected Poems of Frank O'Hara,* ed. Donald Allen (New York: Alfred A. Knopf, 1991), 449.

74. Bernadette Mayer, telephone interview by author, November 6, 1998.

75. Berrigan, diary entry, April 8, 1964. The lists Berrigan made may be of interest in that they show a very diverse group of people attending poetry readings—far more diverse than the earlier Deux Mégots readings (some names may be misspelled):

    Anne came with her fiancee. Also Barbara Enger and husband, Allen Ginsberg, Peter Orlovsky, Frank O'Hara, Joe LeSeur, Mike Goldberg, Bob Dash, Carl Morse, Al Kaplan, Kathy Fraser, Jack Marshall, Gerry Malanga, Wynn Chamberlain, Lewis Macadams and his girl, Sandy, Tom Veitch, Ron and Pat, Margaret Robbes?, John Keys and Karen, Carol Bergé, Susan Sherman, Allen Katzman, John Stanton, Harry Fainlight, Taylor Mead, Some French boy, Ted Greenwald, Lorenzo Thomas, Jackson Mac Low, 3 unidentified girls, Antoinette's friend Jaime, 2 or 3 unidentified fellows, Harold Dicker, Barbara Guest, Tony Towle, Dennis Shea and Muffin, Joe Brainard.

76. In terms of there being a "second generation," Brad Gooch writes in *City Poet,* "Ted Berrigan . . . used to stand on Avenue A staring up patiently at O'Hara's apartment before they ever met. Ashbery gave the nickname 'Tulsa School of Poetry' to Berrigan and his three teenage friends—Ron Padgett, Dick Gallup, and Joe Brainard. . . . Writer and musician Jim Carroll used to wait outside the museum to trail O'Hara down Fifty-Third street as he left work." Gooch also points out how many of the poets associated with the Second Generation attended O'Hara's and Kenneth Koch's classes at the New School: "Among those taking [O'Hara's] course were the poets Tony Towle, Gerard Malanga, Joseph Ceravolo, James Brodey, Ruth Kraus, Jean Boudin, Anne Fessenden, Frank Lima, and Allan Kaplan" (399–400). Ron Padgett attended Kenneth Koch's classes at Columbia University, the New School, and at Wagner College on Staten Island. However, the New York School certainly did not rule over the Poetry Project; a glance at the reading lists for the first four years of the Poetry Project shows a relatively diverse group of poets.

77. Paul Chevigny, *Gigs: Jazz and the Cabaret Laws in New York City* (New York: Routledge, 1991), 74.

78. For a history of cabaret laws in New York City during the 1950s and 1960s, see chapters 3–5 in Chevigny's *Gigs.*

79. See "Poetic License Needed," *New York Times,* June 8, 1959, 54.

80. Chevigny, *Gigs,* 71, my italics.

81. Alfred G. Aronowitz wrote, in "Why the Espresso Got Cold," *New York Post,* June 13, 1960,

> When—and if—the Fire Dept. decides to close (Cafe Wha?'s) doors, its folk singers will have to find new folkways, its pantomimists will have to say at least goodby, its poets may even have to read to people who understand their poetry and its clientele will have to drink coffee that costs only 10 cents a cup.
>
> But the question at the Cafe Wha? last night was Why?
>
> "Why don't they close down the strip joints and the cabarets and the places that can afford to pay under the table for liquor licenses?" asked Peter Lane, a 23–year-old mime who was dressed in leotards, a striped shirt and a plaintive look.
>
> "Why do they call us beatniks and pick on us?"
>
> With still no answer to the question, the Fire Dept. has already unlit the Gaslight and extinguished the flame beneath the coffee urn at the Cafe Bizarre. And it says it's going to empty the cups at just about every other coffee shop on or off MacDougal St. (4)

82. "Poetic License Needed," 54.

83. "Coffeehouse licensing is Local Law 95/1961, codified as NYC Admin. Code section B32–310"; see Chevigny, *Gigs,* 197.

84. "Article 39, Coffee Houses," *New York City Charter and Administrative Code, Annotated* (Albany, N.Y.: Williams Press, 1961), 4:758, my italics.

85. "Article 39," 758. In *Tales of Beatnik Glory* (New York: Stonehill Publishing, 1975), 31, Ed Sanders fictionalizes events similar to what happened at Le Metro: "When they began to hold poetry readings, Karkenshul picked up the announcements of the readings from the *Village Voice* and sent raiders out to issue summonses, informing the two that they'd have to cringe and beg for a cabaret license if they wanted to continue poetry. There was a law in New York that allowed entertainment in a restaurant by no more than three stringed instruments and a piano: allowing *no* poetry and *no* singing."

86. Billie Holiday, Thelonious Monk, and Charlie Parker were often victimized by these laws, which stated that any performer charged with possession of illicit drugs could not perform in New York City—a policy that was tantamount to forcing these and other musicians into poverty. See Chevigny, *Gigs,* 59–68, for additional information on the repercussions of the cabaret laws on jazz musicians' lives.

87. "Article 39," 760, my italics.

88. Diane di Prima, "Fuzz's Progress," *The Nation,* May 4, 1964, 463–64.

89. Di Prima, "Fuzz's Progress," 463–64.

90. Between the time of acquittal on obscenity charges in Los Angeles (for the second time) and the beginning of the New York obscenity trial, a public protest was signed on behalf of Lenny Bruce. See "Bruce's Trial," *Newsweek,* July 20 1964; the petition is available at www.members.aol.com/dcspohr/lenny/petition.htm. The signers, including poets Gregory Corso, Lawrence Ferlinghetti, Allen Ginsberg, Leroi Jones, Peter Orlovsky and Louis Untermeyer, as well as theologian Reinhold Niebuhr, singer Bob Dylan, writers Susan Sontag, Norman Mailer, John Updike, and many others, wrote in their petition:

We the undersigned are agreed that the recent arrests of night-club entertainer Lenny Bruce by the New York police department on charges of indecent performance constitutes a violation of civil liberties as guaranteed by the First and Fourteenth amendments to the United States Constitution.

Lenny Bruce is a popular and controversial performer in the field of social satire in the tradition of Swift, Rabelais, and Twain. Although Bruce makes use of the vernacular in his night-club performances, he does so within the context of his satirical intent and not to arouse the prurient interests of his listeners. It is up to the audience to determine what is offensive to them; it is not a function of the police department of New York or any other city to decide what adult private citizens may or may not hear.

Whether we regard Bruce as a moral spokesman or simply as an entertainer, we believe he should be allowed to perform free from censorship or harassment.

91. Jackson Mac Low, e-mail to the author, May 20, 1998. Mac Low, Sanders, and others refer to the coffeehouse law as the "cabaret law." While these and other poets thought that the readings were being persecuted in accord with the cabaret laws, they were actually being harassed under the newer and almost identical Coffeehouse License Law. It is easy to understand why poets would refer to the "cabaret" laws, since the outcome of both laws was essentially the same.

92. Mac Low, e-mail.

93. Sanders, telephone interview, April 15, 1998.

94. Mac Low, e-mail. Ironically, Ed Koch would soon be associated with *anti*-coffeehouse ordinances in the West Village. As Paul Chevigny has pointed out, Koch was instrumental in banning musical performances. For additional information on Ed Koch and West Village coffeehouses, see Homer Bigart, "Mayor Aids Drive on 'Village' Cafes," *New York Times,* April 3, 1965; Thomas Buckley, "Civic Aide Linked to Coffeehouses," *New York Times,* November 6, 1964; and John Kifner, "'Village' Coffeehouse District Bustles the Day After Cleanup Order," *New York Times,* December 28, 1967.

95. Sanders, telephone interview, April 23, 1998. In an undated manuscript entitled "What's New?: An Interior Report on the Socio-literary Uses of the Mimeograph Machine," Paul Blackburn Papers, MSS 4, Mandeville Special Collections Library, University of California, San Diego, Paul Blackburn echoed Sanders's sentiments that the Department of Licenses was motivated in part by political reasons:

The recent descent of the license bureau upon Le Metro Cafe on Second Avenue, for permitting poetry without having more than a restaurant license (also that bureau's descent upon theaters showing avant-garde films), represent more current efforts on the part of the bureaucracy to suppress or at least to "license"—to their own taste, of course, the arts. The New York Civil Liberties Union presented a brief in Le Metro case as amicus curiae, which helped immensely in having the case dismissed. Since the defense was purely on constitutional grounds, would that indicate that this section of the administrative code is illegal? I guess so. The poets are now working with Henry Stern of the Borough President's Office, and attorneys from the License Department, New York's cultural commissioner, Jerome Donson, to rewrite the coffee house law.

96. Quoted in "Judge Rules a Café, No Levy Must Pay, for Poetry Per Se," *New York Times,* March 25, 1964, 43.

97. A more recent example of this phenomenon includes the boost in attendance and revenue that the Brooklyn Museum of Art received in 1999 and 2001 as a result of former Mayor Giuliani's attacks on the "blasphemous" nature of some of the materials in the museum's exhibitions (including Chris Ofili's now notorious image of the Virgin Mary created partly out of elephant dung and featured in the museum's *Sensation* show). The museum ended up attracting record numbers because of the ensuing controversy. In 2001, disgusted by Renee Cox's photograph exhibited at the museum of a naked African American woman taking Christ's place at the Last Supper, Giuliani "promised . . . that he would appoint a panel to set what he has called 'decency standards' for art in museums that receive any city money, which includes most museums in the five boroughs"; see Elisabeth Bumiller, "Giuliani Names His Panel to Monitor Art at Museums," *New York Times,* April 4, 2001.

98. Stephanie Harrington Gervis, "City Puts Bomb Under Off-Beat Culture Scene," *Village Voice,* March 26, 1964, 1.

99. Emphasizing the connection between the events at Le Metro and the legal troubles other cultural institutions faced, the text of the flyer stated that the march was held "To Protest: Licensing of films—Censorship of Books—Seizure of films & art works as obscenity—City zoning against loft living—Harassment of Lenny Bruce—Federal seizure of the Living Theatre—Harassment of coffee shops and loft theatres by police, fire, and license departments—Closing of off-Broadway theatres by city license department."

100. Allen Ginsberg, *Howl* (San Francisco: City Lights, 1956), 9.

101. "Judge Rules," 43.

102. Quoted in Holman, "History of the Poetry Project," 10.

103. DeLoach, *East Side Scene,* 15.

104. Ted Berrigan, "Get the Money," *East Village Other* 1, no. 3 (1965): 11. In "Poetry Place Protest," in the first issue of the *East Village Other* (October 1965), however, Ishmael Reed wrote of the poets who continued to attend Le Metro readings:

> The Metro poets left behind will serve any muse, be she a gun moll who hustles graveyard trophies skidding through bang bang whorehouses in St. Valentine Day carnivals, or a swishy little pussy who believes that waterfowls are thrilling. . . . They include some especially insidious cockroach stains who peddle their racist lollygag on Lenox Ave, and come on like Father Dine on Second Ave. for a few funky bedroom wrestles. These are the late Metro Poets. They kiss the toes of Shopkeepers. SEIG HEIL. (55)

105. Quoted in Holman, "History of the Poetry Project," 10.

106. Michael Oren, "The Umbra Poets Workshop, 1962–1965: Some Socio-Literary Puzzles," in *Belief vs. Theory in Black American Literary Criticism,* ed. Joe Weixlmann and Chester J. Fontenot (Greenwood, Fla.: Penkeville Publishing, 1986), 182.

107. Henderson, interview, Café Limbo, New York City, April 8, 1998.

108. Ishmael Reed, "Poetry Place Protest," 5.

109. When I interviewed David Henderson (on April 8, 1998), he said,

> I was hanging out with these anarchists, and we had a loft on Second Street and the Bowery, so I wasn't really hanging out that much at the Metro. This was the Bowery Poets Co-Op. We had fliers, and Allen Hoffman did the drawings, and they had these typical anar-

chist drawings, a bomb with a fuse or some stupid shit like that. But he meant well. So any-
way, most of the Metro poets walked out, and they didn't have anyplace to go. So I invited
them to this loft, and the people who were involved in this loft were people like Allen Hoff-
man, Bob Ernstal, Paul Prinsky. . . . We invited them there, and the readings went on there
for several months until they went on to the church. There is an article in the first issue of
the *East Village Other* about the move to the loft.

In Ishmael Reed's *East Village Other* article, Reed records how "poet David Hender-
son finished the 'untouchables' off when he opened his poets cooperative so that even-
tually the shopkeeper . . . is left alone with the poet whorelocks"; see Reed, "Poetry
Place Protest," 5.

110. John Graffiti, "Lower East Side Funk," *East Village Other* 1, no. 1 (1965): 5.

111. While the administrative staff at the Poetry Project was in place by the summer of
1966, actual readings did not begin until September of that year.

Chapter 3: The Aesthetics of the Little

1. Epigraph: Quoted in *Little Magazine in America,* ed. Elliot Anderson and Mary Kinzie
(Yonkers, N.Y.: Pushcart Press, 1978), 299. Di Prima quoted in Anderson and Kinzie,
Little Magazine, 699. See Tom Clark's *Charles Olson: The Allegory of a Poet's Life* (New
York: Norton, 1991) for a history of Olson's consumption of stimulants (or "speed").
It is possible that Olson's drug use is coyly being referred to here by di Prima.

2. Hettie Jones, *How I Became Hettie Jones* (New York: Grove Press, 1997), 140.

3. In his autobiography, Baraka wrote, "The Floating Bear was coming out regularly
and became the talk of our various interconnected literary circles. It was meant to
be 'quick, fast, and in a hurry.' Something that could carry the zigs and zags of the
literary scene as well as some word of the general New York creative ambience"; see
The Autobiography of LeRoi Jones/Amiri Baraka (New York: Freundlich Books, 1984),
251. In a letter from Robert Kelly to George Economou, July 19, 1963, George
Economou Papers, Rare Book and Manuscript Library, Columbia University, one
learns how the mimeo was perceived as a form for disseminating urgent news:

As you probably know, I get very anxious about the long intervals between Trobars. . . . Af-
ter long thought, I've decided to try to bring out, coincident with in the intervals of Trobar,
a mimeographed newsletter-format publication of prose & verse, edited by me. The name
that comes to mind is MATTER. . . . I see no reason why such a sheet shd injure Trobar . . .
but on the contrary allow us to keep Trobar for the purpose we had in mind all the while, to
print periodically collections of the best original American poetry we can find. Trobar, qua
magazine, is bound to be always expensive. . . . I've never wanted to get Trobar proper in-
volved in statements & manifestoes & reviews & our few essays into such have been mixed
blessings. Yet I feel the need of such things around me, & feel the need is more general in the
country. Folk as different as Ginsberg (in that Exwire piece on him) & Olson apparently feel
that FUCK YOU is one of the best, & largely because of the swiftness & cleanness of that gazette.

Ed Sanders, in the first issue of *Fuck You* (1962), would also highlight the mimeo's
abilities in terms of its speed, as the following editorial statement illustrates:

I LIFT MY SPEEDOPRINT MIMEO BESIDE THE GOLDEN DOOR.

(I'LL STOMP OUT MORE ISSUES AS SOON AS MATERIAL, MONEY, JAIL ETC. PERMIT.)

4. Quoted in James Sullivan, *On the Walls and in the Streets: American Poetry Broadsides from the 1960s* (Chicago: University of Illinois Press, 1997), 61.

5. Ed Friedman, the Poetry Project's current director, lists a few of the mimeos associated with the Project over the years: "The list of magazines published at the Poetry Project included *Telephone, Adventures in Poetry, Un Poco Loco, Mag City,* the *4–3–2 Review,* the *Harris Review, Reindeer,* the *12th Street Rag, Cave Man, Unnatural Acts, Little Light,* and *Tangerine,* as well as many one-shot reviews and anthologies"; quoted in Stephen Clay and Rodney Phillips, *A Secret Location on the Lower East Side: Adventures in Writing, 1960–1980* (New York: Granary Books, 1998), 185.

6. The *Ruse* was published by Sparrow and edited by Violet Snow—both pseudonyms, in the Lower East Side "tradition" of collaborative, anonymous, and pseudonymous writing.

7. In an interview by an unnamed student, Shippenburg, Pa., 1970 (sound recording), Paul Blackburn Papers, SPL 407, Mandeville Special Collections Library, University of California, San Diego, Blackburn was to provide a historical overview of mimeography:

Mimeograph machines worked great miracles in this generation. There are more magazines around now than you could . . . which is beautiful. The first mimeograph I ever heard of was sort of 1951/52, it was called *Contact,* out of Toronto. There were a whole bunch of us before that just sending out poems around to each other. We'd make up an envelope, and everybody would add to it, and add comments, poems of his own, send it on to the next man on the way. In effect, that was a magazine. Nobody knew who was writing what where when. OK, that was 1950, now it's 1970. Mimeograph between the mid-fifties and the mid-sixties did absolute wonders. I still have poems still come out in mimeograph magazines, always have. It's editors working on shoestrings, guys with one idea in their head, but it really does work.

8. In the case of the *Deux Mégots* anthology, Allen DeLoach's *East Side Scene* anthology, and some of the later anthologies related to the Poetry Project, the poets' photographs were also included as part of the overall presentation, thereby emphasizing presence and performativity in ways which other anthologies—the anthology edited by Robert Pack, Donald Hall, and Louis Simpson, for example—did not. See Don Katzman, ed., *Seventh Street, Poems from Les Deux Mégots* (New York: Hesperidian Press, 1962); Allen DeLoach, ed., *The East Side Scene* (Buffalo: University Press, State University of New York at Buffalo, 1968); and Robert Pack, Donald Hall, and Louis Simpson, *New Poets of England and America* (New York: Meridian Books, 1957).

9. Paul Blackburn, "What's New?: An Interior Report on The Socio-literary Uses of the Mimeograph Machine," Paul Blackburn Papers, MSS 4, Mandeville Special Collections Library, University of California, San Diego.

10. John Weiners, "Prose Poem," *C: A Journal of Poetry* 1, no. 5 (1963).

11. Ted Berrigan, "Looking for Chris," *C: A Journal of Poetry* 2, no. 11 (1965).

12. An article in the *New York Post* ("A Poet Laments Time Lost in a Courthouse," *New York Post,* October 19, 1961, 27) describes how Jones, seized by U.S. deputy marshal Joseph Caffery and an FBI agent "while asleep in his apartment at 324 E. 14th St., explained he would have 'liked something to do while sitting around in jail' and 'could have spent the time writing something.'"

The literature the postal inspectors claim is obscene is a copy of a newsletter they co-edit, called "The Floating Bear." The newsletter was first read by postal inspectors at the Rahway, N.J., Reformatory, where a copy addressed to an inmate was intercepted. It contained a brief play by Jones about a homosexual experience between two soldiers. The play, part of a book Jones is writing under a John Jay Whitney Foundation fellowship, is slated for production by the New York Poets Theater in the Off Bowery Theater, 84 E. 10ᵗʰ St. The newsletter also contained a political fantasy about the late President Roosevelt by writer William Burroughs. . . .

Jones, known as one of the leading beat generation poets, contended writing "should be regarded as pornographic only if it is intended to arouse." Both works had "some old Anglo-Saxon words," he said, "but they were necessary for the literary effect."

Both he and Miss DiPrima [sic], 309 E. Houston St., with him at their arraignment before U.S. Commissioner John B. Garrity, said their main objection to the charges was that "they're an inconvenience. . . . This is just the latest in a series of minor annoyances at the hands of the government. It's getting to be a drag."

13. Aldon Nielsen, *Black Chant: Languages of African-American Postmodernism* (Cambridge: Cambridge University Press, 1997), 84. For further information on *The Floating Bear,* see Nielsen's chapter, "A New York State of Mind," in *Black Chant.*

14. Quoted in Alan Golding, *From Outlaw to Classic: Canons in American Poetry* (Madison: University of Wisconsin Press, 1995), 134.

15. Regarding Ed Sander's mimeo *Fuck You,* the editors of *Little Magazine in America* claim that Sanders "initiated the era of mimeograph publishing. *Fuck You* was batted out in an incredibly sloppy way; one often saw footprints on the paper"; see Elliot Anderson and Mary Kinzie, eds., *The Little Magazine in America* (Yonkers, N.Y.: Pushcart Press, 1978), 700–701. Sanders himself remembers, "I was so broke I don't think I had electricity in my apartment, so I would hold a flashlight underneath these stencils and draw them"; telephone interview by author, April 15, 1998.

16. This list in no way implies that other publications like *The Exile* were not as significant in the overall history of small magazine publishing.

17. Felix Pollak, "An Interview on Little Magazines," in *The Little Magazine in America,* ed. Elliot Anderson and Mary Kinzie (Yonkers, N.Y.: Pushcart Press, 1978), 35.

18. Quoted in Ian Hamilton, *The Little Magazines: A Study of Six Editors* (London: Weidenfield and Wicolson, 1976), 23.

19. Ed Sanders, *Fuck You / a magazine of the arts* 9, no. 5 (1965).

20. Golding, *From Outlaw to Classic,* 127.

21. Susan Compton, *The World Backwards: Russian Futurist Books, 1912–16* (London: British Museum Publications, 1978), 8.

22. George Economou, telephone interview by author, May 18, 1998.

23. Something to consider at this point is the fact that many contemporary magazines, thanks to computer technology and the grants mechanisms, look "professional." However, one can point to a magazine like *Exquisite Corpse,* which until its recent demise published relatively avant-garde works and whose title was appropriated from a surrealist writing technique. The *shape* of *Exquisite Corpse*—long and thin—was such that it stuck out of most bookshelves. In terms of its relatively odd size, the *Corpse*

generated a sense of the potential strangeness and "shock of the new" within its pages. *Exquisite Corpse* is now available on-line at www.corpse.org.

24. David Bennett, "Periodical Fragments and Organic Culture: Modernism, the Avant-Garde, and the Little Magazine," *Contemporary Literature* 30 (1989): 480–81. Helpfully distinguishing between a "little" and a conventional periodical, Bennett adds, in reference to Joyce:

> Few of those who subscribed to *transition* in order to keep track of Joyce's "Work in Progress" would have shared the disappointment experienced by readers of Dickens's *Household Words* on the delay or nonappearance of their next weekly installment of its front-line narrative. . . . Narrative continuity and suspense, the historical logic of temporal succession, were characteristically not among the little magazine's strategies for guaranteeing the reproduction of its readership. It was against the "tyranny" of historical imperatives, after all, that modernity and the avant-garde turned their backs. (482)

25. In terms of "little" as a metaphor for community, McMillan describes the artists in *transition* as "a little like the brigades that came in the thirties from all over Europe and America to fight in the Spanish republican cause. They came with varying levels of commitment to theory and to those who called for them to come, but they came to assert the right to common liberties. . . . It was *transition* that proclaimed the poet's right to more direct presentation of the unconscious, greater linguistic experimentation, and freer development of personal mythic structures"; see Dougald McMillan, *transition: The History of a Literary Era, 1927–1938* (London: Calder and Boyars, 1975), 5. This characterization of *transition* in terms of revolutionary political activity combined with avant-garde writing practices is typical of descriptions of many "littles" published throughout the twentieth century.

26. Quoted in McMillan, *transition,* 6.

27. Golding, *From Outlaw to Classic,* 122.

28. Reva Wolf, *Andy Warhol, Poetry and Gossip in the 1960s* (Chicago: University of Chicago Press, 1997), 38.

29. The conception of a readership as an extended social group was itself a modernist inheritance. An editorial in *transition* stated, "We should like to think of the readers as a homogenous group of friends, united in a common appreciation of the beautiful— idealists of a sort." Quoted in McMillan, *transition.*

30. Objections could be made for not including (for example) Lita Hornick's *Kulchur,* Allen DeLoach's *Intrepid,* George Montgomery's *Yowl,* and so on. However, the almost arbitrary boundaries that are set up in the following section are meant more as a way to contain discussion than to name all the major players living in or associated with the Lower East Side poetic community.

31. See Ron Sukenick, *Down and In: Life in the Underground* (New York: Beech Tree Books, 1987), 175–76.

32. Ed Sanders, *Fuck You / a magazine of the arts* 1, no. 4 (August 1962).

33. Sanders, *Fuck You / a magazine of the arts* 1, no. 5 (December 1962).

34. See Ed Sanders's "Siobhan McKenna Group Grope," in *Tales of Beatnik Glory* (New York: Stonehill Publishing, 1975), 135–43.

35. Sanders, *Fuck You / a magazine of the arts* 1, no. 1 (1962). This dedication was not repeated word for word in every issue, though a variation of this dedication was always published on the front covers.

36. Sanders, *Fuck You / a magazine of the arts* 7, no. 5 (September 1964).

37. Sanders, *Fuck You / a magazine of the arts* 4, no. 1 (August 1962).

38. Taylor Mead, *On Amphetamine and in Europe,* vol. 3 of *Excerpts from the Anonymous Diary of a New York Youth* (New York: Boss Books, 1968), 31. For a more detailed record of the status of homosexuality in New York City during the 1960s, see Martin Duberman, *Stonewall* (New York: Dutton, 1993).

39. Lawrence Stevens, "Does Mental Illness Exist?" www.antipsychiatry.org/exist.htm.

40. Taylor Mead was often harassed for his homosexuality. As he said in an interview by the author, Joe's Bar, New York City, March 25, 1998,

    Once in a Washington Square toilet I was taking a piss, and this guy is standing next to me. I looked over, and he said to me, "You got a place to go?" And I said, "No, no." And then he said, "Oh, *you* got a place to go," and he took me into the janitor's small room, and there's another big detective there. You know, they were 200 pounds, 6 foot 2 each, and they were ready to beat me up unless I said, "Oh, yes, I'm gay." And the motherfucking court wrote my father—I must have been in my early twenties—and my father, hypocritical as usual, says, "I don't know how this happened, he was so well brought up." He knew what to say to the judge, he really didn't care. So, the second time a detective in Bryant Park—we were sitting next to each other on a bench and talking—and then I put my hand on his knee and he pulled out a badge. I just threw myself over the wall, but he landed right on top of me. And they asked me how much money I had in the bank. I had no money in the bank, of course. The court sent me to the Quaker emergency service people, God forbid, who were these psychiatrists. One of them said, "Maybe you should go to our place in the country," and I said, "With a high fence around it?" He said, "Well, yes." You know, the motherfuckers wanted to send me out to get shock treatment.

41. Sanders, *Fuck You / a magazine of the arts* 5, no. 1 (December 1962).

42. Al Fowler, "Caroline: An Exercise for Our Cocksman Leader," *Fuck You / a magazine of the arts* 5, no. 1 (December 1962).

43. Ed Sanders, telephone interview by author, April 23, 1998. In *Tales of Beatnik Glory,* Sanders actually domesticates the events described in the original Editorial Board "cornholing" of the eight-year-old by reframing it as a consensual adult orgy or "bunch punch": "And Cynthia rolled upon the floor filling her mouth with the carnal cob of Nelson Saite, drama editor, as he lined her ravening buttocks up against the steam-valve of the radiator and completed the metal node within her"; see 192–95.

44. Kathleen Fraser, e-mails to the author, May 25 and 26, 2002.

45. Reva Wolf, in her discussion of Sanders's agreement not to speak the words *fuck you* during an interview by WNET for a public television series, says, "Sanders's seemingly willing concession to the censorship laws of television is consistent with his broader aim to reach large audiences. This aim, which was fairly common among 'underground' figures of the 1960s, had at its roots two distinct objectives: changing the world and achieving fame. These objectives, the one altruistic and the other self-centered, are seldom mutually exclusive, as both Sanders and Warhol well understood"; see *Andy Warhol,* 55.

46. *Life*, February 17, 1967.

47. Sanders, telephone interview by author, April 15, 1998.

48. "The Platonic Blow" was published in *Fuck You / a magazine of the arts* 5, no. 8 (March 1965). For a description of Auden's reaction to this publication, see Humphrey Carpenter's *W. H. Auden: A Biography* (Boston: Houghton Mifflin, 1981).

49. Sanders, interview, April 15, 1998.

50. Sanders, *Fuck You / a magazine of the arts* 7, no. 5 (September 1964). This issue featured poets anthologized in *The New American Poetry,* ed. Donald Allen (New York: Grove Press, 1960), including Olson, Wieners, Creeley, Blackburn, Ginsberg, Corso, Duncan, Philip Lamantia, Snyder, Whalen, and McClure, along with peers like William Burroughs, Norman Mailer, and Carl Solomon and Deux Mégots–Le Metro poets including Robert Kelly, Judith Malina, Al Fowler, and Harry Fainlight. Also, this issue featured *Fuck You*'s first translations—in this case Artaud and Arnaut Daniel. In the same issue, Carl Solomon's essay on Artaud, "The Lunatic and Modern Art," posits an interesting articulation of a kind of avant-garde "tradition":

> Sub-normality and sub-reality are the theme and tone of the late Artaud and his followers. For Artaud and for Genet and even, to an extent, for Michaux, and for the Lettrists, neologisms, screams, belches, and the passing of wind are substituted for the written word.
>
> Ridiculous as all this sounds, it has actually existed as a post-war trend in painting as well as in literature (in the *art brut* of Dubuffet and others). Call it latter-day Dada and you are well.
>
> There is actually a literary tradition to back up this sort of thing. If you are a poet who has read late Artaud and wishes playfully to experiment, you are apt to be bound up in a strait-jacket by the nearest psychiatrist and given no credit for your research until you get a scholarly article on the subject published in the *Partisan Review.*
>
> Dada is dangerous today because the police, among others, don't understand what it's all about (being readers of the *News* and not of the *Partisan,* let alone of *The Evergreen Review,* or even of *Poetry* or even of *Time*) and probably mistake you for the dumbbell you are attempting satirically to mimic.

51. The *Fuck You* "Talk of the Town" page mocked the eponymous column in the staid *New Yorker,* going so far as to duplicate the *New Yorker* image of an aristocratic monocle-wearing gentleman.

52. At a reading he gave at the Poetry Project, St. Mark's Church, New York, October 11, 1967 (sound recording), Paul Blackburn Papers, SPL 400, Mandeville Special Collections Library, University of California, San Diego, former Fugs member Tuli Kupferberg said,

> There was a time when poetry was the leading art on the scene. Then the rock-and-roll thing came in, and it sort of really displaced it. The ideal solution is the idea that we are all going to create a popular music that's going to be poetry, that's where it was in the beginning back in Greek times. Song should be poetry, music should be poetry. The trick is to write songs that are good poetry. The question is what happens to a poem when you put them with music. Sometimes you can deceive yourself. The music can make a poem that isn't so good sound better. Songs tend to want to be simple—the only one who's really mastered it has been Dylan. It's questionable to take the ideas that poems are meant to carry and set them to music.

53. Sanders, *Fuck You / a magazine of the arts* 5, no. 8 (March 1965).

54. Sanders, *Fuck You / a magazine of the arts* 3, no. 5 (May 1963).

55. Sanders, "Sheep Fuck Poem," *Fuck You / a magazine of the arts* 1, no. 3 (1962).

56. In the fifth stanza of Ginsberg's "Sunflower Sutra," the speaker, upon seeing the sunflower, "rushed up enchanted—it was my first sunflower, memories of Blake—my visions." See James Bogan's and Fred Goss's *Sparks of Fire: Blake in a New Age* (Richmond, Calif.: North Atlantic Books, 1982) for essays written by avant-garde writers regarding their views of Blake.

57. Quoted in Bogan and Goss, *Sparks of Fire* 17.

58. William Blake, "Songs of Innocence and Experience," *Blake's Poetry and Designs,* ed. Mary Lynn Johnson and John E. Grant (New York: Norton, 1979), 21.

59. Ed Sanders, interview by Lisa Jarnot, *Poetry Project Newsletter* 168 (1998): 5.

60. Allen Ginsberg, *Howl* (San Francisco: City Lights, 1956), 21.

61. Ginsberg, "Sunflower Sutra," *Howl,* 30.

62. Sanders, interview by Jarnot, 5.

63. Sanders, interview by Jarnot, 5.

64. Sanders, *Fuck You / a magazine of the arts* 6, no. 5 (April 1964).

65. Wolf, *Andy Warhol,* 80.

66. Allan Katzman, "Poet Arrested on Obscenity," *East Village Other* 1, no. 5 (February 1–15, 1966): 6–7.

67. Katzman, "Poet Arrested," 6–7.

68. *Ed Sanders Newsletter,* April 1966, Ed Sanders Archive, Thomas J. Dodd Research Center, University of Connecticut Libraries, Storrs.

69. *Ed Sanders Newsletter.*

70. Sanders, telephone interview, April 15, 1998. Kenneth Koch (interview by author, author's home, New York, October 12, 1998), remembers,

> Ed had a civil liberties lawyer who kept on waiting to get a good judge. Every month or so I'd get a phone call saying, "This might be the day for your appearance. Be ready." I was told to wear a Brooks Brothers suit. This particular day I was aware I might be called down to testify, but I was scheduled to play tennis. At the tennis court, a big announcement came over the loudspeakers on all the Central Park courts. "Kenneth Cock! Kenneth Cock!" I jumped into my gray flannel suit and grabbed my tennis racket. John Ashbery was already there. They were just starting the trial. They dismissed the case. Here's why. This was after the big *SCREW* magazine case, in which I think the decision had been made that obscenity could only be against the law if it encouraged other people to engage in it. So, our lawyer had sort of tricked the opposition lawyer into concentrating his case entirely on the solicitation of people to be filmed during the Mongolian Cluster Fuck. Now, the judge was someone with a sense of humor and a brain, and our lawyer had explained to him, "You don't really believe that they're going to make a movie called *Mongolian Cluster Fuck!* What is that? Obviously, this is a joke, so this doesn't fall under the purview of the law." So the judge explained this to the other lawyer and dismissed the case. I had prepared a list of about ten things I thought were socially redeeming about *Fuck You,* but I never got a chance to state what they were.

71. Ed Sanders, undated press release, Ed Sanders Archive, Thomas J. Dodd Research Center, University of Connecticut Libraries, Storrs.

72. Bourdieu's analysis of the earlier avant-garde's conferring "ready-mades" with economic value and art status is applicable to Sanders's pubic-hair salesmanship. After all, it is arguable whether selling pubic hair is any crazier than Duchamp's presentation of a urinal as art. The artist who succeeds in such a positioning owes his or her "magic efficacy" to, as Bourdieu reads it, "a whole logic of the field that recognizes and authorized him." A "John Ashbery Matchbook" or a Philip Whalen pubic hair can only be successful within a social milieu that Bourdieu characterizes as "a universe of celebrants and believers who are ready to produce it as endowed with meaning and value by reference to the entire tradition which produced their categories of perception and appreciation"; see Pierre Bourdieu, *The Rules of Art: Genesis and Structure of the Literary Field* (Stanford: Stanford University Press, 1992), 169.

73. Sanders, interview, April 15, 1998.

74. In his introduction to *The East Side Scene,* DeLoach writes,

> Other prominent poets who have been generationalized and represent the historical milieu in the Allen anthology but who were variously, if limitedly, active with or on the Lower East Side include: John Ashbery and Frank O'Hara, who were of the "uptown" New York School; Ray Bremser, who was in jail during most of this period; Gregory Corso, who remained essentially on a private scene; LeRoi Jones, who was becoming very active both politically and with the significant Black Arts scene, *and whose omission here is by his own choice;* Denise Levertov, Ed Marshall and Gilbert Sorrentino, who were not, in regards to the scene, part of the nucleus but instead moved in and out of the phenomenon. (vi, my italics)

75. Jon Panish, *The Color of Jazz: Race and Representation in Postwar American Culture* (Jackson: University Press of Mississippi, 1997), 30.

76. Nielsen, *Black Chant,* 125.

77. Michel Oren, "The Umbra Poets' Workshop, 1962–1965: Some Socio-Literary Puzzles," in *Belief vs. Theory in Black American Literary Criticism,* ed. Joe Weixlmann and Chester J. Fontenot, Studies in Black American Literature, vol. 2 (Greenwood, Fla.: Penkeville Publishing, 1986), 184–85.

78. David Henderson, interview by author, Café Limbo, New York City, April 8, 1998. In his essay "Alea's Children," Lorenzo Thomas adds, "The relative lack of racial animosity—at least among the artists—was a notable feature of life on the Lower East Side. The fact that this atmosphere changed in the middle of the decade has, perhaps, more to do with the realities of the nation at the time than with any failure of heart among the practitioners of the avant-garde"; see "Alea's Children: The Avant-Garde on the Lower East Side, 1960–1970," *African American Review* 27, no. 4 (Winter 1993): 578.

79. Baraka was aware of and friendly with the *Umbra* poets, as he indicates in *The Autobiography of LeRoi Jones/Amiri Baraka* (New York: Freundlich Books, 1984):

> Sometime later I began to get some word of *Umbra,* a magazine that began to come out from the Lower East Side that featured black writers. Lorenzo Thomas, who published as a very young person in some of the places that the New York school writers published, I think I was aware of first. His work appeared about the same time that Ted Berrigan and Ron Padgett

and Joe Brainard, the Oklahoma free association semi-surrealists began to appear. . . . One later afternoon . . . I wandered into the Five Spot . . . [and] one guy says to me, "You LeRoi Jones?" I probably just nodded or grunted. One of these dudes is sort of big-headed and bulky, the other taller, with midnight-dark glasses and a rough complexion of skin stretched tight in what I'd have to call an ambiguous smile. The big-headed one says, "I like your prose. I don't like your poetry." The other guy just continues smiling like he knows a secret.

[T]hen [the big-headed one] introduced himself and his companion.

"My name is Ishmael Reed. This is Calvin Hernton." (268)

80. Editor's statement, *Umbra* 1, no. 1 (1963): 3–4.

81. Editor's statement, 4.

82. Lorenzo Thomas, telephone interview by author, September 6, 1998.

83. Oren, "Umbra Poets' Workshop," 181.

84. Henderson, interview, April 8, 1998.

85. Lorenzo Thomas, Ishmael Reed, and David Henderson have all read at the Poetry Project, and Reed and Henderson were employed as writing workshop leaders.

86. Henderson, interview.

87. Henderson, interview.

88. Thomas, interview.

89. Nielsen, *Black Chant*, 107.

90. Nielson, *Black Chant*, 100.

91. Eugene Redmond, "Stridency and the Sword: Literary and Cultural Emphasis in Afro-American Magazines," in *The Little Magazine in America,* ed. Elliot Anderson and Mary Kinzie (Yonkers, N.Y.: Pushcart Press, 1978), 558. *Umbra* promoted other publications with a more heightened sense of political engagement. At the back of *Umbra* 1, no. 2 (December 1963), for example, there is an ad for the "*National Guardian:* the progressive newsweekly," whose copy reads, "Its concern with peace, equal rights and journalistic integrity makes it must reading for thinking people." There is also an ad for the magazine *Freedomways (A Quarterly Review of the Negro Freedom Movement).* On a more radical note, there is also an ad for *LIBERATOR Magazine*'s special issue entitled "Black America Speaks: The Coming Revolution." The text for this ad reads, "*LIBERATOR* is the voice of the Negro protest movement in the United States and the liberation movement of Africa. Each month *LIBERATOR* brings you the best combination of information on the civil rights struggle, the all-black third party developments and self-defense vs. passive resistance."

92. Henderson, interview. Michel Oren writes, "*Umbra* did not go through these phases in a vacuum. In the background were the developing Civil Rights Movement in the South, its more skeptical and nationalistic counterpart represented by Malcolm X in the North, the Harlem riots of 1964, and the efflorescence of the Black Arts Movement itself, which is thought to have peaked around 1970"; see "The Umbra Poets' Workshop," 182–83.

93. Patrice Lumumba was the first prime minister of the Republic of the Congo (now the Democratic Republic of the Congo). Lumumba was known as an intellectual and a charismatic speaker and was a role model for many young black people around the

world. He became president of the multiethnic National Congolese Movement, and when the Congo attained independence in 1960, he became prime minister. Soon dismissed by President Joseph Kasavubu, Lumumba was later arrested and then assassinated. Lumumba was made a national hero and martyr in 1966; before that, black activists and artists in the United States and elsewhere made Lumumba a subject of much of their work, and many of the left-leaning poets at the time believed that the CIA was implicated in Lumumba's killing. In his autobiography, Baraka recalls participating in a Lumumba-related demonstration outside the UN with Mae Mallory and Calvin Hicks. In the paragraph following the description of his and Calvin Hicks's arrest, Baraka describes how he met "Askia Touré (then Rolland Snellings)" (267). Calvin Hicks was the husband of Nora Hicks, who is listed as "Secretary" in *Umbra* 1. Snellings is listed as "circulation manager" in the same issue. David Henderson also remembers that, following the killing of Lumumba, there were "demonstrations at the UN that we went to. Calvin Hicks and other *Umbra* poets were kind of instrumental in that" (Henderson, interview).

94. Lorenzo Thomas, "A Tale of Two Cities," *Umbra* 1, no. 1 (1963): 36–37. Thomas was published consistently in *Umbra* as well as in mimeographed magazines, including Berrigan's *C*.

95. Ginsberg, *Howl*, 9.

96. Ishmael Reed, "Patrice," *Umbra* 1, no. 2 (1963): 36. The Congo once was a Belgian colony. Belgium had particular interest in the Congo because of the Congo's natural resources, including diamonds and petroleum.

97. Charles Olson, "Projective Verse," *Selected Writings* (New York: New Directions, 1966), 22–23.

98. Nielsen, *Black Chant*, 152.

99. Lorenzo Thomas, "Neon Griot: The Functional Role of Poetry Readings in the Black Arts Movement," in *Close Listening*, ed. Charles Bernstein (New York: Oxford University Press, 1998), 309.

100. Thomas, "Neon Griot," 315.

101. "Tom" is Tom Dent, the poet and Umbra member whose apartment served as the meeting space for Umbra workshops; Thomas, interview.

102. In his essay "Alea's Children," Thomas has made much of the relatively unique integration of black and white artists specific to the Lower East Side scene:

> The most remarkable thing about the Lower East Side scene was that, while race remained a powerful engine of social upheaval, the artists seemed able to work together almost in spite of it. Wilmer F. Lucas, for example, produced a record album of poets reading their work that featured two black and two white writers: Umbra's Calvin Hernton and Norman H. Pritchard with Jerome Badanes and Paul Blackburn. Hernton's amazing long poem, "The Passengers," brilliantly dramatized by his voice on the recording, was dedicated to Allen Ginsberg. . . . Because they were all outsiders in an immigrant community, the avant-garde artists became a community. Because those who were African Americans came there to become artists, not to avoid being black, there was a kind of integrated society that did not seem to exist elsewhere. (575–76)

103. Calvin Hernton, *The Sexual Mountain and Black Women Writers: Adventures in Sex, Literature, and Real Life* (New York: Anchor Books, 1990), 153.

104. The point should also be made that the Lower East Side white ethnic community often did not look on integrated relationships with the same grace as did the artistic subculture. In "Alea's Children," Thomas recalls the enlightened social environment at Stanley's Bar but goes on to qualify his praise of the neighborhood: "However, not every local establishment was as accommodating as Stanley's. The little tavern directly across from Tom Dent's East 2nd street apartment had only a bar and three or four tables, but it was somebody's idea of heaven. One afternoon Tom and I dropped in, and the handful of red-nosed old Ukrainian sots in attendance made it clear to the barmaid—in two languages—that our visit should not be encouraged to become a custom" (574–75).

105. Lorenzo Thomas, "South Street Blues," *Umbra* 1, no. 2 (1963): 38.

106. Panish, *Color of Jazz,* 31.

107. Panish, in *Color of Jazz,* 29, addresses the tensions between black poets associated with *Umbra* and their white counterparts in his discussion of the East Village, which he argues was a place where African American avant-gardists were subject to the same forms of racism that existed outside the Village at the time:

    It was because of these factors that these African American avant-gardists decided to band together to form Umbra, a social and cultural collective. However, this gathering of progressive African Americans developed out of more than their small numbers; their common experiences were also a factor in their association. Sarah E. Wright explains, "I was not alone among the writers of our workshop in enduring the injuries of racism. And it was a frequent topic of our conversation—not just the crude bigotries, but particularly the paternalistic racism of liberal whites who prided themselves on what they thought to be their cosmopolitan and enlightened views."

108. David Henderson, "The Ofay and the Nigger," *Umbra* 1, no. 1 (1963): 41–42.

109. Jack Kerouac, *On the Road* (Cutchogue, N.Y.: Buccaneer Books, 1975), 180.

110. Dick Hebdige, *Subculture: The Meaning of Style* (London: Methuen, 1979), 47.

111. Henderson, interview.

112. David Henderson, *Felix of the Silent Forest* (New York: Poets Press, 1967). This book was published by Diane di Prima, at this point sole editor of *The Floating Bear.*

113. Economou, interview, May 18, 1998.

114. In terms of the relationship between *Poems from the Floating World* and *Trobar,* Economou stated in an interview, May 18, 1998:

    First of all, Jerome Rothenberg was a friend. It was a confluence of poetic interests. We weren't obviously going to seek out people like Robert Pack or Donald Hall. The first *Trobar* came out in 1960. There was a certain amount of overlap of what you might call program or agenda—*The Floating World* had come out sometime in 1959. Part of the similarity was the deep image. Jerry was closely identified with the deep image, and he wrote several things about it. We published him in every issue of the magazine. In a sense, both magazines had been identified as instruments for deep image.

115. Paul Christensen, *Minding the Underworld: Clayton Eshleman and Late Postmodernism* (Santa Rosa, Calif.: Black Sparrow Press, 1991), 35.

116. Economou, interview, May 18, 1998.

117. While Margaret Randall's *El Corno Emplumado* devoted much of its space to translation, the texts were predominantly from North, Central, and South America, whereas poetry in *Floating World* and *Trobar* had a more internationalist editorial approach. For a history of *El Corno Emplumado* (which, though published in Mexico City, was widely read on the Lower East Side and published many of the writers mentioned here), see *The Little Magazine in America,* ed. Elliot Anderson and Mary Kinzie (Yonkers, N.Y.: Pushcart Press, 1978). It should be noted that there were two benefits in the West and East Village for *El Corno;* the first was at the Judson Church, Friday, November 23, 1962. Flyers for that reading show that more than thirty poets read, including Paul Blackburn, Carol Bergé, Julian Beck, George Economou, Jackson Mac Low, Amiri Baraka, Taylor Mead, Jack Marshall, Rochelle Owens, Jerome Rothenberg, Ed Sanders, Armand Schwerner, Susan Sherman, Gil Sorrentino, and Diane Wakoski. The second benefit—showing how the arc from Les Deux Mégots to Le Metro to the Poetry Project was in all senses a real one—was held at the Poetry Project on March 29, 1967, and featured many of the readers that participated in the first benefit.

118. Economou, interview, May 18, 1998.

119. One of these four books (the others were books by Rothenberg, Rochelle Owens, and Blackburn) was Louis Zukofsky's *I's (Pronounced Eyes),* which Economou remembers (interview) had a rather amusing history:

> I have a confession regarding that one. On the cover there's a Japanese scroll—it's upside down. Zukofsky got upset. When I showed him the copies he grumbled, "You guys put the cover on upside down!" I showed him the original photograph he sent us, which did not indicate which end was up. We did our best. . . . I don't know how he expected us to know. Ultimately Louis said, "Oh, that's OK. I understand, these things happen." He hadn't quite at that point gotten the major attention that he got in the last few years of his life.

120. Economou, interview, May 18, 1998.

121. Jerome Rothenberg and Robert Creeley, "An Exchange," *Kulchur* 2, no. 6 (1962): 35.

122. The internationalist inclination is clear by looking at the contents page in the first issue of *Poems from the Floating World,* which included poems from writers as disparate as Rafael Alberti, James Wright, Robert Bly, André Breton, Walt Whitman, and Pablo Neruda.

123. Ezra Pound, *Gaudier-Brzeska* (New York: New Directions Press, 1970), 89.

124. In his *Ezra Pound's Cathay* (Princeton: Princeton University Press, 1969), Wai Lim Yip has said of the word *apparition* that it is "a word that calls forth not one definite shade of meaning, but several levels of suggestiveness" (60). In terms of this "suggestiveness," we see that the phrase "the apparition" is precisely what keeps the poem from becoming a clever bit of photographic juxtaposition, in that it (among other things)

    A.   conjures up the ghost associated with the word "apparition."

    B.   makes the crowd and the writer himself appear tenuous—as if perception itself is necessarily relative, associative, not grounded in reaction to a fictional autonomous "thing."

C. suggests classical Greek myth, due to the fact that Pound is underground—i.e., Hades, the place of the fabled damned.

"In a Station of the Metro," often perceived as the Ur-text of Pound's imagist phase, can be read as particularly allusive in this light, simply because we pay a little more attention here to the opening phrase "the apparition" than we otherwise might.

125. William Blake, "The Marriage of Heaven and Hell," *Blake's Poetry and Designs,* ed. Mary Lynn Johnson and John E. Grant (New York: Norton, 1979), 90.

126. Jerome Rothenberg, "The Double Vision," *Poems from the Floating World* 1 (1959): 10.

127. In terms of the deep image and its Blakean rejection of Cartesian rationality and linearity, Rothenberg wrote to Creeley ("Exchange," 34):

I connect "deep image" with *perception as an instrument of vision,* i.e., a visionary consciousness opening up through the senses, grasping the phenomenal world not only for its outward form (though this also, of necessity) but winning from a compassionate comprehension of that world a more acute, more agonizing view of reality than by rational interpretation, etc. So there are really two things here, conceivable as two realities: 1) the empirical world of the naive realists, etc. (what Buber and the hasidim call "shell" or "husk"), and 2) the hidden (floating) world, yet to be discovered or brought into being: the "kernel" or "sparks."

128. Christensen, *Minding the Underworld,* 35.

129. Takis Sinopoulos, "Ionna Raving," *Poems from the Floating World* 2 (1960): 4.

130. Jackson Mac Low, "Leather Costs," *Poets at Le Metro* 3 (1963). While the scope of this project does not allow for an extended discussion of the Fluxus movement initially developed in New York by George Maciunas and others, we should remember that Mac Low participated in this dada-inspired coterie of which former Fluxus member Ken Friedman has said, "Twelve ideas summarize the how and why of Fluxus: globalism, the unity of art and life, intermedia, experimentalism, chance, playfulness, simplicity, implicativeness, exemplativism, specificity, presence in time and musicality"; see his comments on his edited book *The Fluxus Reader* (London: Academy Editions, 1998) at www.amazon.com. One can conclude that such values aided Mac Low in developing and promoting his chance-determined and highly social work.

131. One can imagine that the repetitive words and phrases in these poems were particularly appropriate for a poetry reading. The repetitions in a sense make it easier for a listener to follow the trajectory of a text when the printed version of that text is not available (as is so often the case at poetry readings).

132. Rothenberg and Creeley, "Exchange," 34.

133. Robert Kelly, "Notes on the Poetry of the Deep Image," *Trobar* 2 (1961): 14.

134. It is significant that Nahuatl poems were being translated by members of the Lower East Side poetic community; Charles Olson's visit in 1951 to the Yucatán Peninsula, site of Nahuatl culture, was discussed by many of the Lower East Side poets who looked to Olson as significant predecessor. Olson had written extensive correspondence to Creeley about his time in the Yucatán, which itself was eventually published in Olson's book *Mayan Letters* (London: Cape, 1968).

135. "Poem for Warriors," trans. Jerome Rothenberg, *Trobar* 2 (1961): 10.

136. Christensen, *Minding the Underworld,* 39 (my italics).

137. Christensen, *Minding the Underworld,* 39.

138. Christensen, *Minding the Underworld,* 35.

139. Jerome Rothenberg, "The Deep Image Is the Threatened Image," *Trobar* 4 (1962): 43.

140. Economou, interview, March 10, 1998.

141. Pierre Joris, e-mail to the author, December 11, 1998. "Iron John" refers to the poet Robert Bly, who wrote a book entitled *Iron John* (Reading, Mass.: Addison-Wesley, 1990), which outlined many of the ideas associated with the so-called men's movement of the late 1980s and 1990s.

142. Jed Rasula makes an interesting point when discussing Bly's relationship to "deep imagists," in that he emphasizes how Bly took on the tag to promote himself as poetic personality in distinction to Rothenberg, Robert Kelly, and Economou's more community-oriented practice: "Bly . . . distanced himself from other young poets working on 'deep image' in New York in the late fifties. . . . . The result was that Jerome Rothenberg and Robert Kelly became known as 'deep imagists,' while Bly took on the role of Midwestern maverick using the same terminology as if by coincidence. This is characteristic, in that it has been a familiar syndrome in American poetry to deny the poetic efficacy of collective action; to insist on the integrity of the heroic ego; and to mistrust anything that smacks of the committee room"; see Jed Rasula, *The American Poetry Wax Museum: Reality Effects, 1940–1990* (Urbana, Ill.: National Council of Teachers of English, 1996), 275.

143. Christensen, *Minding the Underworld,* 38.

144. Geoff Ward, *Statutes of Liberty* (New York: St. Martin's Press, 1993), 178.

145. Libbie Rifkin, *Career Moves* (Madison: University of Wisconsin Press, 2000), 129.

146. Ted Berrigan to Sandy Berrigan, March 20, 1962, Ted Berrigan Papers, Rare Book and Manuscript Library, Columbia University, New York.

147. Koch, interview.

148. Ted Berrigan, diary entry, December 18, 1962, Ted Berrigan Papers, Rare Book and Manuscript Library, Columbia University, New York.

149. Jon Cott (later a rock critic for *Rolling Stone* magazine) was a close friend of future Poetry Project director Anne Waldman and inspired Waldman and Lewis Warsh to name their magazine and press *Angel Hair.* Waldman remembers, "'Angel Hair sleeps with a boy in his head' was the line from the Jonathan Cott poem that caught Lewis Warsh's and my fancy, our duetted 'ear,' and we settled on Angel Hair as the name for our magazine and press. Jon was an old high school friend from New York, where we'd been literary pals exchanging Rilke, Watts, Huxley, Murasake, Beckett plays, Berryman's 'Homage to Mistress Bradstreet,' various 'little' magazines (Jon gave me a copy of *C* magazine), and our own early and awkward poems"; quoted in Clay and Phillips, *A Secret Location,* 177.

150. Ron Padgett, interview by author, Teachers and Writers Collaborative, New York City, March 3, 1998.

151. Padgett, interview.

152. Padgett, interview.

153. Padgett, interview. The "scandal" Padgett refers to involved the Beta Theta Pi fraternity, which was "placed on 'social probation' by the Columbia College Dean's Office for physical abuse of pledges during 'Hell Week' initiation rites Feb. 10"; see "Frat at Columbia Put on Probation," *New York Post,* March 12, 1963, 18.

154. Padgett, interview.

155. Padgett, interview. Padgett describes the aftermath to the *Columbia Review:* "[N]ew editors took over the Columbia Review. One of them was a classmate of mine, Philip Lopate, who instantly published a story of his own, a *scandalous* story about a priest having sexual relations with a young boy, much more explicit and scandalous than what we had proposed to publish. But *we* had made such a stink about censorship, interviews on television, articles in the *Post,* and so on."

156. Berrigan, diary entry, March 14, 1963.

157. "Seven Editors Quit Columbia Review in Protest," *New York Post,* March 12, 1963, 80.

158. Padgett, interview.

159. Berrigan, diary entry, April 13, 1963.

160. Berrigan, diary entry, April 28, 1963.

161. Publications included *Literary Days* by Tom Veitch, *Hinges* by Dick Gallup (with drawings by Brainard), *In Advance of the Broken Arm* by Ron Padgett, and *Homage to Arthur Rimbaud* (poem and drawings) by Ted Berrigan and Joe Brainard. See Clay and Phillips, *A Secret Location,* 160–65, for more information on these texts.

162. "Editorially the predecessor to all the second-generation New York School little magazines, the *White Dove Review* was started by high school student Ron Padgett. The associate editor was Dick Gallup, and the art editors were Joe Brainard and Michael Marsh. The first issue contained poems by Paul Blackburn (described as a 'well known poet living in New York') as well as Clarence Major and Ron Padgett, . . . "; see Clay and Phillips, *A Secret Location,* 159. These teenage poets from Tulsa already had started corresponding with poets associated with the Lower East Side poetic community and practicing the social and networking skills that were to prove valuable when they moved to New York City in the early 1960s. In a letter to Paul Blackburn (December 30, 1958, Paul Blackburn Papers, Mandeville Special Collections Library, University of California, San Diego), Ron Padgett wrote,

Dear Mr. Blackburn:

I am sixteen years old and the editor of a small magazine. The staff of this magazine is composed of three other boys about my age, two of whom are very good artists. We have been able to get enough capital in contributions that we shall not lose money. Perhaps we shall die, like so many others. But that is not our intention.

My question (almost a plea) to you might seem ridiculous, even wild. Simply enough, I (and the rest of the staff) would be deeply honoured and gratified if you could save that poem you are considering tearing up, and send it to us. Or perhaps a small essay. We are preparing our first issue, and your help would be a great boon to us. Or you may laugh and, instead, tear this to shreds. Regardless, keep us in mind.

163. Berrigan, diary entry, May 19, 1963.

164. Frank O'Hara, "Why I Am Not a Painter," *Collected Poems of Frank O'Hara,* ed. Donald Allen (New York: Knopf, 1991), 261–62.

165. Ted Berrigan, review of Frank O'Hara's "Lunch Poems," *Kulchur* 5, no. 17 (1965): 91.

166. See Rifkin, *Career Moves,* 108–35.

167. Rifkin, *Career Moves,* 123.

168. Stephen Ratcliffe and Leslie Scalapino, eds., *Talking in Tranquility: Interviews with Ted Berrigan* (Bolinas, Calif.: Avenue B; Oakland, Calif.: O Books, 1991), 160, my italics.

169. Berrigan, diary entry, June 9, 1963.

170. Quoted in Ratcliffe and Scalapino, eds., *Talking in Tranquility,* 76, my italics. Berrigan adds, "The human singing voice, singing songs that are of my own time and seem to deal with my own time, influences me very much because I write songs for the human speaking voice and I'm interested again in what you can do with the singing voice that you can't do when you write in the speaking voice and vice versa and maybe you can translate between those two. Yes, I am just influenced by my ears, that's really it actually"; see Barry Alpert, "Interview with Ted Berrigan," in *Talking in Tranquility,* ed. Ratcliffe and Scalapino, 82.

171. Ted Berrigan to Sandy Alper Berrigan, August 1963, Ted Berrigan Papers, Rare Book and Manuscript Library, Columbia University, New York.

172. Ted Berrigan to Sandy Alper Berrigan, March 6, 1962.

173. Ted Berrigan to Sandy Alper Berrigan, March 17, 1962.

174. Ted Berrigan to Sandy Alper Berrigan, March 19, 1962.

175. Ted Berrigan to Sandy Alper Berrigan, March 26, 1962. Ted Berrigan had married Sandy Alper after meeting her on a weekend trip to Florida. After the marriage, Alper's parents institutionalized Sandy in a mental hospital. These letters were written to Sandy by Ted while Sandy was in the hospital.

176. Charles Bernstein, "Writing Against the Body," in *Nice to See You: Homage to Ted Berrigan,* ed. Anne Waldman (Minneapolis: Coffee House Press, 1991), 154.

177. Arthur Rimbaud, "A Season in Hell," in *Complete Works* (New York: Harper & Row, 1967), 195.

178. Ginsberg, *Howl,* 34.

179. Ted Berrigan, "Words for Love," *C: A Journal of Poetry* 1, no. 2 (1963).

180. Bernstein, "Writing Against the Body," 154.

181. *Locus Solus* was edited by John Ashbery, Kenneth Koch, Harry Mathews, and James Schuyler and was published in Lans-en-Vercors, France, during the years 1961–1962. The magazine was named after the eponymous novel by French surrealist Raymond Roussel, whose work John Ashbery had briefly considered writing a dissertation on; see David Lehman, *The Last Avant-Garde: The Making of the New York School of Poets* (New York: Doubleday, 1998), 147–50. Published in five issues in four volumes, *Locus Solus* was characterized as "the overseas wing of the New York School poets.

Each squat and plain issue looked like the serious literature of the French, a toned-down Gallimard volume perhaps," according to Clay and Phillips in *A Secret Location,* 169. Berrigan noted his publication in *Locus Solus* in a diary entry dated "4 Dec, 1962." Reading this note, it is once again clear that association with the New York School was the most coveted association of all: "*Locus Solus* number V came out yesterday, and to my complete surprise and delight had a poem by me in it. How good that my first major publication was in the magazine edited by Koch + Ashberry [*sic*], w/ poems also by them + O'Hara" (Berrigan, diary entry, December 4, 1962).

182. O'Hara's poems "Mary Desti's Ass," "Madrid," "Poem (beginning with the line 'Twin spheres full of fur and noise')," "Blue Territory," and "Lebanon"; John Ashbery's poem "Into the Dusk-Charged Air"; Kenward Elmslie's poems "Cave In," "Marbled Chuckle in the Savannahs," and "Circus Nerves and Worries"; Barbara Guest's poem "Candies"; Daisy Aldan's poem "Facility Phrases"; a Denby poem, "Snoring in New York: an Elegy"; Kenneth Koch's poems "The Islands" and "The Departure from Hydra"; and James Schuyler's "April and Its Forsythia," "Grand Duo," and "Looking Forward to See Jane Real Soon" were all featured in this volume.

183. In an interview with Ed Foster, Ron Padgett suggests that his and Berrigan's working-class roots also served to differentiate them from first-generation predecessors; see Ed Foster, "An Interview with Ron Padgett," *Postmodern Poetry: The Talisman Interviews, Interviewed by Ed Foster* (Hoboken, N.J.: Talisman House, 1994):

> My work was a little more "down home." It seemed to come more out of the working class. My Arkansas Ozark ancestors are wandering around in my work. The work of the others was more sophisticated, urbane, and witty. But my work was quick and light, with a lot of the cowboy-hillbilly that was natural to my feeling, that I didn't find in theirs. It isn't an accomplishment, it's just something you get in being who you are. . . . Ted had a blue-collar background also, and he was a guy living on the edge, an outlaw type. And there was a lot of spunkiness and orneriness and street urchin bad-boy stuff in there that you don't get so much in the older poets that we had admired so much.

184. Ted Berrigan, review of Ron Padgett's "In Advance of the Broken Arm," *Kulchur* 5, no. 17 (1965): 101.

185. Ron Padgett, "I'd Give You My Seat if I Were Here," *C: A Journal of Poetry* 1, no. 7 (February 1964).

186. See the discussion of Lorenzo Thomas's poem "A Tale of Two Cities," above.

187. Ron Padgett, "Ash Tarzan," *C: A Journal of Poetry* 1, no. 2 (June 1963).

188. Padgett, interview, March 3, 1998.

189. *Locus Solus* 2 was entitled "A Special Issue of Collaborations" and had a big influence on Padgett and Berrigan. This issue included texts like "On Hope," by Abraham Cowley and Richard Crashaw; two passages from Coleridge and Southey's "Joan of Arc"; and "Surrealist Proverbs," by Paul Eluard and Benjamin Peret translated by Koch—another indication of the debt owed to surrealism by the New York School crowd.

190. Padgett, interview, March 3, 1998.

191. Ted Berrigan, "Sonnet II," *C: A Journal of Poetry* 1, no. 1 (1963).

192. Frank O'Hara, "The Day Lady Died," *Lunch Poems* (San Francisco: City Lights Books, 1964), 325.

193. Wolf, *Andy Warhol,* 94.

194. Ron Padgett, ed., *Handbook of Poetic Forms* (New York: Teachers and Writers Collaborative, 1987), 40.

195. Gerard Malanga to Bill Berkson, September 1, 1963, Gerard Malanga Archive, Harry Ransom Center, University of Texas, Austin.

196. Ward, *Statutes of Liberty,* 103.

197. Lehman, *Last Avant-Garde,* 228–29.

198. Quoted in *C: A Journal of Poetry* 1, no. 2 (1963).

199. In our personal correspondence, Padgett has stated, "You've overanalyzed here," in reference to my reading of his "Sonnet." So be it.

200. John Perreault, "John Perreault," *C: A Journal of Poetry* 1, no. 7 (1964).

201. The social politics associated with the Edwin Denby issue of *C* magazine are discussed at length by Reva Wolf, *Andy Warhol.*

202. In *Last Avant-Garde,* 293, David Lehman has pointed out the apolitical nature of the First-Generation New York School, and he connects the omission of overt political content in poetry with an historical avant-garde: "Freedom for an artist meant precisely freedom from politics. Baudelaire, whose prose poems advised the reader to 'get drunk all the time' and to 'beat up beggars,' condemned didacticism outright. He had witnessed the cataclysmic failure of the French Revolution of 1848 and now saw the danger and futility of subordinating art to politics."

203. Lorenzo Thomas, "Political Science," *C: A Journal of Poetry* 1, no. 5 (October/ November 1963).

204. Thomas, interview.

205. Frank O'Hara, "Personal Poem," in *Collected Poems,* 335; "For the Chinese New Year and Bill Berkson," *Collected Poems,* 392. Geoff Ward points out other poems of O'Hara's that appear to contain racial themes, including "The Day Lady Died" and "his most successful Odes . . . 'Salute to the French Negro Poets'"; see *Statutes of Liberty,* 136.

206. Rifkin, *Career Moves,* 115.

207. Rifkin, *Career Moves,* 130.

208. Ward, *Statutes of Liberty,* 178.

209. Rifkin, *Career Moves,* 111.

210. Rifkin, *Career Moves,* 111.

211. Kenneth Koch to Ted Berrigan, July 21, 1963, Ted Berrigan Papers, Rare Book and Manuscript Library, Columbia University, New York.

Chapter 4: The Poetry Project at St. Mark's Church

1. Aldo Giunta, "The Maverick Church: St. Mark's in the Bouwerie," *East Village Other* 1, no. 3 (December 1965): 6.

2. Humphrey Carpenter, *W. H. Auden: A Biography* (Boston: Houghton Mifflin, 1981), 433.

3. Steve Facey, telephone interview by author, February 17, 1999.

4. Christopher Mele, *Selling the Lower East Side: Culture, Real Estate, and Resistance in New York City* (Minneapolis: University of Minnesota Press, 2000), 167.

5. John Cale, a founding member of the Velvet Underground, had worked earlier with composer and musician LaMonte Young, who had been romantically involved with the poet Diane Wakoski (a regular presence at Les Deux Mégots and Le Metro).

6. See www.fillmore-east.com/showlist.html for a list of performances at the Fillmore East.

7. Mele, *Selling the Lower East Side,* 168.

8. Giunta, "Maverick Church," 6.

9. Anne Waldman, e-mail to the author, March 10, 2001.

10. Waldman, e-mail to the author, March 10, 2001.

11. I am indebted to Bob Holman's unpublished "History of the Poetry Project," 1978, Poetry Project Archives, St. Mark's Church, New York, for the information in this paragraph.

12. Waldman, e-mail to the author, March 10, 2001.

13. Bob Holman, "History of the Poetry Project," 14.

14. Poets who read at this event included Deux Mégots and Le Metro regulars Allen Ginsberg, Peter Orlovsky, Alan Katzman, Jackson Mac Low, Armand Schwerner, Carol Bergé, and Jerome Rothenberg.

15. Kenneth Koch, interview by author, in Koch's home, New York, October 12, 1998. Koch elaborates on his approach toward overtly political content:

> A reading that had a big influence on me was one which was held up at Columbia University that Allen Ginsberg did, in the late 1960s, with John Hollander. It was around the time of the Vietnam War, and I had never written a political poem since I was a teenager. I thought, "Why am I not writing about this terrible war, which I don't like?" So I started to write, directly inspired by that reading, my poem "The Pleasures of Peace." I worked on this poem for more than a year, maybe two years. It was very hard for me to work on a poem about the war. You know sometimes your body rejects an artificial heart? Well, my poetry rejected everything about the war. All that was about suffering and destruction. So it turned out to be a poem about the pleasures of the peace movement.

Additionally, John Shoptaw writes in *On the Outside Looking Out: John Ashbery's Poetry* (Cambridge, Mass.: Harvard University Press, 1994), 102:

> The Vietnam War was rapidly escalating. Ashbery wrote a commemorative article on O'Hara's career, "Frank O'Hara's Question," in *Book Week* (25 September 1966) in which he remarked that O'Hara's irreverent poetry incited participation in all causes rather than in a particular program or movement. The piece angered the poet Louis Simpson, an editor of the 1957 formalist anthology *The New Poets of England and America.* Writing in a special issue of *The Nation,* Simpson badly misinterpreted Ashbery's tribute to his friend as an insult to "anti-war" poets: "John Ashbery . . . complimented [O'Hara] on not having written poetry about the war. This struck me as a new concept of merit—praising a man for

things he has not written. But it was not amusing to see a poet sneering at the conscience of other poets." Ashbery wrote an angry letter to *The Nation* in which he quoted his *Book Week* article: ["]Frank O'Hara's poetry has no program and therefore it cannot be joined. It does not advocate sex and dope as a panacea for the ills of modern society; it does not speak out against the war in Vietnam or in favor of civil rights; it does not paint gothic vignettes of the post-atomic age; in a word, it does not attack the establishment. It merely ignores its right to exist, and is thus a source of annoyance to partisans of every stripe . . . It is not surprising that critics have found him self-indulgent: his *culte du moi* is overpowering; the poems are all about him and the people and images who wheel through his consciousness, and they seek no further justification: "This is me and I'm poetry, Baby," seems to be their message, and unlike the message of committed poetry, it incites one to all the programs of commitment as well as to every other form of self-realization: interpersonal, dionysian, occult or abstract.["]

Ashbery also pointed out, lest his protest against Simpson's attack be likewise misunderstood, that he had "signed and contributed money to the petition protesting the war circulated by the Committee of the Professions and published in the *Times* last June 5; was a sponsor of the anti-war fast and poetry read-in at St. Mark's Church last January; and participated in the April 14 [1966] Spring Mobilization march."

16. Renato Poggioli, *The Theory of the Avant-Garde,* trans. Gerald Fitzgerald (Cambridge, Mass.: Harvard University Press, 1968), 183.

17. Allen Ginsberg, "Who Will Take Over the Universe?" *Collected Poems, 1947–1980* (New York: Harper & Row, 1984), 265.

18. In the introduction to *Out of This World: An Anthology of the St. Mark's Poetry Project, 1966–1991* (New York: Crown Books, 1991), 4, Anne Waldman remembers how, prior to the grant from the Office of Economic Opportunity, "Paul Blackburn had moved the poetry reading series from The Metro coffeehouse on Second Avenue to the parish hall of the church. Like a real trooper, he lugged his old Wollensack tape recorder to every reading, dutifully recording the evening and passing the hat for the featured reader."

19. Holman, "History of the Poetry Project," 5.

20. Quoted in Holman, "History of the Poetry Project," 5.

21. The Reverend Michael J. Allen et al., "Creative Arts for Alienated Youth" (grant proposal, Department of Health, Education, and Welfare, Washington, DC, 1966). Joel Sloman, former assistant director of the Poetry Project, was kind enough to send me a copy of the grant, which he's held in his files since 1966. All quotations regarding the grant stem from this source. As the grant is awkwardly and inconsistently paginated, I will not list page numbers.

Michael Allen, received his A.B. (cum laude) from Harvard in history, 1950, and his B.D. from the Episcopal Theological School. He was a senior writer for *Look* Magazine in 1951–54. Allen did Clinical Pastoral Training, Boston State Hospital, in the summer [of] 1955, and at the Boston Psychopathic Hospital in the summer of 1956. He was Assistant Minister, director of youth work, at Grace Church, New York, 1957–59, Assistant Episcopal Chaplain at New York University, 1957–59, and Chairman, College Division, at the Episcopal Diocese of New York, 1959–1961. He began his Rectorship at St. Mark's in the Bouwerie in 1959.

Harry Silverstein received his A.B. from N.Y.U. in Sociology, 1955, and did graduate work at Columbia University from 1955–1961. He was a member of the National Psychological Assn. For Psychoanalysis, 1961, Assistant to the Director, Cross Cultural Study of Youth, U. of Notre Dame, 1963–1965, Senior Research Associate at the Center for the Study of Man, U. of Notre Dame, and a Lecturer in Sociology at Hunter College.

Bernard Rosenberg received his AB from the University of Michigan, his M.S.Sc. at the New School in 1947, and his Ph.D. from the New School in 1949.

22. On the grant application form, the introductory text reads, "Application is hereby made for a grant to support a project for the prevention or control of juvenile delinquency or youth offenses."

23. The Reverend Michael Allen recalled, "The money going to the New School turned out to be an administrative disaster. The second year we administered the funds ourselves, & hired Steve Facey to administer the Arts Projects. He also rewrote the budget"; quoted in Holman, "History of the Poetry Project," 21.

24. Quoted in Holman, "History of the Poetry Project," 5.

25. Joel Sloman, e-mail to author, February 1, 1998. Additionally, Lewis Warsh, editor of the Poetry Project magazine *The World*, remembers, "The whole goal of these projects was to involve the neighborhood youth, but obviously that wasn't what the projects were about. That was the umbrella or pretense for getting this money"; Warsh, interview by author, in author's home, New York, June 8, 1998.

26. Bernadette Mayer, telephone interview by author, November 6, 1998.

27. It should also be noted that by 1968 there were alternative programs based at the church designed to help neighborhood youth. Poets associated with the Poetry Project often assisted in implementing these community-based programs, as Steve Facey recalled in my interview with him:

By 1968 I had started the Preservation Youth Project. This was an organization that lasted for twenty-five years. This was a project that started as street organizing and turned into a work project. These grants weren't linked in any real way, though this was a time when the so-called dropout hippie community was flocking to the church and the Lower East Side. Michael Allen was known as the hippie priest, and Inspector Fink at the Ninth Precinct was known as the hippie cop. He was commander there for years. He once had a meeting with Mike Allen, and he said, "You know, Mike, we're really in the same business." The work-training program came out of a generation of Polish-Ukrainian-Italian kids that still lived in the neighborhood, and then that project gradually spread all the way to Avenue D, so it was predominantly African American and Hispanic. Those were kids in street gangs in the immediate vicinity. We opened the doors to the artists in 1967, so these kids were looking for *their* place in the church. It all linked into what was pioneer urban preservation, because we had fought for this district to be named an historic district, but the church had no endowment, no resources, the graveyard was falling apart, all the day care centers were just beginning, so we put this work program together initially to reclaim the graveyards as community space. The people who did the training in the early years came out of the arts community, so there were people from the theater program and the Poetry Project who survived by being competent skilled people, so I recruited them.

28. Anne Waldman, e-mail to author, March 10, 2001.

29. Michael Stephens, "Poetry Project Days: Meditations on the Oppenheimer That Was," *Talisman* 20 (Winter 1999–2000): 99–100.

30. Joel Oppenheimer to Charles Olson, July 27, 1966, Charles Olson Archive, Thomas J. Dodd Research Center, University of Connecticut Libraries, Storrs.

31. Joel Sloman to Denise Levertov, July 17, 1966, property of Joel Sloman.

32. Workshops and other activities associated with the poetry, theater, and film projects were held at an old courthouse located on Second Street and Second Avenue, which Michael Allen rented from the City of New York for one dollar a year. The building is currently the site of Anthology Film Archives.

33. Joel Oppenheimer to Paul Blackburn, July 7, 1966, Paul Blackburn Papers, Mandeville Special Collections Library, University of California, San Diego.

34. Paul Blackburn to Joel Oppenheimer, July 26, 1966, Joel Oppenheimer Archive, Thomas J. Dodd Research Center, University of Connecticut Libraries, Storrs.

35. Sara Blackburn, interview by author, in Blackburn's home, New York, August 8, 2000.

36. Other poets wrote letters to Paul Blackburn expressing varying levels of disappointment over Oppenheimer's appointment. On July 17, 1966 (Paul Blackburn Papers, Mandeville Special Collections Library, University of California, San Diego), George Economou wrote:

   Joel Oppenheimer has been named Director of the Poetry Section at the St. Mark's Church under the Anti-Poverty Show! Everyone was quite shocked, really expected that Paul Blackburn was the logical choice. I couldn't get a straight story out of Paul Plummer, so I called Joel who was almost apologetic about it. He wants to continue the present series and to keep the "committee" (though Paul P told Jackson it was going to be abolished).

37. In a letter to Oppenheimer, quoted in Lyman Gilmore, *Don't Touch the Poet: The Life and Times of Joel Oppenheimer* (Hoboken, N.Y.: Talisman House, 1998), 144, Bergé writes,

   I am full of wonderment at your suavity and cool. How you managed, when we met in street (12th) last week, not to mention your great coup, your new $12,500 a year job, not to say how you managed to get it, by-passing such old-timer poetry program pro types as Paul Blackburn, Paul Plummer, Planz, Dicker, Rothenberg, and Bergé of course. I think you are very cool, Joel. How *did* you manage not to mention it? How you sleeping nights?

   I, of course, am *not* noted for my cool, which you know now if you didn't before. I should simply sit tight and hope you give me a reading, the way I gave you one when I headed up the planning at the Church. I am a simple fool. But then, I am only 38, and nobody is paying me 12.5 for anything, and none of us who have worked for seven years running readings is as good as you. Patently. So I might as well tell you how I see it. I think it is shit. Especially by-passing Paul Blackburn. That is the real injustice.

38. Anne Waldman, telephone interview by author, January 27, 1998.

39. George Economou, telephone interview by author, March 10, 1998.

40. Quoted in Holman, "History of the Poetry Project," 16.

41. Holman, "History of the Poetry Project," 15.

42. Gilmore, *Don't Touch the Poet*, 145.

43. Quoted in Gilmore, *Don't Touch the Poet*, 124.

44. Shelby Cooper, "Poetry and Plays Liven Church Youth Program in New York," *Sunday Daily News,* December 4, 1966, 19.

45. Oppenheimer to Olson, July 27, 1966, Charles Olson Archive.

46. Reed resigned from his workshop in February 1967; poets in Oppenheimer's workshops in 1966, 1967, and 1968 included Andrei Codrescu, Michael Stephens, Paul Violi, and Thomas Weatherly.

47. Quoted in Holman, "History of the Poetry Project," 19–20.

48. Joel Sloman, e-mail to author, February 1, 1998. Kathy Boudin was a member of the armed revolutionary group The Weather Underground and participated in several bombings. She went underground for many years, though she was later convicted of manslaughter and other charges stemming from a robbery of a Brinks truck in 1981. She is currently a prisoner at Bedford Hills Correctional Center, where she is an active participant in poetry workshops conducted by Hettie Jones, former *Yugen* editor and ex-wife of Amiri Baraka.

49. Stephens, "Poetry Project Days," 100–101.

50. Quoted in *Talking in Tranquility: Interviews with Ted Berrigan,* ed. Stephen Ratcliffe and Leslie Scalapino (Bolinas, Calif.: Avenue B; Oakland, Calif.: O Books, 1991), 128–29. There were exceptions to the dearth of published women poets in the early part of the 1960s, however. Under Amiri Baraka, Totem/Corinth books published Les Deux Mégots stalwarts Carol Bergé, Barbara Moraff, Rochelle Owens, and Diane Wakoski in the anthology *Four Young Lady Poets.* The title seems so old-fashioned and demure that it appears anachronistic alongside its companions—that is, the other mimeos and publications associated with the Lower East Side scene. However, as Rochelle Owens clarifies (telephone interview by author, March 29, 1998), the title was read by the book's contributors in a variety of ways, many of which allowed for a sense of irony:

> Baraka . . . having a kind of intuitive sensibility that was amenable to an avant-garde poetry position, he wanted an anthology of women. He thought the name—as we all did, too—was kind of an ironical name. *Four Young Lady Poets* was an ironical echo of the lady poet of the early twentieth and late nineteenth century. I liked the work of the poets in the anthology, and of course we were all reading together in public at Les Deux Mégots at the same time. Up until the 1960s, women poets were considered a kind of precious, sentimental, flowery kind of group.

> *Four Young Lady Poets* certainly had an impact on the Lower East Side poetic community, and most reactions to the book played on the absurdity of the genteel significations the title afforded; Ed Sanders described Barbara Moraff as "one of the Four Young Lady Fucks of the Totem/Corinth collection"; see Ed Sanders, *Fuck You / a magazine of the arts* 1, no. 5 (December 1962). Additionally, the actual poetry inside the book in no way corresponded to the Victorian aura of the title. Much of the work in the book was "experimental" in the sense that it did not conform to standard narrative or lyric practices typical of "academic" poetry. Owens's poem "Hera Hera Hera," with lines including
>
> > You Ye; The bee's jail, Puck workhouse
> > YOU Ye zealous spongy devoting to

> Fucking logic, bath-ing in the
> Stream, giggling.

or lines from Moraff's untitled poem

> The wild wind whoops birds   shoots bulls of milk whoops
> birds who claw silence beat darkness out of empty eggshells
> the wild wind whoops the birdfeathers choke aeolus weaving
> spiders millions of them crawling round secausus piglegs .

clearly show a kind of alternative aesthetic at work here. Moraff's heavily alliterated, antinarrative, playful, and vocative language places her in the company of Jackson Mac Low and Yoko Ono. On the most basic level, Owens's use of the word *fucking* was still considered to be rather outrageous in 1962, so its appearance in Owens's poem, even post-Ginsberg, was destined to elicit a shocked response on the part of more conservative readers. Baraka's role in *Four Young Lady Poets* shows that he was an editor not only with an interest in the avant-garde, but also with perhaps some real interest in presenting women poets as avant-garde authorities rather than (more typically) conventional rhymers and domestic bards (á la May Swenson or early Adrienne Rich).

51. Waldman, introduction to *Out of This World,* 2–4.

52. The National Organization for Women was founded in 1966, the same year as the Poetry Project.

53. Andrei Codrescu to Margaret Randall, summer 1968, *Corno Emplumado* Archive, Elmer Holmes Bobst Library, Fales Library, New York University.

54. Clayton Eshleman to the author, July 8, 1999. Poetry in the Schools was an organization that sent poets into public schools to teach students creative writing.

55. Eshleman to the author, July 8, 1999. In our personal correspondence, Mac Low recalls that his performance was based on varying words stemming from the phrase "personnel bombs" and adds that the flag was not in terrible condition.

56. Eshleman to the author, July 22, 1999.

57. Richard F. Shepard, "Galbraith Urges Arts 'Handouts,'" *New York Times,* June 23, 1967, 44.

58. Gilmore, *Don't Touch the Poet,* 141.

59. For an account of Sloman's political activism in Massachusetts, see James D. Sullivan's *On the Walls and in the Streets* (Chicago: University of Illinois Press, 1997), 81–85. Also see Sloman's *Cuban Journal* (Cambridge, Mass.: Zoland Press, 2000), a chronicle in poetry of Sloman's participation in the Venceremos Brigade, which was a group of young radicals who traveled to Cuba in 1970 to participate in the effort to harvest a record ten million–ton sugar cane crop.

60. Joel Sloman, e-mail to author, February 1, 1998.

61. Lorenzo Thomas was the first young poet asked to be assistant director of the Poetry Project. In a telephone interview (by the author, September 6, 1998), he remembers of the job offer:

> Taking the job at the Poetry Project wasn't a serious option for me. Being an arts administrator wasn't what I wanted to do. Effectively, the Project became the center that the cof-

feehouses had been, but [with] a much more congenial atmosphere, a big room, a clean, well-lighted space. It's amazing to me that it's been there for more than thirty years. The pastor was one of those young Episcopal ministers who do amazing stuff, get involved in the community, convince people to become church members.

62. Sloman, e-mail to author, February 1, 1998.

63. Regarding the necessary qualifications for the assistant director position, the grant read: "The artist-directors are conceived of as role models, for significantly the artist is the hero of the subculture of the uncommitted—they are the significant others with whom one can identify. . . . Each program will also have an assistant director who will himself be a member of the youth community, who has begun to create, and has found recognition in the eyes of the youth around him, while still essentially one with them."

64. Sloman to Levertov.

65. Quoted in Holman, "History of the Poetry Project," 17. In his interview with Bob Holman, Allen is determined to distinguish the program's intent from one of socializing youth to one of creating a sense of community: "We were not out to reform kids. It was our commitment that people find their own identities. What we were after was the *opposite* of juvenile delinquency: a serious, meaningful, committed community."

66. *East Village Other* 1, no. 1 (September 1966).

67. Leticia Kent, "Film Head Fired: Alienated Revolt," *Village Voice*, March 9, 1967, 1.

68. "Preston Presents," *East Village Other* 2, no. 8 (March 15–April 1, 1967): 14.

69. Jacobs, in his own defense, is quoted asking, "How could you possibly hope to satisfy the needs of would be filmmakers on the feeble $10,000 which would make a nice personal grant for one filmmaker for a year's work. It's a very expensive art form. I never said I could create an adequate workshop with this money for all these people, however, it would make a workable and basic plan with which we could get donations from foundations to continue on a larger scale"; see "Preston Presents," 14.

70. Quoted in Holman, "History of the Poetry Project," 41.

71. Sloman, e-mail to author.

72. Writers published in the one and only issue of *The Genre of Silence* included Joel Sloman, Robert Creeley, Ray Bremser, Sam Abrams, Robert Kelly, Anne Waldman, Lewis Warsh, Joel Oppenheimer, Clayton Eshleman, Jim Brodey, and Ted Berrigan. There was also a photographic series titled "The Work of the Angry Arts, January 29–February 5, 1967," by Wolf von dem Bussche, with additional photographs by Francine Winham, D. J. Davies, and Karl Bissenger.

73. Joel Oppenheimer, introduction, *The Genre of Silence* 1 (1967): ii.

74. In an article titled "Dissent" (included in its February 11, 1967, "Talk of the Town" section, 29–30), the *New Yorker* described Angry Arts Week as

an eight-day festival of the arts based on contributions from hundreds of writers, painters, sculptors, dancers, actors, musicians, and film-makers, all united on one issue: opposition to the present American policy in Vietnam. The form of the contributions varied from a

"Collage of Indignation"—twelve hundred square feet of canvas covered with anti-war cartoons, drawings, and cutouts by a hundred painters and sculptors—to a recital by Suzanne Bloch of Renaissance music for lute, recorder, and virginals. Surveying the schedule of events, which included such catchall titles as "Broadway Dissents," "Off-Broadway Dissents," "Avant-Garde Musicians Dissent," and "Folk Rock Dissents," we noticed a program called "An Act of Respect for the Vietnamese People," to be held in the Washington Square Methodist Church, on West Fourth Street. . . . Robert Nichols, a Greenwich Village architect and poet, who was coordinating this particular program, explained to the volunteers that each artist would have five minutes in which to illustrate some aspect of everyday life in Vietnam. The first artist was Joel Oppenheimer, a tall man with a beard, who directs the Poetry Project at St. Mark's in-the-Bouwerie. He had prepared a talk on the subject of the difference between conventional warfare and guerrilla warfare. Addressing the members of the audience as if they were Vietnamese villagers gathered for a clandestine briefing, he said that guerrilla forces, unlike conventional armies, value men above weapons. "None of you are to risk loss of life to defend a machine gun, a mortar, an anti-tank gun," he said. "What we capture we will use when we can. If it is lost back to the enemy we still have gained."

Other poets who participated in Angry Arts Week included David Antin, Paul Blackburn, Robert Bly, Robert Creeley, Robert Duncan, Clayton Eshleman, Anthony Hecht, Stanley Kunitz, Denise Levertov, Walter Lowenfels, Allen Planz, Jerome Rothenberg, Gilbert Sorrentino, Tony Towle, and James Wright. The presence of so many purportedly academic poets (Wright, Bly, Hecht, Kunitz) underscored what was to become a growing détente between avant-garde and academic poets as the groups joined in opposition to the Vietnam War. See Jed Rasula, *The American Poetry Wax Museum: Reality Effects, 1940–1990* (Urbana, Ill.: National Council of Teachers of English, 1996), 382–90, for further discussion of the détente between "academic" poets and avant-garde poets in response to the war.

75. Joel Sloman, "Suggested Titles," *The Genre of Silence* 1 (1967): 8–9.

76. Joel Oppenheimer, "Poem in Defense of Children," *The Genre of Silence* 1 (1967): 48.

77. Sam Abrams, untitled, *The Genre of Silence* 1 (1967): 85.

78. Quoted in Holman, "History of the Poetry Project," 21.

79. On Sunday, May 28, 1967, Waldman and Lewis Warsh were married at St. Mark's Church by the Reverend Michael Allen; Waldman and Warsh certainly did not have the politically charged, contentious relationship with Allen that other more "disaffected" poets had.

80. Gilmore, *Don't Touch the Poet,* 154. Gilmore had stated earlier:

[The Church] had in mind an administrator-teacher who would organize the project and its personnel, handle the government funding and its paperwork, and teach occasional poetry workshops. To Joel, administration was an anathema. He was nervous and inept at organizing people, hated dealing with money and printed forms, and didn't believe in office hours. Indeed, he was seldom visible at the church. His first assistant director, the young poet Joel Sloman, says that typically he would meet Joel at the church mid-morning, but by noon they would adjourn for drinks. (147)

81. Stephens, "Poetry Project Days," 100.

Chapter 5: Anne Waldman, *The World,* and the Early Years at the Poetry Project

1. Anne Waldman, e-mail to author, March 10, 2001.

2. Anne Waldman, introduction to *Out of This World: An Anthology of the St. Mark's Poetry Project, 1966–1991* (New York: Crown Books, 1991), 4.

3. Dennis Cooper, contributor's note, *Out of This World,* 632.

4. Waldman, introduction to *Out of This World,* 4.

5. Fagin would often request manuscripts from poets who had just finished reading poems at the Poetry Project and publish the poems that evening or soon after in his *Adventures in Poetry.* For brief histories of this and other magazines associated with the Poetry Project, see Stephen Clay and Rodney Phillips, *From a Secret Location on the Lower East Side: Adventures in Writing, 1960–1980* (New York: Granary Books, 1998).

6. Indeed, by 1966 the poets associated with St. Mark's showed increasing sophistication regarding applying for federal grants to fund their magazines. *Angel Hair* received a grant for $1000 from the Coordinating Council of Literary Magazines (offices at National Institute of Public Affairs, Washington, D.C.) on February 21, 1968. Additionally, *Angel Hair* received several special one-time prizes of $250 for magazine development and $500 for an individual author published in *Angel Hair* from the N.E.A., which was awarding prizes for poems included in *The American Literary Anthology 2,* scheduled for publication in early winter 1968 by Random House. Tom Clark won a prize for his poem "Doors," as did John Wieners for "Invitation Au Voyage II." Carolyn Kizer ran this particular grant program, which was deemed "substantial" by the *New York Times;* see "Books of the Times: Angel Hair, Partisan Review et al.," *New York Times,* June 26 1968. Mrs. Heinz, of the H. J. Heinz Company in Pittsburgh, pledged $250 to *Angel Hair.* Additionally, *o to 9* got a grant from the Coordinating Council of Literary Magazines.

7. Joel Sloman, e-mail to author, February 1, 1998.

8. Berrigan himself consistently articulated the notion of the New York School generations: "My plan for [*C*] Magazine was to publish [Ashbery, Koch, O'Hara, and Schuyler], in conjunction with four or five younger people, myself and people that I knew. The younger people to begin with were Ron Padgett and Dick Gallup, the painter Joe Brainard, and myself. And not too long after that, I met some other people like Jim Brodey and Joe Ceravolo. And I put them in, too. And then I realized that there was such a thing as New York School, because there was a second generation"; quoted in *Talking in Tranquility: Interviews with Ted Berrigan,* ed. Stephen Ratcliffe and Leslie Scalapino (Bolinas, Calif.: Avenue B; Oakland, Calif.: O Books, 1991), 91.

9. The significance of Koch's classes in terms of maintaining and developing a second generation should not be glossed over. Bill Berkson remembers taking a class with Koch at the New School in 1959 (in his unpublished autobiography, "Since When," property of Bill Berkson):

   Kenneth's class was held in the afternoon. Sitting very upright at one end of the long table, he invented as he went, uncertain in spots, but with surges of glee at the edges of his thought.

Part of each lesson, the fun and suspense, was watching him steer the language toward describing graphically the pleasurable aspects of the poetry he liked—the poetry of Whitman, Rimbaud, Williams, Stevens, Auden, Lorca, Pasternak, Max Jacob and Apollinaire, as well as of his friends Frank O'Hara and John Ashbery. Then, too, he would make an analogy between some moment in a poem and the sensibilities of New York painting—the amplitude of a de Kooning, Larry Rivers' zippy, prodigiously distracted wit, or Jane Freilicher's way of imagining with her paint how the vase of jonquils felt to be on the window sill in that day's light. All of these things would dovetail into the writing assignments Kenneth gave us, which were designed to (and really did) help precipitate and sustain energy and surprise in our poems.

Koch's energy and influence have lasted for decades. Bob Holman—now widely known as a leading figure in the orally based, hip-hop-influenced "slam" poetry movement based in part at the Nuyorican Poets Café on East Third Street in the Lower East Side—recalls, "I was in Kenneth Koch's class in 1968, at Columbia. Koch was a brilliant teacher—he came into class on the first day, threw his arms around himself and shouted, 'Walt, I love you!' Thus began our study of U.S. poetics. I'd never been on a first-name basis with a poet before, let alone a dead poet, but Kenneth was. It was a spectacular introduction and everything was done with such passion and love. That gave me a way into the New York School"; Bob Holman, interview with author, in Holman's home, New York, March 3, 1999. Ted Berrigan had taken classes with Koch and credited him with helping him move away from blatant O'Hara impersonations toward something else: "Frank opened all the doors for me. For a while he was a very bad influence on me, because I started getting too close, it was seeming too easy for me, and then Kenneth Koch kindly pointed out to me that Frank was being a very bad influence"; quoted in *Talking in Tranquility,* ed. Ratcliffe and Scalapino, 29. Koch saw his own role as a generative one, and he defined his students as heirs apparent to the New York School moniker (interview by author, in Koch's home, New York, October 12, 1998):

There was a general atmosphere of "They were for us," and they didn't write awful academic poems, and they seemed to write things that were full of air and freshness. I was aware of that, and then after a while it seemed that Ted Berrigan was sort of the daddy of the downtown poets, taking care of everybody and showing them what it was like to be a poet. I taught a number of those guys in various places. I taught Ron [Padgett at Columbia University]. David Shapiro was my student, too, and then I taught a couple of summers at Wagner College, and at the New School. At the New School I had Tony Towle as a student, and Bill Berkson, and then at Wagner College even Ted came as my student. Ted pointed out to me something very interesting. He said, "Kenneth, do you know every time you mention Paul Valery you go like this?" [Puts his right hand on top of his head.] I thought that was very astute of him. I was very embarrassed, so I stopped doing that. Joe Ceravolo was my student at the New School. *That's* a pleasure for a teacher, because he didn't even write poetry before then. I was interested in the existence of more New York School poets. I decided to teach at the New School not only because I wanted a job, but I really thought I knew a *secret* about poetry that nobody knew except John and Frank and me. I knew about this new aesthetic, this new way to write poetry, and I wanted to spread it around, because I thought it was *dumb* to think that these other bad poets were writing poetry. I taught with a lot of enthusiasm. . . . I really had a mission to make this aesthetic clear to people.

Asked what he meant by the word *aesthetic* in terms of the New York School, Koch replied,

> Well, let me tell you, a few assignments I used at the New School. I had people read William Carlos Williams and imitate him. This was to get them rid of meter, rhyme, and fancy subject matter. Ordinary American language, spoken language. I had them write poems about their dreams, I had them write stream-of-consciousness. . . . This was to get their unconscious stuff into their poetry. I had everybody write short plays, prose poems, how to transform an article in a newspaper into a poem, and I had them write sestinas. I wanted my students to break away from "poetry" poetry, and sort of . . . it was something I thought was French. I was very influenced by Max Jacob. From Jacob I learned how to be comic and lyrical at the same time. That was quite a discovery. It helped the determination to get rid of Eliot, and depression, and despair, and inky-dinky meter. So, getting back to your question of what is the New York School aesthetic . . . I don't know, just a lot of fresh air, to have fun with poetry, to use the unconscious, to use the spoken language, to pay attention to the surface of the language.

10. In an interview with Barry Alpert, Ted Berrigan ties figures associated with the First Generation New York School to collaborative writing practices: "[Kenneth Koch, Frank O'Hara, Larry Rivers, Norman Bluhm, and Mike Goldberg] literally re-invented that collaborative process, something which had been done by the Dadaists, for example"; quoted in *Talking in Tranquility,* ed. Ratcliffe and Scalapino, 108.

11. Anne Waldman, telephone interview by author, January 27, 1998.

12. Pointing to dada/surrealist progenitor Marcel Duchamp, Berrigan has said of his own practice of collaboration and collage, "I was never trying to hide what I was doing, but thought that I was extending (at least sideways) ideas used by Duchamp, Warhol, John Ashbery"; quoted in Reva Wolf, *Andy Warhol, Poetry and Gossip* (Chicago: University of Chicago Press, 1997), 94.

13. "As Peter Bürger has argued in his influential formulation of the historical avant-garde, such movements as dada, surrealism, and futurism shared a goal of reintegrating art with social praxis in challenging the function of art's autonomy. In proclaiming themselves as artificial constructs, self-critical texts such as Marcel Duchamp's ready-mades implicitly critiqued the systems of production, distribution, and reception of artwork, thus making 'art as an institution' recognizable"; see John Lowney, *The American Avant-Garde Tradition: William Carlos Williams, Postmodern Poetry, and the Politics of Cultural Memory* (Lewisburg, Pa.: Bucknell University Press; Cranbury, N.J.: Associated University Presses, 1997), 17.

14. Judi Freeman, *The Dada and Surrealist Word-Image* (Cambridge, Mass.: MIT Press, 1989), 17.

15. Larry Fagin, interview by author, in Fagin's home, New York, January 26, 1998. Of his own mimeograph magazine, *Adventures in Poetry,* Larry Fagin said, "I once put out an issue of *Adventures in Poetry*—it was number ten—but the name and number of the magazine weren't attributed, there was no table of contents, and all the works appeared anonymously. Not attaching authorship forced attention on the text as a 'pure' experience, or gave it a different reading. I was interested in that experience."

Further surrealist, dada, and futurist influence can be seen in the illustrated covers of *The World.* "The incorporation of language into futurist works of art had its origin in contemporary books and popular imagery. In his experimentation with *calligrammes*—first called 'figurative poems' or 'ideogrammatic poems'—Apollinaire manipulated type into configuration suggestive of a poem's meaning"; see Freeman, *Dada,* 18. *The World* 3 had a Futuristlike cover by artist George Schneeman that collaged various words and images. Here, the title of the magazine physically leaked into the illustration. The illustration itself contained the alphabetical symbols *A* and *B* and the faint outline of the word *MAG* next to cartoonlike images of women being shot at by a disembodied hand. Schneeman may very well have been influenced by his friends Ron Padgett and Joe Brainard (particularly Brainard's extensive use of cartoon images). Padgett's translations and promotion of Apollinaire (work that itself was partly due to Kenneth Koch's classes on Apollinaire) helped bring the Surrealist influence into the Poetry Project scene.

16. One should note that the title itself obscures the generic distinctions between the words *poem* and *prose;* what part of Brodey's text is poetry and what part is prose is essentially impossible to discern as the lineation remains consistent throughout.

17. An article by Rich Mangelsdorff reviewing Lewis Warsh's "Moving Through Air" is adaptable to this discussion of Brodey's text, in that Mangelsdorff justifies the potentially exclusive nature of listing names in poetry by relating the act to coterie and the significance of place: "Reminds me of court poetry; you can sense the power of references which would really explode given involvement with the intended people and scenes. One way to make the language rock, given a tight enough milieu; that's always been one of the reasons for going to New York, anyway"; see "State of the Art: Young American Poets," *Kaleidoscope* (September 27–October 10, 1968), 12.

18. Frank O'Hara, "The Day Lady Died," *Lunch Poems* (San Francisco: City Lights Books, 1964), 27.

19. Jim Brodey, "A Poem & Prose," *The World* 1 (1967). Of the "I do this / I do that" aesthetic and its relationship to Frank O'Hara and the Poetry Project, Brad Gooch writes, "Most of Ted Berrigan's early poems were bald imitations of O'Hara's 'I Do This, I Do That' poems. This style, more than any other, was fast becoming the preferred style copied by most of the second-generation New York School poets already gathering at the St. Mark's Poetry Project, started in 1966 as the official home of unofficial poetry"; see Brad Gooch, *City Poet: The Life and Times of Frank O'Hara* (New York: Knopf, 1993), 469. Note also that the opening line of Brodey's text echoes Ginsberg's opening line in "Sunflower Sutra," where Brodey's "and sigh" rhymes with Ginsberg's "and cry": "I walked on the banks of the tincan banana dock and sat down under the huge shade of a Southern Pacific locomotive to look at the sunset over the box house hills and cry," *Collected Poems, 1947–1980* (New York: Harper & Row, 1984), 138.

20. See chapter 2, where Berrigan is quoted as saying, "My own line of descent is Beatnik cum Frank O'Hara."

21. Quoted in Gooch, *City Poet,* 279–80. For an extended discussion on O'Hara's relationship with Beat and Black Mountain designation writers, see Marjorie Perloff's *Frank O'Hara: Poet Among Painters* (New York: G. Braziller, 1977), 13–18.

22. Quoted in *Talking in Tranquility,* 114.

23. Both Berrigan and Kerouac were notorious for their use of speed, and street names for Benzedrine at that time included the word *goofballs*. In terms of the use of words like *sidekick* and *gunslinger-type,* it is possible that Brodey was alluding to poet Ed Dorn, who had written books including *Hands Up* and whose manuscript *Gunslinger* was circulating among various poetic communities before its official publication.

24. Brodey, "Poem & Prose."

25. Jack Kerouac, *On the Road* (Cutchogue, N.Y.: Buccaneer Books, 1975), 11.

26. O'Hara, "The Day Lady Died," 27; Brodey, "Poem & Prose."

27. Blackburn was still very active in the poetry-reading scene, however. He ran a popular reading series at Max's Kansas City, and later at a bar on Seventy-third Street and Second Avenue called Dr. Generosity's. After Blackburn's death, the poet Marguerite Harris was in charge of the series. Of Dr. Generosity's, Charles Bernstein remembers (interview by author, in Bernstein's home, New York, March 15, 1999),

   In 1975, I moved back to New York, and that's when I started to attend poetry readings an enormous amount. Mac Low, I saw between 1975 and 1985 more than anyone else at the time. He used to read up at Dr. Generosity's, and I used to go up to that series quite a bit. That was interesting—it was very small, on the Upper East Side, an excellent interesting group of people, very much within that Mac Low, Rothenberg, Blackburn, Economou sort of context. Very non–New York School, non–St. Mark's of that moment.

   In a letter to Blackburn from Diane Wakoski (September 28, 1970, Paul Blackburn Papers, Mandeville Special Collections Library, University of California, San Diego), one learns, "Some of us are trying to maintain the noble tradition which you established last year—poetry readings on weekend afternoons in bars. We will continue at Dr. Generosity's on Saturday's at 3 P.M. as you organized the readings. Rather than Max's Kansas City for Sundays, we will hold the readings at St. Adrian's Company at 2 P.M."

28. Lewis Warsh, interview by author, in author's home, New York, June 8, 1998.

29. Ginsberg and Orlovsky both read at the Blackburn memorial, and Orlovsky gave a particularly moving reading, performing a poem that described his last encounter with Blackburn. The final lines of his poem depict an emaciated Blackburn, throat so sore he was incapable of eating, having a smoke with Orlovsky: "Two weeks I felt he would live / and two weeks later he died. / It was so sad. / For sure we will never both smoke again." Unfortunately, Orlovsky's representative refused to grant me permission to reproduce this wonderful reading on CD.

30. Berrigan, quoted in *Talking in Tranquility,* 57.

31. See Brad Gooch's *City Poet* and David Lehman's *The Last Avant-Garde: The Making of the New York School of Poets* (New York: Doubleday, 1998) for accounts of the social world of the First-Generation New York School.

32. Warsh, interview, June 8, 1998.

33. Frank O'Hara, "Adieu to Norman, Bon Jour to Joan and Jean-Paul," *Collected Poems,* 328–29.

34. Ron Padgett, interview by author, Teachers and Writers Collaborative, New York, March 3, 1998.

35. Warsh, interview, June 8, 1998.

36. Warsh recalls (interview, June 8, 1998):

> Ted Berrigan, Ron Padgett, Dick Gallup, and Joe Brainard were all old friends. Initially, Anne and I were treated along the lines of "Who are these guys? So they edit a magazine, so what?" Eventually Ted decided to check us out, and he started coming over. We told him that we thought he and his friends were pretty snotty—and he couldn't believe it. We'd go to parties, and all these people would treat us like outsiders—we thought they were a bunch of jerks. Ted couldn't believe that we would actually talk this way about him and his friends! And after that he never left, he came over every night. And then Dick started coming over, and for months the four of us would sit around, listening to music, smoking dope, talking about poetry.

37. Ted Berrigan and Dick Gallup, "80th Congress," *The World* 3 (1967).

38. In the same issue of *The World*, the poem "Early Sonnet" by Ted Berrigan echoes the idea that Schjeldahl has gained admission into the New York School: "Peter exists / so he's in as who isn't? Isn't / that what it's all about?"

39. Tom Clark, telephone interview by author, March 30, 2001. Interestingly, Clark became poetry editor of the *Paris Review* at the invitation of George Plimpton, who met Clark in England and asked him to work as poetry editor. Tom Clark lived in the Lower East Side only from February of 1967 through April of 1968, though he would continue collaborating with and publishing poets associated with the Lower East Side after he moved to Bolinas, California.

40. Tom Clark and Peter Schjeldahl, "Easter," *The World* 3 (1967).

41. Anne Waldman to Bernadette Mayer, March 23, 1971, Bernadette Mayer Papers, Mandeville Special Collections Library, University of California, San Diego.

42. Sloman, e-mail, February 1, 1998.

43. Waldman, introduction to *Out of This World,* 4.

44. Warsh, interview, June 8, 1998.

45. Alice Notley, e-mail to author, February 7, 1999.

46. Lewis Warsh, "French Windows," *The World* 3 (1967).

47. Andrew Ross, in *The Failure of Modernism: Symptoms of American Poetry* (New York: Columbia University Press, 1986), discusses the apparently nonpolitical stance of the New York School, particularly that of Ashbery and O'Hara:

> If Ashbery and O'Hara flagrantly refuse the poet's prophetic voice, they do not seek to challenge the unearned privileges of that voice, for this would be to fall into the same circuit of aggression. The "nuptial quality," as O'Hara puts it, of Ashbery's writing means that "he is always marrying the whole world," which is to say that the poets' polygamous inheritance is not poethood itself, nor its privileges, but the whole symbolic, or social, order which comes with a given language. Once the language is accepted, then the only oppositional activity proper to the poet is to expose and thereby impoverish an established class of looking and writing that has been standardized and conventionalized within that language.
>
> As a result of this, the political appeal of Ashbery's work is low on the scale of visibility. There is no significant attachment to socio-economic markers . . . nor any passionate revolt against an elitist literary knowledge . . . and neither is there any "committed" adop-

tion of language as an instrument of terror leveled against a "bad" political object. Ashbery's response, by contrast, is to the universality and prolixity of the language system as a whole. . . . The insatiable systematicity of this discourse recalls Olson's threat of an endless or unstoppable oralizing, but it operates beyond the willfulness of any one single mouth. (177–78)

48. Frank O'Hara, "In Memory of My Feelings," *Collected Poems*, 256.

49. Geoff Ward, *Statutes of Liberty* (New York: St. Martin's Press, 1993),79.

50. In James Schuyler's "The Morning of the Poem," Schuyler wrote, "I was deep in the clotted Irish rhetoric (as Frank O'Hara said about Dylan Thomas, 'I can't stand all that Welsh spit')"; see Schuyler's *Collected Poems* (New York: Farrar, Straus and Giroux, 1993), 286.

51. By *serious* I refer readers to Eshleman's use of mythic archetypes and personae in his poetry.

52. Lehman, *Last Avant-Garde*, 349.

53. James D. Sullivan, *On the Walls and in the Streets: American Poetry Broadsides from the 1960s* (Chicago: University of Illinois Press, 1997), 21.

54. Larry Fagin has said of his *Adventures in Poetry*, "Working at the Project and attending hundreds of readings over the years was a big advantage. If I heard something I especially liked at a reading, I would rush to the podium and claim the manuscript for *Adventures*. I was rarely refused"; quoted in Clay and Phillips, *From a Secret Location*, 195.

55. Quoted in Clay and Phillips, *From a Secret Location*, 187–88.

56. Michael Davidson, *Ghostlier Demarcations: Modern Poetry and the Material World* (Berkeley and Los Angeles: University of California Press, 1997), 198.

57. Michael Davidson, *The San Francisco Renaissance: Poetics and Community at Mid-Century* (New York: Cambridge University Press, 1989), 55.

58. In 1981 a double album titled *The World Record: Readings at the St. Mark's Poetry Project, 1969–1980* (New York: Poetry Project) was released. Edited by poets Bill Berkson and Bob Rosenthal, the record featured excerpts from readings by poets including Charles Reznikoff, Ted Berrigan, Anselm Hollo, and Bernadette Mayer. Hopefully, more recordings from the Poetry Project tape archives will be restored, rerecorded, and widely distributed.

59. Davidson, *Ghostlier Demarcations*, 207.

60. Instances of acknowledging the audience not as alienated viewers but as active participants and friends are heard over and over again in tape recordings of early Poetry Project readings. One example out of the dozens available is by Denise Levertov, who read at St. Mark's on March 20, 1967: "As I know that many of the people here have been to a lot of read-ins, the napalm reading and so forth, and because last night I was involved in a kind of napalm reading at Vassar, where I read dozens of poems about the war, my own and others, I thought I wouldn't read tonight my poems about the war. But if anyone in the second set wants to hear any of those poems, please ask me to read them"; Levertov, poetry reading (sound recording), Paul Blackburn Papers, SPL 301, Mandeville Special Collections Library, University of California, San Diego.

61. Anne Waldman, "Poem in New York," poetry reading, St. Mark's Church, New York, November 8, 1967 (sound recording), Paul Blackburn Papers, SPL 382, Mandeville Special Collections Library, University of California, San Diego.

62. Koch, interview, October 12, 1998.

63. In his bio included in the Paul Carroll anthology *The Young American Poets* (Chicago: Follett, 1968), 456–57, Newkirk writes of himself,

> Back in Detroit there were two years at Wayne State University and revolutionary politics. No degree. I then became associated with the artists' workshop in Detroit where friend John Sinclair introduced me, happily, to the projective of Charles Olson. Poetry became more of a possibility for me via the work of LeRoi Jones, Gil Sorrentino, and Ed Dorn. I now live in NYC where I am a director of the Center for Paleocybernetic Research which considers social and cultural revolution within the context of our more general evolution out of those civilizations founded upon, and certainly still pushed by, neolithic technology. The center is also the spiritual home of Guerrilla Press which publishes pamphlets and the newspaper *Guerrilla.* I am convinced that men are weird and lovely mammals with swollen speech centers and that poetry is our major tool to recover our animal status, image and grace."

64. There is some disagreement about whether Newkirk walked up to the stage from the rear of the parish hall or through a side door connecting the parish hall with the sanctuary.

65. Padgett, interview by author, Teachers and Writers Collaborative, New York, February 13, 1999.

66. Werner Sollors, *Amiri Baraka: The Quest for a Populist Modernism* (New York: Columbia University Press, 1978), 6. Baraka's charges were later thrown out on appeal. Baraka's poem "Black People" contains the oft-quoted lines "Up against the wall mother / fucker this is a stick up!"; see *Evergreen Review* 50 (1967): 49.

67. "When Baraka became involved with the Newark ghetto rebellion of 1967, [his poem 'Black people'] was used as evidence of his 'evil' intentions"; see Sollors, *Amiri Baraka,* 201.

68. A rather unfortunate coda to this incident is to be found at a reading Kenneth Koch, John Ashbery, and Allen Ginsberg gave in the Barnard College auditorium just a week after the Koch "assassination." As Koch began to read at Barnard, a student threw a pie in his face. Koch remembers this was supposed to have something vaguely to do with the Columbia student strike, which he supported. "I gave my glasses, which were smeared with cake, to Allen to hold. As I stood on the stage, I heard a great roar of laughter, and I thought to myself, 'Oh, good, I've pulled myself out of this one.' What the audience was actually laughing at, though, was Allen, who was licking the cake off my glasses and making lots of 'mmm' noises while doing so"; Koch, interview, February 11, 1999.

69. Warsh, interview, June 8, 1998.

70. Poets included in the Carroll anthology who read regularly at the Poetry Project or were generally associated with the Lower East Side poetic community included Vito Acconci, Bill Berkson, Ted Berrigan, Clark Coolidge, Jon Cott, Kenward Elmslie, Gerard Malanga, Ron Padgett, John Perreault, Aram Saroyan, Peter Schjeldahl, Tony Towle, Allen Van Newkirk, Diane Wakoski, Robert Kelly, Sotere Torregian, Anne Wald-

man, and Lewis Warsh. From the introduction to *Young American Poets,* 9, Dickey writes,

[T]here are some attempts here at the kind of calculated boldness that one associates with the experimentalism of the 1920s. On the other hand, a few of them have tried to write rather complacent formal exercises in rhyme and regular meter that show into what a mortuary a misunderstood classicism can lead poems. . . . But the important thing to note is that the writers in this anthology are attempting in a new way to speak with as much real boldness as they can summon of passion and involvement, rather than in the distant and learnedly disdainful tone of Eliot or with manic scholarliness of Pound.

71. From the preface to *A Controversy of Poets: An Anthology of Contemporary American Poetry* (Garden City, N.Y.: Anchor Books, 1965), Paris Leary and Robert Kelly write, "This anthology is designed to turn the attention of the reader to the contemporary *poem,* away from movements, schools or regional considerations. Hitherto some of these poets have been referred to by commentators more enthusiastic than accurate as belonging to this or that rival—and hostile—school. Such poetasting has only served to distract the reader from the *poem* and to divert his attention to supposed movements or schools, whereas the only affiliation finally relevant is that apparent from the work itself."

72. Photograph of Diane Wakowski, *Young American Poets,* 467.

73. Carroll, a poet living in Chicago and former editor of *Big Table,* was himself anthologized in Allen's book.

74. Mangelsdorff, "State of the Art," 12–13.

75. Warsh, interview, June 8, 1998.

76. Christopher Mele, *Selling the Lower East Side: Culture, Real Estate, and Resistance in New York City* (Minneapolis: University of Minnesota Press, 2000), 177.

77. Robert Creeley, "Bolinas and Me," in *On the Mesa,* ed. Lawrence Ferlinghetti (San Francisco: City Lights Books, 1971), 29.

78. Lytle Shaw's discussion in "On Coterie: Frank O'Hara," *Shark* 2 (1999): 118, is useful in recognizing that the act of including proper names into poetry has sociability as its guiding principle:

Voice emerges not as the property of a decontextualized "I," but as the enunciations of "someone" situated within the intersubjective networks his poems explore from a variety of angles. These situating networks operate not at an archetypal level (husband/wife; father/son) but at a particularized, socialized level, and include literary history not as an abstract "tradition" (as it often is for Eliot and Lowell) but as specific engagements with authors and texts that mark the poems with proper names.

79. By the mid-1970s, there was even talk of a Third-Generation New York School based on poets such as Eileen Myles, David Trinidad, and Tim Dlugos.

80. Padgett, interview, February 13, 1999.

81. Kenneth Koch, "Fresh Air," *The New American Poetry,* ed. Donald Allen (New York: Grove Press, 1960), 75.

82. Tomaž Šalamun, "111/73," *The Selected Poems of Tomaž Šalamun,* ed. Charles Simic (New York: Ecco Press, 1988), 31.

83. For a diaristic account of the Bolinas scene, see Joe Brainard, *Bolinas Journal* (Bolinas, Calif.: Big Sky Press, 1971).

84. Warsh, interview, February 3, 1999.

85. Mele, *Selling the Lower East Side*, 175–76.

86. Andrei Codrescu to Margaret Randall, summer 1968, *El Corno Emplumado* Archive, Elmer Holmes Bobst Library, Fales Library, New York University.

87. Quoted in Bob Holman, "History of the Poetry Project," 1978, Poetry Project Archives, St. Mark's Church, New York, 31.

88. Anne Waldman to Bernadette Mayer, March 14, 1970, Bernadette Mayer Papers, Mandeville Special Collections Library, University of California, San Diego. Jean Boudin was Frances LeFevre Waldman's (Anne Waldman's mother's) friend.

89. Anne Waldman to Gerard Malanga, January 1968, Gerard Malanga Archive, Harry Ransom Center, University of Texas, Austin.

90. Holman, "History of the Poetry Project," 23.

91. Steve Facey, telephone interview by author, February 17, 1999. Regarding grants received in the mid-1970s, Facey remembers,

> We got a grant from the N.E.A. in 1975 from a program that I think only lasted for one or two years called "City Spirit." It was trying to link up community development and arts activity. The Ford Foundation created their program to fund experimental theater right at the time when the federal grant ran out, so Theater Genesis got one of those five grants, which was two or three years' support. We did get funding at one point from the parks department, and Anne Waldman had to take a basketball exam. She actually went up and took a recreational exam or something, so they could see how good she was.

92. Anne Waldman, e-mail to author, February 13, 1999.

93. Padgett remembers (interview, February 13, 1999),

> It was David Shapiro's idea. But David didn't want to tackle the project alone, so he invited me to join him. David and I had a kind of aesthetic gut feeling about what poets might be interesting together. David also had a good possibility for a publisher, namely Holt, Rinehart and Winston, which had published David's first book of poetry. The editor there, Arthur Cohen, liked David's work a lot. Arthur also signed up my translation of Apollinaire's "The Poet Assassinated." He asked us for our recommendations of contemporary poets. David and I both pitched John Ashbery, and in fact Arthur did sign up *Rivers and Mountains*— obviously not just because of us. Anyway, David and I put together the anthology, in 1967, but shortly thereafter Arthur quit the publishing business.
>
> Another editor at Holt, Robert Cornfield, suggested we take it to Random House. There was a copy editor at Holt named Carol Sims, who was married to an editor at Random House named Bennett Sims. Bennett signed the book up right away. When he left Random House, his agreeable colleague Christopher Serf took over the project and saw it through publication, in 1970, in simultaneous hard- and soft-cover editions. By the way, Random House's design department unilaterally changed the colors on the cover of the cloth edition. Joe [Brainard] had designed a white cover with red images. It was gorgeous. Random did a black cover with the images in grotesque metallic green, red, and blue inks. Notice, by the way, that the book is not called *The New York Poets*, it's not called *The New York School*

Poets, and it's not called *The Anthology of New York Poets.* The little article *An* was a conscious choice on our part.

94. Ron Padgett has said, "New York can be a difficult place to live in. Lewis MacAdams would come in and freak out and leave after three months. Tom Clark left after maybe a year. The city's atmosphere was sometimes hostile and grimy, and the 'vibes' drove a lot of people out. Tom Veitch left and became a Benedictine monk in Vermont. It's just the nature of New York. It attracts and it repels"; quoted in Holman, "History of the Poetry Project," 31, and revised by Padgett in May 1999.

95. Ed Friedman, the current director of the Poetry Project, remembers (interview with author, St. Mark's Church, New York City, February 3, 1999) that by the early 1970s,

> I realized that a lot of people had left. I was at a party at Anne Waldman's, and I remember Michael Brownstein saying, "I wish Ted Berrigan was here." So Ted wasn't around. Lewis Warsh was in Bolinas, Jim Carroll was away, Ron Padgett was kind of in and out—he was gone for a period in the 1970s. You also have to remember that Richard Nixon was president and the screws were being turned on all progressive cultural and political activities. The antiwar movement had recently met up with state troopers and their bullets. Pop music changed some, becoming more mellow—at least on the radio. A lot of people had died or been shot, and youth were being targeted as a supposedly corrupting force within the society. For me, it was exciting to be living in New York and coming to the Poetry Project, but the counterculture, of which the Poetry Project was very much a part—and which had a lot to do with the Project being founded—was waning. Paul Blackburn, who we think of as the founder of the Poetry Project, died in 1971, also.

96. Notley, e-mail to author, February 7, 1999.

97. According to John Giorno, Ron Gold "got busted for grass—Ron was just somebody who was part of Theater Genesis. He wasn't famous, he was an actor who wasn't famous, which was great, because the feeling then was you didn't have to be a celebrity to have people get together and help you get out of jail for something as ridiculous as a marijuana arrest"; John Giorno, interview by author, in Giorno's home, New York, February 25, 1999.

98. Giorno said in the interview,

> I remember that around 1963, Andy Warhol and I went to some gallery to see John Ashbery, Frank O'Hara, and Kenneth Koch give a reading. It was really crowded, and it was the energy of this young New York School crowd, you know? We were standing in the back, because it was really crowded, and there was no PA system. There was no thought given to presentation—it didn't exist. There we were, standing around with hundreds of people, and we couldn't hear a thing. Andy started whispering to me, "Oh John, it's so boring, why is it so boring?" Those words of Andy's, "Why is it so boring, *why* is it so boring," became one of those treasures that propelled me. I didn't know it at the time, but poetry readings didn't have to be boring—people were just making it boring.

99. Giorno, interview.

100. Giorno, interview.

101. Giorno, interview.

102. Giorno, interview.

103. Anne Waldman to Bernadette Mayer, January 16, 1970, Bernadette Mayer Papers.

104. Ted Berrigan, quoted in Holman, "History of the Poetry Project," 30.

105. Harris Schiff, quoted in Holman, "History of the Poetry Project," 30.

Chapter 6: Bernadette Mayer and "Language" in the Poetry Project

1. Libbie Rifkin, *Career Moves* (Madison: University of Wisconsin Press, 2000), 158. Rifkin has made a case for Berrigan's continuing underground status; however, Penguin Books reissued Berrigan's *Sonnets* in 2000, and the number of scholarly essays on Berrigan is rising. Such activity might indicate a possible movement toward mainstreaming Berrigan.

2. Richard Kostelanetz, ed., *The Avant-Garde Tradition in Literature* (Buffalo, N.Y.: Prometheus Books, 1982), 5.

3. The first issue appeared in February 1978 (*L = A = N = G = U = A = G = E* 1, no. 1).

4. "'My Little World Goes on St. Mark's Place': Anne Waldman, Bernadette Mayer, and the Gender of an Avant-Garde Institution," *Jacket* 7 (1999). Available at www.jacket.zip.com.au/jacket07/rifkin07.html.

5. In his essay "Repossessing the Word," which also serves as an introduction to the writing found in *The L = A = N = G = U = A = G = E Book,* ed. Bruce Andrews and Charles Bernstein (Carbondale and Edwardsville: Southern Illinois University Press, 1984), Charles Bernstein writes, "The idea that writing should (or could) be stripped of reference is as bothersome and confusing as the assumption that the primary function of words is to refer, one-on-one, to an already constructed world of 'things.' Rather, reference, like the body itself, is one of the horizons of language, whose value is to be found in the writing (the world) before which we find ourselves at any moment. It is the multiple powers and scope of reference (denotative, connotative, associational), not writers' refusal or fear of it, that threads these essays together" (ix).

6. In terms of language writers questioning the value placed on the poem as an emotional construct, one can look to the magazine *L = A = N = G = U = A = G = E* 1, no. 2 (April 1978), where editors Charles Bernstein and Bruce Andrews published Jackson Mac Low's answer to their question, "Are you interested in having emotion in your process-oriented, programmatic poetry?" Mac Low replied,

   To most readers of poetry this wd seem a remarkable question! . . . But (paragraphs are emotional, said Stein) that may not be what you mean by "having emotion:" if that were all you meant I cd say that of course I've always been interested in the fact that sounds, words, &c., no matter how "randomly" generated, arouse emotions "willy-nilly." But if your question means, Do I allow my own emotions to influence my systematically generated work, I must answer that they can't help doing so: my choices of means, materials, &c., can't help being influenced by emotions, & I'd be foolish if I thought they weren't.

7. This is not to say that language writers do not recognize their debt to New York School predecessors. As Geoffrey Ward rightly points out, "The Language group . . . are responsible for keeping Jack Spicer's work in the arena of debate, and who have helped clear an access to Robert Duncan's poetry that avoids the equally distracting mythologies of San Francisco occultism and Black Mountain College . . . Charles Bernstein,

Clark Coolidge, Ron Silliman and others have never ceased to lay stress on the importance of O'Hara's and John Ashbery's work, through both Language criticism and poetry"; see *Statutes of Liberty* (New York: St. Martin's Press, 1993), 181.

8. Regarding the language poets' rhetoric and poetry as indicating a new avant-garde markedly different from postwar American poetics, Michael Davidson writes, in "'Skewed by Design': From Act to Speech Act in Language Writing," *Aerial* 8 (1995): 241–42:

If one wanted to discover a change between the "new American poetry" of the 1950's and 1960's and that which it spawned in the 1970's and 1980's, one could usefully speak of the latter's revision of the term "gesture," now used to describe the speech act rather than the act of speech. Whereas gesture for the generation of Olson and Ginsberg implied single expressive moments, recorded spontaneously on the page and realized in the oral performance, for writers of a more recent generation gesture refers to the interactive, social web in which language exists. This has been particularly the case with language-writing which offers the most thorough critique of expressivism in postwar writing, even while building upon the earlier generation's accomplishments.

9. Charles Bernstein, interview by author, in Bernstein's home, New York, March 15, 1999.

10. Ann Vickery, *Leaving Lines of Gender: A Feminist Genealogy of Language Writing* (Middletown, Conn.: Wesleyan University Press, 2000), 37.

11. Ron Silliman to Bernadette Mayer, September 9, 1973, Bernadette Mayer Papers, Mandeville Special Collections Library, University of California, San Diego.

12. Bernadette Mayer, telephone interview by author, November 6, 1998. Mayer's relationship with language writers was, however, at times contentious. She believes language writers so politicized and deromanticized poetry that the writing was subsumed by dry theory and rigid rules:

I remember saying to Charles Bernstein, who was spouting off in this really pretentious way, I said, "We're not at Harvard now." Alas, language writers took it in this funny direction. I remember saying to Edmund Leites who was the sort of resident philosopher of the language school—he used to lecture in my workshop—I remember saying to him, "You guys say you're Marxists, how come you all have cars?" And they did! It was amazing. They were the wealthiest Marxists I've ever met. They would have a sexual response to a statement like that, a macho dismissal. I wasn't supposed to have theories like this because I was a female.

Additionally, Bruce Andrews has pointed out that he never participated in Mayer's workshops, despite Mayer's published comments indicating otherwise.

13. Bernstein, interview, March 15, 1999. Larry Fagin adds to this list of predecessor "fragmented" poetry by listing O'Hara's "2nd Avenue" and "Biotherm"; Philip Whalen's work; Ginsberg's poem "Ignu"; Michael McClure's "Ghost Tantras"; Larry Eigner's "On My Eyes"; and concrete poetry coming out of Europe, emphasizing how these poems indicated a breakdown of syntax; Larry Fagin, interview by author, in Fagin's home, New York, January 26, 1998.

14. Vickery, *Leaving Lines of Gender*, 31.

15. Tom Clark, "Stalin as Linguist," *Partisan Review* 54, no. 2 (1987): 300.

16. The magazine $L = A = N = G = U = A = G = E$ in particular would serve a function of examining how poetic reputation and coterie classifications were produced.

17. Of the varied influential sources on $L = A = N = G = U = A = G = E$, Bruce Andrews states, "St. Mark's doesn't have the huge effect as it might seem to, because basically all the original activity took place beginning in 1971. That's when I started corresponding with Silliman, whom I was put in touch with through Jerome Rothenberg. Dick Higgins, who edited Something Else Press, was also very helpful. Jackson Mac Low was also involved. From 1971 through 1975, there was some anthologizing of the work. Ron Silliman put together some of our work in a magazine called *Occident* magazine, which came out of Berkeley, and one in Rothenberg's *Alcheringa*. These were mini-anthologies. All of this was done in the mail. I published people like Jackson and Coolidge." Bruce Andrews, interview, at Andrews's home, New York, May 10, 1999.

18. Bernadette Mayers, "Experiments," quoted in *The L = A = N = G = U = A= G= E Book*, 81–83.

19. Frank O'Hara, quoted in *The New American Poetry*, ed. Donald Allen (New York: Grove Press, 1960), 419.

20. "Bernadette Mayer's Writing Experiments," *The Poetry Project at St. Mark's Church*, 1996. Available at http://www.poetryproject.com/mayer.html.

21. Ron Silliman, "For Language," in *The L = A = N = G = U = A = G = E Book*, 16.

22. In his essay "The Objects of Meaning," Bernstein wrote, "We are initiated by language into a (the) world, and we see and understand the world through the terms and meanings that come into play in this acculturation, a coming into culture where culture is the form of a community, of a collectivity"; see *The L = A = N = G = U = A = G = E Book*, 60.

23. Writers associated with language writing also formed communities in Washington, D.C., and San Francisco. For a more in-depth account of the language school as social and poetic community, see Ann Vickery's chapter "Cities and Communities: Circling Out of Equivalence" in her book *Leaving Lines of Gender*.

24. Ward, *Statutes of Liberty*, 181, my italics.

25. Bruce Andrews, "Writing Social Work and Political Practice," in *The L = A = N = G = U = A = G = E Book*, 134.

26. One should also look to Barthes's book *The Pleasure of the Text* (New York: Hill and Wang, 1975) as another potential influence on Andrews's sensualist rhetoric.

27. Of his relationship with the Poetry Project, Bruce Andrews has said (interview by author, in Andrews's home, New York, May 3, 1999),

    Socially, I was hanging out on the fringe of the Poetry Project a little more than Charles Bernstein. It was the only nonmainstream institutional nexus in the city. In late 1975 through 1976, people that coalesced around [$L = A = N = G = U = A = G = E$-oriented] Roof Books and Language were kind of on the fringe of the St. Mark's social possibility—we read at the Church on Mondays and Wednesdays. The "language" community in the Bay Area was done all from scratch—they had Robert Duncan and Michael Palmer, but not much else. They tended to be a little proud of themselves for that. For us, it was a little more complicated, because there was St. Mark's—we all had to negotiate some kind of relationship with St. Mark's.

28. Andrews, interview, May 10, 1999.

29. Ron Silliman, *What* (Great Barrington, Mass.: The Figures, 1988), 59.

30. Bernstein, interview, March 15, 1999.

31. Roland Barthes, "The Death of the Author," *Critical Theory Since Plato,* ed. Hazard Adams (New York: Harcourt Brace Jovanovich College Publishers, 1992), 1132.

32. Of his public readings in San Francisco, Silliman has written (e-mail to University of Buffalo Poetics discussion group, www.listserv.acsu.buffalo.edu/archives/poetics .html, December 3, 1998),

    It was a solo reading of the whole of Ketjak, in September 1978 (20 years ago!), at the orig- inal branch of the Bank of America, #1 Powell Street, directly in front of the cable car turn- around, and then, several years later (1982 or 83), a reading of the whole of Tjanting at the Church Street Muni Metro station with some 26 odd (some very odd) people assisting. The latter would have been in a BART station if I could have gotten permission to do so, but I was able to wrangle it from Muni because I knew two members of the Public Utilities Com- mission, one from my work as a political organizer and the other being John Sanger, whom the sharp-eyed on this list will recognize as having been (1) the producer of the David Lynch film _The Elephant Man_; (2) Michael Palmer's upstairs neighbor during much of the 1970s; (3) the director of the very last TV episode of Twin Peaks.

33. Ward, *Statutes of Liberty,* 185.

34. In terms of the profusion of extraliterary material associated with the Language po- ets, Geoffrey Ward adds, "The [Language poets] could certainly not be faulted on [their] efforts in getting poetry, and these debates about its contexts, out into the work- ing world; the quantity of interviews, transcriptions of panels and workshops, state- ments and other back-up materials, is breathtaking. The clear intention is to rejuve- nate the idea of a successful social intervention by a poetic vanguard movement"; see *Statutes of Liberty,* 181.

35. Paul Mann, *The Theory-Death of the Avant-Garde* (Bloomington: Indiana Univer- sity Press, 1991), 7.

36. Andrews, interview, May 10, 1999.

37. Ed Friedman, interview by author, at St. Mark's Church, New York, February 3, 1999.

38. This mimeo published works by "a phalanx of literary experimentalists, including the minimalist works of Aram Saroyan and Clark Coolidge, along with the graphic works of artists Sol LeWitt, Michael Heizer, and Robert Smithson, and performance- oriented work by Jackson Mac Low, Steve Paxton, and Acconci himself"; see Stephen Clay and Rodney Phillips, *A Secret Location on the Lower East Side: Adventures in Writ- ing, 1960–1980* (New York: Granary Books, 1998), 207.

39. *0 to 9,* no. 2 (August 1967): 20, 23.

40. Friedman, interview.

41. Charles Bernstein, *Content's Dream: Essays, 1975–1984* (Los Angeles: Sun & Moon Press, 1986), 40–41.

42. *Unnatural Acts* 2 (August 1967).

43. Mayer, interview.

Epilogue: Bob Holman, the Poetry Project, and the Nuyorican Poets Cafe

1. For an in-depth analysis of the spoken-word scene, see Christopher Beach, *Poetic Culture: Contemporary American Poetry Between Community and Institution* (Evanston, Ill.: Northwestern University Press, 1999), 119–49.

2. Miguel Algarín, introduction, in *Aloud: Voices from the Nuyorican Poets Cafe,* ed. Miguel Algarín and Bob Holman (New York: Henry Holt, 1994), 16.

3. Christopher Beach, *Poetic Culture,* 119.

4. Bob Holman, "Invocation," in *Aloud,* 1.

5. Reg E. Gaines, "Please Don't Take My Air Jordans," in *Aloud,* 65.

6. Although slam poetry is by no means a solely African American phenomenon, at a slam, one is likely to see a remarkably multicultural crowd both attending and performing. The point here is that much slam poetry (like much popular music) is highly performative and accessible upon first hearing.

7. Marcella Durand, "Publishing a Community: Women Publishers at the Poetry Project," *Outlet* 4/5 (1999): 76–77.

8. Jonathan Dee, "But Is It Advertising?" *Harpers* (January 1999): 68. XYZ responded to Dee's attack in a letter published in *Harper's:* "Dee seems to think that doing a commercial for Nike took me from obscurity to a terrible fame. Wrong! I am just as obscure as ever, only I'm a little less in debt and my graduate-student husband and I own our first car—an '86 Toyota Tercel. I got my B.A. as an adult, I work full-time, and I am paying back major college loans. For me, that Nike ad was a godsend. But it did not make me rich, it did not make me famous, and it does not mean that my work is up for sale"; see Emily XYZ, "How Much Is That Artist in the Window?" (letter to the editor), *Harper's,* April 1999, 6.

9. Bob Holman, interview by author, in Holman's home, New York, March 3, 1999.

10. Bob Holman, interview, March 3, 1999.

11. Beach, *Poetic Culture,* 149.

12. Bob Holman, interview, March 3, 1999.

13. Maria Damon, *The Dark End of the Street: Margins in American Vanguard Poetry* (Minneapolis: University of Minnesota Press, 1993), 337.

Bibliography

Abrams, Sam. Untitled. *The Genre of Silence* 1 (1967): 85.

Adams, Hazard, ed. *Critical Theory Since Plato.* Rev. ed. New York: Harcourt Brace Jovanovich College Publishers, 1992.

Allen, Donald. Letters. Donald Allen Collection. MSS 3. Mandeville Special Collections Library, University of California, San Diego.

———, ed. *The New American Poetry.* New York: Grove Press, 1960.

Allen, Michael J., Rev., et al. "Creative Arts for Alienated Youth." Grant proposal. Department of Health, Education, and Welfare, Washington, D.C., 1966. Available at St. Mark's Church.

Alpert, Barry. "Interview with Ted Berrigan." In *Talking in Tranquility,* edited by Stephen Ratcliffe and Leslie Scalapino, 31–54. Bolinas, Calif.: Avenue B; Oakland, Calif.: O Books, 1991.

Anderson, Elliot, and Mary Kinzie, eds. *The Little Magazine in America: A Modern Documentary History.* Yonkers, N.Y.: Pushcart Press, 1978.

Andrews, Bruce. "Writing Social Work and Political Practice." In *The L = A = N = G = U = A = G = E Book,* edited by Bruce Andrews and Charles Bernstein, 133–36. Carbondale and Edwardsville: Southern Illinois University Press, 1984.

Ant, Howard. Introduction to *Seventh Street: Poems from Les Deux Megots,* edited by Don Katzman, Allen Katzman, and Robert Lima. New York: Hesperidian Press, 1962.

Appolinaire, Guillaume. *The Poet Assassinated and Other Stories.* Translated by Ron Padgett. San Francisco: North Point Press, 1984.

Aronowitz, Alfred G. "Why the Espresso Got Cold." *New York Post,* June 13, 1960, 4.

Artaud, Antonin. "No More Masterpieces." *Evergreen Review* 2, no. 5 (1958): 150–59.

"Article 39, Coffee Houses." *New York City Charter and Administrative Code, Annotated.* Albany, N.Y.: Williams Press, 1961, 4:757–60.

Ashbery, John. *The Mooring of Starting Out: The First Five Books of Poetry.* Hopewell, N.J.: Ecco Press, 1997.

———, et al., eds. *Locus Solus* 1–5 (Winter 1961–1962).

Auslander, Philip. *The New York School Poets as Playwrights: O'Hara, Ashbery, Koch, Schuyler, and the Visual Arts.* New York: P. Lang, 1989.

Banes, Sally. *Greenwich Village 1963: Avant-Garde Performance and the Effervescent Body.* Durham: Duke University Press, 1993.

Baraka, Amiri. Article responding to Cecil Helmley's review of *The New American Poetry. The Floating Bear* 2 (1961).

———. *The Autobiography of LeRoi Jones/Amiri Baraka.* New York: Freundlich Books, 1984.

———. "Black People." *Evergreen Review* 50 (December 1967): 49.

———. "Cultural Revolution and the Literary Canon." In *Disembodied Poetics: Annals of the Jack Kerouac School of Poetics,* edited by Anne Waldman and Andrew Schelling, 1–21. Albuquerque: University of New Mexico Press, 1994.

———. *The LeRoi Jones/Amiri Baraka Reader.* New York: Thunder's Mouth Press, 1991.

———. "Poetry Christmas." Interview by David Ossman for WBAI, New York. N.d. Sound recording. Paul Blackburn Papers. MSS 4. Mandeville Special Collections Library, University of California, San Diego.

———, ed. *Four Young Lady Poets.* New York: Totem Press, 1962.

———, and Hettie Cohen, eds. *Yugen,* nos. 1–7 (1958–1962).

———, and Larry Neal, eds. *Black Fire: An Anthology of Afro-American Writing.* New York: Morrow, 1968.

Barr, Nelson. "A Bouquet of Fuck You's." *Fuck You / a magazine of the arts* 3, no. 5 (May 1963).

Barthes, Roland. "The Death of the Author." In *Critical Theory Since Plato,* edited by Hazard Adams, 1131–33. New York: Harcourt Brace Jovanovich College Publishers, 1992.

Bartlett, Lee. *Talking Poetry: Conversations in the Workshop with Contemporary Poets.* Albuquerque: University of New Mexico Press, 1987.

Beach, Christopher. *Poetic Culture: Contemporary American Poetry Between Community and Institution.* Evanston, Ill.: Northwestern University Press, 1999.

———, ed. *Artifice and Indeterminacy: An Anthology of New Poetics.* Tuscaloosa: University of Alabama Press, 1998.

Beatty, Paul. *Big Bank Take Little Bank.* New York: Nuyorican Poets Cafe, 1991.

Bell, Ian F. A. *Ezra Pound: Tactics for Reading.* London: Vision Press Limited, 1982.

Bennett, David. "Periodical Fragments and Organic Culture: Modernism, the Avant-Garde, and the Little Magazine." *Contemporary Literature* 30 (1989): 480–502.

Bergé, Carol. Archive. Harry Ransom Center, University of Texas, Austin.

———. "An Informal Timetable of Coffee-House Activities in New York." *Magazine-2.* New York: Crank Books, 1965.

———. *The Vancouver Report.* New York: Fuckpress, 1964.

Berkson, Bill. *Blue Is the Hero: Poems, 1960–1975.* Kensington, Calif.: L Publications, 1976.

———. *Saturday Night.* Berkeley: Sand Dollar, 1975.

———. *Serenade: Poetry and Prose, 1975–1989*; drawings by Joe Brainard. Cambridge, Mass.: Zoland Books, 2000.

———. "Since When." In the author's possession.

———, and Joe Le Sueur, eds. *Homage to Frank O'Hara.* Bolinas, Calif.: Big Sky, 1978.

———, and Bob Rosenthal, eds. *The World Record: Readings at the St. Mark's Poetry Project, 1969–80.* New York: The Poetry Project, 1981. Record album.

Bernstein, Charles. *Close Listening: Poetry and the Performed Word.* New York: Oxford University Press, 1998.

———. *Content's Dream: Essays, 1975–1984.* Los Angeles: Sun & Moon Press, 1986.

———. *My Way.* Chicago: University of Chicago Press, 1999.

———. "Repossessing the Word." In *The L = A = N = G = U = A = G = E Book,* edited by Bruce Andrews and Charles Bernstein. Carbondale and Edwardsville: Southern Illinois University Press, 1984.

———. "Writing Against the Body." In *Nice to See You: Homage to Ted Berrigan,* edited by Anne Waldman, 154–57. Minneapolis: Coffee House Press, 1991.

———, ed. *The Politics of Poetic Form.* New York: Roof Books, 1990.

Berrigan, Ted. Diary and letters. Ted Berrigan Papers. Rare Book and Manuscript Library, Columbia University, New York.

———. "Early Sonnet." *The World* 3 (1967).

———. "Get the Money." *East Village Other* 1, no. 3 (December 1965): 11.

———. "Homage to Jim Brodey." *Poets at Le Metro* 8 (1963).

———. *Many Happy Returns.* New York: Corinth Books, 1969.

———. *On the Level Everyday: Selected Talks on Poetry and the Art of Living.* Jersey City, N.J.: Talisman House, 1997.

———. Poetry reading. St. Mark's Poetry Project, New York. Fall 1967. Sound recording. Paul Blackburn Papers. SPL 403. Mandeville Special Collections Library, University of California, San Diego.

———. "Review of Frank O'Hara's *Lunch Poems.*" *Kulchur* 5, no. 17 (Spring 1965): 91–94.

———. "Review of *In Advance of the Broken Arm.*" *Kulchur* 5, no. 17 (Spring 1965): 100–102.

———. *Selected Poems.* New York: Penguin Books, 1994.

———. *So Going Around Cities: New and Selected Poems.* Berkeley: Blue Wind Press, 1980.

———. "Sonnet II." *C: A Journal of Poetry* 1, no. 1 (1963).

———. "Sonnet LVIII." *C: A Journal of Poetry* 1, no. 3 (1963).

———. "Sonnet LXXXIV." *C: A Journal of Poetry* 1, no. 7 (1964).

———. *The Sonnets.* New York: Grove Press, 1967.

———. Untitled poem. *Poets at Le Metro* 7 (1963).

———. "Words for Love." *C: A Journal of Poetry* 1, no. 2 (1963).

———, and Dick Gallup. "80th Congress." *The World* 3 (1967).

———, and Ron Padgett. *Bean Spasms.* New York: Kulchur Press, 1967.

———, et al. "Benefit Poetry Reading for Andrei Codrescu." St. Mark's Church, New York. March 4, 1968. Sound recording. Paul Blackburn Papers. SPL 395. Mandeville Special Collections Library, University of California, San Diego.

———, et al. "Memorial Reading for Charles Olson." St. Mark's Poetry Project, New York. February 4, 1970. Sound recording. Paul Blackburn Papers. SPL 349. Mandeville Special Collections Library, University of California, San Diego.

Bigart, Homer. "Mayor Aids Drive on 'Village' Cafes." *New York Times,* April 3, 1965.

Blackburn, Paul. *The Cities.* New York: Grove Press, 1967.

———. "Clickety-Clack." May 22, 1964. Brooklyn Civic Center. Sound recording. Paul Blackburn Papers. SPL 407. Mandeville Special Collections Library, University of California, San Diego.

———. *Early, Selected y Mas: Poems 1949–1966.* Los Angeles: Black Sparrow Press, 1972.

———. "The Grinding Down." *Kulchur* 3, no. 10 (1963): 9–18.

———. *Halfway Down the Coast: Poems and Snapshots.* Northhampton, Mass.: Mulch Press, 1975.

———. "The International Word." *The Nation,* April 21, 1962, 357–60.

————. Interview by David Ossman. WBAI, New York. 1960. Sound recording. Paul Blackburn Papers. SPL-161. Mandeville Special Collections Library, University of California, San Diego.

————. Interview by an unnamed student. Shippensburg, Pa. 1970. Sound recording. Paul Blackburn Papers. SPL 407. Mandeville Special Collections Library, University of California, San Diego.

————. *The Journals.* Los Angeles: Black Sparrow Press, 1975.

————. Papers. MSS 4. Mandeville Special Collections Library, University of California, San Diego.

————. *The Parallel Voyages.* Tucson: SUN/Gemini Press, 1987.

————. *Proensa: An Anthology of Troubadour Poetry.* Berkeley: University of California Press, 1978.

————. "The Sullen Art." Interview by David Ossman. *Nomad* 10–11 (1962): 8–10.

————. "What's New?: An Interior Report on the Socio-literary Uses of the Mimeograph Machine." N.d. Paul Blackburn Papers. MSS 4. Mandeville Special Collections Library, University of California, San Diego.

————. "Writing for the Ear." *Big Table* 1, no. 4 (1960): 127–32.

————, Joel Oppenheimer, and Amiri Baraka. In conversation. January 30, 1962. Sound recording. Paul Blackburn Papers. SPL 161. Mandeville Special Collections Library, University of California, San Diego.

Blake, William. *Blake's Poetry and Designs.* Edited by Mary Lynn Johnson and John E. Grant. New York: Norton, 1979.

Bloedow, Jerry. "Scene 10." *Seventh Street, Poems from Les Deux Mégots,* edited by Don Katzman. New York: Hesperidian Press, 1962.

Bogan, James, and Fred Goss, eds. *Sparks of Fire: Blake in a New Age.* Richmond, Calif.: North Atlantic Books, 1982.

"Books of the Times: Angel Hair, Partisan Review et al." *New York Times,* June 26, 1968.

Bourdieu, Pierre. *The Rules of Art: Genesis and Structure of the Literary Field.* Palo Alto, Calif.: Stanford University Press, 1992.

Brainard, Joe. *Bolinas Journal.* Bolinas, Calif.: Big Sky Press, 1971.

————. *I Remember.* New York: Full Court Press, 1975.

————. "A Play." *C: A Journal of Poetry* 1, no. 1 (May 1963).

Brodey, Jim. "A Poem & Prose." *The World* 1 (1967).

"Bruce's Trial." *Newsweek,* July 20, 1964. Available at members.aol.com/dcspohr/lenny/brtrial.htm.

Buckley, Thomas. "Civic Aide Linked to Coffeehouses." *New York Times,* November 6, 1964.

Bumiller, Elisabeth. "Giuliani Names His Panel to Monitor Art at Museums." *New York Times,* April 4, 2001.

Bürger, Peter. *Theory of the Avant-Garde.* Minneapolis: University of Minnesota Press, 1984.

Butterick, George, ed. *Charles Olson and Robert Creeley: The Complete Correspondence.* Santa Barbara: Black Sparrow Press, 1980.

Caplan, David. "Who's Zoomin' Who?: The Poetics of www.poets.org and wings.buffalo.edu/epc." *Postmodern Culture* 8, no. 1 (1997).

Carpenter, Humphrey. *W. H. Auden: A Biography.* Boston: Houghton Mifflin, 1981.

Carroll, Paul, ed. *The Young American Poets.* Chicago: Follett, 1968.

Chevigny, Paul. *Gigs: Jazz and the Cabaret Laws in New York City.* New York: Routledge, 1991.

Christensen, Paul. *Minding the Underworld: Clayton Eshleman and Late Postmodernism.* Santa Rosa, Calif.: Black Sparrow Press, 1991.

Clark, Tom. *Charles Olson: The Allegory of a Poet's Life.* New York: W. W. Norton, 1991.

———. *Late Returns: A Memoir of Ted Berrigan.* Bolinas, Calif.: Tombouctou, 1985.

———. "Stalin as Linguist." *Partisan Review* 54, no. 2 (1987): 299–304.

———, and Peter Schjeldahl. "Easter." *The World* 3 (1967).

Clay, Stephen, and Rodney Phillips. *A Secret Location on the Lower East Side: Adventures in Writing, 1960–1980.* New York: Granary Books, 1998.

Codrescu, Andrei. *License to Carry a Gun.* Chicago: Big Table, 1970.

Compton, Susan P. *The World Backwards: Russian Futurist Books, 1912–16.* London: British Museum Publications, 1978.

Cook, Albert Spaulding. *The Reach of Poetry.* West Lafayette, Ind.: Purdue University Press, 1995.

Cooper, Shelby. "Poetry and Plays Liven Church Youth Program in New York." *Sunday Daily News,* December 4, 1966.

Corso, Gregory. Archive. Harry Ransom Center, University of Texas, Austin.

———. *Elegiac Feelings American.* New York: New Directions, 1970.

———. "The Rebel." *Poets at Le Metro* 3 (1963).

Creeley, Robert. "Bolinas and Me." In *On the Mesa,* edited by Lawrence Ferlinghetti, 28–32. San Francisco: City Lights Books, 1971.

Damon, Maria. *The Dark End of the Street: Margins in American Vanguard Poetry.* Minneapolis: University of Minnesota Press, 1993.

Davidson, Michael. "Compulsory Homosociality: Charles Olson, Jack Spicer, and the Gender of Poetics." In *Cruising the Performative,* edited by Sue-Ellen Case, Philip Brett, and Susan Leigh Foster, 197–216. Bloomington, Ind.: Indiana University Press, 1995.

———. *Ghostlier Demarcations: Modern Poetry and the Material Word.* Berkeley and Los Angeles: University of California Press, 1997.

———. "Postwar Poetry and the Politics of Containment." *American Literary History* 10, no. 2 (1998): 266–90.

———. *The San Francisco Renaissance: Poetics and Community at Mid-Century.* New York: Cambridge University Press, 1989.

———. "'Skewed by Design': From Act to Speech Act in Language Writing." *Aerial* 8 (1995): 241–47.

Dawson, Fielding. *An Emotional Memoir of Franz Kline.* New York: Pantheon Books, 1967.

———. *Krazy Kat & 76 More: Collected Stories, 1950–1976.* Santa Barbara: Black Sparrow Press, 1982.

———. *Tiger Lilies: An American Childhood.* Durham, N.C.: Duke University Press, 1984.

———, et al. "Memorial reading for Charles Olson." St. Mark's Poetry Project, New York. February 4, 1970. Sound recording. Paul Blackburn Papers. SPL 349. Mandeville Special Collections Library, University of California, San Diego.

Dee, Jonathan. "But Is It Advertising?" *Harper's,* January 1999, 61–72.

DeLoach, Allen. "Hotel Earl." *Poets at Le Metro* 4 (1963).

———, ed. *The East Side Scene.* Buffalo: University Press, State University of New York at Buffalo, 1968.

———, ed. *Intrepid* 1–5 (March 1964–March 1965).

Dembo, L. S. "An Interview with Paul Blackburn." *Contemporary Literature* 13, no. 2 (1972): 133–43.

Denby, Edwin. *The Complete Poems.* New York: Random House, 1986.

Dent, Thomas. "Umbra Days." *Black American Literature Forum* 14, no. 3 (1980): 105–8.

Dickey, James. Introduction to *The Young American Poets,* edited by Paul Carroll, 9. Chicago: Follett, 1968.

di Prima, Diane. "Fuzz's Progress." *The Nation,* May 4, 1964, 463–64.

———. *Revolutionary Letters.* San Francisco: City Lights, 1968.

———. *Selected Poems, 1956–1975.* Plainfield, Vt.: North Atlantic Books, 1975.

"Dissent." *New Yorker,* February 11, 1967, 29–31.

Dorn, Ed. *The Collected Poems.* Bolinas, Calif.: Four Seasons Foundations, 1975.

———. *Gunslinger.* Los Angeles: Black Sparrow Press, 1968.

———. *Hands Up!* New York: Totem Press, 1969.

Drucker, Johanna. "Visual Performance of the Poetic Text." In *Close Listening: Poetry and the Performed Word,* edited by Charles Bernstein, 131–61. New York: Oxford University Press, 1998.

Duberman, Martin. *Black Mountain: An Exploration in Community.* New York: W. W. Norton, 1994.

———. *Stonewall.* New York: Dutton, 1993.

Duncan, Robert. "Poetry Christmas." Interview by David Ossman. WBAI, New York. N.d. Sound recording. Paul Blackburn Papers. MSS 4. Mandeville Special Collections Library, University of California, San Diego.

DuPlessis, Rachel Blau. "Manifests." *Diacritics* 26, nos. 3–4 (1996): 31–53.

Durand, Marcella. "Publishing a Community: Women Publishers at the Poetry Project." *Outlet* 4/5 (1999): 66–77.

Economou, George. "Crazy-Eyed Cowboys." In *The East Side Scene,* edited by Allen De Loach, 81. Buffalo: University Press, State University of New York at Buffalo, 1968.

———. *The Georgics.* Los Angeles: Black Sparrow Press, 1968.

———. Papers. Rare Book and Manuscript Library, Columbia University.

———. "Some Notes Towards Finding a View of the New Oral Poetry." *boundary 2,* no. 3 (1975): 653–63.

Elledge, Jim, ed. *Frank O'Hara: To Be True to a City.* Ann Arbor: University of Michigan Press, 1990.

Ellis, Albert. "Introduction." *Femora* 2 (1964).

Emerson, Ralph Waldo. "The American Scholar." In *Masters of American Literature,* edited by Henry A. Pochmann and Gay Wilson Allen, 711–20. New York: Macmillan, 1949.

Eshleman, Clayton. Archives. Elmer Holmes Bobst Library. Fales Library, New York University.

———, et al. "Benefit for Andrei Codrescu." Poetry reading. St. Mark's Church, New York. March 4, 1968. Sound recording. Paul Blackburn Papers. SPL 395. Mandeville Special Collections Library, University of California, San Diego.

"Eskimo Songs." *o to 9* 2 (August 1967): 20.

Fagin, Larry, ed. *Adventures in Poetry* 1–12 (March 1968–Summer 1975).

Feinstein, Sascha. *Jazz Poetry: From the 1920s to the Present.* Westport, Conn.: Greenwood Press, 1997.

Ferlinghetti, Lawrence. "Horn on Howl." *Evergreen Review* 1, no. 4 (1957): 145–58.

———, and Nancy Peters. *Literary San Francisco: A Pictorial History from Its Beginnings to the Present Day.* San Francisco: City Lights Books, 1980.

Fish, Stanley. *Is There a Text in This Class?: The Authority of Interpretive Communities.* Cambridge: Harvard University Press, 1980.

Fitch, Noël Riley. *Literary Cafés of Paris.* Washington, D.C.: Starrhill Press, 1989.

Foster, Edward Halsey. "An Interview with Ron Padgett." In *Postmodern Poetry: The Talisman Interviews, Interviewed by Ed Foster,* 99–114. Hoboken, N.J.: Talisman House, 1994.

———. *Understanding the Black Mountain Poets.* Columbia: University of South Carolina Press, 1994.

Fowler, Al. "Caroline: An Exercise for our Cocksman Leader." *Fuck You / a magazine of the arts* 5, no. 1 (December 1962).

Fox, Robert Elliot. *Conscientious Sorcerers: The Black Postmodernist Fiction of LeRoi Jones / Amiri Baraka, Ishmael Reed, and Samuel R. Delany.* New York: Greenwood Press, 1987.

Fraser, Kathleen. *Translating the Unspeakable: Poetry and the Innovative Necessity.* Tuscaloosa: University of Alabama Press, 2000.

"Frat at Columbia Put on Probation." *New York Post,* March 12, 1963.

Freeman, Judi. *The Dada and Surrealist Word-Image.* Cambridge, Mass.: MIT Press, 1989.

Friedman, Ken, ed. *The Fluxus Reader.* London: Academy Editions, 1998.

Frost, Robert. *Robert Frost's Poems.* Edited by Louis Untermeyer. New York: Washington Square Press, 1960.

Gaines, Reg E. "Please Don't Take My Air Jordans." In *Aloud: Voices from the Nuyorican Poets Cafe,* edited by Miguel Algarín and Bob Holman, 65–67. New York: Henry Holt, 1994.

Gervis, Stephanie. "William Carlos Williams (1883–1963)." *Village Voice,* March 7, 1963.

Gilmore, Lyman. *Don't Touch the Poet: The Life and Times of Joel Oppenheimer.* Hoboken, N.Y.: Talisman House, 1998.

Ginsberg, Allen. *Allen Verbatim: Lectures on Poetry, Politics, Consciousness.* Edited by Gordon Ball. New York: McGraw-Hill, 1974.

———. *Collected Poems, 1947–1980.* New York: Harper & Row, 1984.

———. Foreword to *Out of This World: An Anthology of the St. Mark's Poetry Project, 1966–1991,* edited by Anne Waldman, xxvii. New York: Crown Publishers, 1991.

———. *Howl.* San Francisco: City Lights, 1956.

———. Introduction to John Wieners poetry reading. St. Mark's Church, New York. January 3, 1968. Sound recording. Paul Blackburn Papers. SPL 388–89. Mandeville Special Collections Library, University of California, San Diego.

———. *Journals, Early Fifties, Early Sixties.* New York: Grove Press, 1992.

———. *Selected Poems, 1947–1995.* New York: HarperCollins, 1996.

———, et al. "Benefit for the Committee for Non-Violence." Poetry reading. St. Mark's Church, New York. April 1966. Sound recording. Paul Blackburn Papers. SPL 261–62. Mandeville Special Collections Library, University of California, San Diego.

———, et al. Roundtable discussion. Vancouver Poetry Conference. Vancouver, British Columbia. August 5, 1963. Sound recording. Paul Blackburn Papers. SPL 203. Mandeville Special Collections Library, University of California, San Diego.

———, and Kenneth Koch, with Ron Padgett. *Making It Up: Poetry Composed at St. Mark's Church on May 9, 1979.* New York: Catchword Papers, 1994.

Giorno, John. "I'm Tired of Being Scared." In *An Anthology of New York Poets,* edited by Ron Padgett and David Shapiro, 267. New York: Random House, 1970.

Giunta, Aldo. "The Maverick Church: St. Mark's in the Bouwerie." *East Village Other* 1, no. 3 (December 1965): 6.

Golding, Alan. *From Outlaw to Classic: Canons in American Poetry.* Madison: University of Wisconsin Press, 1995.

Gooch, Brad. *City Poet: The Life and Times of Frank O'Hara.* New York: Knopf, 1993.

Graffiti, John. "Lower East Side Funk." *East Village Other* 1, no. 5 (1965): 5.

Gruen, John. *The New Bohemia: The Combine Generation.* New York: Shorecrest, 1966.

Guiney, Mortimer. "Reverdy in New York." *World Literature Today* 59, no. 4 (1985): 538–43.

Halburg, Robert von. *Politics and Poetic Value.* Chicago: University of Chicago Press, 1987.

Hamilton, Ian. *The Little Magazines: A Study of Six Editors.* London: Weidenfeld and Nicolson, 1976.

Harrington Gervis, Stephanie. "City Puts Bomb Under Off-Beat Culture Scene." *Village Voice,* March 26, 1964.

Harris, Mary Emma. *The Arts at Black Mountain College.* Cambridge, Mass.: MIT Press, 1987.

Hebdige, Dick. *Subculture: The Meaning of Style.* London: Methuen, 1979.

Helmley, Cecil. "Within a Budding Grove." *Hudson Review* 13, no. 4 (1960–61): 626–31.

Henderson, David. *Felix of the Silent Forest.* New York: Poets Press, 1967.

———. "For the Sweet Black Boy." In *Seventh Street, Poems from Les Deux Mégots,* edited by Allen Katzman, Don Katzman, and Robert Lima, 30. New York: Hesperidian Press, 1962.

———. Interview by Lisa Jarnot. *Poetry Project Newsletter* 163 (December/January 1996–97): 5–9.

———. "The Ofay and the Nigger." *Umbra* 1, no. 1 (1963): 41–42.

———. ed. *Umbra: Blackworks from the Black Galaxy.* New York, 1970.

Hernton, Calvin. *The Sexual Mountain and Black Women Writers: Adventures in Sex, Literature, and Real Life.* New York: Anchor Books, 1990.

Herron, Don. *The Literary World of San Francisco and Its Environs.* San Francisco: City Lights Books, 1985.

Hobbs, Stuart D. *The End of the American Avant-Garde.* New York: New York University Press, 1997.

Hodgson, Godfrey. *America in Our Time.* Garden City, N.Y.: Doubleday, 1976.

Hollander, John. Introduction to *Walt Whitman's Leaves of Grass,* edited by Justin Kaplan, xi–xxvi. New York: Random, 1992.

Holman, Bob. "History of the Poetry Project." 1978. Poetry Project Archives, St. Mark's Church, New York.

Howe, Susan. "Since a Dialogue We Are." *In Relation* 10 (1989): 166–72.

Jones, Hettie. *How I Became Hettie Jones.* New York: Grove Press, 1997.

"Judge Rules a Café, No Levy Must Pay, for Poetry Per Se." *New York Times,* March 25, 1964.

Kalaidjian, Walter. *Languages of Liberation: The Social Text in Contemporary American Poetry.* New York: Columbia University Press, 1989.

Katzman, Allan. "Poem for the Poet." *Poems Collected at Les Deux Megots* 2 (January 1963).

———. "Poet Arrested on Obscenity." *East Village Other* 1, no. 5 (February 1–15, 1966): 1, 7.

Kelly, Robert. "Notes on the Poetry of the Deep Image." *Trobar* 2 (1961): 14–16.

———. Poetry reading. Café Cino, New York. 1960. Sound recording. Paul Blackburn Papers. SPL 158. Mandeville Special Collections Library, University of California, San Diego.

Kendrick, Laura. *The Game of Love: Troubadour Wordplay.* Berkeley and Los Angeles: University of California Press, 1988.

Kent, Leticia. "Film Head Fired: Alienated Revolt." *Village Voice,* March 9, 1967.

Kerouac, Jack. *On the Road.* Cutchogue, N.Y.: Buccaneer Books, 1975.

———. *Scattered Poems.* San Francisco: City Lights Books, 1971.

Kifner, John. "'Village' Coffeehouse District Bustles the Day After Cleanup Order." *New York Times,* December 28, 1967.

Kirby, Michael, and Victoria Nes Kirby. *Futurist Performance: With Manifestoes and Playscripts Translated from the Italian by Victoria Nes Kirby.* New York: Dutton, 1971.

Koch, Kenneth. "Fresh Air." In *The New American Poetry,* edited by Donald Allen, 229–38. New York: Grove Press, 1960.

Kostelanetz, Richard, ed. *The Avant-Garde Tradition in Literature.* Buffalo, N.Y.: Prometheus Books, 1982.

Kuh, Richard H. *Foolish Figleaves? Pornography in and out of Court.* New York: Macmillan, 1967.

Kupferberg, Tuli. Poetry reading. St. Mark's Church, New York. October 11, 1967. Sound recording. Paul Blackburn Papers. SPL 400. Mandeville Special Collections Library, University of California, San Diego.

Lacey, Henry C. *To Raise, Destroy, and Create: The Poetry, Drama, and Fiction of Imamu Amiri Baraka (LeRoi Jones).* Troy, N.Y.: Whitston Publishing, 1981.

Lane, Mervin, ed. *Black Mountain College: Sprouted Seeds: An Anthology of Personal Accounts.* Knoxville: University of Tennessee Press, 1990.

Leary, Paris, and Robert Kelly, eds. *A Controversy of Poets: An Anthology of Contemporary American Poetry.* Garden City, N.Y.: Anchor Books, 1965.

"Legalize Poetry." *East Village Other* 2, no. 5 (February 1–15, 1967): 15.

Lehman, David. *The Last Avant-Garde: The Making of the New York School of Poets.* New York: Doubleday, 1998.

———. "The Whole School." *Poetry* 119, no. 4 (1972): 224–33.

Levertov, Denise. Introduction to *Seventh Street: An Anthology of Poems from Les Deux Mégots,* edited by Allen Katzman, Don Katzman, and Robert Lima. New York: Hesperidian Press, 1962.

———. Poetry reading. St. Mark's Church, New York. March 20, 1967. Sound recording. Paul Blackburn Papers. SPL 301. Mandeville Special Collections Library, University of California, San Diego.

Lewis, Felice Flanery. *Literature, Obscenity, and Law.* Carbondale: Southern Illinois University Press, 1976.

Lewis, Harry. "The Circuit/New York City Public Readings: A Short History." In *The Poetry Reading,* edited by Stephen Vincent and Ellen Zweig, 85–90. San Francisco: Momo's Press, 1981.

The Little Magazine and Contemporary Literature: A Symposium Held at the Library of Congress, 2 and 3 of April, 1965. Washington, D.C., Library of Congress, 1965.

Lockwood, Lee. "Still Radical After All These Years." *Mother Jones* (September/October 1993). Available at www.motherjones.com/mother_jones/5093/lockwood.html.

Lowell, Robert. *Robert Lowell, Interviews and Memoirs.* Ann Arbor: University of Michigan Press, 1988.

———. *Selected Poems.* New York: Farrar, Straus and Giroux, 1976.

Lowney, John. *The American Avant-Garde Tradition: William Carlos Williams, Postmodern Poetry, and the Politics of Cultural Memory.* Lewisburg, Pa.: Bucknell University Press; Cranbury, N.J.: Associated University Presses, 1997.

Lykiard, Alexis, ed. *Wholly Communion.* New York: Grove Press, 1965.

Mackey, Nathaniel. *Discrepant Engagement: Dissonance, Cross-Culturality, and Experimental Writing.* New York: Cambridge University Press, 1993.

Mac Low, Jackson. "The Coffeehouse Poetry Reading Scene in New York, 1960–1967." In *Light Years,* an anthology of memoirs about the coffeehouse readings in New York from 1959 through the 1960s, edited by Carol Bergé (unpublished). In author's possession.

———. "Dick Higgins, 1938–1998." *Poetry Project Newsletter* 174 (May 1999): 6.

———. "Leather Costs." *Poets at Le Metro* 3 (1963).

———. Papers. MSS 180. Mandeville Special Collections Library, University of California, San Diego.

———. Poetry reading. St. Mark's Church, New York. February 14, 1968. Sound recording. Paul Blackburn Papers. SPL 393. Mandeville Special Collections Library, University of California, San Diego.

———. *Representative Works: 1938–1985.* New York: Roof Books, 1986.

Magee, Michael. "Emancipating Pragmatism: Emerson, Jazz, and Experimental Writing." Ph.D. diss., University of Pennsylvania, 1999.

Malanga, Gerard. Archive. Harry Ransom Center, University of Texas, Austin.

———. Untitled article. *Poetry* 123 (1974): 236–41.

Mangelsdorff, Rich. "State of the Art: Young American Poets." *Kaleidoscope* (September 27–October 10, 1968), 12–13.

Mann, Paul. *The Theory-Death of the Avant-Garde.* Bloomington: Indiana University Press, 1991.

Mayer, Bernadette. *A Bernadette Mayer Reader.* New York: New Directions, 1992.

———. "Bernadette Mayer's Writing Experiments." *The Poetry Project at St. Mark's Church.* 1996. Available at www.poetryproject.com/mayer.html.

———. Interview by Lisa Jarnot. *Poetry Project Newsletter* 168 (February/March 1998): 6–7.

———. Papers. MSS 420. Mandeville Special Collections Library, University of California, San Diego.

McMillan, Dougald. *transition: The History of a Literary Era, 1927–1938.* London: Calder and Boyars, 1975.

Mead, Taylor. *On Amphetamine and in Europe.* Vol. 3 of *Excerpts from the Anonymous Diary of a New York Youth.* New York: Boss Books, 1968.

Mele, Christopher. *Selling the Lower East Side: Culture, Real Estate, and Resistance in New York City.* Minneapolis: University of Minnesota Press, 2000.

Micheline, Jack. "Happiness, Happiness, Happiness, Jelly Roll!" *Poems Collected at Les Deux Megots* 2 (January 1963).

Middleton, Peter. "The Contemporary Poetry Reading." In *Close Listening: Poetry and the Performed Word,* edited by Charles Bernstein, 262–99. New York: Oxford University Press, 1998.

Montgomery, George. "A Poem for Ray and Bonnie B." *Poets at Le Metro* 5 (June 1963).

Moore, Alan, and Josh Gosciak, eds. *A Day in the Life: Tales from the Lower East: An Anthology of Writings from the Lower East Side, 1940–1990.* New York: Evil Eye Books, 1990.

Morgan, Bill. *The Beat Generation in New York: A Walking Tour of Jack Kerouac's City.* San Francisco: City Lights Books, 1997.

Mullen, Harryette. "Poetry and Identity." *West Coast Line* 19 (Spring 1996): 85–89.

Nelson, Cary. *Repression and Recovery: Modern American Poetry and the Politics of Cultural Memory, 1910–1945.* Madison: University of Wisconsin Press, 1989.

The New York Beat Generation Show: Women and the Beats. Thin Air Radio, 1994. Videocassette. Available at New York University's Bobst Library.

Nielsen, Aldon Lynn. *Black Chant: Languages of African-American Postmodernism.* Cambridge: Cambridge University Press, 1997.

O'Hara, Frank. Article on Franz Kline. *Evergreen Review* 2, no. 6 (1958): 58.

———. *The Collected Poems of Frank O'Hara.* Edited by Donald Allen. New York: Alfred A. Knopf, 1991.

———. *Lunch Poems.* San Francisco: City Lights Books, 1964.

Oliver, Douglas. *Poetry and Narrative in Performance.* New York: St. Martin's Press, 1989.

Olson, Charles. Archive. Thomas J. Dodd Research Center, University of Connecticut Libraries, Storrs.

———. *Charles Olson Reading at Berkeley, as Transcribed by Zoe Brown.* San Francisco: City Lights Books, 1966.

———. *The Collected Poems of Charles Olson.* Berkeley and Los Angeles: University of California Press, 1987.

———. *The Maximus Poems.* New York: Jargon, Corinth Books, 1960.

———. *Mythologos: The Collected Lectures and Interview.* Edited by George Butterick. Bolinas, Calif.: Four Seasons Foundation, 1978.

———. *Selected Writings.* New York: New Directions, 1966.

Oppenheimer, Joel. Archive. Thomas J. Dodd Research Center, University of Connecticut Libraries, Storrs.

———. *In Time: Poems, 1962–1968.* Indianapolis: Bobbs-Merrill, 1969.

———. Introduction to *The Genre of Silence* 1 (1967).

———. "Morning Song." *Yugen* 7 (1961): 50.

———. "Poem in Defense of Children." *The Genre of Silence* 1 (1967): 48.

Oren, Michel. "The Umbra Poets' Workshop, 1962–1965: Some Socio-Literary Puzzles." In *Belief vs. Theory in Black American Literary Criticism,* edited by Joe Weixlmann and Chester J. Fontenot, 177–223. Studies in Black American Literature, vol. 2. Greenwood, Fla.: Penkeville Publishing, 1986.

Orlovsky, Peter. *Clean Asshole Poems & Smiling Vegetable Songs: Poems, 1957–1977.* San Francisco: City Lights Books, 1978.

———, et al. "Memorial Reading for Paul Blackburn: Thirty-five Poets Read Blackburn's and Their Own Work." St. Mark's Church, New York. October 13, 1971. Sound recording. Jerome Rothenberg Papers. SPL 458. Mandeville Special Collections Library, University of California, San Diego.

O'Sullivan, Maggie, ed. *Out of Everywhere: Linguistically Innovative Poetry by Women in North America and the U.K.* London: Reality Street, 1996.

Pack, Robert. *Affirming Limits: Essays on Mortality, Choice, and Poetic Form.* Amherst: University of Massachusetts Press, 1985.

———. *The Long View: Essays on the Discipline of Hope and Craft.* Amherst: University of Massachusetts Press, 1991.

———, Donald Hall, and Louis Simpson, eds. *New Poets of England and America.* New York: Meridian Books, 1957.

Padgett, Ron. "Ash Tarzan." *C: A Journal of Poetry* 1, no. 2 (June 1963).

———. *The Big Something.* Great Barrington, Mass.: Figures Press, 1990.

———. *Great Balls of Fire.* Chicago: Holt, Rinehart and Winston, 1969.

———. "I'd Give You My Seat if I Were Here." *C: A Journal of Poetry* 1, no. 7 (February 1964).

———. "Judging the Judges." *Columbia Spectator,* April 24, 1964. Ted Berrigan Papers. Rare Book and Manuscript Library, Columbia University, New York.

———. "Sonnet to Andy Warhol." *C: A Journal of Poetry* 1, no. 7 (February 1964).

———, ed. *The Handbook of Poetic Forms.* New York: Teachers and Writers Collaborative, 1987.

———, and Clark Coolidge. *Supernatural Overtones.* Great Barrington, Mass.: Figures Press, 1990.

———, and David Shapiro, eds. *An Anthology of New York Poets.* New York: Random House, 1970.

Panish, Jon. *The Color of Jazz: Race and Representation in Postwar American Culture.* Jackson: University Press of Mississippi. 1997.

Parry, Albert. *Garrets and Pretenders: A History of Bohemianism in America.* New York: Dover Publications, 1960.

Paul, Sherman. *Olson's Push: Origin, Black Mountain, and Recent American Poetry.* Baton Rouge: Louisiana State University Press, 1978.

Perelman, Bob. "Speech Effects." In *Close Listening: Poetry and the Performed Word,* edited by Charles Bernstein, 200–217. New York: Oxford University Press, 1998.

Perloff, Marjorie. *Frank O'Hara: Poet Among Painters.* New York: G. Braziller, 1977.

Perreault, John. "John Perreault." *C: A Journal of Poetry* 1, no. 7 (February 1964).

———. "Three Poetry Events." *0 to 9* 5 (January 1969): 14.

"Poetic License Needed." *New York Times,* June 8, 1959.

"A Poet Laments Time Lost in a Courthouse." *New York Post,* October 19, 1961.

Poggioli, Renato. *The Theory of the Avant-Garde.* Translated by Gerald Fitzgerald. Cambridge, Mass.: Harvard University Press, 1968.

Pollak, Felix. "An Interview on Little Magazines." In *The Little Magazine in America,* edited by Elliot Anderson and Mary Kinzie, 34–49. Yonkers, N.Y.: Pushcart Press, 1978.

Pound, Ezra. *Gaudier-Brzeska.* New York: New Directions Press, 1970.

———. *The Letters of Ezra Pound, 1907–1941.* Edited by D. D. Paige. New York: Harcourt, Brace, 1950.

———. *Personae.* New York: New Directions, 1926.

"Preston Presents." *East Village Other* 2, no. 8 (March 15–April 1, 1967): 14.

Quartermain, Peter. "Sound Reading." In *Close Listening: Poetry and the Performed Word,* edited by Charles Bernstein, 217–30. New York: Oxford University Press, 1998.

Randall, Margaret, ed. *El Corno Emplumado/The Plumed Horn.* Correspondence and manuscript collection, 1959–1969. Elmer Holmes Bobst Library, Fales Library, New York University.

Rasula, Jed. *The American Poetry Wax Museum: Reality Effects, 1940–1990.* Urbana, Ill.: National Council of Teachers of English, 1996.

———. "Understanding the Sound of Not Understanding." In *Close Listening: Poetry and the Performed Word,* edited by Charles Bernstein, 233–62. New York: Oxford University Press, 1998.

Ratcliffe, Stephen, and Leslie Scalapino, eds. *Talking in Tranquility: Interviews with Ted Berrigan.* Bolinas, Calif.: Avenue B; Oakland, Calif.: O Books, 1991.

Redmond, Eugene. "Stridency and the Sword: Literary and Cultural Emphasis in Afro-American Magazines." In *The Little Magazine in America,* edited by Elliot Anderson and Mary Kinzie, 538–74. Yonkers, N.Y.: Pushcart Press, 1978.

Reed, Ishmael. "The Ghost in Birmingham." *Liberator* 3, no. 11 (November 1963): 21.

———. "Patrice." *Umbra* 2 (December 1963): 36.

———. "Poetry Place Protest." *East Village Other* 1, no. 1 (October 1965): 5.

Rembrar, Charles. *The End of Obscenity.* New York: Random House, 1968.

Rexroth, Kenneth. "San Francisco Letter." *Evergreen Review* 1, no. 2 (1957): 5–14.

———. Untitled article on poetry readings. *Evergreen Review* 2, no. 6 (1958): 14.

Rifkin, Libbie. *Career Moves.* Madison: University of Wisconsin Press, 2000.

———. "'My Little World Goes on St. Mark's Place': Anne Waldman, Bernadette Mayer, and the Gender of an Avant-Garde Institution." Paper presented at the Page Mothers Conference, University of California, San Diego, 1999. Available at www.jacket.zip.com .au/jacket07/rifkin07.html.

Rimbaud, Arthur. *Complete Works.* New York: Harper & Row, 1967.

Ross, Andrew. *The Failure of Modernism: Symptoms of American Poetry.* New York: Columbia University Press, 1986.

Rothenberg, Jerome. "The Deep Image Is the Threatened Image." *Trobar* 4 (1962): 43.

———. "The Double Vision." *Poems from the Floating World* 1 (1959): 10.

———. "Introduction." *Poems from the Floating World* 3 (1961): inner cover.

———. *Sightings.* New York: Hawk's Well Press, 1964.

———, ed. *Alcheringa* 1 (Fall 1970).

———, ed. *Poems from the Floating World* 1–5 (1959–1963).

———, trans. "Poem for Warriors." *Trobar* 2 (1961): 10.

———, and Robert Creeley. "An Exchange." *Kulchur* 2, no. 6 (1962): 32–37.

———, and David Guss, eds. *The Book, Spiritual Instrument.* New York: Granary Books, 1996.

Šalamun, Tomaž. *The Selected Poems of Tomaž Šalamun.* Edited by Charles Simic. New York: Ecco Press, 1988.

Sanders, Ed. *1968, a History in Verse.* Santa Rosa, Calif.: Black Sparrow Press, 1997.

———. Archive. Thomas J. Dodd Research Center, University of Connecticut Libraries, Storrs.

———. *Ed Sanders Newsletter.* April 1966. Ed Sanders Archive. Thomas J. Dodd Research Center, University of Connecticut Libraries, Storrs.

———. *Hymns to the Rebel Cafe.* Santa Rosa, Calif.: Black Sparrow Press, 1993.

———. Interview by Lisa Jarnot. *Poetry Project Newsletter* 166 (October/November 1997): 5–6, 8–9, 28–29.

———. "Poem Describing the Cover of the Next Issue of *Fuck You,* Issue 5 Volume 5." *Poets at Le Metro* 8 (1963).

———. *Poem from Jail.* San Francisco: City Lights Books, 1963.

———. Poetry reading. St. Mark's Church, New York. April 1967. Sound recording. Paul Blackburn Papers. SPL 306. Mandeville Special Collections Library, University of California, San Diego.

———. "Sheep Fuck Poem." *Fuck You / a magazine of the arts* 1, no. 3 (1962).

———. *Tales of Beatnik Glory.* New York: Stonehill Publishing, 1975.

———, et al. "Memorial Reading for Charles Olson." St. Mark's Church, New York. February 4, 1970. Sound recording. Paul Blackburn Papers. SPL 349. Mandeville Special Collections Library, University of California, San Diego.

Sanders, Ed, ed. *Fuck You / a magazine of the arts* 1, no. 1–5, no. 9 (1962–1965).

Saroyan, Aram. *Friends in the World.* Minneapolis: Coffee House Press, 1992.

Schorer, Mark. "On Lady Chatterley's Lover." *Evergreen Review* 1, no. 1 (1957): 149–78.

Schuyler, James. *Collected Poems.* New York: Farrar, Straus and Giroux, 1993.

"7 Editors Quit Columbia Review in Protest." *New York Post,* March 12, 1963.

Shaw, Lytle. "On Coterie: Frank O'Hara." *Shark* 2 (1999): 112–29.

Shepard, Richard F. "Galbraith Urges Arts 'Handouts.'" *New York Times,* June 23, 1967, 44.

Shoptaw, John. *On the Outside Looking Out: John Ashbery's Poetry.* Cambridge, Mass.: Harvard University Press, 1994.

Silliman, Ron. E-mail to University of Buffalo Poetics discussion group. December 3, 1998. www.epc.buffalo.edu/poetics/early_archive.

———. "For Language." In *The L = A = N = G = U = A = G = E Book,* edited by Bruce Andrews and Charles Bernstein, 16. Carbondale and Edwardsville: Southern Illinois University Press, 1984.

———. *What.* Great Barrington, Mass.: Figures Press, 1988.

Simpson, Megan, ed. *Poetic Epistemologies: Gender and Knowing in Women's Language-Oriented Writing.* Albany: State University of New York Press, 2000.

Sinopoulos, Takis. "Ionna Raving." *Poems from the Floating World* 2 (1960): 4.

Sloan, Mary Margaret, ed. *Moving Borders: Three Decades of Innovative Writing by Women.* Jersey City, N.J.: Talisman House, 1998.

Sloman, Joel. *Cuban Journal.* Cambridge, Mass.: Zoland Press, 2000.

———. Letter to Denise Levertov. July 17, 1966.

———. "Suggested Titles." *The Genre of Silence* 1 (1967): 8–9.

Smith, Alexander. *Frank O'Hara: A Comprehensive Bibliography.* New York: Garland Publishers, 1979.

Sollors, Werner. *Amiri Baraka: The Quest for a Populist Modernism.* New York: Columbia University Press, 1978.

Solomon, Carl. "The Lunatic and Modern Art." *Fuck You / a magazine of the arts* 7, no. 5 (September 1964).

Spahr, Juliana. *Everybody's Autonomy: Connective Reading and Collective Identity.* Tuscaloosa: The University of Alabama Press, 2001.

Stein, Gertrude. "In." *0 to 9* 2 (1967): 23.

Stephens, Michael G. "Poetry Project Days: Meditations on the Oppenheimer That Was." *Talisman* 20 (Winter 1999–2000): 91–109.

Stevens, Lawrence. "Does Mental Illness Exist?" www.antipsychiatry.org/exist.htm.

Suárez, Juan. *Bike Boys, Drag Queens, and Superstars: Avant-Garde, Mass Culture, and Gay Identities in the 1960s Underground Cinema.* Bloomington: Indiana University Press, 1996.

Sukenick, Ronald. *Down and In: Life in the Underground.* New York: Beech Tree Books, 1987.

Sullivan, James D. *On the Walls and in the Streets: American Poetry Broadsides from the 1960s.* Chicago: University of Illinois Press, 1997.

Thibodaux, David. *Joel Oppenheimer: An Introduction.* Columbia, S.C.: Camden House, 1986.

Thomas, Lorenzo. "Alea's Children: The Avant-Garde on the Lower East Side, 1960–1970." *African American Review* 27, no. 4 (Winter 1993): 573–78.

———. "Neon Griot: The Functional Role of Poetry Readings in the Black Arts Movement." In *Close Listening: Poetry and the Performed Word,* edited by Charles Bernstein, 300–323. New York: Oxford University Press, 1998.

———. "Political Science." *C: A Journal of Poetry* 1, no. 5 (October/November 1963).

———. "The Shadow World: New York's Umbra Workshop and Origins of the Black Arts Movement." *Callaloo* 4 (Oct. 1978): 53–72.

———. "South Street Blues." *Umbra* 1, no. 2 (1963): 38.

———. "A Tale of Two Cities." *Umbra* 1, no. 1 (1963): 36–37.

Tompkins, Jane, ed. *Reader-Response Criticism: From Formalism to Post-Structuralism.* Baltimore: Johns Hopkins University Press, 1980.

Torgensen, Eric. "Cold War in Poetry: Notes of a Conscientious Objector." *American Poetry Review* 11, no. 4 (July–August 1982): 31–35.

Vickery, Ann. *Leaving Lines of Gender: A Feminist Genealogy of Language Writing.* Middletown, Conn.: Wesleyan University Press, 2000.

Wakoski, Diane. *Emerald Ice: Selected Poems, 1962–1967.* Santa Rosa, Calif.: Black Sparrow Press, 1988.

Waldman, Anne. *Autobiography.* Contemporary Authors Autobiography Series 17. Detroit: Gale Research, 1993.

———. *Fast-Speaking Woman: Chants and Essays.* San Francisco: City Lights Books, 1996.

———. *Helping the Dreamer: New and Selected Poems.* Minneapolis: Coffee House Press, 1989.

———. Introduction to *Out of This World: An Anthology of the St. Mark's Poetry Project, 1966–1991.* New York: Crown Books, 1991.

———. *Life Notes.* Indianapolis: Bobbs-Merrill, 1973.

———, ed. *The Beat Book: Poems and Fiction of the Beat Generation.* Boston: Shambhala, 1996.

———, ed. *Nice to See You: Homage to Ted Berrigan.* Minneapolis: Coffee House Press, 1991.

———, ed. *Out of This World: An Anthology of the St. Mark's Poetry Project, 1966–1991.* New York: Crown Books, 1991.

———, ed. *The World Anthology: Poems from the St. Mark's Poetry Project.* Indianapolis: Bobbs-Merrill, 1969.

———, and Jim Brodey. Poetry reading. St. Mark's Church, New York. November 8, 1967. Sound recording. Paul Blackburn Papers. SPL 382. Mandeville Special Collections Library, University of California, San Diego.

———, et al. "Memorial Reading for Paul Blackburn: Thirty-five Poets Read Blackburn's and Their Own Work." St. Mark's Church, New York. October 13, 1971. Sound recording. Jerome Rothenberg Papers. SPL 458. Mandeville Special Collections Library, University of California, San Diego.

———, and Andrew Schelling, eds. *Disembodied Poetics: Annals of the Jack Kerouac School of Poetics.* Albuquerque: University of New Mexico Press, 1994.

———, and Lewis Warsh, eds. *The Angel Hair Anthology.* New York: Granary Books, 2001.

——— , and Lewis Warsh, eds. *Angel Hair Magazine* 1–5 (1966–1968). Elmer Holmes Bobst Library, Fales Library, New York University.

Wallace, Mark and Steven Marks, eds. *Telling It Slant: Avant-Garde Poetics of the 1990s.* Tuscaloosa: University of Alabama Press, 2002.

Ward, Geoff. *Statutes of Liberty.* New York: St. Martin's Press, 1993.

Warsh, Lewis. "French Windows." *The World* 3 (1967).

———. *Part of My History.* Toronto: Coach House Press, 1972.

———. *The Suicide Rates.* Eugene, Ore.: Toad Press, 1967.

Watson, Steven. *Strange Bedfellows: The First American Avant-Garde.* New York: Abbeville Press, 1991.

Whitman, Walt. *Complete Poetry and Collected Prose.* Edited by Justin Kaplan. New York: Library of America, 1982.

Wieners, John. Poetry reading. Le Metro, New York. September 11, 1963. Sound recording. Paul Blackburn Papers. SPL 186. Mandeville Special Collections Library, University of California, San Diego.

—————. Poetry reading. St. Mark's Church, New York. January 3, 1968. Sound recording. Paul Blackburn Papers. SPL 388–89. Mandeville Special Collections Library, University of California, San Diego.

—————. "Prose Poem." *C: A Journal of Poetry* 1, no. 5 (1963).

Wolf, Reva. *Andy Warhol, Poetry and Gossip in the 1960s.* Chicago: University of Chicago Press, 1997.

Woodward, Kathleen. *Paul Blackburn: A Checklist.* San Diego: Archive for New Poetry, University of California, San Diego, 1980.

XYZ, Emily. "How Much Is That Artist in the Window?" Letter to the editor. *Harper's,* April 1999, 6–7.

Yip, Wai-lim. *Ezra Pound's Cathay.* Princeton: Princeton University Press, 1969.

Young, La Monte, ed. *An Anthology of Chance Operations.* Munich: Heiner Friedrich Gallery, 1970.

Zumthor, Paul. *Oral Poetry: An Introduction.* Minneapolis: University of Minnesota Press, 1990.

Sources and Permissions

The section of chapter 3 relating to Ed Sanders and *Fuck You / a magazine of the arts* was previously published in a slightly different form in *Arshile: A Magazine of the Arts* 11 (1999): 82–111. Reprinted by permission.

Grateful acknowledgment is made for permission to print or reproduce material from the following sources:

Text

Vito Acconci, letter to Clayton Eshleman, March 26, 1969, from the Clayton Eshleman Archives, Elmer Holmes Bobst Library, Fales Library, New York University. Reproduced by permission of Vito Acconci.

Bruce Andrews, personal interview at Andrews's home, May 10, 1999.

John Ashbery, personal interview at Ashbery's home, February 1999.

Bill Berkson, e-mail to the author. February 21, 1999.

Charles Bernstein, personal interview at Bernstein's home, March 15, 1999.

Ted Berrigan, Untitled poem, from *Poets at Le Metro* 7 (1963). "Homage to Jim Brodey," from *Poets at Le Metro* 8 (1963). Diary entries dated December 4, 1962, December 18, 1962, February 22, 1963, March 14, 1963, April 13, 1963, April 28, 1963, May 1963, May 19, 1963, June 9, 1963, August 6, 1963, September 13, 1963, April 8, 1964, and April 1965, from the Ted Berrigan Papers, Rare Book and Manuscript Library, Columbia University. All reproduced by permission of Alice Notley, Literary Executrix of the Estate of Ted Berrigan. Letters to Sandy Alper Berrigan dated March 6, 1962, March 17, 1962, March 19, 1962, March 20, 1962, March 26, 1962, and August 1963, from the Ted Berrigan Papers, Rare Book and Manuscript Library, Columbia University. Reproduced by permission of Sandy Alper Berrigan.

Paul Blackburn, letter to Joel Oppenheimer, July 26, 1966, from the Joel Oppenheimer Papers, Thomas J. Dodd Research Center, University of Connecticut, Storrs. Letter to Charles Olson, December 8, 1950, from the Charles Olson Archive, Thomas J. Dodd Research Center, University of Connecticut, Storrs. Interview of Paul Blackburn by an unnamed student and selection from "What's New? An Interior Report on the Socio-literary Uses of the Mimeograph Machine," from the Paul Blackburn Papers, Mandeville Special Collections Library, University of California, San Diego. All items © 2002 Joan Miller Cohn.

Jerry Bloedow, personal interview at New York University, April 29, 1998.

Andrei Codrescu, letter to Margaret Randall, from *El Corno Emplumado* Archive, Fales Library, New York University. Reproduced by permission of Andrei Codrescu.

Kirby Congdon, letter to Ed Sanders, August 27, 1962, from the Ed Sanders Archive, Thomas J. Dodd Research Center, University of Connecticut, Storrs. Reproduced by permission of Kirby Congdon.

George Economou, personal telephone interviews, March 10 and 18, 1998.

Clayton Eshleman, letter to the author, July 27, 1999.

Steve Facey, personal telephone interview, February 17, 1999.

Larry Fagin, personal interviews at Fagin's home, January 26, 1998, and February 19, 1999.

Kathleen Fraser, e-mails to the author, May 25 and 26, 2002.

Ed Friedman, personal interview at St. Mark's Church, New York City, February 3, 1999.

John Giorno, personal interview at Giorno's home, February 25, 1999. "I'm Tired of Being Scared," from *An Anthology of New York Poets,* edited by Ron Padgett and David Shapiro. Reprinted by permission of John Giorno.

David Henderson, personal interviews at Limbo Café, New York City, February 28 and April 8, 1998. "The Ofay and the Nigger," *Umbra* 1 (1963). Reprinted by permission of David Henderson.

Bob Holman, personal interview, March 3, 1999. *A History of the Poetry Project,* © 1978, St. Mark's Church Poetry Project Archives. Reprinted by permission of Bob Holman.

Pierre Joris, e-mail to the author, March 19, 1999.

Robert Kelly, letter to George Economou, July 19, 1963.

Kenneth Koch, personal interviews, October 12, 1998, and February 11, 1999.

Jackson Mac Low, e-mail to the author, May 20, 1998. "The Coffeehouse Poetry Reading Scene in New York 1960–1967," written for "Light Years" (unpublished), an anthology of memoirs about the coffeehouse readings in New York from 1959 through the 1960s, edited by Carol Bergé. Reprinted by permission of Jackson Mac Low.

Gerard Malanga, letter to Bill Berkson, September 1, 1963, from the Gerard Malanga Archive, Harry Ransom Center, University of Texas, Austin. Reproduced by permission of Gerard Malanga.

Bernadette Mayer, personal telephone interviews, October 10 and November 6, 1998.

Alice Notley, e-mail to the author, February 7, 1999.

Joel Oppenheimer, letters to Charles Olson, July 27, 1966, and February 19, 1968, from the

Charles Olson Archive, Thomas J. Dodd Research Center, University of Connecticut, Storrs. Letter to Paul Blackburn, July 7, 1966, from the Paul Blackburn Papers, Mandeville Special Collections Library, University of California, San Diego. All reproduced by permission of Theresa Maier, Literary Executrix of the Estate of Joel Oppenheimer.

Ron Padgett, personal interviews, October 10, 1997, March 3, 1998, March 24, 1998, and February 13, 1999. Letter to Paul Blackburn, December 30, 1958, from the Paul Blackburn Papers, Mandeville Special Collections Library, University of California, San Diego. Reprinted by permission of Ron Padgett.

Ezra Pound, letters to Paul Blackburn, July 4, 1950, and September 20, 1950, from the Paul Blackburn Papers, Mandeville Special Collections Library, University of California, San Diego. © 2001 by Mary de Rachewiltz and Omar S. Pound. Reprinted by permission of New Directions Press.

Ishmael Reed, "Patrice," *Umbra* 2 (December 1963). Reprinted by permission of Ishmael Reed.

Jerome Rothenberg, "The Double Vision," from *Poems from the Floating World* 1 (1959). Reprinted by permission of Jerome Rothenberg.

James Schuyler, letter to Gerard Malanga, January 9, 1962, from the Gerard Malanga Archive, Harry Ransom Center, University of Texas, Austin. Reproduced by permission of Darragh Park, Literary Executor of the Estate of James Schuyler.

Ron Silliman, letter to Bernadette Mayer, September 9, 1973, from the Bernadette Mayer Archive, University of California, San Diego. E-mail to the University of Buffalo Poetics discussion group 3, December 1998. Reprinted by permission of Ron Silliman.

Joel Sloman, e-mail to the author, February 1, 1998. Letter to Denise Levertov, July 17, 1966. Reprinted by permission of Joel Sloman.

Lorenzo Thomas, personal telephone interview, September 6, 1998. "A Tale of Two Cities," *Umbra* 1, no. 1 (1963). Reprinted by permission of Lorenzo Thomas.

Diane Wakoski, letter to Paul Blackburn, September 28, 1970, from the Paul Blackburn Papers, Mandeville Special Collections Library, University of California, San Diego. Reprinted by permission of Diane Wakoski.

Anne Waldman, personal interview, January 27, 1998. E-mail to the author, February 13, 1999. Letters to Bernadette Mayer, January 16, 1970, March 14, 1970, March 23, 1971, from the Bernadette Mayer Archive, University of California, San Diego. Letter to Gerard Malanga, January 1968, from the Gerard Malanga Archive, Harry Ransom Center, University of Texas, Austin. Reprinted by permission of Anne Waldman.

Lewis Warsh, personal interviews in the author's home, June, 8, 1998, and February 3, 1999.

John Wieners, letter to Paul Blackburn, April 4, 1958, from the Paul Blackburn Papers, Mandeville Special Collections Library, University of California, San Diego. Reprinted by permission of John Wieners.

Compact Disc

Track 1: Denise Levertov, "O Taste and See," St. Mark's Church, New York City, March 20, 1967. © 2001 by the Denise Levertov Literary Trust, Paul A. Lacey and Valerie Trueblood Rapport, Cotrustees. All rights reserved.

Track 2: Paul Blackburn, "Clickety-Clack," Brooklyn Civic Center, Brooklyn, New York, May 22, 1964. Published in *The Collected Poems of Paul Blackburn,* © 1985 by Joan Miller Cohn. Reproduced by permission of Persea Books, Inc. (New York).

Track 3: Jackson Mac Low and Anne Tardos, excerpt from "Phoneme Dance in Memoriam John Cage" (1993), by Jackson Mac Low and Anne Tardos, first included on the compact disc *Open Secrets* (XI 110), © 1993 by Jackson Mac Low, (P) 1993 Experimental Intermedia Foundation. Reproduced by permission of Jackson Mac Low, Anne Tardos, and Phill Niblock.

Track 4: David Antin, "Who Are My Friends," Café Le Metro, New York City, September 1, 1965. The full text of this poem was included in Antin's *Code of Flag Behavior* (Los Angeles: Black Sparrow Press, 1967) and republished in *Selected Poems 1963–1973* (Los Angeles: Sun and Moon, 1991). Reproduced by permission of David Antin.

Track 5: Jerome Rothenberg, "A Valentine, No, a Valedictory for Gertrude Stein," Café Le Metro, New York City, September 1, 1965. Originally published in Jerome Rothenberg's *Poems for the Game of Silence* (New York: New Directions), © 2000. Reproduced by permission of Jerome Rothenberg.

Track 6: Armand Schwerner, selection from "The Tablets," St. Mark's Church, New York City, April 6, 1966. Reproduced by permission of Adam Schwerner.

Track 7: Clayton Eshleman, "Notebook Entry 1968," St. Mark's Church, New York City, March 4, 1968. Clayton Eshleman's most recent collection of poetry is *From Scratch* (Los Angeles: Black Sparrow Press, 1998). His most recent collection of essays is *Companion Spider* (Middletown, Conn.: Wesleyan University Press, 2001). Reproduced by permission of Clayton Eshleman.

Track 8: Robert Creeley, "The Charm," "A STEP," and "KATE'S," St. Mark's Church, New York City, May 17, 1967. © by Robert Creeley. Reproduced by permission of Robert Creeley.

Track 9: Robert Kelly, Troubadour text, translated by Robert Kelly, Café Cino, New York City, 1960. Reproduced by permission of Robert Kelly.

Track 10: John Wieners, "Poem for Cocksuckers," Café Le Metro, New York City, 1963. Reproduced by permission of John Wieners.

Track 11: Allen Ginsberg, "A Supermarket in California," Pacifica Studios, Berkeley, California, Oct 25, 1956. Previously available on the compact disc *Holy Soul Jelly Roll,* Rhino Records, 1994. Reproduced by permission of Bob Rosenthal.

Track 12: Amiri Baraka, "A Poem Some People Will Have to Understand," Poetry Society of America, New York City, December 26, 1963. Published in *Black Magic: Sabotage, Target Study, Black Art; Collected Poetry, 1961–1967* (Indianapolis: Bobbs-Merrill, 1969). Reproduced by permission of Amiri Baraka.

Tracks 13 and 14: John Ashbery, "They Dream Only of America" and "Thoughts of a Young Girl," Washington Square Gallery, New York City, August 23, 1964. Reproduced by permission of John Ashbery and George Borchardt, Inc., Literary Agency. © 1962 by John Ashbery. All rights reserved.

Tracks 15 and 16: Frank O'Hara, "Naphtha" and "Poem (Lana Turner Has Collapsed!)," State University of New York, Buffalo, 1964. Published in *Lunch Poems* by Frank

O'Hara (San Francisco: City Lights Books, 1964). © 1964 by Frank O'Hara. Reproduced by permission of Maureen O'Hara Granville-Smith.

Track 17: Kenneth Koch, "To My Audience," St. Mark's Church, New York City, January 10, 1968. Reproduced by permission of Kenneth Koch.

Track 18: Bill Berkson, "I Feel Free," St. Mark's Church, New York City, May 29, 1969. Reproduced by permission of Bill Berkson.

Track 19: Bill Berkson, "Poem," read over phone to author. Published in *Serenade* (Cambridge, Mass.: Zoland Books, 2000). Reproduced by permission of Bill Berkson.

Tracks 20, 21, and 22: Ron Padgett, "Detach Invading," "Joe Brainard's Painting 'Bingo,'" and "Nothing in That Drawer," originally taped on "Susan Howe with Poetry" radio show, WBAI, New York, June 17, 1975. Reproduced by permission of Ron Padgett.

Track 23: Joe Brainard, selections from *I Remember,* venue and date unknown. Reproduced by permission of John Brainard, executor of the estate of Joe Brainard.

Track 24: Dick Gallup, "Where I Hang My Hat," St. Mark's Church, New York City, September 27, 1967. Reproduced by permission of Dick Gallup.

Track 25: "Five Leaf Clover," St. Mark's Church, New York City, May 16, 2001. Reproduced by permission of Lorenzo Thomas. © 2001 by Lorenzo Thomas.

Track 26: Anne Waldman, "Poem in New York," St. Mark's Church, New York City, November 8, 1967. Reproduced by permission of Anne Waldman.

Track 27: Ted Berrigan and Anne Waldman, selection from "Memorial Day," St. Mark's Church, New York City, Memorial Day, 1974. The excerpt from "Memorial Day" (© 1974) is from the compact disc *Alchemical Elegy,* produced at Naropa University, 2001. © 2001 by Fast Speaking Music.

Track 28: "Sonnet I," "Sonnet II," "Sonnet III," and "A Final Sonnet," St. Mark's Church, New York City, 1968. Published in *The Sonnets* by Ted Berrigan. © 2000 by Alice Notley, Literary Executrix of the Estate of Ted Berrigan. Used by permission of Viking Penguin, a division of Penguin Putnam Inc.

Track 29: Clark Coolidge, "Machinations Calcite," Franconia College, Franconia, New Hampshire, circa 1971. Reproduced by permission of Clark Coolidge.

Track 30: Alice Notley, "How to Really Get an Apartment," University of California, San Diego, Revelle Formal Lounge, April 25, 1989. Reproduced by permission of Alice Notley.

Tracks 31 and 32: Joe Ceravolo, "A Song of Autumn" and "Drunken Winter," recorded at Ceravolo's home, Bloomfield, New Jersey, Spring 1968. Initially included on an LP in *Mother* 9 (Spring 1968), ed. Duncan McNaughton and Lewis MacAdams. Reproduced by permission of Rosemary Ceravolo, Literary Executrix of the Estate of Joe Ceravolo, and Coffee House Press.

Tracks 33 and 34: Bernadette Mayer, "Sonnet—You Jerk, You Didn't Call Me Up," "Warren Finney," and "Sonnet—Other Than What's Gone On in Stupid Art," University of California, San Diego, Price Center, Room 5, November 15, 1989. Reproduced by permission of Bernadette Mayer.

Index

Tracks on the compact disc are represented in italic type with the abbreviation CD followed by the track number.

Abrams, Sam, 140, 150
abstract expressionism, 3, 116
academia, 3, 4, 42–43, 99–100, 215n47.
   See also names of universities
Acconci, Vito Hannibal, xix, 154, 188, 198
Adams, Leonie, 42
Addison, Lloyd, 81
Adventures in Poetry, 154, 168, 257n5, 259n15,
   263n54
African American poets/poetics. *See* Black
   Arts movement; *Umbra;* Umbra poets;
   names of individual poets
Aldan, Daisy, 105
Algarín, Miguel, 203, 206; *Aloud: Voices from
   the Nuyorican Café,* 203, 204, 205
Allen, Donald, 8, 11, 17, 35. See also *The New
   American Poetry: 1945–1960*
Allen, Michael, 123, 124, 125, 250n21; departure
   from St. Mark's, 187; and federal funding,
   129, 130, 136, 127, 255n65; and firing of
   Jacobs, 145–48; and Ron Gold reading, 183,
   185
Allen anthology. See *The New American Poetry:
   1945–1960*
Aloud: Voices from the Nuyorican Café, 203, 204,
   205
Amini, Johari, 85
Anderson, Margaret, 2, 61

Andrews, Bruce, 191, 197–98, 270n27; "Writ-
   ing Social Work and Political Practice," 194
Angel Hair, 153, 154, 156, 244n149
Angry Arts Week, 149, 150, 255–56n74.
   See also *Genre of Silence*
The Anonymous Diary of New York Youth
   (Mead), 66–67
Ant, Howard, 34, 35
An Anthology of New York Poets, 182,
   266–67n93
Antin, David, 142; Angry Arts Week, 149,
   150; antiwar movement, 66, 79; attack
   on, 181; and Poetry Project, 141–43; St.
   Mark's benefit readings for, 16, 126–28;
   "Who Are My Friends," *CD4*
Antonius, Brother, 40
appropriation, 46–47, 110–11, 112–18, 120,
   154, 157–59, 259nn10,12
Artaud, Antonin, 13, 34, 236n50
Ashbery, John, 41; as apolitical, 262–63n47;
   "How Much Longer Shall I Be Able to
   Inhabit the Divine Sepulcher?" 114; "Last
   Month," 46; and New York vs. Black
   Mountain schools, 24; on O'Hara's poetics,
   249–50n15; Padgett on, 42, 43; on role
   of readings, xvi-xvii; *The Tennis Court
   Oath,* 191; "They Dream Only of Amer-
   ica," *CD13;* "Thoughts of a Young Girl,"

Ashbery, John *(continued)*
   CD14; "To a Waterfowl," 114; as witness
      for Sanders, 78
Aspen Writers Conference, 135
Atelier East Gallery, 56
Auden, W. H., xvii, 61, 82, 123, 126; *Platonic
   Blow,* 70
audience participation, 31, 33, 171–73, 263n60
audio tape, 6, 169–70, 263n58
avant-garde. *See names of individual
   movements and schools*

Bakhtin, Mikhail, 128
Banes, Sally, 87
Baraka, Amiri, 3–4, 13, 29, 80, 238n74; con-
   viction of, 171, 172, 173; defense of *New
   American Poetry,* 9–10; "The Eighth Ditch,"
   216n57; in *Evergreen Review,* 9, 13; *Four
   Young Lady Poets,* 253–54n50; legal charges
   against, 15, 60, 216n57, 232–33n12; on
   natural rhythms of poetry, 27; Olson's
   influence on, 19, 23, 218n71; open readings
   at Le Metro, 41; "A Poem Some People
   Will Have to Understand," *CD12;* and
   Umbra poets, 238–39n79. See also *The
   Floating Bear*
Barnard College, 264n68
Barr, Nelson, 39, 225n46
Barthes, Roland, 188, 195
Barzini, Benedetta, 156
Barzun, Jacques, 14, 102, 215–16n51
Beach, Christopher, 12, 204, 207
Bearden, David, 102, 103, 104
Beat poets, xiii, xiv, 1, 3, 34; Ashbery on,
   xvii; and black culture, 88–89; chance-
   determined writings of, 38; lack of
   publishing opportunities for, 29; and
   Le Metro, 39; and New York School, 42,
   109–12, 158–59. *See also names of individual
   poets*
Beatty, Paul, 204
bebop, 29, 43–44
Beck, Julian, 50
Beckett, Samuel, 63
benefit readings, 16, 126–28, 141, 183
Bergé, Carol, 1, 8, 20, 22, 253–54n50; on
   directorship of Poetry Project, 136; in *Fuck
   you,* 65; and Les Deux Mégots readings, 34,
   39; as organizer, 36, 41; in *Poets at Le Metro,*
   45; and police crackdowns, 51; post–New
   York, 180
Berger, Art, 79
Berger, Martin, 77

Berkeley Defense League, 183
Berkeley Poetry Conference, 121, 153
Berkson, Bill, 105, 176, 177; "I Feel Free,"
   CD18; "Poem," *CD19*
Bernstein, Charles, 110, 111, 141, 188; on devel-
   opment of language school, 190, 191; on
   naturalness, 200; on readings, 196
Berrigan, Phil, 16, 17
Berrigan, Sandy Alper, 101, 109, 46n175
Berrigan, Ted, 1, 206–7, 217n66, 246n170,
   247n183; and Alper, 246n175; and appro-
   priation and collaboration, 46–47, 110–11,
   113–18, 120, 259nn10,12; "Ash Tarzan," 113;
   Beat and New York Schools, blending of,
   108–12, 158; censorship of, 102–4, 215–
   16n51; on contemporaries, 101; departure
   of, 176, 183, 185–86; "80th Congress" (with
   Gallup), 164; as establishing Second-
   Generation New York School, 106–8,
   227n76, 257n8; Folklore Center readings,
   56; "Get the Money," 54; "Homage to
   James Brodey," 46–47; "Improvised
   Monday, Sept. 23rd 1963" poems, 45–
   46; influence on Poetry Project, 154, 157;
   and Le Metro, 41, 43, 45–48, 54; "Looking
   for Chris," 59; mainstream status of, 187,
   268n1; "Memorial Day" (with Waldman),
   CD27; on New York vs. Black Mountain
   schools, 23–24, 26; and O'Hara, 109;
   "Poem in the Traditional Manner," 111;
   and poet as outsider, 59; post–New York,
   176, 179; readings at Poetry Project, 42;
   "Sonnet LVIII," 8; *The Sonnets,* 19, 46, 107,
   161, 164, 182; "Sonnets I, II, III," and "A
   Final Sonnet," *CD28;* "Sonnet II," 113;
   success of, xix, 198; "Tambourine Life,"
   169; and use of vernacular, 8; "Waterloo
   Sunset" (with Padgett), 167–68; on women
   poets, 140–41. See also *C: A Journal of
   Poetry*
Berryman, John, 95
Beyond the Blues, 81
Black Arts movement, 82, 85. See also *Umbra;*
   Umbra poets; *names of individual poets*
Black Arts Repertory Theater and School, 79
Blackburn, Paul, 1, 21, 24, 221n111; attitude
   toward New York School, 41, 226n58;
   "Clickety-Clack," *CD2;* and Greenwich
   Village readings, 29–30; memorial for,
   160–61, 261n29; Olson's influence on, 19;
   as organizer of Le Metro readings, 40, 41,
   54, 225–26n55; poetic influences of, 7, 9;
   in *Poets at Le Metro,* 45; in *Poets at Les*

Deux Mégots, 36; and Poetry Project, 36, 135–37; and troubadour poetry, 72; on vernacular in poetry, 32; "What's New?: An Interior Report on the Socio-literary Uses of the Mimeograph Machine," 58, 229n95

Blackburn, Sara, 22

Black Mountain College, 38

Black Mountain school, xiii, 1, 3, 34; at Atelier East Gallery, 56; and Le Metro scene, 39, 163; vs. New York School, 24–26. *See also names of individual poets*

black nationalism, 79–80, 81

Black Panthers, 133, 181

black poetics, 79–90. *See also* Black Arts movement; *Umbra;* Umbra poets

Blake, William, 74, 93, 94

Bloedow, Jerry, 38, 40, 50, 54

Bly, Robert, 99, 100, 244nn141,142

Bolinas, California, xix, 176–78, 179

bombings, 180–81

Borregaard, Ebbe, 176

Boudin, Jean, 139

Boudin, Kathy, 139, 253n48

Bourdieu, Pierre, xiv, 32, 238n72

Bowery Poets Co-Op, 230–31n109

Bowes, Ed, 189

Brainard, Joe, 25, 56, 78, 105, 176; *I Remember,* 39, 95, 115, *CD23*

Bread and Puppet Theater, 50

breath, in poetry, 27–28, 30

Brennan, Paul, 81

Bridge Theater, 77

British Renaissance poets, 11

Broderick, Vincent, 78

Brodey, Jim, 41, 46, 206, 227n72; "A Poem & Prose," 158–59, 260nn16,17,19

Brown University, 4

Bruce, Lenny, 15, 51, 53, 69, 103, 228–29n90

Buddhism, 153, 165

Buffalo Poetics List, 196

Burroughs, William, 15, 38, 40, 61; "Roosevelt at the Inauguration," 216n57

cabaret laws, xvi, 48–49, 138, 209n5, 228nn81,86

Café Au Go Go, 51

Café Bizarre, 49, 228n81

Café Cino, 30, 91

Café Des Deux-Mégots (Paris), 34, 65–66

Café Le Metro. *See* Metro, Le (coffeehouse)

Café Wha?, 49, 228n81

Cage, John, 38, 116

C: A Journal of Poetry, xvii, 100–122; group poetics in, 120; as model for *The World,* 155; origin of, 102–5; publication of First-Generation New York School poets, 42, 121–22. *See also* Berrigan, Ted

Carrington, Harold, 60

Carroll, Jim, 72, 176

Carroll, Paul, 175; *The Young American Poets,* 175–76, 264–65n70

Carson, Devereaux, 176

Caterpillar, 154

Catonsville 9 benefit reading, 16, 141

The Censored Review, 104

censorship, 102–4, 215–16n51

cento poetry, 114

Ceravolo, Joe, 122, 155, 227n76, 257n8, 258n14; "Drunken Winter," *CD32;* "Fits of Dawn," 191; "A Song of Autumn," *CD31*

chain magazine, 7

Chelsea and *Chelsea Review,* 90–91

Christenberry, Robert K., 14

Christensen, Paul, 91, 98, 100

City Lights Books, 45

civil rights movement, xviii, 13, 66, 80, 81, 82

Clark, Angelica, 176

Clark, Tom, 56, 164, 262n39; *Air,* 182; in Bolinas, 176; "The Book of Love," 177; "Easter" (with Schjeldahl), 165, 166; on language poets, 192; "Stalin as Linguist," 192; *Stones,* 182

Codrescu, Andrei, 141, 167, 172, 176, 179, 180

coffeehouse license law, xv, xvi, 49–50, 229nn91,95

coffeehouses. *See names of individual coffeehouses*

Coleman, Ornette, 89

collaboration, 154; Berrigan and, 46, 110–11, 113–18, 120, 259nn10,12; and mimeographed magazines, 169; in *Unnatural Acts,* 199–201; at Warsh/Waldman home, 161–64; in *The World,* 157–59, 163, 165

collagism, 157. *See also* appropriation; dada

Coltrane, John, 28

Columbia Review, 102–4, 245n155

Columbia University, 14, 15, 42, 102–4, 215–16n51, 245n153

Congdon, Kirby, 4

A Controversy of Poets, 175, 265n71

Cook, Ralph, 145

Coolidge, Clark, 56, 175, 210n9; "Machinations Calcite," *CD29; Polaroid,* 189; *Space,* 182

Cooper, Dennis, 154

Corman, Cid, 37, 63. See also *Origin*
Corno Emplumado, El, 242n117
corporate sponsorship, 205, 272n8
Corso, Gregory, 109, 159, 226n63, 238n74;
    "Birthplace Revisited," 111
Cott, Jonathan, 102, 156, 164, 244n149
Counter Intelligence Program
    (COINTELPRO), 181
cowboy aesthetic, xiv, 17–23, 217nn66, 68
Cowley, Malcolm, 14, 34
C Press, 104
Crane, Hart, 63
Creative Arts for Alienated Youth, 130, 146.
    See also Millennium Film Workshop;
    Poetry Project at St. Mark's Church;
    Theater Genesis
Creeley, Robert, 8, 29, 176, 210–11n11;
    "Bolinas and Me," 177–78; "The Charm,"
    CD8; "I Remember Joanne," 178;
    "KATE'S," *CD8;* "A STEP," *CD8*
Cunningham, Merce, 36, 116

dada, xiv, xviii, 5, 38, 105; and little magazines,
    61–64; and Poetry Project, 154, 157
The Dada Painters and Poets (Motherwell), 188
Dangerfield, Harlan (pseud.), 162
Daniel, Arnaud, 30
Dawson, Fielding, 19
Dee, Jonathan, 205, 272n8
Deep Image poetics, xvii, 1, 34, 91–100,
    243n127. See also *Poems from the Floating
    World; Trobar*
de Kooning, Willem, 3, 116
DeLoach, Allen, 35, 54
Denby, Edwin, 45, 105
Dent, Tom, xvii, 54–55, 82
De Sapio, Carmine, 51
Deutch, Babette, 42
Deux Mégots, Les (coffeehouse), readings at,
    17, 34–39, 208, 222–23n27; and literary
    genealogy, 5; and poem as speech act, 26;
    San Francisco readings as predecessor to,
    28; and sex, 65; women poets at, 20
"Dial-A-Poem," 183–84
Dicker, Harold, 7
Dickey, James, 175
di Prima, Diane, 9, 15, 41, 60, 180; "Fuzz's
    Progress," 50; *Revolutionary Letters,* 58
Dlugos, Tim, 186
Dorn, Ed, 217n68
downtown poets. *See* Lower East Side poetic
    community; *names of individual poets*
Dragonette, Ree, 34

Dr. Generosity's, 261n27
drugs (illegal), xviii, 6, 40, 59–60, 132, 185, 186
Duchamp, Marcel, 68, 73, 86, 105, 238n72,
    259nn12,13
Duncan, Robert, 11, 27; "Africa Revisited," 37;
    "At the Poetry Conference: Berkeley after
    the New York Style," 121
Durand, Marcella, 205
Dylan, Bob, 45

Eastern religion, 165
East Side Review, 126
The East Side Scene (De Loach), 35, 54, 79
The East Village Other, 54, 55, 76, 124, 145, 146,
    224n40; on legal proceedings against poets,
    15–16; on St. Mark's Church, 125
Economou, George, 1, 9, 30, 41, 91, 136–37;
    "Crazy-Eyed Cowboys," 19
Eighth Street Bookshop, 45, 144
Electric Circus, 124
The 11th Street Ruse, 58
Eliot, T. S., xvii, 4, 11, 61; *Four Quarters,*
    214–15n38; *The Waste Land,* 25
Ellis, Albert, 20
Elmslie, Kenward, 48
Emerson, Ralph Waldo, 167
"The End" (Doors), 169
Epitome (coffeehouse), 49
Eshleman, Clayton, 91, 92, 100, 142, 154, 168;
    "Notebook Entry 1968," *CD7*
"Eskimo Songs" (anonymous), 198–99
Evergreen Review, 9, 11, 12, 13, 17, 214n36
Experiments in Art and Technology (E.A.T.),
    212n16
Exquisite Corpse, 233–34n23

Facey, Steve, 124, 187
Fagin, Larry, 154, 157, 161, 168, 187, 257n5,
    263n54
Femora, 20, 219n72
Ferini, Vincent, 23
Ferlinghetti, Lawrence, 11, 214–15n38; *A Coney
    Island of the Mind,* 45; *On the Mesa: An
    Anthology of Bolinas Writing,* 176–77
Fillmore East, 124, 142
Finley, Karen, 68
Finnegans Wake (Joyce), 63, 116
First-Generation New York School. *See* New
    York School, First-Generation
Five Spot Café, 3, 28, 136, 220–21n5,
    238–39n79
The Floating Bear, 9, 15, 57, 60, 64, 231n3
Fluxus movement, 243n130

Folklore Center, 56
Ford, John, 22
Four Young Lady Poets, 253–54n50
Fowler, Al, 67, 68
Fraser, Kathleen, 1, 20, 54, 68–69
Freilicher, Jane, 105
Friedman, Ed, 198, 199, 200
frontier mentality, 17–18
Fuck you/a magazine of the arts, xv, xvii, 39,
    64–79, 236nn50,51; availability of, 64;
    dedication of, 66, 235n35; demise of,
    76–79; and homosexuality, 67; legal battles
    relating to, 60, 61, 71; look of, 66, 233n15;
    politics of, 72; and sexual deviance, 65,
    66, 67–68; third anniversary issue, 71–72.
    See also Sanders, Ed
Fugs, xv, 32, 45, 70, 72, 77, 78, 79
funding, federal, for Poetry Project, xviii,
    129–34
futurism, 5, 6, 33, 61–64, 211–12n15

Gaines, Reg E., 204–5
Galbraith, John Kenneth, 143
Gallup, Dick, 42, 48, 104; "80th Congress"
    (with Berrigan), 164; *Where I Hang My
    Hat,* 182, CD24
Garcia, David, 125
Gaslight, 49
Genet, Jean, 13, 15, 77
Genre of Silence, 149–51, 154, 255n72
gentrification, of Lower East Side, 18
Gestetner mimeograph machine, 58
Gillespie, Dizzy, 29
Ginsberg, Allen, xvii, 1, 90, 206; "America,"
    110; on cut-up, 224–25n42; and Eastern
    religion, 165; in *Evergreen Review,* 9, 11, 13;
    "Footnote to Howl," 74; and *Fuck you,* 61,
    73, 75–76; *Howl,* 10–11, 53, 68, 89, 103,
    206, 214n36; "Howl," 83; and hyperbole,
    68; *Kaddish,* 68; and mainstream accept-
    ance, 69, 210–11n111; memorial for, 72; on
    O'Hara, 159; and Orlovsky, 73; on Poetry
    Project, xiii, and "poets as community,"
    xiv; and police crackdowns, 51; Rexroth
    on, 12; and Sanders, 75; in San Francisco,
    28; at St. Mark's antiwar reading, 126–27;
    "Sunflower Sutra," 74, 237n56, 260n19;
    "A Supermarket in California," CD11;
    "Who Will Take Over the Universe?" 128;
    "Wichita Vortex Sutra," 126
Giorno, John, 117, 200, 212n15,16; "I'm Tired
    of Being Scared," 5–6; and Radio Free
    Poetry, 132, 183–85

Giuliani, Rudolph, xvi, 230n97
Glassco, John, 30
Gold, Ron, 183, 184, 185, 267n97
Goldberg, Mike, 105, 106
Goodman, Paul, 63
Graham, Bill, 124
grants: for *Angel Hair* and other magazines,
    257n6; federal, for Poetry Project, 129–
    34, 250–51n21, 251nn22,23,25, 255n63;
    nongovernment, for Poetry Project,
    266n91
Grateful Dead, 124
Green Mill, 206
Greenwald, Ted, 164, 180
Greenwich Village, 2, 29, 34
Grove Press, xiv, 9–17, 216n55. See also
    *Evergreen Review; The New American
    Poetry: 1945–1960*
Gruen, John, 18
Gude, Ellen, 104
Gude, Lorenz, 100, 104
Guest, Barbara, 41, 101, 105, 121
Guggenheim Museum, 139
Gysin, Brion, 38, 45

Hacker, Marilyn, 141
Hall, Donald, 13; *New Poets of England
    and America,* 13, 43, 60, 215n47
Hall, Mitchell, 102, 103–4
Hanrahan, Captain William, 11
harassment of the arts, 48–54
Hardware Poets Theater, 50
Haring, Keith, 69
Harper's magazine, 205
Harris, Frank, 15
Harris, Marguerite, 31, 41
Harvard University, 4, 43
Hawkins, Bobby Louise, 176
Heliczer, Piero, 142
Helmley, Cecil, 9
Henderson, David, 1, 230–31n109; on being
    an outsider, 17; at Le Metro, 48, 55; "The
    Ofay and the Nigger," 87–89; on Umbra
    poets, 80. See also *Umbra;* Umbra poets
Herndon, Venable, 90–91
Hernton, Calvin, 80–81, 86
Higgins, Dick, 6, 212n18
Hill, Joe, 61
hip-hop, 204, 205
hippie counterculture, 44, 124–25, 176, 180,
    181
Holiday, Billie, xvi, 51, 89, 220n5, 228n86
Hollo, Anselm, 105, 179

Holman, Bob, xix, 129, 137; and slam poetry, 203, 204, 206, 207, 208
homosexuality, 9, 24, 67, 111, 219n81, 235n40
Howard, Richard, 187
Howe, Susan, 22
How(ever), 69
Hudson Review, 9
Huncke, Herbert, 41
Hunter, Charlene, 82

Imagism, 91
improvisation, 43–44, 46
intermedia, 6
interracial couples, 65, 87, 241n104
"Intersection" reading series, 179
I's (Zukofsky), 242n119
Italian futurists, 5, 6, 33, 211–12n15

Jacobs, Ken, 145–48, 255n69
Jarnot, Lisa, 16, 17, 32, 74
jazz: clubs, xvi; connection to poetry, 86; jazz-poetry readings, 28, 220–21n5; musicians' presence in Lower East Side scene, 3; role of, in poetic community, 28, 29, 30, 89
Jefferson Airplane, 124
Joans, Ted, 81
Johns, Jasper, 105
Jolas, Eugene, 61, 116
Jones, Hettie, 17, 57
Jones, LeRoi. *See* Baraka, Amiri
Joplin, Janis, 124
Joris, Pierre, 99, 212n19
Joyce, James: *Finnegans Wake,* 63, 116; *Ulysses,* 14, 61, 63, 103
Judson Church, 21, 129
Jung, Carl, 86, 91

Kandell, Lenore, 20, 140
Kapelner, Alan, 139
Kaplan, Ed, xiii
Katz, Alex, 105
Katzman, Allen, 34, 38, 41, 51, 55, 76
Katzman, Trudy, 55
Kazin, Alfred, 14
Kelly, Joan (a.k.a. Joby), 91
Kelly, Robert, 1, 54, 100, 175, *CD9;* and 1960 reading at Café Cino, 30; "Notes on the Poetry of the Deep Image," 97; poetic influences of, 9; and *Trobar,* xvii, 90–91
Kendrick, Laura, 30, 37
Kenyon Review, 63

Kerista Free Love Society, 65
Kerouac, Jack, 11, 90, 158–59; *The Dharma Bums,* 165; *Mexico City Blues,* 86; *On the Road,* 88–89, 112
Kerouac School of Disembodied Poetics at Naropa College, 186
Khlebnikov, Velimir, 62
Kinks, 124
Kirby, Michael, 33
Kline, Franz, 3
Koch, Ed, 51, 52, 229n94
Koch, Kenneth, 24, 128; "assassination" reading, 171–73, 264n64, *CD17;* on contemporaries, 101; "Fresh Air," 25, 179; on jazz-poetry readings, 28; Padgett on, 42–43; pie in face, 264n68; "The Pleasures of Peace," 173, 249–50n15; as teacher, 257–59n9; "To My Audience," 171–72, *CD17;* "When the Sun Tries to Go On," 191; as witness for Sanders, 78, 237n70
Kostelanetz, Richard, 5, 175, 188
Krauss, Ruth, 139, 141
Kray, Betty, 142
Krim, Seymour, 139
Kruchenykh, Alexei, 62
Kuh, Richard H., 15
Kulchur, 112
Kunitz, Stanley, 42, 126
Kupferberg, Tuli, 72, 77, 236n52
Kyger, Joanne, 141, 176, 177–78

Lacan, Jacques, 191
Lady Chatterley's Lover (Lawrence), 13–14, 103
La Mama Theater, 53, 77
L = A = N = G = U = A = G = E, xix, 188, 190, 191, 200, 268n6, 269n16, 270n17; Mayer's influence on, 192; as political critique, 194
language school, 188–97, 268–69n7, 271n34; and Mayer, 188, 190–91, 192–93, 269n12; performativity of, 189, 195–97; poetics of, 268nn5,6, 269n8, 270n22; vs. slam poetics, 207; as subversive, 194–95
Laughlin, James, 63
Lawrence, D. H., 13, 103
Leary, Paris, 175
Lehman, David, 105, 115, 168
Le Metro coffeehouse. *See* Metro, Le (coffeehouse)
Les Deux Mégots coffeehouse. *See* Deux Mégots, Les (coffeehouse)
Levertov, Denise, 71, 134, 144–45, 238n74, 263n60; "O Taste and See," *CD1*

Lewis, Mort, 50
Lines, 47, 154
list poems, 95, 115, 150
little magazines, 60–64, 116, 234n24. *See also*
    magazines, mimeographed; *names of indi-*
    vidual magazines
The Little Review, 61, 63
Living Theatre, 50
Locus Solus, 24, 111, 114, 156, 246–47n181,
    247n182; collaboration issue, 162, 247n189
Loewisohn, Ron, 16
Lowell, Robert, 95
Lowenfels, Walter, 55
Lower East Side poetic community: African
    American poets in, 79–90; as alternative,
    xiii, xiv, xvi, 3, 17, 28, 210–11n11; in
    Bolinas, 176–78; changes in, 163, 174–76,
    179–80, 267n95; as communal, 7–8, 33–34,
    75, 76; and Deep Image poetics, 90–100;
    emphasis on immediacy, 169; extraliterary
    practices of, xiv, 76; and frontier mentality,
    18–19; and Grove Press, 9–17; heterosexism
    of, 21; informality of, 31; lack of publishing
    opportunities for, 2, 29; and magazines,
    45, 57–64; and Olson, 23; outside of New
    York, 176–83; and politics, 60, 127; and
    Pound and Williams, 6–7; race relations
    in, 87, 238n78, 240n102, 241n104, 241n107;
    San Francisco scene as predecessor to, 13,
    28, 214n37; and slam poetry, 208; as trans-
    national and transgenerational, 177; and
    Umbra poets, 79–90
Lower East Side neighborhood, 217n64; 1960s'
    changes in, 44, 124–25; as marginal, 3, 18;
    as slum, 180; working-class history of, 3
LSD, xviii, 6, 132, 185
Lumumba, Patrice, 83, 239–40n93

MacAdams, Lewis, 175, 176; *The Poetry Room,*
    182
machismo: of Black Mountain poets, 24–26;
    of Lower East Side scene, 140, 214n36
Maciunas, George, 51, 243n130
Mackey, Bill, xiii, 34, 38–39
Mackey, Nathaniel, 28–29
Mac Low, Jackson, 1, 96, 222n24; "The Blue-
    bird Asymmetries," 33; "Leather Costs,"
    96; on Lower East Side reading venues,
    35; "Phoneme Dance in Memoriam John
    Cage" (with Tardos), *CD3;* in *Poets at Les
    Deux Mégots,* 36; on police crackdowns,
    51–52; and typographical innovation, 5, 6
magazines, little, 60–64, 116. *See also* maga-

zines, mimeographed; *names of individual
    magazines*
magazines, mimeographed, xv, 56, 57–64;
    collaboration in, 169, 199–201; and com-
    munity, 63, 170; defense of *New American
    Poetry* in, 9; as embodying poetics of
    Lower East Side, 45, 59, 60; end of, 175–
    76, 182; immediacy of, 169, 231n3; and
    language poets, 197–98; and police crack-
    downs, 53, 60; as social registers, 159; as
    traces of oral readings, 36–37; women
    poets in, 20. *See also* magazines, little;
    magazines, rexograph; *names of individual
    magazines*
magazines, rexograph, 36–38, 43, 223n33
Mailer, Norman, 89
Major, Clarence, 55
Malanga, Gerard, 18, 47, 48, 72; "I Wrote
    the Word *Love* and You Wrote the Word
    Why?" (with Waldman and Warsh), 156;
    3 Poems for Benedetta Barzini, 156
Malcolm X, 80
Mallarmé, Stéphane, 25, 34
Mama Theater, La, 53, 77
Mann, Anthony, 22
Marcabru, 30
march, in protest of harassment of the arts,
    53, 230n97
Margules, Cindy, 41
Margules, Maurice (a.k.a. Moe), xiii, 40, 41,
    54, 55; police summons of, 50, 51, 52
marijuana, xvii, 6, 79
Marinetti, Filippo, 211–12n15
Marvell, Andrew, 11
Mathews, Harry, 105, 111
Matthiessen, F. O., 22
Max's Kansas City, 39, 225n44, 261n27
Mayer, Bernadette, 125, 141; and language
    poets, 188, 190–91, 192–93, 201, 269n12;
    at Le Metro, 48; and *o to 9,* xix, 198–99; as
    outside of norm of poetry scene, 189, 198;
    on sex at St. Mark's Church, 16; "Sonnet—
    Other Than What's Gone On in Stupid
    Art," *CD34;* "Sonnet—You Jerk, You
    Didn't Call Me Up," *CD33;* on St. Mark's
    social scene, 132; and *Unnatural Acts,*
    199–201; "Warren Finney," *CD33*
Mayo, Mary, 65, 68
Mead, Taylor, 12, 66–67
medieval poets, 09
Mekas, Jonas, 77
Mele, Christopher, 217n64
Meridian Books, 13

Metro, Le (coffeehouse), readings at, 1, 34, 35, 39–56, 229n95; connection between place and poetry, 32; demise of, 54–56; drugs at, 40; and hippie counterculture, 44; location and logistics of, 39, 40; and mimeographed magazines, 58; mixing of poetic schools at, 39; and New York School poets, 41–43, 47; and poem as speech act, 26; San Francisco readings as predecessor to, 28; Wieners reading at, 31; women poets at, 20

Micheline, Jack, 36

Millennium Film Workshop, 126, 129, 139; firing of Ken Jacobs, 145–48

Miller, Henry, 15, 68

mimeographed magazines. *See* magazines, mimeographed

mimeograph machines, 58, 79, 163, 168, 232n7

minorities, in Lower East Side, 3, 18

mixed-race couples, 65, 87, 241n104

modernism, 5, 62–64

Molinaro, Ursule, 90–91

Monk, Thelonius, 28, 29, 228n86

Monnier, Adrienne, 116

Montgomery, George, 20

Moog, Bob, 6, 212n16

Moore, Marianne, xvii

Moraff, Barbara, 20, 253–54n50

Motherwell, Robert, 188

Mus, David, 175

Museum of Modern Art (MOMA), 41, 43

music: and cabaret laws, 48, 209n5; of Lower East Side, 124; poets' choice of, xiv; popular, 169; rock, and link to poetry, 72, 236n52; and slam poetry, 204. *See also* jazz

Myles, Eileen, 186

Nahuatl translations, 97, 243n134

Naked Lunch (Burroughs), 15

Naropa College, 186

National Organization for Women, 141, 254n52

Navire d'Argent, Le, 116

The New American Poetry: 1945–1960, 9–10, 13, 14, 17, 35, 212n20; and Berrigan, 101, 106; defense of, 213–14n31; Koch poem in, 25; Lower East Side poets in, 40, 71, 213n30; vs. *New Poets of England and America,* 215n47; success of poets in, 210n8, 210–11n11; women poets in, 141

New Critics, 11, 12, 13, 73, 91, 99, 214–15n38, 215n44

New Directions, 63

"New Jazz for Old" reading, 30

Newkirk, Allen Van, 172, 173, 264nn63,64

New Poets of England and America, 13, 43, 60, 215n47

New School, 129, 130, 136, 146, 227n76, 257–59n9

New Year's Day readings, 126

New York Civil Liberties Union (N.Y.C.L.U.), 52, 77–78, 229n95

New York School artists, 105–6

New York School, First-Generation, xiii, 1, 3; and absence of poetics, 25; aesthetics of, 166–67; as apolitical, 167, 248n202, 262–63n47; and Beat poets, 42, 109–12, 158–59; and Berrigan, 104–12, 257n8; vs. Black Mountain School, 24–26; and *C: A Journal of Poetry,* 58; dissemination of poetics of, 178–79; and homosexuality, 24–26, 111, 219n81; influence on Poetry Project, 41–42, 48, 154–61, 227n76; and Le Metro, 39, 41–43, 47, 48; poetics of sociability, 162; vs. Second-Generation, xvii, 109. *See also names of individual poets*

New York School, Second-Generation, xvii, 42, 161, 227n76; appropriation and collaboration by, 112–18; Berrigan and *C* as establishing, 106–8, 155; and language school, 189, 190, 191, 192, 267–68n7; publishing success of, 182; resistance to seriousness of, 165–67; and speed of composition, 167–68; at Warsh/Waldman home, 161, 163–64. *See also names of individual poets*

New York School, Third-Generation, 186

92nd Street Y poetry readings, 16, 139, 142, 144

Nixon, Richard, 181

Nodland, Jayne, 176

North Beach (San Francisco), 12, 179, 215n41

Norton Anthology of Modern Poetry, 187

Notley, Alice, 141, 166, 176, 183; "How to Really Get an Apartment," CD30

Nuchim, Paul, 77

Nuyorican Poets Café, 186, 203, 204, 205–7, 208

obscenity charges, 77; against Baraka, 216n57; against Bruce, 51, 228–29n90; by Columbia University, 102–4; against Grove Press, 10–11; and mimeographed magazines, 15, 60; against Sanders, 76–78

Ofili, Chris, 68, 230n97

O'Hara, Frank, xvii, 23, 24–26, 41, 42–43; "Adieu to Norman, Bon Jour to Joan and Jean-Paul," 162; on *New American Poetry,* 213–14n31; and Berrigan, 47, 106, 109;

"The Day Lady Died," 113, 114, 158–59, 220n5; in *Evergreen Review,* 9, 13; "For the Chinese New Year and for Bill Berkson," 119; influence on Mayer, 193; "In Memory of My Feelings," 167; and Le Metro readings, 43; *Lunch Poems,* 106, 109; and naming of names, 178; "Naptha," *CD15;* "Personal Poem," 119, 213–14n31; "Poem (Lana Turner Has Collapsed!)" 47, 168, 227n73, *CD16;* and politics, 119–20, 248n205, 262–63n47; speed of composition, 168; "Why I Am Not a Painter," 106

Olson, Charles: "As the Dead Prey Upon Us," 22; "At Yorktown," 22; "The Death of Europe," 22; "Diaries of Death," 22–23; field poetics of, 220n2; influence on Lower East Side poets, 19–20, 218n70, 243n134; "The Kingfishers," 22; "La Préface," 25; *Maximus,* 22, 25; networking of, 63; and *New American Poetry,* 17, 23–24, 210–11n11; performativity of, 196; Pound's influence on, 8; "Projective Verse," 17, 19, 21, 26, 29, 84, 218n71

On the Mesa: An Anthology of Bolinas Writing, 176–77

Oppenheimer, Joel, 1, 24, 217–18n68; and antiwar movement, 16, 143–44, 148; as director of Poetry Project, 134–40, 143, 149–51, 252nn36,37, 256n80; and firing of Jacobs, 145–48; "The Great American Desert," 21; Olson's influence on, 19; Pound's influence on, 8; readings at Poetry Project, 36; reading of Williams's poems, 40; *Women Poems,* 140; "Zen You," 156

orality: Berrigan on, 108; connection with mimeographed magazines, 59; oral tradition, 37, 86, 97; and slam poetry, 208. *See also* readings

Origin, 37, 60, 61, 63

Orlovsky, Peter, 1, 41, 73, 127

Ossman, David, 21, 31

o to 9, xix, 154, 188–89, 194, 198–99, 271n38

"outrider" poetry aesthetic, 17

Owens, Rochelle, 41, 92; "Hera Hera Hera," 253–54n50

Pack, Robert, 13; *New Poets of England and America,* 13, 43, 60, 215n47

Padgett, Ron, 1, 41, 245n162; and appropriation, 112–13, 115; censorship of, 15; chronology of alternative tradition, 8–9; "Detach Invading," *CD20; Great Balls of Fire,* 182; "I'd Give You My Seat If I Were Here,"

112; *In Advance of a Broken Arm,* 112; "Joe Brainard's Painting 'Bingo'" *CD21;* and Le Metro, 40, 43, 47, 48; mainstream status of, 187; on New York School poets, 42–43; "Nothing in That Drawer," *CD22;* readings at Poetry Project, 42; on rexographs, 43; as Second-Generation New York School poet, 25, 247n182; "Sonnet to Andy Warhol," 116–17; "Waterloo Sunset" (with Berrigan), 167–68

Palmer, Michael, 16

Paris Review, 164

Parker, Charlie, xvi, 29, 228n86

Partisan Review, 192

Paulson, Elin, 67, 68

Peace Eye, xv, 76–77, 78

Perdomo, Willie, 207

performativity, 211n15; in jazz, 29; and language poets, 189, 195–97; and mimeographed magazines, 58; in *o to 9* and *Unnatural Acts,* 198–99; of slam poetry, 207

Phoenix Bookshop, 45, 71

Pietri, Pedro, 207

Pinsky, Robert, 187

Piombino, Nick, 141, 188

Pitcher, Oliver, 81

Plath, Sylvia, 95

Plummer, Paul, 129

Poems from the Floating World, 90–100, 198, 241n114, 242n122. *See also* Deep Image poetics

poetic schools. *See names of individual schools*

poetry: as communal, 73, 75, 76, 178; as healing, 98–99; as heard thing, 108; as living art, 81; as political forum, 82; as song, 72; as speech act, 27, 96, 169, 195–96, 208; speed of composition of, 168; as visual, 36–37, 220n2

Poetry Committee, 129, 137

Poetry Flash, 192

Poetry in the Schools, 142, 254n54

Poetry Machine, 38

Poetry Project at St. Mark's Church, xiii, 16, 26, 35; and antiwar movement, 141–43; audience participation at, 171–73, 263n60; benefit readings at, 16, 141, 183; changes in, xviii–xix, 174–76, 178, 179–80, 267n95; criticisms of, 148; effects of, on youth, 133; as familial, 170; frequency of readings at, xviii, 225n49; and *Genre of Silence,* 149–51; government grant, xviii, 129–134, 250–51n21, 251nn22,23,25, 255n63; incep-

Poetry Project at St. Mark's Church *(continued)*
tion of, 36, 56; influence of New York
School poets on, xviii, 41–42, 48, 154–61;
lack of diversity at, 203, 204, 205; and
language school, 188, 192; link to rock
music, 72–73; mimeograph machine, 58;
Oppenheimer as director of, 134–40, 143,
149–51, 252nn36,37, 256n80; post–federal
funding, 181–83, 266n91; publications of,
232n5; Ron Gold reading, 183, 184, 185;
and slam poetry, xix, 203, 207, 208; and
tape recording, 169–70; women poets in,
214n36
poetry slams, xix, 203–8, 272n6
Poets at Le Metro, 43, 44, 45, 46, 141, 155
Poets at Les Deux Mégots, xv, 36–38, 43, 45, 141,
155
Poets Co-Op, 55–56
police harassment and crackdowns, 2, 15,
48–54, 60, 61, 67
Pollak, Felix, 61, 63
Pollock, Jackson, 116
pop art, 48, 116–17. *See also* Warhol, Andy
Porter, Fairfield, 24, 105
The Postmoderns, 210n8
Pound, Ezra, xiv, 7, 8, 39, 43, 61; as Black-
burn's "grampaw," 7; *Cantos,* 70; "Homage
to Sextus Propertius," 86; Imagism, 62, 91,
93, 94; "In a Station of the Metro," 93–
94, 242–43n124; *The Letters of Ezra Pound,*
8; Poundian contractions, 8, 212–13n23,
213n25; and *Trobar,* 92
Presley, Elvis, 89
PROJECTION, 126
Promethean, 144
protest, against harassment of the arts, 53,
230n97

Queneau, Raymond, 188

race relations, 64, 87, 238n78, 240n102,
241n104, 241n107. *See also* Black Arts
movement; *Umbra;* Umbra poets
Radio Free Poetry, 132, 184–85
Rafael, Lennox, 55
rally, in protest of harassment of the arts, 53,
230n97
Ranaldo, Lee, 72
Randall, Margaret, 141
Ransom, John Crowe, 12
rap music, 204, 205, 206
reading lists, 188
readings, xvi; audience participation at, 31,

33, 171–73, 263n60; and authorship, 30;
Berrigan and, 108, 120; and Black Arts
movement, 85; as boring, 267n98; as
communal experience, 30–34; and lan-
guage poets, 195–96; Lower East Side
venues for, 35, 223n32; and poet's body,
27–28; tape recording of, 169–70. *See also*
slam poetry; *names of individual reading
venues*
Reed, Ishmael, 8, 54, 139, 238–39n79; *The
Freelance Pallbearers,* 86; "Patrice," 83–84;
"Poetry Place Protest," 55
Reed, Lou, 45, 72
"The Return of the Warriors" (anonymous),
97–98
Reverdy, Pierre, 93
rexograph magazines, 36–38, 43, 223n33
Rexroth, Kenneth, 11–12, 28, 215n41
Ricard, Rene, 164
Rimbaud, Arthur, 34, 109; "A Season in Hell,"
110
Rivers, Larry, 28, 105; *O'Hara Nude with Boots,*
24
rock music, 72–73. *See also* Fugs
Roethke, Theodore, 105
Ron Gold Defense Fund reading, 183, 184, 185
Rosenquist, James, 148
Rosset, Barney, 11
Rothenberg, Jerome, 21, 22, 93, 100; "The
Double Vision," 94; "An Exchange," 96;
as organizer, 30, 36, 48; "A Valentine, No,
a Valedictory for Gertrude Stein," CD5;
White Sun Black Sun, 97. *See also* Deep
Image poetics; *Poems from the Floating
World*
Rothko, Mark, 220n5
Royal Albert Hall reading, 34
Rubinstein, Carol, 129
Ruskin, Mickey, xiii, 34, 38–39, 222–23n27

Šalamun, Tomaž, 179
sale, of poets' memorabilia, 78–79, 238n72
Sanchez, Sonia, 85
Sanders, Ed, xv, 23; on art as a happening, 32;
"The Editorial Conference," 68; *The Ed
Sanders Newsletter,* 77; Folklore Center
readings, 56; "A Fuck You Position Paper:
Resistance Against Goon Squads," 71; and
Ginsberg, 75; "Gobble-Gang Poems," 127;
and Le Metro readings, 41, 48; and literary
ownership, 70; obscenity charges against,
15, 61, 76–78, 237n70; "Poem Describing
the Cover of the Next Issue of *Fuck You,*

Issue 5 Volume 5," 44; and police crack-downs, 51, 52; and public eye, 68–69, 235n45; readings at Poetry Project, 36; sale of poets' memorabilia, 78–79, 238n72; and sexual content, 44–45, 65, 68; "Sheep Fuck Poem," 73; "Siobhan McKenna Grope Grope," 65. See also *Fuck You/a magazine of the arts*
San Francisco, 10–11, 28, 179, 215n41
San Francisco Renaissance, xiii, xiv, 11, 29, 72, 214nn36,37, 220n3
Saroyan, Aram, 47, 154, 176
Sartre, Jean-Paul, 34, 66
Saxon, Dan, 36, 41, 43, 45
Schiff, Harris, 186
Schjeldahl, Peter, 164, 262n38; "Easter" (with Clark), 165, 166
Schneeman, George, 105, 161
schools of poetry. *See names of individual schools*
Schuyler, James, xvii, 18, 24, 41
Schwerner, Armand, 22, 30, 41; "The Tablets," *CD6*
Seaton, Peter, 191
Second-Generation New York School. *See* New York School, Second-Generation
Sedgwick, Edie, 124
Selby, Hubert, Jr., 15
Serrano, Andrés, 68
sex: in *Fuck you*, 65, 66, 67–68; male poets and, 22; at St. Mark's Church, 16
sexual liberation, xviii, 65
Shepard, Sam, 125
Sherman, Susan, 41
Shoptaw, John, 24, 111
Silliman, Ron, 193–94, 207, 271n32; "The Dwelling Place," 190; "For L = A = N = G = U = A = G = E," 193; *Tjanting*, 307; "What," 195–96
Silo, 153
Silverstein, Harry, 129–34, 145, 250n21
Simpson, Louis, 13, 249–50n15; *New Poets of England and America*, 13, 43, 60, 215n47
Sinopoulos, Takis, 95–96
slam poetry, xix, 203–8, 272n6
Sloman, Joel, 155, 166; and antiwar movement, 143–44, 148, 254n59; as assistant director of Poetry Project, 131, 134, 144–45; "Strike," 4; "Suggested Titles for St. Mark's Literary Journal," 150; *Virgil's Machines*, 145
Smith, Jack, 77
Smith, Marc, 206
Smith, Patti, 72

Snyder, Gary, 11, 165
sociability, in poetry, 178
Solomon, Carl, 41
Sonic Youth, 72
Sorrentino, Gil, 40, 238n74
spacing, innovative, 84
speed, of composition, 167–68, 169, 171
Spellman, A. B., 29, 82, 105
Spicer, Jack, 11
spoken-word poetry, xix, 203–8, 272n6
Stein, D. D., 17–18
Stein, Gertrude, xiv, 63, 189; "IN," 199
Stella, Frank, 105
Stephens, Michael, 133, 140, 151, 217–18n68
St. Mark's Church: as antiestablishment, 138; antiwar benefit reading at, 126–28; damage to, 183; as gathering place, 132, 195; history of, 123–24; Reading Series Committee, 36; as spirit of 1960s Lower East Side, 124–25, 126. *See also* Poetry Project at St. Mark's Church
Stockhausen, Karlheinz, 45
Strand, Mark, 175
Stuyvesant, Peter, 123, 138
Summerfield, Arthur, 14
Sun Arts Festival benefit, 141
surrealism, xiv, 13, 38, 62–64, 105, 154

tape recording, 6, 169–70, 263n58
Tardos, Anne, *CD3*
Te li le, 62
Tenth Street Coffeehouse, xiii, 34, 35, 48, 222n26
Theater Genesis, 125, 130, 145
33 St. Mark's Place, 161–65, 182, 186, 262n36
Thomas, Dylan, 63, 167
Thomas, Lorenzo, 1, 13, 119–20, 254–55n61; "Alea's Children," 240n102, 241n104; "Five Leaf Clover," *CD25*; at Le Metro, 47, 48, 55; "Neon Griot: The Functional Role of Poetry Readings in the Black Arts Community," 85; "Political Science," 119; "South Street Blues," 87; "A Tale of Two Cities," 83; on Umbra poets, 80, 85–86
Three Penny Poetry Reading, 142, 254n55
Torres, Edwin, 204
Touré, Askia Muhammed, 85
transatlantic review, 116
transition, 61, 63, 116, 234nn24,25,26
translations, 91, 95, 97, 115, 242n117
Trilling, Diana and Lionel, 213–14n31
Trinidad, David, 186

Trobar, xvii, 30, 90–100, 198, 231n3; diversity of poets in, 99; origin of, 91–92, 241n114. *See also* Deep Image poetics
troubadour poetry, xvii, 9, 30, 37, 72, 208
typography: innovative, 5, 115, 211nn12,15; and Umbra poets, 84, 85; word-processing, 212n19

Ulysses (Joyce), 14, 61, 63, 103
Umbra, 17, 55, 79–90, 239nn91,92
Umbra poets, 55, 79–90, 241n107; appropriation of Lower East Side poetics and scene, 81–82, 85; as political activists of Lower East Side community, 82, 83, 90; workshops, 17, 81
Unnatural Acts, 194, 199–201

Vega, Suzanne, 72
Velvet Underground, 124, 161
Verlaine, Paul, 34
vernacular, 8, 31–32
Vietnam War, xviii, 16, 58, 61, 181. *See also* antiwar movement
Village Voice, 52, 140, 146, 184
Voznesensky, Andrei, 142
V Tre, 51

Wakoski, Diane, 1, 20, 22, 48, 175, 253–54n50
Waldman, Anne, 17, 23, 42, 125, 144, 153; apartment of, 161–65, 262n36; *Baby Breakdown,* 182; on changes in New York City, 180–81; as director of Poetry Project, 151; "I Wrote the Word *Love* and You Wrote the Word *Why?*" (with Malanga and Warsh), 156; "Memorial Day" (with Berrigan), *CD27;* on New York, 170–71, 216–17n61; on Oppenheimer, 136; *Out of This World,* 154, 166; "Poem in New York," 170, *CD26;* on production of *The World,* 168; "The Reject Paper," 156; and Warsh, 179–80, 256n79; and women in poetry scene, 140, 141; *The World Anthology,* 182
Warhol, Andy, 45, 48, 118, 124, 161; *Sleep,* 116–17
War Resisters League, 66
Warsh, Lewis, 42, 144, 153, 167; apartment of, 161–65, 262n36; in California, 176–78, 179; "French Windows," 166; "I Wrote

the Word *Love* and You Wrote the Word *Why?*" (with Malanga and Waldman), 156; *Part of My History,* 156; and Waldman, 179–80, 256n79
Weather Underground, 180, 181, 253n48
Weiner, Hannah, 141, 188
West Village, xvi, 2, 3; as center for avant-garde, 2
Whalen, Philip, 179
White Dove Review, 105, 245n162
Whitehead, Alfred, 188
Whitman, Walt, xiv, 25
Wieners, Dana, 23
Wieners, John, 12, 23, 59, 159, 222n15; "Acts of Youth," 31; audience participatory reading, 171; at Le Metro, 31, 41, 45; "Mole Proposes Solitude," 31; as part of San Francisco reading scene, 28; "Poem for Cocksuckers," *CD10;* "Prose Poem," 59
Wilentz, Ted, 45, 144
Williams, Flossie, 39
Williams, William Carlos, 7, 8, 12, 39, 212n21, 225n48
Wilson, Bob, 45
Wittgenstein, Ludwig, 188, 191
women poets, 20–21, 140–41, 214n36, 253–54n50
Woodstock, 177
workshops: at St. Mark's, xix, 139–40, 141; *Umbra,* 17, 81
The World, xviii, 154–60, 194; collaboration in, 157–59, 163, 169; as creating community, 170; evolution of, 174; nonseriousness of, 165–67, 174; production of, 168–69; and Warsh/Waldman home, 161; women poets in, 141
The World Anthology, 182
Wright, James, 99, 126

X, Malcolm, 80
XYZ, Emily, 205, 272n8

Yeats, William Butler, 61
Young, Andrew, 82
The Young American Poets, 175–76, 264–65n70
youth programs, 251n27
Yugen, 57

TEXT 10.5/13 ADOBE GARAMOND   **DISPLAY** AKZIDENZ GROTESK
DESIGN NICOLE HAYWARD   **COMPOSITION** INTEGRATED COMPOSITION SYSTEMS   **PRINTING + BINDING** THOMSON-SHORE, INC.

Playlist for Compact Disc

See pages 291–93 for a list of sources and permissions.

1. Denise Levertov, "O Taste and See" (0:47)
   St. Mark's Church, New York City, March 20, 1967

2. Paul Blackburn, "Clickety-Clack" (3:00)
   Brooklyn Civic Center, Brooklyn, New York, May 22, 1964

3. Jackson Mac Low and Anne Tardos, excerpt from "Phoneme Dance in Memoriam John Cage" (4:00)
   From the compact disc *Open Secrets* (XI 110), Experimental Intermedia Foundation, 1993

4. David Antin, "Who Are My Friends" (3:07)
   Café Le Metro, New York City, September 1, 1965

5. Jerome Rothenberg, "A Valentine, No, a Valedictory for Gertrude Stein" (0:23)
   Café Le Metro, New York City, September 1, 1965

6. Armand Schwerner, selection from "The Tablets" (5:06)
   St. Mark's Church, New York City, April 6, 1966

7. Clayton Eshleman, "Notebook Entry 1968" (3:03)
   St. Mark's Church, New York City, March 4, 1968

8. Robert Creeley, "The Charm," "A STEP," and "KATE'S" (1:30)
   St. Mark's Church, New York City, May 17, 1967

9. Robert Kelly, Troubadour text, translated by Robert Kelly (0:42)
   Café Cino, New York City, 1960

10. John Wieners, "Poem for Cocksuckers" (1:08)
    Café Le Metro, New York City, 1963

11. Allen Ginsberg, "A Supermarket in California" (2:44)
    Pacifica Studios, Berkeley, California, October 25, 1956. From the compact disc *Holy Soul Jelly Roll,* Rhino Records, 1994

12. Amiri Baraka, "A Poem Some People Will Have to Understand" (1:10)
    Poetry Society of America, New York City, December 26, 1963

13. John Ashbery, "They Dream Only of America" (1:07)
    Washington Square Gallery, New York City, August 23, 1964

14. John Ashbery, "Thoughts of a Young Girl" (0:40)
    Washington Square Gallery, New York City, August 23, 1964

15. Frank O'Hara, "Naphtha" (1:45)
    State University of New York, Buffalo, 1964

16. Frank O'Hara, "Poem (Lana Turner Has Collapsed!)" (0:44)
State University of New York, Buffalo, 1964

17. Kenneth Koch, "To My Audience" (2:24)
St. Mark's Church, New York City, January 10, 1968

18. Bill Berkson, "I Feel Free" (1:14)
St. Mark's Church, New York City, May 29, 1969

19. Bill Berkson, "Poem" (0:41)
Read over phone, November 2000

20. Ron Padgett, "Detach Invading" (1:05)
Originally taped on "Susan Howe with Poetry" radio show, WBAI, New York City,
June 17, 1975

21. Ron Padgett, "Joe Brainard's Painting 'Bingo'" (1:05)
Originally taped on "Susan Howe with Poetry" radio show, WBAI, New York City,
June 17, 1975

22. Ron Padgett, "Nothing in That Drawer" (0:29)
Originally taped on "Susan Howe with Poetry" radio show, WBAI, New York City,
June 17, 1975

23. Joe Brainard, selection from *I Remember* (1:13)
Venue and date unknown

24. Dick Gallup, "Where I Hang My Hat" (0:33)
St. Mark's Church, New York City, September 27, 1967

25. Lorenzo Thomas, "Five Leaf Clover" (1:07)
St. Mark's Church, New York City, May 16, 2001

26. Anne Waldman, "Poem in New York" (1:04)
St. Mark's Church, New York City, November 8, 1967

27. Ted Berrigan and Anne Waldman, selection from "Memorial Day" (4:55)
St. Mark's Church, New York City, Memorial Day, 1974

28. Ted Berrigan, "Sonnet I," "Sonnet II," "Sonnet III," and "A Final Sonnet" (3:37)
St. Mark's Church, New York City, 1968

29. Clark Coolidge, "Machinations Calcite" (2:06)
Franconia College, Franconia, New Hampshire, circa 1971

30. Alice Notley, "How to Really Get an Apartment" (0:48)
University of California, San Diego, April 25, 1989

31. Joe Ceravolo, "A Song of Autumn" (0:54)
Recorded at Ceravolo's home, Bloomfield, New Jersey, Spring 1968

32. Joe Ceravolo, "Drunken Winter" (0:23)
Recorded at Ceravolo's home, Bloomfield, New Jersey, Spring 1968

33. Bernadette Mayer, "Sonnet—You Jerk, You Didn't Call Me Up" and "Warren Finney" (2:02)
University of California, San Diego, November 15, 1989

34. Bernadette Mayer, "Sonnet—Other Than What's Gone On in Stupid Art" (0:52)
University of California, San Diego, November 15, 1989